The American Exploration and Travel Series

Joseph Reddeford Walker
and the Arizona Adventure

Joseph Reddeford Walker

AND

the Arizona Adventure

By *DANIEL ELLIS CONNER*

Edited by *DONALD J. BERTHRONG*
and *ODESSA DAVENPORT*

UNIVERSITY OF OKLAHOMA PRESS ᓚᕒ *Norman*

Library of Congress Catalog Card Number 56-11227
ISBN 978-0-8061-5286-8 (paper)

Copyright 1956 by the University of Oklahoma Press, Publishing Division of the University. Paperback published 2016. Manufactured in the United States of America.

Acknowledgments

Our greatest debt of gratitude is owed to Edwin W. Sandison of Wilmington, California, who preserved Daniel Ellis Conner's original manuscript for more than forty years. Many people aided in the gathering of information, but in particular Jane Hudgins, director of the Phoenix Public Library; W. C. Lefebvre and James Barney of Phoenix, Arizona; Mrs. Lucile M. Reynolds, Los Angeles Public Library; and Orris E. Carter, Jr., Phillips Collection, University of Oklahoma Library, contributed their assistance most generously. Professors Harley P. Brown, Edward A. Frederickson, George J. Goodman, and George M. Sutton, all of the University of Oklahoma, provided information in fields where the editors had little, if any, competence. We are also especially indebted to Professor Stanley K. Coffman and to Rhio Berthrong for their constructive criticisms.

DONALD J. BERTHRONG
ODESSA DAVENPORT

September 5, 1956

Contents

Acknowledgments	vii
Introduction	xiii
1. Following Joe Walker's Trail	3
2. "I Want Him Dead"—the Betrayal of Mangas Coloradas	10
3. Pinos Altos to Tucson over the Old Southern Route	43
4. Opening Central Arizona's Mines	67
5. A Solitary Journey from Prescott to the Colorado River	106
6. The Apaches Begin Rifle Negotiations	133
7. Lead or Strychnine—the Pinole Treaty	155
8. A Visit to the Mohaves with Joe Walker	185
9. The Perils of Prospecting	216
10. The Fight at Battle Flat	242
11. The Last Campaign of Sugarfoot Jack	263
12. Mining the Quartz Lodes	283
13. Visits to Sonora and La Paz	309
14. Taste All Gone—the Adventure Ends	327
Bibliography	353
Index	359

Illustrations

	facing page
Joseph Reddeford Walker and His Squaw	10
Portrait of Joseph Reddeford Walker	58
Daniel Ellis Conner	90
King Woolsey	122
Iretaba, Chief of the Mohaves	170
Ed Peck	202
Governor Richard C. McCormick	234
Prescott, Arizona	298

	page
Map: The Route of the Walker Party	2

Introduction

BY THE MID-1850's the gold-bearing sands of the Feather, Yuba, and San Joaquin had played out; nuggets and gold no longer appeared in the pans and rockers of the individual prospector. He was being supplanted by wealthy corporations that moved in heavy machinery to reduce the quartz lodes; one by one the old mining districts were being deserted by miners who became farmers, ranchers, or city dwellers. Yet the lure of gold was still irresistible to some of these miners who refused to believe that a fortune in gold was not their destiny. North to the Fraser River, south to Baja California, and east to Colorado and the Comstock, the luckless miners began to drift.[1] Thus, nineteen men, recently of the Tuolumne district, gathered at Keyesville, California, in 1861 and placed themselves under the leadership of Joseph Reddeford Walker for another try at new, unexhausted gold fields. Their destination was uncertain—but not their dreams. In the mountains of Colorado, on the upper reaches of the Río Grande, or even in the unexplored country north of the Gila they would at last strike it rich.

[1] John Walton Caughey, *Gold Is the Cornerstone*, 295 ff.

INTRODUCTION

Joe Walker, their choice for leader, possessed, if it lay within human power, the ability to lead them safely across the trackless desert, through the dangers of Indian country, and over the tortuous mountain ranges. From the Missouri to the San Joaquin, from the Gila to the Yellowstone, Joe Walker had spent most of his life trapping beaver in the ice-fringed mountain streams, bartering with the Crow, Ute, Cheyenne, Arapaho, and Shoshone Indians for their pelts and skins, droving horses, mules, cattle, and sheep, and guiding emigrants and explorers. His skills were acquired over nearly forty years of continuous experience in the Far West, dating from his first trek to Santa Fé in 1820.[2] Now his hair was white, but old Joe Walker still possessed the keenness of mind, the alertness to danger, and the ceaseless vigilance of a veteran mountain man so necessary for survival in the Far West where both nature and its children—the Indians—were ready to snuff out life in the unwary and careless traveler.

Born in Roane County, in eastern Tennessee on December 13, 1798, Walker moved with his family to the vicinity of Fort Osage on the Missouri frontier around 1818. Only two of the five Walker brothers, Joe and Joel, lived out their natural lives, for family tradition relates that John died at the Alamo, Isaac was killed in battle with the Mormons, and Samuel failed to survive a plains crossing in 1849.[3]

At twenty-nine, Walker, a strapping six-foot, two-hundred-pounder, was elected sheriff of Jackson County, Missouri, thus assuming responsibility for keeping the peace in the boisterous frontier town of Independence, the county seat which he selected and named.[4] While occupying the sheriff's office for four years, Walker manifested the characteristics which were to win respect for him throughout his career. Never a braggart,

---

[2] Douglas S. Watson, *West Wind: The Life Story of Joseph Reddeford Walker*, 8, says Walker went to Santa Fé in the spring of 1820, but Robert Glass Cleland, *This Reckless Breed of Men*, 276, maintains that Walker went to Santa Fé with Becknell's expedition of 1821.

[3] Watson, *West Wind*, 6.

[4] Cleland, *Reckless Breed of Men*, 277.

soft spoken, yet capable of maintaining discipline, his sharp blue eyes sometimes snapped with anger, but more often twinkled with kindly and humane humor.

In February, 1831, while leading a party to the Cherokee Nation to obtain horses which would then be sold to fur traders' outfits, he met Captain Benjamin L. E. Bonneville at Fort Gibson. Captain Bonneville undoubtedly approached Walker to explain his contemplated fur-trading expedition to the Rocky Mountains, and after Bonneville obtained the necessary financial backing in the East, Walker spent the rest of 1831 and the spring of 1832 preparing for that great venture. Fort Osage was the point of departure for the party on May 1, 1832. The journey across the Kansas River at Independence and up the Platte River to the mountains was uneventful until they reached the western slope of the Rockies on July 25, and the Green River rendezvous on July 27, 1832.[5] Here Lucien Fontenelle of the American Fur Company lured away many of Bonneville's best men and his Delaware Indians, teaching him his first lesson in the fur trade. To offset this, Bonneville sent Walker and a single companion to intercept the free trappers before they made their way to the rendezvous, offering them a buyer's market for their beaver. Profits for the Eastern backers, however, could not be realized by such techniques. After dividing the party, Walker led one group across the Tetons to Horse Prairie, where Indians surprised him in a sudden attack. Thereafter he maintained unceasing vigilance which paid its most evident reward—no Indian ever counted coup over Joe Walker's scalp.

Slowly the trappers made their way back to the winter rendezvous and all told the same story: the Indians refused to trade and the beaver catches were small. Trapping parties were sent out again in the spring of 1833, one returning an utter failure and the others with meager results. When the returns were totaled, Bonneville had collected only four thousand pounds of beaver skins, an amount insufficient to cover ex-

[5] Watson, *West Wind*, 31.

penses. He still had most of his trade goods and supplies, however, and recalling Walker's tale told while riding up the Platte a year earlier of Jedediah Smith's journey to California, a legend well known in the fur trade, Bonneville was fired with a desire to recoup his losses by a trapping expedition into the untouched streams far to the west and south. When the rendezvous broke up on July 24, 1833, Walker was given about fifty men, each with four horses and a year's supplies and instructed to rendezvous a year later on the Bear River.[6]

On the Bear River Walker and his men staged a buffalo hunt for meat and were also joined by Joe Meek and other free trappers. In the blazing heat of mid-August they made their laborious way over the desert west of the Great Salt Lake, finding no relief until they reached Ogden's River, now the Humboldt. This they trapped with disappointing results, because it had been cleaned out by a Hudson's Bay Company brigade led by Edward Rose and Jim Bridger.[7]

Near the Humboldt Sink, Indians began to gather around the party in considerable numbers. All along the Humboldt, trappers lost their traps to thieving Indians until finally a mountain man's temper blazed and he shot an Indian. For this act, Walker severely reprimanded the mountain man because he wished to avoid a conflict if possible. After this incident, the Indians continued to harass the party. When finally eighty to a hundred of them came tauntingly close, Walker now felt that there was no alternative left but to chastise the sullen and warlike Indians. According to Zenas Leonard, clerk to Walker and chronicler of the expedition, thirty-two men surrounded the Indians and, after killing thirty-nine, completely routed the survivors. To make the victory complete, Walker ordered some of the men to take the bows of the fallen, wounded warriors and to kill them. Leonard justifies the action as necessary for the safety of the party, but admits that the

---

[6] Zenas Leonard, *Narrative of the Adventures of Zenas Leonard*, 105.
[7] Bernard DeVoto, *Across the Wide Missouri*, 147.

INTRODUCTION

"severity with which we dealt with these Indians may be revolting to the heart of the philanthropist." [8]

The party entered California in what is present-day Mono County and pushed westward along the watershed between the Merced and Tuolumne rivers, finally reaching the San Joaquin Valley.[9] After touching the Pacific Coast, where they met Captain John Bradshaw, master of the *Logoda,* who was hunting sea otters along the coast, the party recruited their animals in the Santa Cruz Mountains. Although Walker visited Monterey, the expedition remained near San Juan Bautista. Apparently the stay in California was pleasant to some of the men, for a few of the party, such as George Nidever, remained there.[10] Finally, in January, 1834, after once again returning to Monterey for supplies, Walker led his men out of California, traversing Walker's Pass for the first time. Following brutal periods of hardship and considerable disagreement, when Walker had to use the utmost patience and leadership to control the group, they reached the old trail in May.[11] Instead of proceeding directly to Salt Lake, they took a northern route to the Snake River and reached the Bear River on July 3, 1834. A week later they rode into Captain Bonneville's camp as agreed a year earlier—but without beaver. Although they had performed a prodigious feat, Washington Irving, reciting the life and adventures of Bonneville, chose to ignore the significance of the California expedition and blamed Walker for the ultimate failure of the whole Bonneville venture. Irving concluded that the "failure of this expedition was a blow to his pride, and a still greater blow to his purse. The Great Salt Lake still remained unexplored; at the same time, the means which had been furnished so liberally to fit out this favorite expedition, had been squandered at Monterey; and all the

[8] Leonard, *Adventures of Zenas Leonard,* 110, 116.
[9] Francis P. Farquhar, "Exploration of the Sierra Nevada," *California Historical Quarterly,* Vol. IV, No. 1 (March, 1925), 6–7.
[10] George Nidever, *The Life and Adventures of George Nidever, 1802–1883,* 34.
[11] Leonard, *Adventures of Zenas Leonard,* 208.

peltries, also, which had been collected on the way." [12] Evidence appearing since, however, has completely vindicated Walker and any faulty judgment now rests upon the shoulders of Bonneville.[13]

Despite what Irving interpreted as Walker's malfeasance, Bonneville and Walker continued their relationship, and the latter took fifty-five men to trap on the upper Missouri River, agreeing to rendezvous in June, 1835. After trapping the Yellowstone, Tongue, Powder, and Musselshell rivers, Walker finally headed back to the Popo Agie, where he met Bonneville as planned. Apparently the Captain had had his fill of the mountains and the pitfalls of the fur trade, and he resolved to leave the fur trade to the Hudson's Bay and American Fur companies, because he failed to attend the rendezvous he had ordered for 1836 with Walker. This left Walker to bring back to St. Louis the results of the 1835–36 trapping season.[14]

Walker's activities now become vague and hard to follow until the period covered by this volume. It appears that after severing connections with Bonneville he remained in the mountains in the service of the American Fur Company for four years. During 1840 and 1841 he traded between California and Santa Fé. In February, 1841, Joe Walker and Henry Fraeb appear on the account books of Abel Stearn, an early Los Angeles merchant, credited with 417 pounds of beaver pelts valued at $1,147 with which they obtained supplies, horses, and mules to trade in Santa Fé.[15] Two years later Walker led the J. B. Chiles party, which contained the first wagons to pass overland from Salt Lake to California.[16]

On December 25, 1843, Walker obtained a passport to New Mexico and joined the annual caravan going there. When out

[12] Washington Irving, *The Adventures of Captain Bonneville*, II, 113.
[13] Hiram Martin Chittenden, *The American Fur Trade of the Far West*, II, 396–97.
[14] Leonard, *Adventures of Zenas Leonard*, 226 ff.
[15] LeRoy R. and Ann W. Hafen, *Old Spanish Trail: Santa Fé to Los Angeles*, 184.
[16] Dale Morgan, *The Great Salt Lake*, 160; John Walton Caughey, *California*, 215–16.

INTRODUCTION

on the trail, he learned that John C. Frémont, guided by Kit Carson, was traveling ahead. Leaving the caravan, he finally overtook Frémont's party at Mountain Meadows, Utah, over the Rockies through the Colorado parks, and finally to old Bent's Fort, which they reached July 1, 1844.[17] There Carson and Walker left Frémont to go south to Taos and Santa Fé, but agreed to rejoin him on his next California expedition. When Frémont appeared at Bent's Fort again on August 2, 1845, Carson and Walker joined him and his sixty-man party. Walker stayed with Frémont until the latter's retreat from Hawk's Peak in February, 1846, an act which thoroughly disgusted Walker, who demanded and obtained his release from the expedition.[18] Gathering up four hundred or five hundred horses, Walker went to the Green River and on to Santa Fé, where he disposed of them to troops about to engage in the Mexican War, and then returned to Missouri.[19]

After spending several years with relatives in Missouri, Walker returned in 1849 to California, where he and a nephew, James T. Walker, supplied beef and mutton to the mining camps. This activity must have held his interest for a short time only, because in February, 1850, he made an extended expedition to the upper reaches of the Virgin River, and to the Zuñi and Moqui villages. Returning to California, he went to Santa Fé in 1851 to buy sheep, which, however, were priced too high for purchase. He spent three years in the vicinity of John Gilroy's ranch, in California, but in 1854 explored the region of Mono Lake, California. Upon his return from Mono Lake he purchased a cattle ranch in Monterey County, but in 1859 he was on the trail again, this time as a scout and guide in the campaigns against the Colorado River Indians.[20]

As we have seen earlier, the last of Joe Walker's expeditions began in 1861. Authorities disagree as to the origins of this last venture. Orick Jackson maintains that Walker, in the company

[17] Allan Nevins, *Frémont, Pathmarker of the West*, 184.
[18] Watson, *West Wind*, 93 ff.
[19] Morgan, *Great Salt Lake*, 158.
[20] Watson, *West Wind*, 100–105.

of Kit Carson and Pauline Weaver, had visited central Arizona some twenty years before and had determined then to return some day.[21] James H. McClintock insists that Walker's and Jack Ralston's finding gold on the Little Colorado River about 1860 led directly to the formation of the Keyesville party.[22] Although disagreement also exists over the route from Keyesville, a member of the original party, Samuel C. Miller, apparently related that they traveled from Keyesville through Death Valley, to the Colorado, and into the Navajo country, from where they ventured into Colorado.[23] There, six members of the group remained, including John Walker, a nephew of Joe Walker. Evidently the prospects of Colorado did not tempt the old mountain man, because Walker recruited additional miners to join a party for a mining exploration through New Mexico and Arizona. Shortly after this, when the party was on the Mountain Branch of the Santa Fé Trail, they were joined by our author, Dan Conner.

Daniel Ellis Conner was born December 24, 1837, at Bardstown, Kentucky, where he was brought up by relatives. He attended Hanover College, Hanover, Indiana, between 1856 and 1858, after which time he went to Missouri, hoping to find employment as a civil engineer on the railroads. Unable to find suitable work because of the curtailment of railroad constructions following the Panic of 1857, he lived with relatives at Ridgeley, Missouri, until 1859, when he joined a party at Leavenworth, Kansas, which was about to depart for the Colorado gold fields. For the next three years he prospected, finally leaving Georgia Gulch in 1861 and going to the vicinity of Pueblo, where he worked at a military station near what is now Beulah Valley. Encountering difficulties because of his sympathy for the Confederacy, he sought out in the fall of

[21] Orick Jackson, *The White Conquest of Arizona: History of the Pioneers*, 12.
[22] James H. McClintock, *Arizona, Prehistoric—Aboriginal—Pioneer—Modern*, I, 107.
[23] Daniel Ellis Conner to Miss [Sharlot M.] Hall, May 14, 1910. CONNER MANUSCRIPTS, Arizona State Library, Phoenix, Arizona.

INTRODUCTION

1862 the Walker party, which he found south of Raton Pass in northern New Mexico.

Conner remained with the party until its dissolution at Prescott in 1863, and continued to prospect and fight Indians until 1867, when he left for California. Finally, he returned to his home town of Bardstown, where he wrote his thousand-page narrative from notes taken while in the Far West. Little is known of Conner's life thereafter, but in 1869 he had a civil engineering office in Cincinnati. Then he sinks into obscurity again until he appears back in California as the city engineer in Wilmington. When Wilmington was consolidated within the city of Los Angeles on August 5, 1909, Conner lost his position. Some time in 1911 or 1912 he moved to Elsinore, a small town south of Riverside, California, where he again practiced his profession of civil engineering. When his health failed, he entered the Riverside County Hospital, now the General Hospital of San Bernardino County, on May 5, 1917, remaining there until his death on June 19, 1920.

The manuscript written by Conner posed many problems to the editors. First, it is too long for publication in a single volume, and only that portion specifically dealing with New Mexico and Arizona is presented here. A second volume containing Conner's overland trip from Leavenworth, Kansas, to Colorado will appear later. Second, Conner's descriptions of locale are often so vague and confused that only approximations of the location of an event or place can be given. Third, Conner sometimes employs only initials in referring to individuals participating in an event. Often these persons can be identified by internal evidence or other sources, but unfortunately on occasions men will have to remain nameless unless additional documents appear. Fourth, Conner was not a great stylist, grammarian, or speller. We have retained Conner's spelling of names and places, but for ease of reading we have corrected other words and certain punctuation to conform to modern usage. Certain passages have been shortened or deleted where Conner is repetitious or addicted to meaningless or flowery phrases, but no points of fact, opinion, or conclusions have been eliminated.

Despite Conner's efforts to publish his manuscript and his almost pathetic attempts to interest the officials of Arizona in his writings, no previous publication has reproduced his original text. This document is important because it gives the only known eyewitness account of the last years of Joe Walker's travels in the Far West before his death in Contra Costa County, California, on October 27, 1876—a hitherto almost unknown portion of his life. The Conner manuscript is also a contribution to our knowledge of the Southwest because it contains the only known authentic accounts of the death of Mangas Coloradas, of the Pinole Treaty, and of the opening of central Arizona's mines. Finally, it offers in straightforward terms a slice of American exploration and travel in the West which is on a par with the most adventurous accounts we possess for the first two-thirds of the nineteenth century.

Joseph Reddeford Walker
and the Arizona Adventure

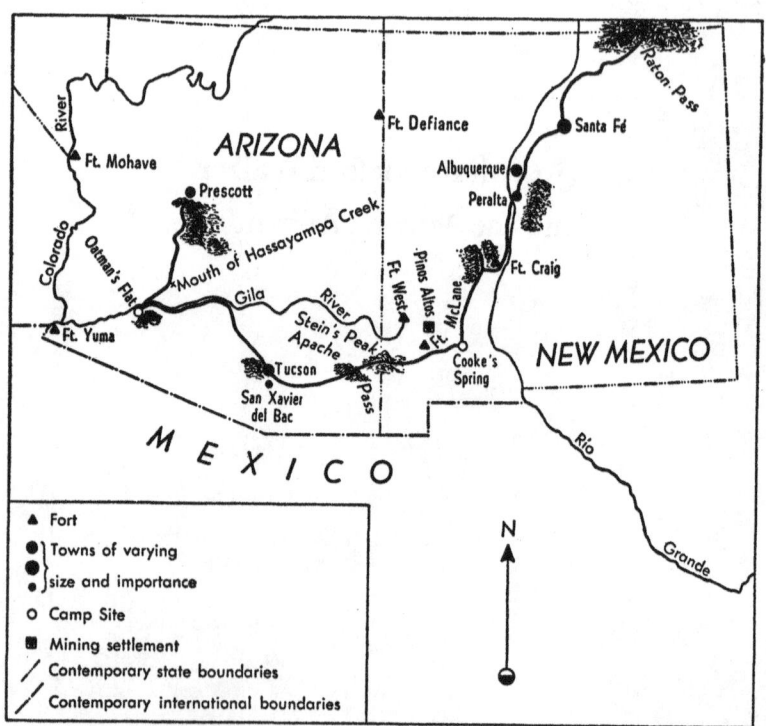

The route of the Walker Party into "the last unexplored wilderness."

Following Joe Walker's Trail

[DAN CONNER no longer found Colorado a hospitable place when the bitterness of the Civil War began to find its way into the mining districts. Southern sympathizers, of whom Conner was a member, attempted to organize a regiment in an effort to aid the Confederate States, but Federal forces, now alerted to danger, began a thorough search for all those who might aid the Southern cause. Conner managed to avoid capture until October, 1862, when a friend, Jim Gray, advised him to join the Walker party, which had passed near by.]

His last advice was accepted, which was to pass on and attempt to catch a citizen exploring party that had passed his house three days previously, en route for Arizona under the leadership of Capt. Joseph R. Walker, a contemporary and friend of Kit Carson. I was informed that I would have to take to the mountains if I followed Walker's trail, for the reason that he didn't follow trails, but rather made them. His thirty men and fifty pack animals left quite a path wherever they went as his mode of travel was that of single file. This gentleman came out again before daylight to be sure that I departed in good time and bade me good-bye. . . . I arose on that morning, feeling that my task of hunting through a hostile Indian country for Walker's party, then probably a hundred miles away, was no ordinary undertaking. Especially without food or the presence of a single white resident within the scope of hundreds of miles. I must confess that the prospect was a wickedly gloomy one. But I rode off from that place in the gray dawn of morning to make the attempt whatever might be the result. I kept up the creek until broad daylight and saw a Mexican slaughtering a sheep, taken from the soldier's herd, which they had driven with them.

I rode up to him and offered him a half-dollar silver piece for some meat. He quickly slashed off a mutton shoulder, and tied it to my saddle. These were Spanish sheep and very small and similar to the usual stock seen in New Mexico, and therefore my piece was small. . . . [A short time later] I saw quite a number of unarmed men, recruits—in the distance, coming, riding in haste. After they passed on within about three hundred paces of me I turned directly up one of the ravines leading up the Ratone Mountain,[1] and began the task of crossing this, my first obstacle between myself and imaginary relief.

I struggled hard all day with the pathless, roadless cañons and gorges. To turn back frequently was a matter of course, in view of so many trifling and so many imposing obstacles to pass. I arrived on the top of the main divide just before sundown and dismounted for the first time during the day and took a seat upon a large rock to contemplate the whole country of which I now had so splendid a view. I could still distinctly see Pike's Peak, a hundred and fifty miles or more away.[2] I felt that I was now forty miles at least from any civilized human creature, and as yet had not seen any sign of Capt. Walker's trail. But I knew that it must lay between me and the front range of the Rocky Mountains, which stupendous ridge now loomed up like an impassable wall,

[1] Conner probably did not mean Raton Mountain, which can be reached from a northerly direction only after an ascent through the Raton Mountains. Another landmark commonly mentioned in this area is Raton Pass, which was utilized by the Mountain Branch of the Santa Fé Trail, running from old Bent's Fort through Raton Pass and joining the main trail at Santa Clara Spring. The Raton Mountains are on the Colorado–New Mexico boundary.

[2] Pikes Peak is closer to 130 miles from the area of Raton Pass.

by which the plains and the mountains were permanently separated. This ridge of imposing peaks and spurs meandered in each direction along the border of the plains as far as the eye could distinguish anything and until they were lost in the distance. I sat in silent contemplation of the sun, which was now large, red, and burning and about passing down behind the range out of my sight.

All was silent and still except the distant, melancholy howl of the wolf—borne upon this exceedingly light atmosphere, it seemed to mellow into more piteous tones than ever. . . . I mounted my horse and directed my course down the opposite side of Ratone Mountain, bearing a little to the right hand, toward the foot of the main range. I had not proceed[ed] more than a mile or two before night and the tall pines on the side of the mountain closed out all light and all my efforts to proceed further.

I selected a grassy plot near a tall pine and picketed my horse to graze. On searching for my mutton shoulder I found that it was missing. I felt that it was a curious fact that I had not missed it nor even thought of it since I had tied it to the rear of my saddle in the morning.

But it was gone and that much was certain. I made no light and it was very dark. So having no supper to be bothered with, nor other camp duties to perform, I rolled myself in my blanket and placed my saddle at the picket pin for a pillow and lay me down to sleep and rest. . . .

[When morning came] I mounted my horse and bore down and toward the main front range foothills which constituted my only guide, and observed closely for signs of Capt. Walker's fresh-made trail. At the distance of about four miles . . . I came across the trail. I entered this plainly beaten fresh path and bent my energies and all of those of my horse to the task of overtaking the party. . . . I . . . hurried on, following my lonely trail until late in the night and until my horse began to fag and show signs of being too much worried and I halted. I hid away in the shade of some scattering trees in a little hollow where it was very dark and picketed my horse to grass, and again slept at the picket pin, rolled in my blanket, with my saddle for my pillow. I now began to feel sick and faint for the want of nourishment. It seemed an age since the Mexican gave me my last humble meal before daylight on the Las Animus river, beyond the Ratone Mountain.[3]

I arose on the following morning and felt well rested and hungry. My horse was in good condition, after feeding all night on luxurious grass. . . . I began my lonely journey again and continued it until about noon, when I again had another run away. I rode suddenly around a little sharp angle of rocks and so close to a grizzly bear that the horrible brute "fetched" a snort like a frightened hog and frightened me and the horse into a sudden stampede which lasted for two hundred yards. . . . I rode on for a few miles and halted for the horse to graze and rest. Here I made up my mind to shoot any game that I could find, for I really felt that I was in a starving condition and my pluck and courage began to grow feeble.

I searched all the little hollows about there, while my horse was feeding. But I found no living thing, not even a bird. I stretched myself on my blanket and forced myself to the conclusion that I didn't need anything to eat, nor wouldn't yet for several days. I mounted again and rode on, following what I now began to believe to be [the] longest trail in the world, to be such a fresh one. Dark again came on and found me as usual, plodding this weary, weary trail. I now really felt the full meaning of discouragement. I had never before known what discouraged resignation did for the overtasked mortal body. Three days of perfect fasting had passed and during which three days great fatigue had been overcome.

Mental anxiety as to the result gave its share of burden, and all together I felt compelled to admit that that kind of pastime was becoming monotonous. The trail looked the same that it

---

[3] The Las Animas River to which Conner is referring is also known as the Purgatoire or the Picketwire. It is the largest tributary of the Arkansas River flowing from the south.

did when I first saw it over a hundred miles to the rear in the foothills of the Ratone Mountain. I began to feel that I was not wanting food—that was not what was the matter, but my reason forced a different conclusion, and I knew this fact alone was the worst feature of the whole matter. At any rate I determined never to stop again until the horse failed completely, whether it was night or day, and therefore I continued my journey in the night. A little before midnight I heard in the distance ahead of me the sharp and businesslike howl of the coyote wolf. It didn't have the twang of sorrow in it. I knew that there was something ahead to engage the attention of howling wolves.

I urged my tired horse to greater efforts for an hour, when I suddenly came in sight of smouldering campfires that appeared only a few hundred yards off, but in reality they were nearly a mile away. I kept traveling, however, but the anxious inquiry uppermost in my mind was, who built those fires, Indians or white men. But as soon as I became near enough to see the dark herd of mules, all huddled together against the side of the mountain, I knew it was not an Indian camp, for they allow their animals to scatter everywhere they choose to go. I rode within a hundred yards and hailed the guard. I soon observed the form of a man slowly passing around the herd of mules and directed his course toward me for some ten paces and stopped. I hailed him again, upon which he came a little farther and asked, "Who are you?" "A friend," I replied, and that was true too, for I felt that I was no enemy to anybody on earth just then. "Come up nearer," was the next order. I put my horse in motion again for the distance of probably twenty paces and was ordered to stop again. I stopped. "Are you an Indian, Mexican, or a white man?" was the next query. "I am a white man." "Who is with you?" "No one." "Where did you come from?" "Colorado." "Ride up nearer." I rode up to within ten paces and was halted again and further questions were put, and the first reply I made, my voice was recognized by an acquaintance, who quickly called my name and asked me if he was right. I now had the privilege of riding up to the two guardsmen and dismounting. It was a mutual surprise, for I recognized in the person of this acquaintance our old friend F. G. Gillilan [4] who had such a race down the ridge from a grizzly bear in Colorado and who only saved himself by making a terrific leap for the lone tree on the ridge. My horse was turned into the herd and I was in the camp of Captain Walker. I was plied with many questions about how I came to go crazy and undertake such a foolish trip alone, but I waved all else except the subject of something to eat. I insisted that I was unable to talk until I had refreshments. F. G. G. informed me that I had another acquaintance in the camp and directed me where to find his bed on the far side of the camp. . . . I followed his directions and awoke S——, who also knew my voice and arose and gave me a hearty supper, a part of which consisted of fresh venison, the first food that I had eaten since I had started on this arduous and dangerous trip. It was long after midnight and after learning that the party was now encamped on a creek in the Rocky Mountains of New Mexico and on the Atlantic side of the Cordillera, I retired to sleep, the first safe sleep, that I had had for several days. . . .

I here joined the Walker Party and traveled with it in the Rocky Mountains for a year and until it was disbanded finally, in Arizona. The strangest story that I told this party on catching up with them was that of not seeing any Indians. They had seen them frequently and were compelled to guard their stock closely on account of their threatening attitude. And they were all surprised that I had run the gauntlet so successfully, without even seeing any of them. This party had obtained a pass from the Governor of Colorado and it was required to obtain one from the authority of New Mexico.[5] Hence the party when be-

[4] Francis G. Gilliland was listed as a native of Kentucky by Conner and was twenty-four years old at the time of the Walker expedition to Arizona. Daniel E. Conner to Miss Hall, Wilmington, California, May 1, 1910, CONNER MANUSCRIPTS.

[5] During the Civil War the military commanders demanded that individuals traveling through their jurisdictions take an oath of allegiance to the United States. An example of this is the proclamation issued by General James H. Carleton when he assumed command of the Territory of Arizona as its military governor on June 8, 1862.

"I. No man who has arrived at lawful age shall be permitted to reside within

coming familiarized with the unrestrained freedom of the wild woods and landscapes felt a great inconvenience by having to travel more than a hundred miles out of the way just to get a pass. But it was done. The party changed its course to bear in the direction of the settlements of New Mexico to obtain the required pass under protests. But Capt. Walker who was well and personally acquainted with Gen. Carleton, whose headquarters were located at Santa Fe, felt that it was his duty to obtain the required pass if it did cost time and trouble.[6] Then this inconvenience was repaid in part by the opportunity it offered for us to observe some of our Mexican brethren's costumes in our newly acquired territory. The settlements, so called, were exceedingly sparse and had rather a nomadic finish about them.

---

this Territory who does not without delay subscribe to the oath of allegiance to the United States.

"II. No words or acts calculated to impair that veneration which all good patriots should feel for our country and Government will be tolerated within this Territory or go unpunished if sufficient proof can be had of them.

"III. No man who does not pursue some lawful calling or have some legitimate means of support shall be permitted to remain in the Territory. . . ." *The War of the Rebellion: A Compilation of the Official Records of the Union and Confederate Armies*, Series I, Vol. IX, 561-62. Hereafter cited as *Official Records of the Union and Confederate Armies*. See also Clarence C. Clendenen, "General James Henry Carleton," *New Mexico Historical Review*, Vol. XXX, No. 1 (January, 1955), 41.

[6] General James Henry Carleton commanded the California Column, which moved west from California in the spring of 1862 to regain control of Arizona and New Mexico, temporarily occupied by Confederate forces under General Henry H. Sibley. General Carleton assumed command of the Union troops in New Mexico in September, 1862. General Order No. 84, Headquarters Department of New Mexico, Santa Fé, New Mexico, September 18, 1862, *Official Records of the Union and Confederate Armies*, Series I, Vol. IX, 582. For a history of the California Column, see William A. Keleher, *Turmoil in New Mexico 1846-1868*, 213 ff.; George H. Pettis, "The California Column," *Papers of the Historical Society of New Mexico*, No. 11.

"I Want Him Dead"—
the Betrayal of Mangas Coloradas

CAPT. JOSEPH R. WALKER, who had been chosen as the leader of this expedition, was a native of West Tennessee, a contemporary and friend of Kit Carson. He went to the Rocky Mountains, and thence to California in 1832, and had roamed and lived in some part of these mountains and Pacific country continuously every since. He was between sixty and seventy years of age and still a fine specimen of physical manhood. He weighed about two hundred pounds and stood over six feet in height; had broad shoulders, black eyes, and luxuriant growth of hair and unshaven beard. He stood erect and was well preserved for his age—walked and moved as easily and nimbly apparently as a boy. Taken in all ways he was still a dignified and reticent man of strong unobtrusive will and deliberate judgment—a good judge of human nature and always apparently cool and fearless. Walker and Carson were associates up to the date of Gen. Fremont's crossing the mountains, when he took Kit Carson with him as a guide to California.[1] I traveled with

[1] After guiding the Chiles party to California in 1843, Walker joined the annual westbound caravan to Santa Fé. When he learned that Frémont and Carson

Courtesy Walters Art Gallery

Joseph Reddeford Walker and his squaw, by Alfred Jacob Miller (1837).

"I WANT HIM DEAD"—THE BETRAYAL OF MANGAS COLORADAS

Capt. Walker through the Rocky Mountains for more than a year, and in the midst of and during all the hardships and dangers of mountain, desert, and vale, I never saw him excited or agitated but once, and that was when his orders were disobeyed during an important and critical situation. And during my whole experience with him I never heard him dwell upon any of his own exploits, nor tell any wonderful story for the edification of those present. Yet he roamed the Rocky Mountains continuously for thirty years and that too during a period when this illimitable romantic wilderness was almost totally unknown by the masses of the people of our country. . . .

This party had no tents, but took the weather as it came. But the preparations for the protection of the necessary supplies &c were efficient and quite sufficient. Each pack mule was provided with two boxes or pockets made of rawhide with the hair outward and had attached near the back upper edge two loops of the same material, by which to hang the box on one side, to the packsaddle. The other box was similarly hung on the opposite side to balance the load; the sides of these two boxes, which lay next and against the animal, extended high enough to be drawn over the top of the box and tied down to keep out the rain. These boxes were made large enough to contain seventy-five pounds of flour to each, sack and all, and were constructed too stout and tight to endanger the safety of anything put into them. Each mule carried two of those pockets, besides the cooking utensils placed on the top and covered with blankets &c, before binding the whole with pack ropes. One of the mules thus caparisoned, was loaded with mule shoes and nails and hammers

---

were traveling ahead of the caravan, Walker overtook them at the site of Mountain Meadow, Utah. From that point Walker guided Frémont's party to Utah Lake, through the Colorado parks, and on to old Bent's Fort which was reached early in July, 1844. Conner is in error at this point, however, because both Carson and Walker accompanied Frémont to California. This expedition was organized at Bent's Fort and left very early in August, 1845. Watson, *West Wind*, 86, 90, 93; John C. Frémont, *Report of the Exploring Expedition to the Rocky Mountains in the Year 1842, and to Oregon and North California in the Years 1843-'44*, 271, 288; Edwin L. Sabin, *Kit Carson Days*, 238-39; Allan Nevins, *Frémont, Pathmarker of the West*, 207 ff.

&c, with which to put them on. The party was prepared to live for an indefinite time in the wilderness by all conveniences except tents. We had to take the weather as it came.

On the following morning from my arrival in camp the party arose early and took up the usual single file march with Captain Walker at the head of the line. The pack mules would follow him just where ever he chose to go, whether the ground was rough or smooth. When one of them ventured to turn aside to select a better road than marked by the animal next in front, he generally received such kicks and cuffs from the next following rider as were necessary to teach him his error and to warn him not to leave the trail again. I now easily understood how this party had made such a neat trail for me to follow. We made many camps on many different days and nights and killed wild game in abundance until we began to draw near to Taos. We came out of the roughest mountains, taking the nearest direction to Santa Fe to get the requisite passport to entitle us to the privilege of exploring this desert wilderness. We arrived at the old circular rock corral which has been known by the oldest citizens for fifty years, and camped. This was eight miles or thereabout from Santa Fe.[2] We visited the city from this old camp several times during several days.

But we moved off a mile further to a spring and bivouacked for a few days. While we were here the Indians came within sight and captured a herd of sheep and the Mexican boy with them. They always took the herder as well as the herd, in order to have a slave to continue the care of the sheep captured.... Finally Gen. Carleton, who was stationed at Santa Fe, sent out an officer and company of soldiers to investigate us. On arriving in sight they halted long enough to form in line and then came up to within twenty paces of our camp in "big" style and halted in line. The officer in command quickly dismounted, as though he fully appreciated the greatness of the occasion, and came for-

---

[2] Abraham Robinson Johnston, *Journal of Abraham Robinson Johnston, 1846*, in Ralph P. Bieber, (ed.), *Marching with the Army of the West*, 316, places the Rock Corral eight miles from Santa Fé on the Santa Fé Trail.

"I WANT HIM DEAD"—THE BETRAYAL OF MANGAS COLORADAS

ward *à la militaire,* and informed Capt. Walker that his men would have to take the oath of allegiance to the United States before they would be permitted to proceed further. Our old captain asked why Carleton didn't come out, and continued coolly, "I expected him, after receiving word to that effect. I have known Carleton for many years and have had many games of euchre with him, but had I have known that he was not coming I should not have waited here nearly a week for a pass simply because I can take these men and pass anywhere in this wilderness without fear or favor. I only waited here to be courteous to my old friend." [3] We proceeded toward the Rio Grande, passing to the left of Albuquerque and in the direction of Peralta on the Rio Grande, where we expected to cross the river.[4] This country was comparatively unsettled, only on the creeks. We had now passed through enough of New Mexico to observe the foreign aspect of everything. The surface of the country presented every character and degree of existing condition thought to be necessary to engage the domestic attention of domestic interests and welfare. The high, dry land covered in some sections with dry, short, and thinly settled grass, and in other with loose drifting sand and rocky neighboring spurs projecting from hills, peaks, and ridges which stand, lay, and extend in all directions, certainly offer a sufficient variety of landscape from which to select a satisfactory location for someone else's home at least. The strips of timber growing here and there over a great portion of the Territory seem to be generally confined to the ridges and rolling hills and consists for the most part of scrubby pine, piñon, and cedar. The little towns are composed of houses that

[3] This statement is difficult to understand. Carleton and Walker might have been friends, but certainly we can wonder what Walker meant by an "old friend." Carleton did not appear on the frontier until 1841 and served for a period of time at Forts Leavenworth and Gibson. After the Mexican War, Carleton was stationed in New Mexico from 1851 to 1856, but during this time Walker spent the greater portion of his time in California as far as the records show. Perhaps their acquaintance dates from this period or from the autumn of 1858 when Carleton rejoined his company at Fort Tejon, California. Clendenen, "General Carleton," *New Mexico Historical Review,* Vol. XXX, No. 1 (January, 1955), 26–33.

[4] Peralta is located on the east bank of the Río Grande about eighteen miles south of Albuquerque.

appear in the distance to be a collection of small brick kilns and are built of adobe.

The alcaldes and padres are generally the only personages of any consequence in the whole country and are usually found about the little villages, lazily engaged in a game of cards, or else they are asleep. The houses seldom have any other than a solidly beaten dirt floor and the major part of the people live and reside at their homes without a table or a chair, knife or fork about the establishment. Their houses inside and out looked as void of comfort or conveniences or even of household plunder as a chicken-coop, and frequently without a fireplace.

I came across a grist mill, which I examined minutely, as I thought that I might not see another like it. But in this particular I was mistaken, for these Mexicans seemed to have the same kind of knack for making similar things out of similar materials that birds have in constructing their nests. This mill stood, as all the others did, in a little hollow on four legs, and covered a square surface of about eight feet. A floor was built on the top of these legs and upon this floor was erected a little room about six feet high. One mill-stone was laid on the floor and made fast and the other was placed on the first one. A rude wooden shaft with wooden gudgeons, stood perpendicularly under the center of the floor in a socket in a rock, and the top of the shaft extended through the floor and the first stone and was made fast to the upper one. The lower end of the shaft was bristled with numerous rude paddles which were driven into it horizontally and were about three feet in length. A little stream of water was flowing down the hill through an artificial ditch, and was guided against the paddles by a small trough. The corn was poured by hand into a hole in the center of the upper stone and the meal came out from between the two stones all around their circumferences, and fell on the floor ready to be scraped up for use. If there was a particle of iron about this mill, even as much as a nail, it was not visible.

Their vehicles, like their mills, were all about the same pattern, from one end of the Territory to the other. This contrivance consisted of two wheels, an axle, a pair of thills, and a rude bed. The wheels were about four inches thick and about two and a half feet in height and each was composed of three pieces of cottonwood slabs and fastened together into one piece, out of which the wheel cut round, or nearly so. It was amusing to see a little Mexican ox hitched to one of these carts and pulling a load. The vehicle was connected to a board which was first firmly bound to the animal's horns. Having to draw the load entirely by the horns and forehead, the little animal would project his nose to the front with his forehead horizontal, pull his best as he traveled and kept constantly licking out his tongue and rolling his eyes with great efforts to see the ground, and would patiently prolong these exertions until I began to feel tired myself from looking on at such desperately hard work. The custom of carrying wood on these little harmless and docile donkeys, I presume, is one of the oldest established modes of obtaining firewood by the Mexicans. They carry miraculous loads on these little burros. It was not an uncommon sight those days to see a Mexican driving a donkey with a square load of wood on him that looked in the distance like there might be a half cord of it. The donkey is the most useful animal that the Mexicans have and they treat them cruelly. They mount the little animal when they want to ride him, from behind, after the fashion of leap frog.

I never saw or heard of a blacksmith shop in the Territory. Rawhide takes the place of iron in Mexico. In great portions of the country where timber is scarce and hard to obtain for firewood the Mexican will search on the desert country for a certain kind of wood which mostly develops itself in the ground and beneath the surface. Its presence is generally indicated by a switch or possibly a half-dozen of them growing out of the ground. On prospecting the place, with a pick and shovel, there may be found a half cord of good wood or roots, the pieces of which may in some instances be eight or ten inches in diameter. It seemed to me an odd way of obtaining fuel, as wood, but as I before stated, everything looked foreign and was foreign to all customs known by the writer at the time. The Mexicans even dug their soap out of the ground. A plant which botanists attempted to conceal under the name of *Yucca Augustifolia*, palmillo of the Spaniards, but in plain Anglo-American lingo—"soap plant"—was universally sought after, for the purpose of washing and laundering.[5] The root alone was used and being succulent and soft, it would all wash away like a bar of soap except a slight remnant of sinewy fiber, which had the appearance of a quantity of entangled white thread.

Numbers of the little handfuls of this fiber would be found lying about neighboring water holes after wash day. The plows used by the Mexicans all through New Mexico for cultivating the soil were as nearly alike in construction as are those manufactured in the United States. They were of the most simple, primitive order, consisting of and formed from the fork of a tree. One fork was cut short and sharpened to go into the ground, while the other extended horizontally for a beam by which it was drawn. The main trunk of the tree from which the model seemed to have been taken extended back a sufficient length to support a handle by which to guide the machine. The handle was usually a straight stick bound on firmly with a rawhide thong cut for the purpose. There was no iron used in the construction of the Mexican plow. When those people went on a trip, either for business or pleasure with their women, they generally rode in pairs. The man first mounted the pony or burro or donkey and took the woman before him, after the style of our fathers, carrying children on horseback. The custom of the people on meeting each other was to embrace with one arm instead of shaking hands, like the barbarous Anglo-Americans. Men, women, and children greeted each other thus. One pretty Mexican lady, who had heard of our approach, not far from

---

[5] E. O. Wooton and Paul C. Standly, "Flora of New Mexico," *Contributions to United States National Herbarium, 1915,* 136, identify this plant in the following way: "This is the common narrow leaved Yucca of southern New Mexico, known as 'palmilla,' or 'soapweed.' The roots termed 'amole,' are often used as a substitute for soap. . . ." This species of the Yucca is found from West Texas to Utah and from Arizona to northern Mexico.

Santa Fe, came to a neighboring house where some of our party halted a few moments. There was a priest present who smiled upon us benignantly after embracing each of us, as also did the lady.

But there was one of our "boys" behind, who had not seen the affectionate salutations, and who was not acquainted with the style. As he came up and dismounted with the rest of us, the woman being the nearest stepped to his side and embraced him before he knew what was going on. He let go of his bridle rein and started back a little, with his eye on the woman in surprise and quickly exclaimed, "Look here, what in the d—l are you going to do?" The woman understood the tenor of his remarks, although she couldn't speak English. She smiled pleasantly at what she considered the fellow's ignorance, while the balance of the party laughed heartily at his confusion. Until the matter was explained to him he thought that it was a made-up trick to impose upon his ignorance. The Mexican women are far superior to the men and almost universally amiable and have pretty forms. Their kindliness of disposition greatly contrasts with the sour and suspicious glances of their treacherous men. The women were modest and retiring in their deportment and generally wore at this period a kind of shawl wrapped about the head and face, which they called a *rebozo*. Their arms and shoulders were naked, except when the *rebozo* would extend over them. The rest of the dress was similar to that of American ladies.

The men who had means to do so dressed after our fashion, but by far the greater number, when they dressed at all, wore leather breeches tight around the hips and open from the knee down. Sometimes the open trouser leg would have a row of buttons and button holes on either side, with which to close it in case of necessity or pleasure. The first act of a Mexican after purchasing a pair of new pants is to rip the outer seam from the hip to the foot, in order to expose his white undergarment. They take great pride in wearing pure and spotless white underclothing and in this respect are superior to their corresponding class of Americans. The Mexicans are our superior in horsemanship, as they are also in politeness. Naturally graceful in their movement, their salutations at a little distance are rather upon the order of a cultivated military salute. They evidently cultivate this art even amongst the lower classes. But they are all really paupers in New Mexico. They would visit our camps as we passed through their vicinity, and sit around with their *sarapes* drawn tightly around their manly, worthless shoulders, holding the customary number of three eggs, three onions &c, for which they wanted twenty-five cents, or eight and a third cents apiece.

Another would come only a few hundred yards, riding a donkey, for he was afraid of looking like he belonged to the lower class if he walked. He would dismount and let his donkey loose. But if the donkey moved, he would check it by a prolonged Sh-e-e-e—like driving the chickens out of a garden. This is their only command to a horse, mule, or donkey to quiet it, or bring it to a halt. They stop a dog by the same serpent-like hiss, which we use to set him on.

But however, this is enough of the Mexican just now. His mode of worship in churches without seats has nothing to do with this outline, for they have no seats anywhere except on the ground, and in particular they were as well off as the members of our party. We were again several days without seeing a single residence and were glad to feel that we were departing from all their settlements. We arrived in an unsettled, pretty, grassy valley, and encamped by an old deserted adobe house of one room and roofless. There was also an adobe wall or corral for stock connected with the house and about six feet high, with prickly pears and other species of cactus planted all around the top of it. This had been a stock ranch and had been robbed and plundered by the Apaches. I was on guard with others, and a cold bleak night it was. On this occasion I saw the first eclipse of the moon. None of the party were aware of the approaching eclipse and consequently none but the guards saw it. It took us by surprise, growing dark so rapidly, and hid our animals totally from sight. We lost an animal that night and failed to find it again until long after daylight. In our dark search for the brute each of us climbed over the wall and received a share of the cactus prickles, which had been planted for defense.

Capt. Walker was displeased by the carelessness that lost the animal, but we pleaded the eclipse as the cause. We passed on and at the end of several days crossed the Rio Grande some distance above Peralta. One of our party first rode across the river to test its depth and safety. But his crossing was soon observed to have disturbed the quicksand to such an extent that the water, which was only belly deep to the horse going over, was a few moments later deep enough to have drowned a giraffe. Our party crossed single file, each going further up the river to avoid the route just previously taken by some other one of the party. This was continued until the last one going over started from a point a half mile above where the first passage was made. But the section of the river thus crossed would have floated a steamboat a few minutes after we were all safely over.

Our direction now lay down the river. We passed Peralta, Valencia, Tome, Limitar, and many other little towns on each side of the river. The Mexicans, men, women, and children, fled from our approach as though we were demons. They would flee from the houses in any convenient direction across the vineyards, corn patches, &c, shouting at every jump "Tehanas, Tehanas, Tehanas," as though Sibley's vanguard was surely coming again. They had all seen a little of the conflicts of 1861, between the armies of Gen. Sibley and Canby.[6] We were many days reaching the battle ground of Valverde and one and a half miles above Ft. Craig. We camped under the large cottonwood trees where Canby had his artillery planted. The Indians showed themselves below the gap through which the army of

[6] Colonel E. R. S. Canby commanded the Union troops at the battle of Valverde which began February 21, 1862. The Confederate forces, although numerically inferior to the Union troops and led by Brigadier Gerenal Henry H. Sibley, drove the Union army to Fort Craig. Keleher, *Turmoil in New Mexico*, 169–72; William I. Waldrip, "New Mexico During the Civil War," *New Mexico Historical Review*, Vol. XXVIII, Nos. 3 and 4 (July, October, 1953), 177–79; *Official Records of the Union and Confederate Armies*, Series I, Vol. IX, 486–87, 505–506.

Sibley passed down to the river to the position in which they contested the battle of Valverde. They fired a few shots at us and drew off, over the mountain out of our sight, passing through this gap which lies between the Mesa da la Jordana and Sierra del Oso. We left this camp and passed up a little nameless creek coming in from the right hand until we came near the edge of the plain upon which Ft. Craig is situated.

We passed the fort and encamped for a day or two in a bend of the river surrounded by a rolling plain. The commandant at Ft. Craig sent us a five-gallon keg of whiskey, which resulted in extreme happiness of the major part of our party. Capt. Walker took in the situation easily and ordered for the first time that all the animals be "side lined" for the night.

This process consisted in buckling the end of a leather strap around the hindmost ankle. Then to draw the hindmost foot up nearly to the foremost foot to which the other end of the strap is buckled. Thus the two feet of the animal on the same side are secured so near to each other that the animals cannot be stampeded, for the want of the use of their legs. We were now a long distance from even Mexican settlements. All was quiet until about midnight. The attempt of the stock to run, together with three or four quick, successive shots, aroused our camp thoroughly. We always shaped our campground in a circle of thirty or forty yards in diameter; hence the beds and campfires were always in a circle. Each member crawled out of his blankets in the dark and remained quiet when this alarm came. The mules were in motion, hobbling toward our campground, followed by the guard. There had not yet been a word spoken and it was very dark. So dark that the animals were really within the circle before their guard knew it.

Capt. Walker walked across the right and stopped the mules after stirring up a light. He caught G[eorge] L[ount] putting a charge in his gun and halted, and the following conversation took place. "Why Mr. L[ount], didn't I give orders particularly that all the guns should be loaded tonight?" "Yes sir, but I cleaned my gun just before dark and thought that I would wait for it to get dry before reloading it." "Does it take your gun half the night to dry after cleaning it?" "No, reckon not that long." "Well, why didn't you reload it?" "I didn't think that there was any use of it, because I thought there were no danger here." "No danger, no danger," broke in the old Captain, "no danger—I have seen a great many 'no danger' men since I have been in the mountains and I have got the first one yet to see that it is worth a d—n for anything. You are always in danger in an Indian country." After a few random shots were fired into camp all became quiet and the guard was doubled, and the remainder retired in peace to their blankets to sleep.

On the following morning the headdress of an Indian was picked up and brought into camp. The red paint off of the wearer's forehead was fresh coated on to this crown. We took our leave of this place and turned directly into the wilds of Arizona and where our next camp was located cannot be described. There was no landmarks sufficient known to know where we were ourselves. Suffice it [to] say after two or three days travel directly into the Apaches' stronghold, their signal smokes could be seen in all directions almost continuously and especially early in the morning. Capt. Walker called it Indian telegraphy. One morning when I awoke I was surprised to find our camp the center of a circle of Indian signal smokes. It now took the neatest kind of caution to avoid their traps.

Day after day these smokes would loom up in a line with each other and in a direct line with the course that we were going, yet we could see no Indian.

Time and again they would have our party surrounded entirely and we would pass out of their lines upon the highest ground which lay in our direction, and sometimes succeed without firing a shot. There were only thirty-three in our party and therefore our policy was to avoid them rather than to seek battle. But Capt. Walker kept them laying plans for two weeks without giving them any satisfaction. They would fortify a gap and wait for us, but we would never go through the right one. They would lay in wait at the limited watering places, but we would camp in a dry desert or on a dry hill for the night and get water as we crossed it in the daytime. If we became entangled in rough and craggy places so near night that we could not find an open place to occupy during the night, we would huddle together on the summit of a little peak until daylight. We fired on a grizzly on the side of a mountain among the rocks and chaparral. The hill was so steep that the bear tumbled down it and the Indians on the opposite side of the narrow ravine took a position to command the approach to the dead bear, and we had to leave it to them or run the risk of losing some of our mules or men. We therefore passed on and made a tedious passage out of this rugged position.

We found the Indians too strong for us in this continuous and apparent endless expanse of terribly broken country. Serious obstacles were continuously confronting us, necessitating a slow and uncertain progress. We found a long sharp ridge and took up our march to its top. It was rocky and craggy and covered sparsely with low chaparral. A sharp, precipitous ravine divided this ridge from a similar one, which was occupied by a strong force of Indians. The occupants of both ridges traveled nearly all day parallel with each other and kept up an irregular skirmish across this nearly impassable ravine, all day.

They had the advantage of their ridge as a breastwork for their footmen, but we could not always keep our mules out of sight behind our ridge and therefore had some of them wounded, but the wounds of our men were inconsiderable.

We had the advantage of better and heavier guns and therefore the responsibilities on each side were somewhat equal at last. But we finally reached a comparatively open country into which the Apaches failed to follow. The Apache loves to play the cunning, at which game he is an adept, but an open fight away from rocks and trees has no charms for him unless he greatly outnumbers the enemy. Even then the white man with his repeating rifle supported by a reserve of two heavy six-shooters, was regarded by them as a dangerous animal.

Capt. Walker concluded that to force our way through this

rugged unexplored country to central Arizona with so small a force was nearly hopeless, in view of the rapidly increasing resistance offered by the savages in addition to the apparent impassable, broken country. We therefore changed to a southwest course. Capt. Walker said that there was a spring known as "Kook's Spring" in that direction, which he had visited once, which had been nearly thirty years previously.[7] He said that it was the only landmark that he knew by which he could be safely guided. Therefore to find it was desirable. We traveled nearly constantly for two days without finding any water. On the morning of the third day we found ourselves in quite a good grazing country, but without water. The party stopped and unpacked the animals for a temporary rest. It was about noon and both man and beast suffered greatly from the want of water. Then there was much anxiety felt, if not expressed, as to our old Captain's doubtful guess at the true position of a spring that he had only seen once, in such a rugged country as this, and that, too, after the expiration of thirty years. While resting here, he selected five of us to go ahead and look out for the spring, faced with a large, flat square rock high up the mountain and overlooking the spring. We took the direction he indicated and went afoot, for our animals were so worn down that we could beat them traveling. We were informed that the party would follow us pretty soon and we were ordered that if we found the water, to not go to it until the party came up. Our Captain remarked that there would be Indians always found at the watering in such a desert country and we would be therefore liable to surprise. We walked briskly until about the middle of the afternoon when we descried a large flat rock in the side of a mountain four or five miles away and ahead of us. Feeling conscious that the party were following in our rear, we redoubled our speed until we were in a half-mile of the mountain and standing

[7] Cooke's Spring was near present Deming, New Mexico, and was named after Philip St. George Cooke, who commanded the Mormon Battalion on its overland march to California in 1846–47. Later, it was a station on the Butterfield Overland Mail route, and Fort Cumming was established near it. Roscoe P. and Margaret B. Conkling, *The Butterfield Overland Mail, 1857–1869*, II, 113.

on the border of the highlands overlooking a little valley at our feet, which was lying between us and the mountain. We halted here and became convinced that we had found the place sought. Whilst sitting on the ground looking down onto the little narrow valley, we espied a small squad of probably a half-dozen Indians crossing the narrow opening at the lower end on a fatigued looking dog-trot toward a long, sharp rocky spur that joined the mountain. We were now satisfied that the old Captain was right and the spring was near.

We guessed that the party was not far behind us and therefore concluded to descend into the valley and hunt the spring, which we did and found it, and got a "big" drink, contrary to orders. But its well-used banks and recent moccasin prints impressed us with an intuition that urged our departure immediately after getting the drink. Subsequent events proved the wisdom of the Captain's caution, for on raising the hill toward the highland in the direction that we had come, a long-ranged volley was sent after us from the rocks at the foot of the mountain. We were not hit and hurried on to meet the party, which we did, but were much longer doing it than expected. We gave the glad tiding that the mountain described was surely the place where the spring was because the large rock was there and because the Indians were there and had fired on us in the distance.

We failed to tell Captain Walker that we had gone to the spring and drank, and after thinking it over, we begun to fear that we had left our tracks in our haste, to detect our disobedience. But all's well that ends well. The party arrived and detailed an advance guard to scour the foot of the mountain to clear away all resistance, before taking the animals to water, and before the men could go to drink, as thirsty as they were.

We couldn't stay at the spring, however, but went into a camp a distance from it, and when we wanted water we would detail "drawers of water" to get it while the rest kept the Indians in the rocks, by rifle exercise, at all available hiding places in gunshot of the water.

"I WANT HIM DEAD"—THE BETRAYAL OF MANGAS COLORADAS

We left this point for the mountainous sections toward the west. We had lost all dates and days but knew that [we] were traversing a country whose soil may be said to have no history, or at least none whatever, except what may be taken from an obscure tradition. The pre-historic man of Arizona is destined to cut a sorry figure in the history of that country unless his claims to consideration are couched in the mists of fiction and poetry. From my own observation he had a history and maybe an important one, but badly lost. There are many evidences, plainly visible in that extensive wilderness, which indicated to a certainty that a previous condition of the inhabitants has existed, which was vastly superior to that of its present population.

It appeared indeed strange that we could constantly travel and traverse a new region by the day, week, and year, without ever seeing a single instance of care, toil, or evidence of other consideration for future want, more considerate than are usually provided by wild animals. A stump from which a tree had been cut, or the print of an edged tool on anything would have looked like a strange dream here in this land of purely original aspect....

There are only a few acres to an averaged thousand throughout the Territory fit for cultivation. For months we strayed about habitless plains, waterless deserts, and treeless mountains, searching for gold diggings and wild game.

We would sometimes find game in superabundance, and then perhaps for the next month, do without because we unluckily happened to blunder into a section whose only inhabitants were lizards, rattlesnakes, horned toads and coyote wolves. There were great scopes of this sort of country to cross from time to time, where the adventurer loses all interest in everything save his own trifling existence alone in such an inanimated, lifeless, inert, and waterless region. The picture might be said to have been finished by an eternal, brooding silence, which would drown every animated throb in its deluge of delirous nonenity. But even in view of all these facts, there will be circumstances connected, out of which will spring impulses that are quickened into gratification at the sight of any living thing—yea, even at the sight of a snake or horned toad. Now observe yonder lone and distant mountain. It is studded with green pines, piñon, and oaks and looks grand, animated, and beautiful as it seems to command and smile upon the poverty of the surrounding country. The dazzling sun rays are refracted from it in all directions. The heart leans toward that beautiful and inviting retreat instinctively. Hasten over the burning, desert surface until this destination is reached, and of all the disappointments, it is the worst to contemplate. This place was sought with a light heart and a quickened step, while all other considerations were triumphantly dismissed in the midst of the happy contemplations of rest and abundance of fresh water. But alas, the beauty is flown out from amongst these trees. Dry naked ridges and alternate gorges traverse this mountain to its summit, while the scrubby trees hang in the crevices of the rocks and on the dry ground by precarious means. They look sorry and condemned here, as they seem to exist without an object other than to bear with painful submission, this continuous, unbroken, and murderous silence. No animal nor living thing seemed to inhabit this prodigious pile of granite-mount[ed] craggy defiance of all descriptions as it stands boldly out in the sun-lit desert, like the shattered segments of a sin-stricken world. . . .

But however, we left this artless scenery and continued on a westerly course. We were straightened out in a single file as usual, with our old Captain at the head, and traversing an arid plain which was bordered on our right hand some five miles away, by a range of partially wooded mountains. We observed to our right hand an Indian sitting on his horse, erect, and dignified, and about five hundred yards off. His lance-blade rested in its scabbard fixed about the stirrup, while its long shaft leaned against his left shoulder and projected high above his head. He hailed us in broken Spanish, and desired a pow-wow. Our line halted and the Captain rode a little way toward him and asked him in Spanish to come nearer. The Apache refused to trust, and so did the Captain. Now one of our men espied another "brave" similarly equipped, sitting upon his horse away beyond this fellow, and remarked it to Captain, who then drew out his spyglasses from the case in front of his saddle and discovered a regular line of such sentinels extending entirely to the foot of the range of mountains referred to.

Some of our boys begged the old Captain to allow them to open fire on the suspicious sentinel, but he said that there was nothing to be gained by it, and we passed on, leaving the proud looking savage sitting still, looking after our departure. This was about December, 1862. We encamped that night on this plain and without water. But it was right cold at night and we built fires out of sage-brush.

On the morning following we were again surrounded with signal smokes in the distance, and indeed the savages never failed to have their signals out upon any day afterward. We were again beset by the wily and cunning Apache on every hand. We failed to find an open gap in a high range, and therefore turned toward the old Southern Route to California, and after thirsting for water for nearly three more days, we came in sight of what was known as Stein's Peak.[8] This is a moderately prominent pointed peak covered apparently with piñon trees. We saw what we supposed a signal smoke arising from its foot, but pushed on to find water, which we did and encamped near by. Some of the men went to investigate the cause of the smoke and found three white men, who it seemed had been crazy enough to attempt a passage over this "Southern Route" alone, to California.

They were hanging by their ankles all in a row to a horizontal piñon limb. Their hands were tied behind them and their heads hung to within a foot of the ground and a little fire had been built directly under each head. They were dead and the

---

[8] Stein's Peak, named after Major Enoch Stein of the United States Dragoons, who camped there with his command in March, 1856, while en route to occupy Tucson under the terms of the Gadsden Treaty, is about nineteen miles west of present Lordsburg, New Mexico. Later, it was a station on the Butterfield route. Conkling, *Butterfield Overland Mail*, II, 129.

skin and their hair was burned off of their skulls, giving them a ghastly appearance as they swung there perfectly naked. We re-covered them up with dirt just deep enough, in our haste, for the wolves to scratch them out easily, and left them in their wild and lonely resting place without a name or an epitaph. The savages hung around us all the evening, but kept out of reach. In the morning they fired at us from a ridge, but they were too far to effect anything and we never even replied to their salutations.

We started again for the main Cordillera and surveyed it for weeks without finding an opening through it unoccupied, and therefore were unable to get on to the Pacific side of the Rocky Mountains. Each party maneuvered for days to get an advantage so as to make an effective onslaught, but both parties were too prudent to risk without a certainty.

We knew that our defeat meant destruction and therefore held the enemy aloof by adhering to an open country. The Apache thought that he would out general us in the end and therefore contented himself for a long while with setting cunning traps and making feints to annoy. They would steal around the guardsmen at night and raise quietly from behind a rock or ridge or bunch of bushes, while holding a "bouquet" of brush in the left hand and before the face, so as not to be noticed, until their gun, which was extended through the bouquet, was discharged.

Sometimes they would wear a crown on the head bedecked with brush and oak boughs so as to look in the dark like a bunch of boughs growing slowly up from behind a large boulder some twenty paces off from my beat. I had observed that boulder before dark and knew that if there had been any brush behind it I would have been sure to have noticed it and marked the fact in my memory. I unhesitatingly sent a Sharp's rifle ball to investigate the strange bunch of brush, which disappeared immediately upon the crack of the rifle. On the following morning the crown was there, with some of the sprays shot out of it, and leaving the stubs. I had shot a little too high, or else poor "Lo" had kept his head too low. Our next camp was located on a volcanic plain of perhaps fifty acres or more of level land covered with a luxuriant growth of *grama* grass, interspersed with half-hidden black volcanic rocks that looked like cold, hard lumps of lava slag. The ever industrious John Apache, as he is called on the border, was hovering the edge of the little plain amongst the rocks of the foothills, in force. Their object was to stampede the stock first and then shoot as many men in the mêlée as might be convenient. But the first motion was discovered by one of our dogs in time to countervail their calculations. We had two dogs in the party that lent material aid sometimes. One was a large brindled bulldog and the other, a light and lithe curly shepherd of a grisly, gray color. The latter, from his peculiar color, could hardly be seen at a little distance early in the morning or late in the evening. "Curly" had just seen the Indians as their first arrow was thrown at a mule, and to the surprise of the red skins, the dog made an affrighted leap out of the rocks not far from them and ran for dear life to camp, probably two hundred yards off. But the action of the dog drew the attention of the guard, who now discovered the arrow sticking into a restless mule. The Indians kept as still in the edge of the brush as so many partridges, but the dog indicated the direction from whence the arrow came, by his vigilance in looking that way. Every one of the "boys" now vigorously turned loose a half-dozen balls each into that hillside.

Not a thing was seen to move. But it was afterward discovered that one of the savages who had concealed himself in so rugged a place that when the stray ball killed him, his friends could not get his body out without exposing themselves, and consequently deserted him to the enemy. This was like fighting ghosts, as no one but the dog had ever seen one of these insidious creatures alive on this occasion.

Their signal smokes could now be seen springing up all over the country from one to ten miles distant. On leaving this little rocky prairie on the following morning we were beset by the savages in every direction that we attempted to move. But we at last took the clearest route offered, while the savages played along on the border, keeping parallel to our course and shooting from the rocks in neighboring hillsides all day, without doing any particular injury.

A lonely and scattering volley sometimes would check their bold pretensions for quite a spell. It was decided that we could not get through the worst gorges where the Indians were so numerous and therefore were compelled to take a circuitous route back toward the old "Southern" route to California. After a few more days of travel we encamped within a mile of the old road referred to. We again rested for the night on a little level plot between the mountains. Coyote wolves here strewed the plain. They could be seen everywhere. Some of the men set a couple of beaver traps out a distance from the camp on the desert prairie. In the morning each trap had a wolf by the fore paw. These traps were connected to a long slender chain, and in preparing it for business the opposite end of the chain is made fast to a stake driven into the ground or a bush that is stout enough to hold firmly. A forked stick is obtained with which to hold the wolf at a proper distance while he is being led into camp to do battle with Curly, who was always ready to fight a wolf. The dog and coyote were pretty well matched in all ways except running, but this was obviated by the necessary wounded foot disabled by the trap. Our cruel and mischievous fellows would keep these animals fighting as long as Curly could hold out and then let the old brindled bulldog finish the wolves which was always done with dispatch.

We would sometimes, when times were dry and there was no excitement, have three or four coyote wolves harnessed up ready for battle at one time. Like everything else there were two or three of our party who could make two wolves fight each other and never fail, while all the others would always fail.

We struck the road again and I know not where. This route from the Missouri River to California meandered through mountains, plains, deserts, and valleys for a distance of two thousand miles, hence there were not many points on the route in proportion to the distance which had any name by which to fix an incident to a particular locality. But wherever it was, [we] found eight dead bodies to attest to the industry of poor "Lo." It was not the custom of the Apaches to scalp their victims, but all of these were scalped except one, who had a luxurious suit of long black hair which may or may not have been the reason of their failure to scalp him. One of the bodies was in a sitting posture, reclining a little backward against a bunch of cacti to which he had been bound and burned. All of the body was not consumed and it was still partially supported by some of the unburned thongs. A few of the old firebrands were lying about the sitting body of which there was but little consumed by fire. We covered them over with dirt in one common pile and left the place, and I have never seen it since. It began now to appear impossible for us to reach central Arizona by a direct route. It seemed that we could not get through the main divide onto the Pacific side of the mountains anywhere near the right point.

We took a southwest course and after several days went into camp at an old crater of a volcano which was nearly full of hot water.

The weather was very cold and the ground was frozen. We could see the smoke arising from this ugly hole in the ground for some miles before reaching it, and at first thought that it was another signal smoke. Its throat was about eight feet in diameter and situated in the center of a little knoll, which was not higher than numerous other little hills in the vicinity that it took to constitute merely a rolling country. The knoll was grassy and quite smooth from its base up to the shattered cracked rocks which constituted the lining of this dangerous looking shaft. The circular shape of this wall was evidently what kept it from falling in. The water was blue and clear and stood within a few feet of the top, and indeed so near the top that I could easily dip it up with a quart cup. But I never dipped but one cup full, for as I turned to get away with the water, the rocks grated under my feet treacherously and on making a sudden start the water spilled on my hand and convinced me that the water was not merely warm, but hot. The water was so clear that the bubbles of gas which was constantly coming to the surface, by the "bushel," could be distinctly seen at a great depth and observed easily until its arrival at the surface, where it agitated the water like a boiling chaldron. The gas would cease coming nearly entirely for a short interval and then make up for the deficiency by coming in vast quantities of globules, large and small, and on reaching the surface jump up and create the boiling agitation referred to. There was also a fresh cold-water spring within twenty feet or less of the crater, out of which we obtained our camp supply while tarrying there. . . .

The rock wall of this crater showed the unmistakable evidence of the action of fire and from all of its apparent details this evident throat of Vulcan's fireworks may again awaken the inhabitants of the land from their dreamy indifference to the existence of this silent but living specimen of Nature's artillery We left this locality and proceeded for a day near and along the foot of the Cordillera of the Rocky Mountains and finally departed from it toward the southwest and went into camp in the midst of what might be called a rolling, uneven plain, or rather a prairie country. Our camp was located amongst the ruins of an old fort which had been thrown up for a temporary purpose and made of pine logs. It was from five to ten miles from woodland at the foot of the Cordillera. The old cabins were roofless and had been partially burned, but there was enough debris left to supply us with fuel for some weeks.

The weather was the coldest that I ever experienced in Arizona, it being in February, 1863. This place had been named Ft. McLean and was about eight miles north of the old Southern Route to California and probably temporarily located here to protect the new gold mines discovered by Mexicans just on the eve of the late war.[9] At any rate the mining camp which had

[9] Fort McLane was first established as Camp Webster on September 16, 1860, but was renamed Fort Floyd and finally Fort McLane. It was abandoned July 3, 1861. Fort McLane was located about twelve miles west of a point where the Butterfield route crossed the Mimbres River and about fifteen miles south of the

been previously established on the principal heights of the Rocky Mountain range opposite and twenty miles northerly from this fort, was deserted when the troops left.

This camp was called "Pene Alto," after quite a number of log houses were built there.[10] It was the first camp or town I ever saw that was intended to be permanently established upon the top of a great and principal ridge of the Rocky Mountains.

Our camp at the old fort was situated in the debouchure of the hollow that extended from Pene Alto in our direction. Being twenty miles from Pene Alto and the main range, we could see quite an unobstructed distance. Nearly twenty miles westerly stood "Burro Mountain" in the border of this rolling prairie.[11] The country around us for the most part appeared devoid of convenient places for Indian haunts, but upon our better acquaintance with it, there was discovered to be very many deep arroyos traversing the face of the country which were not seen or known of until approached accidently by some straggling member of our party.

I could see often, during the weeks we remained here, an Indian spy ride out of the foot of the distant mountain and across the rolling prairie and enter the woodland foothills of an

---

Santa Rita copper mines, placing it fifteen miles southwest of present Silver City, New Mexico. Differences in spelling stem from the fact that some officers used the name "Fort McLean" in their official reports. Contemporary maps show hot springs north and east of Fort McLane. In general, the party seemed to be between the Mimbres Mountains and the Río Grande when they encountered these springs. *Official Records of the Union and Confederate Armies*, Series I, Vol. L, Part 2, 296–97; Capt. E. D. Shirland to Capt. William McCleave, January 22, 1863, National Archives, Department of War, Washington, D.C.

[10] Pinos Altos was located on the Continental Divide in Grant County, New Mexico, about six miles north of present Silver City, New Mexico. It was approximately twenty-four miles west of Fort McLane. Gold, according to some accounts, was discovered there in May, 1860. When the California Column came into New Mexico, food was sent to people already located at the Pinos Altos mines because they were starving. Keleher quotes a description written by General Carleton in which distances and directions cannot be accurate. See Keleher, *Turmoil in New Mexico*, 347–48; *Official Records of the Union and Confederate Armies*, Series I, Vol. L, Part 1, 105.

[11] Big Burro Mountain is approximately fifteen miles southwest of Silver City, New Mexico, placing it about thirty miles southwest of the location of Fort McLane.

opposite mountain. They would not venture within less than a mile of us in the daytime. But morning after morning for weeks their signal smokes embellished the mountain peaks all around the border of this prairie, and I often wondered why the savages did not collect force enough to come and overwhelm our little party. There were only thirty-three of us, all told, but we were armed to the effect of an hundred. The worst task we had was to stand guard so continuously, night and day. Each man went on guard for twelve consecutive hours out of every thirty-six the year round, without being excused by rain, snow, or dark freezing nights. A member of each guard's mess always had the additional duty to perform of relieving him while he ate his breakfast, dinner, or supper. Our stock had to be grazed night and day when not in motion, in order that they would be kept in good traveling condition, and especially when we had the grassless scope of desert country to cross for two or three days at a time.

Capt. Walker's intention was now settled on another effort to cross the main ridge to the Pacific side by a western course by the foot of Burro Mountain. But concluded that if we could capture by strategy one of the chiefs of the Apaches, to hold as a hostage for their good conduct, we would be able to proceed with less difficulty, and began to plan a course by which this end might be carried out. The federal head chief of all the Apache tribes was a notorious personage and was known to keep his headquarters near Pene Alto at the time, and had been for some months. The pronunciation of his name by the Mexicans on the frontier settlements of Sonora (a northern state of Old Mexico) was *"Mangus Colorawgh."* These people were probably better acquainted with Mangus (and to whom his name was a terror) than any other people on earth. Mangus took northern Sonora at pleasure. The Mexicans translated this double name of "Mangus Colorawgh" into "Red Sleeves" or probably, more correctly "Colored Sleeve." But the word Mangus seems to have no root in Latin, but may come from *"Manche"* of the French; or it may be for aught I know, a pure Indian word to be correctly spelled any way that pleases the speller. But, however, "Mangus" was the great chief of all the Apache tribes which roamed the Territories of New Mexico and Arizona and a portion of Old Mexico, which extent of country is a vast empire of unsettled wilderness.[12] This is the "big brave" that we concluded to entrap. J. W. S[willing] of our party was the chosen director to accomplish the task.[13] In the meantime while the advance guard of some California troops en route for the war in the states arrived at our encampment under the command of Capt. Sherland of the United States Army. He said that he had espied our fresh trail and tracked us up to see who we were. He had thirty or forty soldiers with him and informed us that several hundred more were behind under the command of Gen. West, Major McClane, and others.[14]

We were glad to see them, being the only white men that we had seen for many months. Our *pro tem* captain, J. W. Swilling,

[12] Mangas Coloradas, or Red Sleeves, rose to power among the Mimbreño Apaches after the massacre of this band at the Santa Rita copper mines in 1837. Juan José had held the band in peace with the whites, but already two factions had appeared among the Mimbreños. The more peaceful of the Mimbreños remained in the camp of Juan José and were called the Copper Mine Indians. The warlike group gathered in the village of Cuchillo Negro (Black Knife) and were called the Warm Spring Indians. Taking the bounty offer of the Mexican government, James Johnson, an adventurer, slaughtered Juan José and many of his followers at Santa Rita in 1837. Mangas was at the time forty years of age and quickly led the united Mimbreños against the whites for the rest of his life. Mangas, although only chief of this band, managed to acquire a considerable following among the other Apache bands by astute marriages of his daughters to other chiefs and leaders. Frank C. Lockwood, *The Apache Indians*, 71 ff.

[13] John W. Swilling, a native of Georgia and more recently of Texas, was a Confederate and served briefly as a captain in the Southern forces in Arizona. He and his men engaged in the only official clash between Union and Confederate troops at Picacho Pass, April 15, 1862. Later, he organized the first irrigation project in the Salt River Valley, called the Swilling Canal Company. Hubert Howe Bancroft, *History of Arizona and New Mexico*, 514; Frank C. Lockwood, *Pioneer Days in Arizona*, 144.

[14] The time of the trapping of Mangas must have been in January of 1863, instead of February as given by Conner. The officers listed by Conner were Captain E. D. Shirland, First Cavalry, California Volunteers; Brigadier General Joseph R. West and Major William M. McCleave, First Cavalry, California Volunteers. *Official Records of the Union and Confederate Armies*, Series I, Vol. XV, 228; L, Part 2, 281, 296–97. There is a minor disagreement about the date of the death of Mangas. Captain Ben C. Butler dates it the eighteenth, but General West dates it the nineteenth, of January.

was ready now to proceed after Mangus and invited the Captain and his soldiers to go with us to Pene Alto, some of whom accepted the invitation. We started, leaving some of each party at the old fort in camp. We arrived at Pene Alto before night and remained until morning and succeeded by hoisting the white flag of drawing some Indians into our sight. The proposition to make a treaty was entertained by the Indians at a distance. The negotiations were conducted in broken Spanish on both sides, and after a long and tedious indulgence of prudential precautions by both parties they approached to a point within easy talking distance. The professions of friendship were here so extremely indulged by both of these high contracting parties, lent at once a patent impunity to a common treachery that froze their words of love into such hostile motives as might offer the best advantage to be taken in deadly conflict. Mangus and three or four of his followers came up, but the main body of his men remained back on the hillside amongst a profusion of boulders, which are the natural breastworks of poor "Lo." Our men now presented their guns and ordered Mangus to stand still and surrender, which he did in surprise. He turned to his companions after he found that they were to be released, and warned them that they were not fooling with Mexicans now, and that they need not look for him until they saw him.

We asked him to tell his people that his safety depended on their good conduct toward us, and that if they would let us travel in peace for "ten moons," we would send him back in safety to them. He talked to his people in gutturals toward the last so that we could not understand him, and his face wore an air of care and perplexity. His dress consisted of a broad-brimmed small-crowned chip or straw hat of Mexican manufacture—a check cotton shirt, breech cloth or clout, and a high pair of moccasins or moccasins with legs to them like boots, only that they fit the legs closely. Mangus was apparently fifty years of age and a large athletic man considerably over six feet in height, with a large broad head covered with a tremendously heavy growth of

"I WANT HIM DEAD"—THE BETRAYAL OF MANGAS COLORADAS

long hair that reached to his waist.[15] His shoulders were broad and his chest full, and muscular. He stood erect and his step was proud and altogether he presented quite a model of physical manhood. If Mangus ever had any or many peers amongst his people in personal appearance, I never saw them during the five years experience in their country. We hurried Mangus off to our camp at old Ft. McLean and arrived in time to see Gen. West come up with his command. The General walked out to where Mangus was in custody to see him, and looked like a pigmy beside the old Chief, who also towered above everybody about him in stature.

He looked careworn and refused to talk and evidently felt that he had made a great mistake in trusting the pale face on this occasion. Our men kept Mangus during that night and on the following day the General concluded that he would take charge of Mangus until the old "brave" accounted for the loss of two plundered government wagons and teams, which were lost on the Rio Grande del Norte some months previously. One of the wagons was loaded with clothing and the other with artillery ammunition, when captured by the Indians, and both were *en route* for Santa Fe, New Mexico, together so these soldiers had been informed. Two soldier sentinels now took charge of Mangus and kept him all day at a fire built of the old cabin logs of the fort, which were lying promiscuously about the camp. Our party had been there long enough to form a regularly beaten path a hundred and fifty paces in length on the west side of the camp by walking sentinel night and day. The soldiery formed their adjoining camp and the sentinel beat at right angles with that of ours, so that the two beats came together, forming a right angle at the fire, where old Mangus was lying on his blanket, a prisoner.

One soldier walked their beat and one citizen walked our beat, and two extra sentinels were placed over the person of

---

[15] Mangas might have been slightly older than estimated by Conner because Lockwood says that the chief was about forty at the time of the slaughter at Santa Rita. There is little agreement about the height of Mangas, but the estimates range from six feet to six feet, six inches, which was most unusual for an Apache.

Mangus. This was the situation when night came on and it was a bitter cold on that bleak prairie. I was on guard for the forepart of the night, which was exceedingly dark. Being cold and disagreeable, all but the guard retired to their blankets early and soon left the camp wrapped in profound silence. No fire was kept burning except the one at the junction of the two guard beats, where Mangus lay upon his blanket with his trinket under his head for a pillow.

A while before midnight I noticed Mangus moving now and then, drawing up his feet restlessly and tucking the lower end of his blanket with which he was covered, over one foot with the other. I would walk up to the fire and then walk off in the dark of my beat to which I had become so accustomed that I could follow it without difficulty this dark night. When I arrived at the far and lower end and turned to come back to the fire I noticed that the soldiers were annoying Mangus in some way and they would become quiet and silent when I was about approaching the fire, and keep so until I again walked off in the dark on my beat. But my curiosity as to what they were doing to the old Indian became aroused and as soon as I departed into the dark far enough to get beyond the reflection of the firelight I walked rapidly to the lower end of my beat, then turned and walked leisurely back and observed the sentinels' pranks.

I could see them plainly by the firelight as they were engaged in heating their fixed bayonets in the fire and putting them to the feet and naked legs of Mangus, who was from time to time trying to shield his limbs from the hot steel. When I came up to the fire each time they would become innocent and sleepy and remain so until I departed on my beat again, when they would arouse themselves into the decided spirit of indulging this barbarous pastime. I didn't appreciate this conduct one particle, but said nothing to them at the time and really I had some curiosity to see to what extent they would indulge it. I was surprised at their ultimate intentions just before midnight when I was about midway of my beat and approaching the firelight. Just then Mangus raised himself upon his left elbow and began to expostulate in a vigorous way by telling the sentinels in Spanish that he was no child to be playing with. But his expostulations were cut short, for he had hardly begun his exclamation when both sentinels promptly brought down their minnie muskets to bear on him and fired, nearly at the same time through his body.

The Chief fell back off of his elbow into the same position in which he had been lying all the forepart of the night. This was quickly followed by two shots through the head by each sentinel's six-shooter, making in all, six shots fired in rapid succession. The old Chief died without a struggle in the precise position that he had occupied continuously since dark. The force of the musket balls marked the frozen ground beyond the body for a distance of five or six feet with an unbroken line of blood plainly indicating the respective directions of the bullets after passing through his body. The four six-shooter balls likewise streamed the old Indian's long hair in strands over his face and straight out upon the ground its full length, indicating the direction of the pistol bullets as they left the victim.[16]

The shooting aroused the whole camp, which soon settled into silence again when the cause was ascertained and the two sentinels retired with the rest of the camp members. Geo. Lount who was to relieve me of guard duty at midnight now promptly took my place, stating that it was not quite midnight but that it

---

[16] The official reports of the army officers cited above make no mention of Walker's party or its participation in the capture of Mangas. Historians of Arizona, however, either follow the account given by Conner entirely or give it in addition to a reminiscence by Clark B. Stocking, a soldier of the California Column who claimed to be present at the death of Mangas. James H. McClintock, *Arizona—Prehistoric—Aboriginal—Pioneer—Modern*, I, 176–78, quotes Stocking as follows: "General, then Colonel West said to the guards, 'Men, that old murderer has got away from every soldier command and has left a trail of blood for 500 miles on the old stage line. I want him dead or alive tomorrow morning, do you understand, I want him dead.'" Stocking claimed that Mangas was persuaded to come into camp by a Captain Sheldon, but Sheldon is not mentioned in official reports as participating in the capture of Mangas. See also Lockwood, *Pioneer Days in Arizona*, 158–60; John C. Cremony, *Life Among the Apaches*, 176. More recently Paul Wellman in *Death in the Desert*, 87–89, uncritically combines the Conner and Stocking versions.

was so near it that he would remain up and go on duty immediately.

I retired to my blankets and slept soundly until morning within less than ten paces of the dead body of Mangus, and arose to find the weather extremely cold and found the body of the Indian in the same position and untouched. I raised his head and took from under it quite a number of curious trinkets, one of which was a rectangular wooden block made of oak. It was about four inches in length by about two and a half inches in width and three quarters of an inch thick. It had a hole through one end by which it was fastened to the other trinkets, temporarily. A stout string passed through the hole with its ends permanently tied together forming a loop large enough through which to pass the hand, and I thought that it was to be worn on the wrist, as it was apparently worn smooth by much handling. This block was marked by hieroglyphics which were burned deeply into the wood with some hot instrument and quite neatly executed. The hole had been burned through the block. I gave them to a lieutenant whose name I don't remember, indeed if I ever knew it.

Quite a number of soldiers came to where I was standing near the corpse, and amongst them there was one who called himself John T. Wright of California, who asked the loan of my butcher knife with which to scalp the Chief. I declined upon the ground that my knife was the only cutlery that I possessed with which to prepare my food &c. He then applied to the soldier's cook, Wm. Lallier, who furnished a large bowie knife, with which the soldier took off the scalp of Mangus. He wrapped the long hair around the scalp and put it in his pocket. I thought that I had never seen the skin about the head of a buffalo much thicker than this scalp of Mangus.

It was as before stated very cold and therefore the operation of taking this scalp was a bloodless one, leaving the inner skin as white as the skull from which it was taken. The body was left where it lay till noon, when it was carried on a blanket and dumped into a gully, blanket and all, and covered up.

"I WANT HIM DEAD"—THE BETRAYAL OF MANGAS COLORADAS

A few nights after this, some soldiers dug Mangus' body out again and took his head and boiled it during the night, and prepared the skull to send to the museum in New York. I afterward saw the skull frequently before the soldiery departed with it.[17] Thus ended the career of the most notorious chief which the Apaches ever boasted of since the United States has owned Arizona and New Mexico.

An hour after Mangus was killed, a portion of the soldiers were started for Pene Alto where they arrived about daylight and attacked the Indians from an old log cabin where they were concealed after having the Indians decoyed to within gunshot, and succeeded in killing two of them. This act confirmed the savages as to the fate of Mangus. They returned in a day or two to our camp and some of our party accompanied them into the mountains north of Pene Alto and surprised a rancheria of them and killed ten Indians. The Indians were stripped of their clothing and the men wore some of this Indian apparel back to camp. They looked grotesque enough, dressed in beaded buckskins, feathered headdresses and high-legged moccasins, as they rode into camp with Indian scalps dangling at their saddles. . . . But these soldiers were green hands at the business of Indian fighting, or they would have had some idea before they put on this Indian rigging, how lousy they would be at the end of a week, but as it was, they inoculated the camp to its highest temperament, when the itch began to prevail pretty generally. The two sentinels who killed Mangus reported to their superiors that he was attempting to make his escape and that report was never questioned while this camp was occupied.

However that may be, Mangus went to his happy hunting ground without any living friend to tell the tale of the manner of starting, and it was useless for any of the members of that camp to affect to believe that the Chief was attempting to escape, for they all knew better, officers and all, before they left

---

[17] McClintock states that the skull of Mangas Coloradas was eventually secured by O. S. Fowler, a phrenologist, and it is not at the Smithsonian Institution, as is supposed by some authorities.

that encampment. The Indians went to war in earnest, which increased our difficulties very materially. We could get over the main range to Pene Alto, but the country west of it was impassable and also a regular stronghold for the Apaches, who now were doubly industrious. They hung on our rear and infested every locality where they could annoy and endanger us. Mangus was a general favorite among them and they seemed bent an avenging his death with all their power....

Captain Walker now said that our stock was well rested and in good condition after this several weeks holiday and ordered that all of us should be ready on the following morning to take our final leave of this tiresome old campground. It was some time in the latter part of March, 1863. We never pretended to try to keep posted as to the days of the week, but attempted to keep pace with the months, and even failed in this sometimes.

Pinos Altos to Tucson over the Old Southern Route

MORNING CAME and found the party in the usual single-file line, traveling toward Burro Mountain and when within a few miles of it we descried a band of Indians whipping and spurring about in all directions near its foot, raising a dense dust from the alkaline soil about the foot of the mountain.

Our departure seemed to arouse the savages' vigilance quickly for signal smokes sprang up rapidly everywhere. We passed through the gap between Burro Mountain and the range to its right without being put to the necessity of exchanging a single shot. We thought perhaps the reason was that the savages expected to see Mangus with us, and were not prepared to fight without a signal from him to that effect. Beyond this place we crossed the Cordillera over the lowest gap that I ever saw in the main range of the Rocky Mountains.[1] We were on the Pacific side of the mountains before we knew it. At the foot of the other side

[1] The party must have traveled southwest from the area of Fort McLane to Burro Mountain and through the open, rolling country east of the Gila until that river was reached. Their destination seemed to be west of Pinos Altos, which could be reached by traveling up the Gila River.

was located what was known by prisoners and Mexican captives as Mangus' rancheria.

It was a pretty place, situated in the lap of the Cordillera on its west side and facing the rolling, rough country beyond. There might have been as much as forty acres of moist, arable land heavily set with wild, coarse grass. The morning shades of the Cordillera overcast the whole of it, giving the place an appearance calculated to make it very inviting for a romantic and pleasant summer's retreat. It bore evidences of previous cultivation. There were no visible signs of there ever having been a shelter there, but undoubtedly there had been from the stories told by escaped captives who had herded sheep for these Indians. A few water ditches were plainly visible and overgrown by rank grass, and in some places, turfed over with firm sod. A plow leaning against the projecting rocks in the hillside bordering the arable land and was in a state of decay.

Anyhow, this was the headquarters of the great Chief for many years, and had witnessed probably very many untold horrible tales. But we found it deserted and silent. The wolves would come and awaken sleepy Nature now and then by their surprise and energetic howls upon so sudden and unexpected discovery of us. Some of our men would whistle for the wolves derisively, as though they were trying to pet and make friends with Mangus' dogs, as they called them. But the old Chief's dogs seemed as loth to trust us as their master had been. It was observed that our levity might yet give away to a more reflective mood before we were a great distance from this—the Capitol of the Apaches. "Yes," responded the wag of the party seriously, "it should not be forgotten that Napoleon quietly took possession of Russia's deserted capitol and his hasty retreat from Moscow may have been less disastrous than our departure hence may yet prove." Speculations were abruptly closed by the usual "catch up" ordered by our old Captain and our mules were soon "caught up," packed and in the usual line coursing toward the Gila River high up in the mountains. Signal smokes mapped out our route everywhere we went and so they did here, but we only saw a few skulking Indians here and there as we proceeded. We came on to a herd of deer so suddenly that they failed to take any general course in their confusion, and scattered in all directions. . . .

In a few days we pitched camp on a high, treeless hill overlooking the Gila. This hill was covered with a fine growth of grama grass and located in the right angle formed by the junction of a little valley on the north and the river on the west. The Gila flowed close to the foot of this hill and hence its side next to the river was very steep. This hill, like the greater part of all prominent points overlooking a stream of water in central Arizona, was fortified on its top and around its brow by ridges of volcanic rock, thrown up to about the height of three feet. The whole space thus enclosed was subdivided into rooms by the same character of ridges like a chess board but without its regularity. Some of the rooms were probably twenty feet square, while some were greater and less in size and a few others were triangular, rectangular, and circular. . . .

Around this hill, for a distance of from two to four miles, there was a rolling country studded promiscuously by small clumps of hills divided by sharp ravines and all covered with a fair growth of grama grass. But little timber was in sight either on this slope just described or on the distant mountain ranges. A few scattering clumps of scrubby oaks marked the ravines and hillsides while perhaps enough cottonwood trees to indicate the direction of Gila grew upon its banks, for there was but little bottom land on this river so high up. I will venture to assert that the Gila is the longest river of its size in the world and that it drains more country than any other stream of its width and depth and yet it has time to go dry in places. Just across the Gila from our hill opposite there was a small knoll which was fortified by a circular wall around its center about ten feet in diameter. It had the appearance of being as old as time itself, and the ground around and about it was strewed profusely with fragments of crockery ware.

But it might be well to state here that this pottery is found about all the old fortified mountain tops and river bottoms in Arizona, and all of it seems to be of about the same character. The largest pieces found are not perhaps more than two or three inches in extent and seem to be made of better and stouter material than is generally used for such ware in the factories of our states. The strangest of all my observations concerning this earthen-ware is that it is painted so well that the color withstands the efforts of time and weather unblemished. Black is the prevailing shade, but blue and red and different shades of these mark these bits of pottery so permanently that the marks look new and the paint fresh and glossy. White was sometimes found to have been used, which was also pure and unsoiled. Evidently this paint was of a quality that would only perish with the decomposition of the fragment upon which it was found. I pulled pieces out of the ground and after cleaning it, it was as bright as any of it. . . . The character of painting was rude and consisted of senseless hieroglyphics for the most part. The prevailing figure was in black and designed to mark a "zig-zag" line similar to an old fashioned rail fence.[2] Such fragments were quite numerous on our camp-hill, scattered about and hidden by the grass. Such was the place where we located our encampment and similar places in the distance seemed to have been selected by the Apaches for their camps, judging from the number of signal smokes daily arising from them. We had not been here many days when to our surprise our soldier friends again tracked us up and a second time pitched camp with us on the top of this hill and amongst the old ruins, aforesaid.

While excavating to form more level ground on the side hill near the summit upon which to sleep, one of the "boys" gave a blow with a pick that sounded hollow and cavernous. On close examination there was discovered an *olla* or spherical

---

[2] For a discussion of the archaeology of this region and Arizona, see Byron Cummings, *First Inhabitants of Arizona and the Southwest*. Painted and fired pottery probably did not come into existence until the Pueblo period, which would date it after A.D. 900.

earthen-ware vessel in perfect preservation and about one-third full of human bones.

It was about two and a half feet below the surface of the ground and had a small aperture in its top, large enough to easily admit a man's hand. This aperture was covered by another sample of pottery which was about the size and shape of an ordinary table saucer. It was turned upside down over the aperture, rendering the vessel water proof. . . . This *olla* was carefully taken out of its secure resting place and examined with considerable interest. The bones, which appeared to be the remnants of a bone-burning or cremating process, were emptied out, ashes and all, on a blanket spread on the ground to receive them. The ashes were of a grayish white color and when disturbed in the least, there would arise from them a light impalpable dust which floated like incense in the light atmosphere. These ashes were the remains of more than one person evidently, for they contained two distinct knee-caps greatly differing in size, but were nearly charred by the action of the fire. We put the bones and the ashes back in the *olla* and fitted the broken fragments of the saucer together again and gave the whole concern to one of the officers, who said that he desired to send it to New York. This earthen vessel did not appear to be made of as good material as were the fragments of pottery found on the top of the ground. This was of a red color and looked like it might be easily broken, while the fragments of the surface were of a hard, gray-looking material, and then the *olla* was not painted nor ornamented in any way but was regular in its proportions. . . .

The soldiery made quite a permanent camp on this hill and called it after Gen. West.[3] It easily took the name of Ft. West and then our party moved back out of sight of the river and downward some two hundred paces into a little hollow on the

[3] Fort West was established as a temporary post by General Carleton on February 1, 1863, to protect the miners of Pinos Altos. It was garrisoned with four companies of the California Volunteers, one-fourth of whom were on furlough, free to prospect. The fort was located about twenty-four miles northwest of present-day Silver City, New Mexico. Keleher, *Turmoil in New Mexico*, 338.

side of the main hill which had a pretty level bottom quite large enough for our party's convenience. Only a few days passed after the arrival of the troops before a trip from this point as a base of operations was projected and preparations followed rapidly. The proposed tour was to be prosecuted westerly toward and to the river Francisco, which was in a direct line to central Arizona, our final destination.[4] The point desired to be reached upon this occasion was about one hundred and fifty miles distant through an unexplored, broken, and terrifically lonesome and craggy country and, withal, a strong-hold of the Apaches—made sacred to them by freedom from invasion and an inherited impunity which had been exercised without being questioned so long that the memory of man runneth not to the contrary. Major McClane, the commandant of Ft. West, was persuaded to join our exploration, and it was but little time getting off under a preparation for a month's absence.[5]

About thirty soldiers and four of our citizen party remained to keep the respective camps in order and to take care of the superfluous plunder &c. The soldier-guard left behind had one company's cavalry horses to graze daily and myself and three comrades had left in our charge four head of mules to care for. Capt. Walker, when on the eve of starting, warned us privately not to trust our mules with the soldier's herd but to graze our four mules alone and attend to them ourselves. He said that the soldiers were too d—ned careless and then he continued to say that Uncle Sam was better able to lose his stock than our party, and that on his return, if he found us alive, he wanted [to] find those mules safe also. . . .

Our camp now consisted of four, which number was divided

[4] Conner here confuses the San Francisco and the Verde rivers. Although they are widely separated, contemporary maps and writers use the names almost interchangeably. The San Francisco River rises south of the Nutrioso village in Apache County, Arizona, flowing generally south, although curving into New Mexico before finally reaching the Gila River in Arizona. The Verde River rises on the west side of the Chino Valley in central Arizona and flows generally east and southeast, entering the Salt River in Maricopa County, Arizona.

[5] Major McCleave, First Cavalry, California Volunteers, is again referred to here by Conner.

into two guards to take a day alternately to graze the mules. When night came on we hitched up to some little scrubby oak trees, a half-dozen of which stood around our camp on the little flat referred to. The company's cavalry horses were sent out in different directions daily to be grazed under a guard of fifteen soldiers, and thus the days were passed for weeks and until the situation became very monotonous. . . . Intimate acquaintance and high appreciation always stand in inverse ratios; and we thought we were acquainted with the Apache right well, and therefore had but little respect for him. And the fact that they did not come and annihilate our weak little camps convinced us that they were not entitled to any consideration whatever, nor wouldn't be if we even had a surplus on hand.

One bright sunny morning just about sunrise, myself and companion took our four mules across the little valley on the same side of the river that our camp was and about a half-mile away, to graze. We were quite concealed by the undergrowth in the edge of a small skirt of scrubby oaks in plain unobstructed view of the camps on the hill, when there suddenly appeared on the little plain between us and the camps twenty or thirty Apaches on horseback, wildly chasing the beef cattle belonging to the soldiers. These soldiers always left the cattle near the camp to be watched by the camp-keepers. But the Indians scattered them in all directions on short notice and followed them on a reckless stampede—shooting their long lances into the poor old terror-stricken cattle at every jump. They continued this crazy, energetic pastime until all of the cattle were lanced to death and lay scattered promiscuously over the little plain to the number of about a dozen. This mêlée was about over before the soldiers in their tents at camp knew or even suspected anything wrong. But when they did become alarmed they rushed out and began to shoot at long range at everything in sight. They were just out in time to see the Indians dart into the inaccessible hills and beyond the valley. They at last espied my friend Jake and myself with the mules in the undergrowth and opened fire upon us.[6] We were afraid to signal too loud to them, so as to stop them from shooting at us because we had been silent spectators of the beef killing and knew that the Indians were in the undergrowth along the valley not far above us and had thus far failed to discover us. They had had us completely cut off from assistance and knew it not, and when our chance to escape began to improve, our friends opened fire upon us, all of which we had to endure until their bullets fell so thick around us that we mounted a mule apiece and spurred for camp across the open plain, affrightedly followed by our two loose animals.

When we emerged from the brush, the soldiery recognized us and ceased shooting, but by then we became the targets for the Apaches, who were concealed up the valley a distance and who now opened upon us with a dozen shots. But we continued to be the recipients of good luck and escaped finally uninjured, notwithstanding the united efforts of friends and enemies to slay us. The soldier boys were a generous set of fellows and regretted exceedingly that they fired on us in such a situation, through sheer carelessness and want of reflection. . . . I always felt since that event that the Indians were more than ordinarily remiss in failing to discover us. For they are so much like a wolf in the ability to see all ways at once and intuitively surmise all that is left unseen that I at one time during their fight with the cattle on this occasion began to believe that they had seen us and were only determined to finish the cattle first, and then turn upon us, and was somewhat surprised when they fled into the brush without doing it, after killing the cattle. However, we were very well pleased with the result and learned a lesson in the meanwhile that was regarded as of considerable value and by which I for one resolved to profit. Only a short time expired before all was again silent and as lonesome as if nothing had happened. . . .

Both camps now met and agreed upon a certain set of rules that were to be engrafted into a mutual understanding to *"estab-*

---

[6] Jake is identified by Conner as Jacob Schneider, age twenty-eight, a native of Germany. Conner to Miss Hall, May 1, 1910, CONNER MANUSCRIPTS.

lish justice, insure domestic tranquility, provide for the common defense," and to promote the general welfare.

The first and only important provision stipulated that no shot should be fired after dark unless an Apache was the target, so that all might know what kind of war a signal shot in the dark meant. . . .

It was now about five weeks since our captain and party had left us. My Dutch guard-mate and myself were agreeably surprised early in the morning when we saw our party's herd of mules coming to us, driven by some of our very welcome "boys." They came up and delivered to us the mules—informed us that the party had gotten back to camp safely, after having reached the Francisco River, one hundred and fifty miles distant or thereabouts. They also seemed very cheerful and satisfied for not having lost a single man, but had had several short fights with the Indians in which quite a number were slightly wounded. My fellow-sentinel Jake and myself united in urging them to leave all the mules in our care and return to camp and persuade Capt. Walker into speedy preparations for a final leave of that place. We assured them that we were heartily tired of it and that a move in any direction would be an improvement as far as we were concerned. But we were destined for a surprise, for the "boys" had not been gone from us more than an hour when thirty or forty mounted Indians dashed out of an arroyo near the soldiers' herd and made a sally on them and their horses so suddenly as to surprise them completely. They begun their fracas by uttering their favorite music—the war-whoop—in order to stampede the stock, while a continued chorus of fire arms rattling kept up the confusion sufficiently to shield them as they darted hither and thither amongst the stock, thrusting their long lances to their hilts into each affrighted horse that ran a contrary direction to that which they desired. Fifteen soldiers were on guard at the time, all of whom discharged their arms without killing a savage, with one exception. One of the soldiers had left his arms hanging on his saddle and was lying flat upon the ground with little thought of danger, when the attack was made and he therefore lost his horse and arms together.

I ran here and there trying to collect our mules into a little nook against the steep hillside, and urged my friend Jake to do likewise and reminded him frequently and hurriedly that he would soon have assistance and could save our mules if we could only keep them for ten minutes longer. I warned him that if the Apaches made a sweep our way, to be sure to shoot his horse instead of himself as there was but little certainty about hitting the rider as he lay behind the horse's neck and on a wild run. A little squad of them made a feint on our mules twice but failed to carry out what their motions indicated and drew off each time after we fired on them. But the greatest source of annoyance to me was the conduct of Jake. That Dutchman stubbornly refused to hurry or to go out of a walk the whole time. He stepped long as he walked about after the mules and swore and grumbled all the time. He appeared perfectly indifferent about his own personal safety and declared that he hoped that the Apaches would take all of the stock anyhow, so that we would be done with all "dis trouble." With the greatest stoicism he would shoot and then damn the Indian because he failed to hit him. When I told him to shoot at the horse instead of its rider he would tell me to attend to my own business and do my own shooting. On one occasion the horse was shot and therefore became unmanageable and his rider quickly deserted him—Jake petulantly hurled his reproof at me with, "Now, dar is hour hoss shot and de tem greaser ish got away." Pretty soon, however, these wild riders had the herd headed toward the adjacent mountains and on a full, reckless stampede, raising a cloud of dust which lingered densely enough in their rear to conceal their flight. All was as silent within the space of five minutes after their departure with the stock as though nothing had happened.

The storm being over the soldiers began to examine their position and found three of their men slightly wounded and about four of their horses left, which were too badly wounded with lances to travel or even to live. We had our mules huddled together close to the hillside and all safe, a fact simply the result of good luck and nothing else. But now another storm came from the direction of our camp. Soldiers and citizens were soon scattering all the way from the camp to the locality of the scene just described, some on horseback and some afoot. They came just in time to see the Apaches preceding their heavy dust in their wild flight across a ridge in the foothills of the distant mountains. Three of our party arrived together ahead of the others, one of whom was a small man and when excited, very talkative and rattling. It was hard to conciliate or to reconcile him and make him believe that we were safe, mules and all. He declared that it was impossible to conceive the cause of our miraculous escape and good fortune, and he could hardly realize yet that it was true. He, however, became pacified and voluntarily took his place on guard with the others, to relieve us of duty immediately, upon the grounds that we had done enough in one day to excuse us for a month. "Suppose our mules were gone," he exclaimed, "Why by G—d we couldn't carry enough provisions to last one-hundredth part of the way to civilization." All became calm however, and the soldiers rode headlong here and there to see where the Indians had gone with the seventy-eight cavalry horses so lately in their possession. Jake and myself took our way to camp and heard many reproofs by the officers dealt out on all sides against the carelessness that lost the stock. They came to inquire how we managed to keep our mules, to all of which we insisted that it was all owing to accidental good luck, which was true. But they put the fellow who lost his arms in a tent that they called the guard house, to punish him for negligence. . . .

On the arrival of these men they presented an aspect of poverty not excelled by the hunger-stricken wolves of the deserts. They had shot nearly one-half of their horses because they gave out and became unable to travel and therefore had to return on foot. There were hardly one of the soldiers who had any pants on at all from the knee down.

They were surely the raggedest set of men I ever saw in one

body, up to that time. This and all experience in the southern part of the mountains in this section taught conclusively the fact that horses cannot undergo as great hardships as mules, and live on grass alone.

It was now remembered by a member of our party that he had been commissioned to see a Mexican, who was in favor with the Indians, and who was supposed to know something of the fate of a missing man by the name of C. P. O—— who left California en route for the states about three years previously, and who was known to have started over the route which passes through southern Arizona, and same upon which we had previously discovered the dead men who were burned by the Apaches.

Some of our party had learned that there were some Mexicans with the Apaches at Pene Alto, when we captured Chief Mangus. One of these Mexicans was supposed to be the one having the knowledge of the missing man C. P. O. This man was said to have started from California with a large amount of gold dust and to have been murdered by the Indians at the instance of Mexicans on the Rio Mimbres.[7] There was discovered by Mexicans, near this river, a mine of copper which is undoubtedly one of the finest veins of copper ore in the country.[8] Our party picked up pieces of the solid metal when we passed it. It was at this time that the Mexicans who assisted in robbery of the missing man, were supposed to have taken the exploited gold dust and thence subsequently to Pene Alto, the place of the Mexicans' retreat, when driven away from the copper mine by the Indians. Now the question was: could the Mexican, who knew the particulars of this last man's fate, be found and interviewed.

To this end our old Captain was persuaded to remain here

[7] The Mimbres River has its source in Grant County, New Mexico, north of present Deming, New Mexico. It flows above the ground until it reaches a point about twenty miles north of Deming and then it flows underground until it reaches a drainless lake in the province of Chihuahua, Mexico.

[8] The Santa Rita copper mines were discovered in 1800 by a Lieutenant Colonel Carrisco, aided by an Indian. They were worked by the Mexicans after 1804 and were mined by the Patties as early as 1825. Ralph Emerson Twitchell, *The Leading Facts of New Mexican History*, I, 475; II, 37.

at our camp on the hill for a few more days. He therefore called for five volunteers to proceed to Pene Alto to find the Mexican and five of us were soon prepared to start. Capt. Walker then gave us our order to the effect that as it was a hair-brained excursion (as he expressed it) we must proceed in the night and return in the night. That the distance was more than fifty miles and that five men would make just the number to steal through the country under the cover of darkness successfully, or to get up a splendid war-dance if we were discovered and taken. He impressed us particularly with the necessity of out-witting the Indians, instead of attempting to fight our way through. "Fight out, if you can, but never fight into their strong-holds," he remarked with emphasis. Some of the soldiers wanted to accompany us, but Capt. Walker objected, saying that a greater number would only serve to insure discovery without adding a fight force sufficient to insure safety.

We mounted a mule apiece and started just as the sun was setting and proceeded in silence. The night was just dark enough for easy concealment and light enough to follow without difficulty the numerous Indian trails that checkered the country, and to distinguish the outline of the Cordillera from the surrounding mountains. It was probably after midnight when we crossed the main divide a little north of Mangus' rancheria and then turned left, keeping in the rugged hills and spurs along the Atlantic side of the main mountain range upon which Pene Alto was to be finally found located somewhere in the distance. We discovered on either side from time to time the campfires of the Apaches, which are always located under some cliff or behind a clump of boulders, or perhaps at the head of some little rough arroyo, where they cannot be seen, only for short distances. This fact was soon impressed upon us, and hence impelled greater caution as we proceeded. At one of those campfires we could easily see the savages pass about the fire. The braying of a mule just then would have ruined us, but it is a fact worthy of consideration that horses and mules, when placed in those wild situations, seem to become instinctively cautious and fearful, as well as men, and on this occasion we had no fault to find with ours, on account of any noise they made, although we urged them to a constant strain throughout the whole night, and until after sunup on the following morning. I was in constant apprehension of an Apache shooting his wicked lance out from the huge rocks amongst which our trail meandered. There were but few patches and lines of trees here and there in this section of country, the greater part being pine and stunted oak. The rest of the space was covered with rocks and chaparral. We arrived in sight of the old mining camp of Pene Alto and halted to cut some bunch grass for our mules about sunup. It was a pretty bright morning and a perfect calm silence brooded over the landscape away upon this high ridge. Quite a woods of pine and scrubby oak lay across the continent's backbone at this point. We unexpectedly found a company of United States soldiers making a short sojourn at Pene Alto and we therefore were disappointed in having our expected opportunity to consult the Mexican.

These soldiers were from New Mexico and would not remain long, but their presence there caused the Indians to skulk and elude all observation, and of course their Mexican friend or prisoner, which ever he may have been, was also hid away in the mountain recesses, out of our reach. Our arduous and dangerous visit was therefore useless; this was close to where Mangus had been captured and killed, and we remained all day and slept until nearly dark. We communicated to an officer in the military the object of our visit, who promised to learn all that he could and communicate it to the proper authorities in the States and in California. When night came on we were loth to undertake our return trip. We knew it to be impossible to go back over the same numerous trails which we came and, therefore, were afraid of marching into some of those Indian rancherias which we had seen or others just like them. Believing that we had avoided discovery by mere accident, we concluded to remain until the following morning, which was the time set for our return to Captain Walker's camp on the Gila. Contrary to orders on the following morning we started bright and early to risk the return trip in the daytime. We passed down off of the main range to its western foot, determined to go back on the side opposite to the route we had come. Following a steep hollow down, we naturally fell into a water course that we called Bear River, believing it to be the same creek which emptied into the Gila about a mile above Capt. Walker's camp at Ft. West, which we found to be true.[9]

But we had not followed it far from its head when we found it to be a narrow gorge bounded on each side by perpendicular rock walls. We traveled hour after hour in this rock-bound crack in the earth until our patience almost gave entirely away. Some places the walls would stand up straight for a hundred feet in height and about eight or ten feet apart. It was a perfectly fatal trap if the Apaches had known of us being in it. The springing of the triggers would have been a small matter, because it was impossible for us to escape out over its side anywhere within a distance of twenty-five miles. The Indians would never have thought of looking into such a place for us, because of it being the last place that they would think of visiting when an enemy was near. But we silently and impatiently threaded our tedious way through this rift until it debouched sufficient to get our animals out upon the mountain side which we did on the first opportunity. We came to a fall in this creek, which was about twenty feet in height, but the water had been forced around the side of the narrow place and wore a second gorge down a little distance over which we drove the mules as far as they would go and push them down the balance of the way on their haunches. After we left this creek bottom our route was selected on a high ridge, thus increasing the danger of discovery, but we arrived safely at our camp in the evening just as the sun was sinking behind the western mountains. We had stopped upon one high point from which we could distinctly see the

[9] Bear River, called also Bear Creek, is a small tributary of the Gila River flowing west from the continental divide in Grant County, New Mexico. Fort West was located just south of the juncture of Bear Creek and the Gila River.

soldier's tents on the hill at our camp, a distance supposed to be at least ten miles. Some of the officers had walked out from their camp about a half-mile and met us.

They stated that as our time having been up for twelve hours they had been sweeping the distant mountains with their spyglasses ever since noon to discover us, and first saw us come in sight on the hill from whence we had seen their tents.

They reckoned the distance to be ten miles, judging from comparing it with other points where we could be seen before arriving. This atmosphere was exceedingly transparent. Our old Captain came up and remarked, "Well you have completed your senseless excursion and nearly killed your mules." He continued to say that if he had not been so troubled about us that he would give us a piece of his mind about disobeying his orders in a way that he did not want it done again under any circumstances.

On our homeward stretch, after leaving this creek we came to a ravine which came from a southeastern direction and connected with a creek within two or three miles of our camp. It was the queerest freak of the kind I ever noticed. It was a broad-bottomed gulch apparently two or three hundred paces across it, filled nearly level full of large boulders without any soil or earth between them, apparently. A large flat trough filled with eggs is the best comparison I can make to illustrate it. It seemed singular why the spaces between the huge boulders did not fill up. And it appeared equally as strange to contemplate such a vast and orderly collection of boulders lying so loose and clean with a general level surface below the level of the adjoining land and extending like a regular water course as far as the eye could trace it toward the southeast. Everything settled back to a comparative peace, but it was not destined to remain so very long. One day I told Capt. Walker that I desired above all things to leave that place. The old gentleman remarked that some other foolish hair-brained adventure would spring into crazy brains in due time and offer employment to those who liked it. I heartily agreed with him that all of these dangerous

Courtesy the Porter Collection

*Joseph Reddeford Walker
—the portrait by Alfred Jacob Miller (1837).*

and foolish adventures were but a waste of time. But still, I considered them as offshots and the legitimate and appropriate branches of the original *big* foolish adventure that brought us into this sterile country at all. The whole must have all of its parts. And to consider this country as a whole, it always presented itself to my mind as a vast blank—a land upon which God had never smiled for one moment since it had been created and one which if He ever addressed at all, it was expressed in the language of serpents, stings, and snakes, and thus left in its silence to be interpreted by those who chose to go read. This is no exaggeration; it was bleak to sterility, and as ugly as sin, and without apparent hope or remedy.

I walked up a ravine one morning to its head and looked over a ridge and down a flat space, and saw a coyote wolf cutting all sorts of pranks with a kind of a ground squirrel which he had scratched out. He would let the little animal escape and enter a hole in the ground, when he would jump at it and scratch like his life depended on his exertions, somewhat after the manner of a playful dog, until he had his victim on top again. So busy was he with the little creature that I walked down the hill some distance toward the spot without attracting his notice. The next spring the wolf made at the ground and began scratching, I leveled my gun to surprise him by a shot, but was surprised myself, when the gun discharged itself with a weak squib and failed to throw the ball fifty paces, all of which was quickly followed by the report of rifles that did send their bullets singing across the ridge high over my head.

A squad of Indians had attacked the guard several ridges to the south of me and a sudden and lively skirmish was the consequence. The wolf retreated out of the range of my gun while I was retreating out of the range of the guns that were throwing balls so fast in my direction. By the time I arrived near the herd of stock and got the gun recharged, the Apaches were gone without getting any stock or killing any of the guard. But they succeeded in wounding one of our men slightly and it was thought that they were damaged considerably worse. Upon examination

I found quite a number of cartridges out of which the powder had wasted. But this little incident was the forerunner of another.

Another company of troops tracked up our party of citizens and soldiers, all of whom we were glad to see. In a very few days thereafter they lost another herd of horses so neatly and easily as to be extremely provoking to the officers. The horses were lazily strolling up the river bottom upon a cloudless, bright morning, followed by five soldiers, who had their muskets slung over their shoulders and suspended by the leather straps on them. They were within gunshot of the tents on the hill and were passing now and then the arroyos which opened onto the level bottom land over which the herd was passing upstream—all quiet and happy. An Indian rode out of the mouth of an arroyo behind the soldiers and the herd, put spurs to his horse, passed within twenty paces of the surprised soldiery on a full run, and entered the herd of stock, passed through the foremost of the herd and rode on in a hurry. But this Indian had been followed by two others, who dashed at the soldiers and shot one apiece with arrows, delivered a terrific war-whoop, which stampeded the horses directly after the foremost Indian who now led the herd his own direction on a wild race. The two hindmost Indians followed the flying herd closely and lying flat upon their horses to escape the musket balls of the soldiers.

The soldiers were so completely surprised and the whole transaction executed so suddenly, that they never got ready to shoot until the Indians, herd and all, were too far away to accomplish anything, but they did shoot after them without any known results, other than to apprise the whole camp of the ill luck. In much less time than it takes to describe it, the Indians and the herd were lost to view, leaving a line of dust behind to settle as quickly as the landscape seemed a few moments after the departure of the Apaches. The soldiers, however, were startled into prompt activity and wanted to fight badly, but there was no enemy to shoot and they therefore had little else to do but look disgusted and puzzled. One of the two who were shot died, and the other was still prostrated when we separated from them and I never heard the result of his fate.

Nine men out of ten who are killed by the Indians in the Far West owe their distruction to mere carelessness. It matters not who they are or howsoever talented they may be, the usual cause can nearly always be safely attributed to carelessness and want of due reflection. It is by the usual depreciation of this wily cunning that the Indian tribes are made so unnecessarily expensive to the Government of the United States. The agents and officers are so often deceived by believing that because the Indian is a savage that he has no intellectual endowments, all of which is a wonderful mistake. We despise his ignorance and thereby overrate our own intelligence.

In April, 1863, we bid our soldier friends of this camp adieu, and never met them again. We took our line of march and traveled nearly constantly until we reached the same old Southern Route to California again.

Signal smokes again marked our course, as usual. We came suddenly and unexpectedly in contact with a rancheria of Indians somewhere in the hills north of the trail and a short sharp conflict ensued, which resulted in routing the savages without any serious consequences to ourselves, other than some flesh wounds.

They left three of their dead and two Spanish mules; the latter we took with us. We arrived at and encamped near the entrance of what was known as Doubtful Pass.[10] It was a deep and narrow gorge through high mountains and about one and a half miles in length. The walls were about perpendicular and in some places very high and in others not over thirty or forty feet in height. It was a fine place in which a few Indians might kill a hundred men by throwing rocks down upon them, without danger to the assailants. About midnight the party were surprised by our Captain's order to "catch up." Our animals were

[10] Doubtful Pass is referred to as Doubtful Canyon and is located with Stein's Peak as its eastern end on the Butterfield route. It was regarded as one of the most hazardous portions of the Butterfield route because the Apaches kept it under constant surveillance. Conkling, *Butterfield Overland Mail*, II, 127, 129.

soon packed and again strung out in the usual single file through this ugly cañon. It was a quiet and silent march as well as a dark one, but we succeeded without difficulty and came out of the other end on to a real desert, upon which we encamped for the remainder of the night, and where we received splendid salutations on the following morning from a cloudless sun as he arose and smiled benignantly upon the surrounding desert waste. Whether the Indians were disappointed or not by our slipping through this dangerous pass in the night, we thought they were, and that was sufficient. All of our "boys" thought well of this little stratagem in behalf of safety, but one whose time on guard duty began at midnight. He stole off amongst the sage-brush and slept until daylight and excused himself by proposing to recommend this strategic move to the officers in the war department at Washington. But our old Captain was never apprised of his default and it was soon forgotten, although the act was very reprehensible.

We steadily pursued our course without unnecessary halt or delay over a desert country for many days and until we arrived at Tucson, which has lately had the honor of becoming the capital of Arizona.[11] Tucson is situated upon a little dry creek that traverses the desert and is called the Santa Cruz River, and which has no particular source for a beginning, and about equally indifferent as to where it ends.[12] It ends in a desert. The town had its beginning by the place having been used as a campground, midway between the settlements of Old Mexico and those of New Mexico, which were five or six hundred miles apart and separated by this vast desert country in the middle of which this town of Tucson grew to a population of three

---

[11] Tucson was the capital of Arizona Territory from 1867 to 1877. Rufus Kay Wyllys, *Arizona: The History of a Frontier State*, 174.

[12] The Santa Cruz River rises in Sonora, Mexico, flowing north and west past Tucson, Arizona. It finally sinks into the desert near Maricopa station on the Southern Pacific Railroad. Father Eusebio Francisco Kino visited this valley as early as 1691 and has received credit for naming the river. Herbert Eugene Bolton, *Rim of Christendom: A Biography of Eusebio Francisco Kino, Pacific Coast Pioneer*, 247; Wyllys, *Arizona*, 41 ff.

hundred inhabitants during a period of three hundred years.[13]

The old church, San Xavier, is situated up stream upon the left bank of the Santa Cruz, about twelve miles from Tucson, and is said to have been built by Mexican Catholic priests in the year of 1760.[14] It is finely finished inside and shows that the skill necessary to the finest workmanship was liberally displayed in its completion. Yet it has stood all of these years alone, in the midst of a vast desert, unprotected, save by the silent patience which seems to live in the atmosphere around it and its sad but successful reproof to all who dare to desecrate and profane these sacred precincts dedicated to the Holy Trinity. A tribe of very black Indians, known as the Jacquois, have had control of this old church as a right handed down by tradition for so long that the "memory of man runneth not to the contrary," and they still approach it with reverential humility.[15] They insist upon all visitors taking their shoes off before entering within this deserted cathedral from year to year with a vestal fidelity. It stands in the midst of the range of the Apaches, whose great numerical force and reputation for reckless cruelty have for many years made their name a terror to the inhabitants of the northern states of Mexico, yet their superstition has always and still forbids their approach to this old chapel.

On the contrary Tucson, twelve miles below, had been captured and pillaged annually for the last half-century by these cruel vagabonds. Whatever may be the age of Tucson and whatsoever history it may have, there is one fact concerning it that I know to be true and that is: that in the spring of 1863 the coyote wolves from the surrounding desert would come and howl at it

[13] A Spanish presidio was located at Tucson in 1776, but it also acquired a population of not more than two thousand people before acquisition by the United States. Wyllys, *Arizona*, 61.

[14] Although the mission or church of San Xavier del Bac became a mission as early as 1732, the actual edifice seen by Conner had its beginning between 1783 and 1785. Wyllys, *Arizona*, 61.

[15] Conner confuses the Yaqui with the Papago Indians who lived about the mission of San Xavier del Bac during this period. J. Ross Browne, *A Tour through Arizona, 1864, or Adventures in the Apache Country*, 140, describes a village of two or three hundred Papago Indians living about the mission.

all night and sneak about its suburbs all day. The poor thin creatures looked too poor and emaciated to cast a shadow in a bright sun. I do not mean to say that Tucson had three hundred residents in the spring of 1863. If there were half that number at that time, they were not at home when we passed through the place. I remember to have seen three white Americans residing there on that occasion—or at least they were there.[16]

After a stay of one day and night at Tucson we took our departure toward the Pima Indian Village, which is about eighty miles westwardly on the Gila River, the same stream which we had encamped upon at Ft. West several hundred miles above.[17]

The country from Tucson to this village was nothing but one continuous desert. The only grass on the route of any consideration was coarse like wheat-straw and stood in bunches six or eight inches in diameter about the desert, with sand drifted against it. What little water we succeeded in finding was of a light mud color and is never known to become clear, nor even the least transparent. When we got about halfway to the Pimas on this trip, we encamped amongst some thinly scattered mesquite trees in the sand to rest at noonday.

It was nearly or quite in the month of May and was becoming very warm. We observed in the distance in the direction of the Gila, some Indians coming and could only make out about five. On closer observation as they drew nearer they proved to be three Pima "braves," two of whom were carrying a papoose, each. Being always friendly and at peace with the whites, they confidently walked into our camp and sat the children on the sand and then walked into our camp and sat unhesitatingly shaking hands with each member of our party, accompanying each greeting with the usual short guttural and emphatic *"How—how."*

[16] The population of Tucson was reduced during the Civil War because of the failure to protect the settlers from the raids of the Apaches. Browne, in *A Tour through Arizona, 1864,* 133, estimated the population in 1854 as from four to five hundred, while Father Joseph P. Machebeuf gave the population as eight hundred in 1858. Wyllys, *Arizona,* 128.
[17] Browne, in *A Tour through Arizona, 1864,* 110, says there were actually ten Pima and two Maricopa villages scattered along the Gila River for several miles. In general, these villages were located about twelve miles east of Maricopa Wells.

After a full exchange of salutation they proceeded to inform us in broken Spanish that they and their tribe had just finished a campaign against the Apaches—had taken ten scalps and four prisoners; two squaws and two papooses. We now knew that the two children they had with them were prisoners. We inquired how many scalps and prisoners they had lost. They replied that that had not lost a single warrior and that the Apaches were not brave enough to take off scalps; hence it was not their custom to scalp their enemy. Upon being asked what they intended to do with the infant captives, they informed us that they always sold them to the Mexicans for slaves and that they were then en route to the frontier Mexican settlements for that purpose. One of the children was a boy about five years of age and the other was a girl somewhat older, apparently. These poor unfortunate little waifs seemed monstrously lost and knew about as much of their destiny as two rabbits. But they were guilty of having Apache ancestry and that was fatal; however innocent or harmless. . . .

These Indians remained until we left, when they did likewise in the direction of Tucson and probably ended their search for a market for the little Apaches in Sonora in Old Mexico; and if they failed to sell them, they surely killed them. But we never saw or heard of any of them again.

. . . We left this camp and waded through the sand the rest of the day and again encamped in it that night. On the following morning the Apaches fired on us from the hills, but without effect other than to awaken a vigorous response from our camp that silenced them. We, however, moved on and in two more days arrived at the Pima Indian Village on the Gila. The Pimas arose *en masse* against us, under the impression that we were the Texans of the Rebel army that they had been cautioned against by the authorities of the United States. Their commotion was general and continuous until they were drawn up in a line of battle. A white flag was improvised on the moment and served the purpose of bringing about a pow-wow, which ended in peace and good understanding. We passed on their little collection of rude huts and encamped below them at a point known as the Maricopa Wells.[18] These wells are little holes of putty-colored water standing along some gullies, which were coursing down from the mountain side toward the Gila. Here the Pimas and Maricopas crowded our camp continuously during the two days we tarried and I noticed that the squaws would now and then depart and bring boiled wheat for their lords to eat, who had not the time to go after it. They were very friendly, however, and boasted that they never knew the color of a white's man's blood.

[18] The station of Maricopa Wells is located in Township 3, Range 3, Section 17, two miles south of the Gila River. Philip St. George Cooke dug the wells whence the site derives its name when the Mormon Battalion which he commanded camped on the site in December, 1846. Conkling, *Butterfield Overland Mail*, II, 169.

Opening Central Arizona's Mines

THERE HAS BEEN so many published conjectures concerning the Pima and Maricopa Indians that it seems useless to venture anything upon the subject.[1] Therefore, in consideration of the fact that I became one of the very first settlers of central Arizona and remained four consecutive years, dating from the building of the first shanty by the Caucasian, I feel that I am in rather conflict with myself as to how to treat the subject. For I am fearful that false steps would do more harm than anticipated.

But believing that a few general remarks may not be amiss to explain some apparent obscure ideas taken mostly from flying trips made by persons who followed the regular beaten routes laid out by hastening military expeditions, I shall remark a few observations taken by an experience, which necessity compelled

---

[1] Early in the nineteenth century the Pimas were joined by the Maricopas, who were of Yuman stock and who had resided up to that time at the mouth of the Gila River where it enters the Colorado. Although the Pimas and Maricopas speak different languages and have other dissimilarities, they have lived together in peace since their union. Leslie Spier, *Yuman Tribes of the Gila River,* 11 ff.

to be slow and deliberate, and were far from the old beaten trails across to California.[2] I shall then proceed with our exploration into the unexplored country west of the Gila into central Arizona, our original destination. This first expedition through the present Territories of Arizona and New Mexico, of which we have any account, was made by three hundred Spaniards and eight hundred Indian followers in 1540–1542, under the leadership of Vasquez Coronado. After passing entirely through this vast territory, this expedition took a northeast course from the source of the Gila and traversed the buffalo plains as far east as the 40th degree of latitude. The principal object of this exploration seemed to have been the discovery of gold, and found none.[3] We now know that gold has since been found throughout this whole extent of country and that very lately. And it might be said that the whole train of this great Cordillera, the main stem of the numberless spurs, angles, and peaks of the Rocky Mountains, has been subsequently, to all expensive and fruitless expeditions made to a late date, found to be one great gold and silver mine extending through the length of the continent. Yet these different and imposing expeditions failed to find gold and, we may add, failed also to learn anything of a definite character upon any subject. This expedition found the seven fabled villages of Cibola and by their description located them in a narrow valley six leagues long on the very source of some one of the branches of the Rio Gila. It is now hardly necessary to say that there are no sources of the Gila which have any valley six leagues long or anything like it. Albert Gallatin wrote a letter to Lieutenant W. H. Emory of United States Topographical Engineers in 1847, directing him to make inquiries concerning these fabled

---

[2] By this time various routes were available across Arizona, such as Kearny's route, Cooke's Wagon Road, the Butterfield route, and Beale's Wagon Road. Wyllys, *Arizona*, 93 ff., 268–69; Lockwood, *Pioneers Days in Arizona*, 71 ff.

[3] Coronado did not traverse the country at the source of the Gila, but reached that river at San Geronimo and crossed the Salt River at Bonito Creek. From this crossing the party traveled generally north to the Zuñi village. For a full discussion of Coronado, see Herbert E. Bolton, *Coronado: Knight of the Pueblos and Plains*.

villages and other matters.[4] Like all other information received from the early explorations, which were explained by inquiries in this letter, they only served to show the limited extent of correct information given in any particular.

All accounts agree that the Pimas and Maricopas were always an agricultural people, while their *anciently* occupied locality is totally surrounded by the Apache country and has always been, as far back as accounts go. It is also agreed that the Indians of the Rio Grande, five or six hundred miles north of the Pimas, were an agricultural people and lived in adobe or mud houses just like the Pimas did, while the Apache country lay between these agricultural peoples and all around each. At the other corner of the triangle, hundreds of miles from the Gila Indians and the Rio Grande Indians on the Little Colorado, are located the Zuni Indians, who are also a peaceable tribe of agricultural people and they too lived in adobe or mud houses, with from two to four stories, like the Pimas and the Rio Grande tribes.[5] The two- and four-storied houses of the two latter tribes are now nowhere to be seen, but those of the Zunis are still standing, and are still entered by the means of movable ladders up above the first story, and if the house has but one story, it is still entered at the top by means of a ladder, just like the other peaceable tribes are said to have done. The only peaches I ever saw in sight of the Rocky Mountains grew at the Zuni village, thus attesting the permanence of the settlement. There was still another tribe called the Soones, who were a peaceable and agricultural people who also lived off to themselves.[6] Now all of these peaceable tribes so called, for there are very few souls of each, live a great way apart from each other under different names,

---

[4] Quoted in W. H. Emory, *Notes of a Military Reconnaissance from Fort Leavenworth, in Missouri to San Diego, in California, including parts of the Arkansas, Del Norte, and Gila Rivers*, 127–30.

[5] Zuñi is a popular name given to a Pueblo tribe residing in a permanent pueblo on the north bank of the upper Zuñi River in Valencia County, New Mexico. Frederick W. Hodge, *Handbook of American Indians North of Mexico*, II, 1015–20.

[6] Soones is only another name given to the Zuñi. Hodge, *Handbook of American Indians*, II, 1144.

with habits, customs &c, alike, and the Apache country lays all around and between each two of them, and always at war with them all. The pottery used by these weak and friendly tribes is all of the same character and differ only from the fragments found strewn through central Arizona in as much that the fragments seem to be of better materials and mostly painted, as before stated in these pages. These fragments are scattered all over the Apache country for hundreds of miles and especially about old fortifications, which are extensively thrown up of black volcanic rocks, without any pretensions toward building a wall.

These numerous and extensive breastworks are in my settled opinion the work of hostile forces and not intended to reside in. I do not consider them *ruins,* as the popular idea has it, but simply ridges of rocks thrown into indifferent squares &c, for breastworks and are now about as perfect, perhaps as they ever were, and as convenient for residences as when first made. They are not confined to the localities of arable soil, but on the contrary mostly located on prominent waterless hills, where it was probably necessary to carry water to the contestants in these earthen vessels which were destroyed or deserted. Some of the earlier accounts say that the peaceable tribe of Soones contained many albinos. This fact was attributed to their customs of living in rooms scooped out of solid rock under the ground, which again appears to me to be ridiculous. He who might have been curious enough to have visited the Zuni village in 1863 and even later, could have seen several albino Indians there who do not nor never did live in the ground.

The Apaches seem to have always been at war with the rest of the human race, together with the Navajos, who undoubtedly are a branch of the Apaches.[7] And they claim and roam over an

---

[7] The Navajos are an Athapascan tribe now occupying a large reservation in northeastern Arizona, northwestern New Mexico, and southeastern Utah. During the period before the United States occupied the Southwest, the Navajos waged war against the whites and the Pueblo Indians. The tribe recognized the United States as their sovereign in 1849, were reduced to peace by Carson's expedition of 1863, and given a reservation by the United States government in exchange for their other lands in 1868. Hodge, *Handbook of American Indians,* II, 41–45; Keleher, *Turmoil in New Mexico,* 296 ff.

immense territory and probably larger than any other tribe of Indians on the continent. In the midst of this great scope of country lays the great triangle whose extreme point marks the homes of the three peaceful and agricultural people mentioned. The country contained inside of this triangle was always regarded the stronghold of the Apaches, whose boast was that white men never escaped who once got into this. Central Arizona is located within these forbidden limits, the place of our destination and which as yet we had failed to reach after going nearly all around it, but still bent on perseverance until the object and place was finally reached if it took us a year to accomplish it.

A few more facts are only necessary to reach my conclusions and then I will have done with the subject. The great Apache nation was a federal institution and subdivided into several lesser nations, each having its own chief.

I could record several of those branches if I knew how to spell their names, but they are made up from broken Spanish and Indian lingo and have not yet appeared in any history at my command. But I shall however attempt some of them as directed by their sound. Mesquilaros, Tantos, Kiotaras, Pinals, Hwalipais, Apachemohaves, and a White Mountain tribe and others.[8]

Some of those names have been previously published but not all of them. The Apachemohaves are of a recent tribe and took the Mohaves part of their name from the necessity imposed on them of seeking the protection of the Mohave tribe against the main body of the Apache nation from whence they had recently seceded. New tribes thus come into existence from time to time under new names like any other people who rebel and claim their independence of the original stock and by treaties unite again under their separate rights like other states. They are all

[8] The Apache Indians comprise a number of differing divisions. Hodge, in *The Indians of North America*, 66, gives an acceptable grouping of the divisions: Querechos or Vaqueros, which include the Mescaleros, Jicarillos, Faraones, Llaneros, and probably the Lipan; Chiricahua; Pinaleños; Coyoteros, which include the White Mountain and Pinal divisions; Arivaipa; Gila, which include the Gileños, Mimbreños, and Mogollones; Tontos.

Apaches and so call themselves. They fight together, live together, go on the warpath together and recognize one common great chief to command all of them when necessary.

They have different customs in many ways from each other, all trifling in effect. Some are known by having two barbs of feathers on their arrows, by which the arrow is made to fly straight and others have three for the same purpose, while others again fix the feathers cylindrically like the threads of a screw to give the arrow a rotary motion like a rifle does its ball. Some of them form their moccasins so as to turn up at the toe. The Tontos cut their hair short and differ in this respect from any other Indians I ever saw. They cut it square in front so that it comes just to the eyes, thus concealing their forehead entirely and giving the wearer a hideous appearance. These are customs which are common to each branch or sub-tribe, but those of each tribe differ with those of the other &c. All the arrows, for instance, of one tribe are alike, but different in pattern from the arrows of all of the other tribes. This might be called a good example of the recognition of states' rights, for a Tonto Indian is an Apache Indian on the same recognized principle that an Ohioan is also a citizen of the United States. It will be remembered that our party captured Mangus, the Great Chief of all those tribes. The English of his name was Red Sleeve. I do not know how the Great Chief succeeds to the position, but it is remembered that Red Sleeve was also their Great Chief during the Mexican war and he must have been an ancestor of the one we captured. One more singular difference of feature even in the same tribe, I will notice and end the speculation. The Maricopa men have aquiline noses and women have *retrousses*.

They surely are of the same tribe and this peculiar difference is very noticeable, while it is remarkable. The conclusion is easily reached from the above facts, and additional ones too tedious to mention here, that these tribes of Indians are all of the same stock originally and have only been changed to their respective present conditions by the ordinary chance capricious of the same treacherous destiny that silently awaits the destined result of all other races of beings. The United States authorities give great praise to the Pima Indians for their long and well-tested good conduct toward the white race, but it is forgotten in the meanwhile that all of these good results are just attributable to the fact that the Mexican Government, through the means of its priests, taught the Pimas the Spanish language, and by that means alone acquired the right to peaceably appoint their chiefs for them. The same Jesuits who superintended the building of the old church previously referred to in 1760 (San Xavier) may have had much to do with starting such of these Indians who would accept their tutorings upon a peace footing to endure for all time to come.

They have the same sort of pestles and mortars with which to grind their corn and wheat that are frequently seen deserted and unused away in the wild mountains of the Apaches, where a Pima would not dare to go. They frequently parch their corn and wheat first and then grind it into a meal, which they call *pinole*. This *pinole* is very nutritious and goes a great way for food on a desert trip and especially when a little sugar is added and the whole stirred in water. I took a survey of their houses &c.

The house is constructed by leaning small poles together at the top at a common center while the lower ends rest upon the ground in a circle of eight feet in diameter probably, forming a frame work some six feet in the center. This skeleton is then thatched with twigs, grass, straw &c, and plastered over with mud on the outside. A hole three or four feet in height is left open in one side through which to enter in a stooping attitude. Their granaries were constructed by driving three stakes into the ground a few feet from the houses, and a platform of wicker work made upon the top of the stakes, a probable height of three feet from the ground. Upon this platform was constructed a platted circular measure of probably three feet in diameter and as many in height, giving a capacity sufficient for the storage of several bushels. All of the outside was thatched and plastered with mud. Some of these rude constructions seemed to have stood so long that they were careened and appeared about to tumble down. My impression was after looking over this village of the marmot order that it would take a terribly mean man to disturb or to distress these semi-civilized, but still barbarous and contented people. It was painful to observe a careworn and infirm old warrior listlessly sitting nearly naked near his two bushel and a half corncrib, patiently depending upon its scanty contents for existence up to his departure for his happy hunting ground. But then they were honest and virtuous and that is about all that human life is worth in the end. The government of the United States was furnishing them with farming implements and condemned muskets with which to defend themselves, for all of which they seemed very grateful and they have undoubtedly paid back to the white man, in different ways, the full amount of their obligations. Our manufacturers might doubt a relator's integrity who would tell them that these Pima Indians wove baskets out of twigs and grass that would hold water. But such is the fact, and the most of the wheat they cook whole is boiled in those baskets of home manufacture by immersing hot rocks into the water put in them.

However, we were getting ready to start on a pretty morning when we were informed by some of the Pimas that we would need a great amount of water if we crossed the Gila Desert. There was an eighty-mile desert over there to cross, before we could go to central Arizona, and the weather was becoming exceedingly hot. But the object of their information was soon made manifest by them fetching us a number of large gourds to use as extra canteens. We traded for them and really found that we needed them before we had passed the desert. We left the Pimas, crossed the Gila, and followed down the river on the opposite side some ten or twelve miles and encamped for the night in sight of an old monument built by surveyors to make an original boundary between the United States and Mexico. This camp we called Sacatone Station, after the grass of that name which we found in abundance at this place.[9] A little fur-

---

[9] Sacatone or Sacaton Station was sixteen miles north of Casa Grande in Pinal County, Arizona, and near the present town of Sacaton, Arizona, on the Gila River.

ther down on the next day, we came to two graves which were covered with rocks and prickly pear plants, and other specimens of the cactus family.

These graves contained some of the bodies of the Oatman family, whose history was a sad one.[10] Father, mother, two daughters, and a son were with some emigrants en route to California. They had quarreled at the Pima Indian Village and Oatman refused to travel with the party any further and waited until the balance of the party had moved on to Ft. Yuma on the Colorado River and then started alone with his one wagon and his family from the Pimas, and had not gone a day's travel before he stalled on a low spur, which descended to the river from the mountains and impinged upon the stream, down which the road lay. Some Apaches came to help him over the hill, and he knew no better than to believe that they were in good faith. When they all began to push the wagon, the Indians turned on Oatman and slew him. His wife, on the surprise of the moment, exclaimed in the tones of despair, "In the name of God, will nobody help us?" That was all she had time to say for her slaughter quickly followed that of her husband. The young man and son was next who was thrust by lances and thrown over the cliff into the river. The two daughters, Olive and the younger sister, were taken prisoners.

The wagon was soon plundered and the savages betook themselves off toward central Arizona with their captives and plunders, and for years they were not heard from. The young man was not killed and when the Indians were gone with his two sisters, he began to crawl back up the river toward the Pima Village, too badly wounded to walk. On the following day the wolves found him and retarded his exertions by crowding around him. He was naked, having been stripped by the savages,

---

It served as a station on the Butterfield route, deriving its name from a species of native grass called *sacate*. Conkling, *Butterfield Overland Mail*, II, 165–67.

[10] The massacre of the Oatman family took place March 28, 1851, at a place now designated as Oatman Flat, which is about eighteen miles east of Agua Caliente on the Gila River. The Indians committing the massacre are identified as Apache-Mohave. Wyllys, *Arizona*, 134; Browne, *A Tour through Arizona*, 86–98.

and the wolves had no fear of him, which compelled him to crawl to a bush upon the treeless desert and keep off the wolves as best he could. This was the situation when he was discovered by two Indians riding in a gallop toward him.

He now considered his time up and wholly despaired of his life. But to his great gratitude, they were Pimas, who drove away the wolves and took him back to their village and cared for him until he recovered from his wounds. He arrived long afterward at Ft. Yuma, California, in safety and raised several short expeditions to search for his sisters, but all was without success and the whole matter died away, and the worst was submitted to, as of necessity. Some years had passed when Mr. G[rinnell], a brother of a well-known New York millionaire, was at Ft. Yuma and vicinity for a short time, and while there, engaged his idle time in prospecting up the Colorado River for some distance. On one of these occasions he was in a rancheria of Mohave Indians and discovered an almost naked and tattooed squaw and at once saw that she was not an Indian, and went up to her, when she refused to look at him.

But he insisted on talking to her as earnestly as she refused to listen, as she sat upon the ground. He intuitively knew that it was Olive Oatman, as it did prove to be. He struck a trade with some of the Indians and gave a number of sheep and ponies for her. But he had some difficulty in making the exchange when the time came at Ft. Yuma, but with the assistance of a half-breed, who has since been traveling with a circus in the states under the name of Comanche Jim, or Captain Jim, he succeeded in making the exchange without a conflict. The young lady was taken to California, thence to New York, since which time she has been lost sight of. Her sister was not stout enough to stand the hardship with the Indians and died somewhere in Arizona at a place unknown to her friends, and probably always will be. The Apaches were going to burn her body after their custom, but the objections of Olive, supported by an old squaw friend, prevailed, and the two were permitted to bury her in a wilderness grave at a spot too badly lost to give any idea where to find it. This girl had been sold by the Apaches to the Mohaves from whom Mr. Grinnell purchased her. This is a rough outline of this melancholy case of destruction in the wilds of Arizona, which has effected many a stout heart to tears more than once since its occurrence. These were the graves of the old people that we came to before departing for the desert.[11] And on the eve of starting we were joined by the Chief of the Mohaves, and a black warrior and a squaw, all of whom were en route for their homes on the Colorado River beyond our destination in central Arizona, and the Chief proffered his services as guide, which were accepted of course.[12] I neglected to name the most important personage of this royal suit. His name was Charley, a Mohave boy, perhaps twenty years of age, who had loafed about Ft. Yuma in California long enough to learn to speak a little

---

[11] On the reverse side of page 312 of the CONNER MANUSCRIPT is found the following signed statement by Conner:

> Mr. Grinnell claimed to be, and no doubt correctly, a brother of the New York millionaire Grinnell who financed an expedition to, or in search of, the South Pole. He was a carpenter by trade and a trader among the quasi friendly Mohaves on the Colorado River and made his headquarters at Ft. Yuma where he was fully trusted as a reliable man. But it is true history that he rescued Olive Oatman who referred to her missing sister as Annie, but that she may have had another name. His associate upon these trading excursions was a half-breed Indian known as "Comanche Jim" and to whom Mr. Grinnell usually referred to as Capt. Jim and who could speak fair English. Mr. Grinnell in the presence of Capt. Jim gave me personally the details of finding Olive Oatman with the Mohaves on the Colorado River whence he rescued her in company with and by the aid of Capt. Jim, in which both spoke of Olive Oatman refusing to answer questions until Mr. Grinnell called her name on suspicion of it being her. She then immediately responded as if her name was the first word she comprehended. The squaws and little Indians protested when they understood she was to be taken away, which culminated into a retreat followed by an increasing crowd of angry savages to Ft. Yuma before safety was secured. I got these details from Mr. Grinnell in 1864, and some ten years subsequently met Capt. Jim with a circus at Owingsville, Ky., where he recognized me and gave me additional details concerning the Oatman tragedy and informed me that Olive Oatman had been married in New York to a New Joursey farmer.
>
> [Signed] D E Conner
> of the old Walker party of Arizona.

[12] The Mojaves, or Mohaves, a tribe of Yuman descent, lived in the vicinity of Fort Mohave on the Colorado River and the Needles. They maintained friendly relations with Yavapai and western Apaches but warred with the Maricopa, Pima, and Papago. A. L. Kroeber, *Handbook of Indians of California*, 726-40.

broken English.[13] In company with this cortège we started and boldly upon the desert for new and unexplored lands. The Chief of his party were on foot, but they proved to be good footmen and traveled equal to our mules. We all agreed pretty well except the Indians and our old bulldog who could not endure each other with much patience.

Although we had to keep moccasins on this old dog so that he could travel, he still kept up a proud spirit and insisted upon commanding personal respect from all parties, and especially the Indians. The curly shepherd was always docile, friendly, and "plucky." While we were at the Pimas some of the "boys" killed a deer and when it was brought to camp, one of the Indians caught ahold of one of the deer's legs to hold while the skin was taken off, and Curly took hold of the Indian's wrist gently and held on until the fellow let go of the deer, when the dog let loose quietly without doing any injury. The Indian shot off some of his mixed and entangled gutturals at the dog for his impudence and refused to help further in butchering the deer. The Chief's name was Irotaba, if the California papers have published his name correctly.[14] Irotaba could not talk a word of English and if he knew any Spanish he kept it to himself. He seemed to be a kind of protector of a little disaffected branch of the Apache nation, which roamed some of the country into which we were going. He could speak their language, but Charley could not, so our information had to be drawn through several channels before its final reception. We learned from the

---

[13] Fort Yuma was located in Imperial County, California. It was originally established as Camp Calhoun in September, 1849, but the name was changed to Camp Yuma in 1851. The post was abandoned for a time and was re-established as Fort Yuma in February, 1852. Will C. Barnes, *Arizona Place Names*, 498–99.

[14] Conner spells the name of the chief of the Mohaves variously but most usually "Irotaba"; therefore, we have adopted this spelling in the text. Government documents, however, spell the name "Iretaba" and contemporary Arizona newspapers give the spelling as "Irataba." Iretaba is credited with having purchased the Oatman girls from the Apaches and having guided the Whipple party in 1854 and the Ives expedition in 1857 through portions of the country continguous to the Mohave lands. He died on May 3, 1874, on the Colorado River. *Report of the Commissioner of Indian Affairs, 1864*, 150; Prescott, *Arizona Weekly Miner*, January 22, 1875.

Chief through Charley, that there was some water in a little clump of hills about midway of the desert, unknown to the pale face, and that he was directing his course to it. We traveled this desert in the night as much as was convenient on account of the heat, for the sun was pouring down its bright straw-colored rays with terrible energy.

We arrived at the clump of hills about noon on the following day and halted for rest and water. The old Indian pointed up to a cliff to indicate the place where the water was to be found, and Charley, followed by some of the men, departed through some gorges out of sight, but they were presently seen scaling a precarious wall upon top of which they finally found the water. They had taken a rope off of one of the pack mules with them, with which they let the water down by suspending to it the canteens, gourds, &c. This water was alive with little flat, scaly bugs about the dimensions of hungry chinches, which are called in the Pacific country waterlice.[15] After percolating a canteen full through a fragment of a cotton flour sack, we could have nearly half-pint of these working, writhing little scab-like bugs. Some of the men who were too thirsty and impatient to await the slow process of filtering, drew their moustaches over their mouths to serve as filters, but were defeated easily in their attempts to get hasty drinks by the declaration of Tom Johnson, who remarked that the "d—n things were so thin that they could go anywhere that water could." As did Jack Lyon. He was a filthy looking object when he took the cup from his mouth, leaving a myriad of these lice scrambling in his moustache. He quietly remarked, while brushing at them, that he wished he had some clear water with which to wash them out. There was no spring here, but some tanks naturally worn under some cliffs held this fragrant water, all of which we used before we left it. We were soon in single file again on a northerly course and traveling toward the mountains bordering the desert in the distance.

[15] This was probably not a water louse but a species of the tadpole shrimp. Henry S. Pratt, *A Manual of the Common Invertebrate*, 378.

This desert was nearly devoid of vegetation, if we except the numerous sorts of the cactus family and the offensive larrea, which no animal will touch as food under any circumstance. But the cactus vegetation stands thick all over this desert and of every variety.

Burs, large and small, round and oval, load the bushes everywhere, while the accumulated crops of years lay upon the sand like chestnut burs in great profusion for mile after mile as we traversed this unhallowed waste. The straw-colored burs imparted a straw-colored tint to the landscape which was softened a little here and there by a reddish tinge given by the predominance of red feldspar at occasional localities. Some portions of the desert was covered deeply with the loose, straw-colored sand while at others the surface was quite solid, but all barren of useful vegetation. The cacti burs would seem to be always to be inclined toward the mules' legs, as we came near them, and the least touch was sufficient apparently to stick tenaciously. A bur would adhere to a mule's shin-bone as certainly as to any other part of the body and when struck with a gun barrel to knock it off the prickles would draw out of the bur and stick to the mule. The points were barbed and of too fine a finish to detect with the naked eye and it creates more pain to withdraw one from the flesh than is felt upon its entering. They are certainly the sharpest instruments ever invented and so well seasoned that they hardly ever decompose in the sand or on the plant. However clean and smooth a prickly pear may appear by looking at it, the stings in the tongue and lips quickly give warning of the presence of thistles, upon attempting to eat it. The only sure plan is to wet them before eating so as to take the flexibility out of the invisible fuzz with which this fruit is invariably coated. There is also a sand bur very diminutive and hidden in the sand and seem to last forever. One may blunder and fall with one hand in the sand for support, but upon taking the hand from the apparent clean nice sand it is invariably covered with adhering prickles and sand burs which have become detached from the burs and accumulated for years in the sand, as afore-stated.[16]

We kept our direct course until night when we were all fearfully thirsty. The dogs had either to be tied upon the packs of the mules or to be deserted and left. So we bound them fast to the packs on two mules and then they came near choking before night came on the day previously. About midnight I dismounted and left my horse to keep his place in the line without any rider. To thus walk awhile was usual in the party, but I turned out of the trail and stretched out flat upon the ground where it was quite solid and rested and longed for water. The ground was still uncomfortably warm and I remained for an hour or more and arose to start when a new idea presented itself to me. I had heard that the large species of the cactus genus which here stood about the desert in numbers were filled with a watery pulp which was good to allay thirst, and harmless to health. So I felt that being alone in the silent desert and under cover of the night, I could take my own time to explore the inside of one of those singular trees and therefore went to work upon one of them with my butcher knife.[17]

As there are so few comparatively who have any knowledge of the existence of such a tree or plant in this country, I will give a short description of one. They grow always in desert land or in the rocks, and sometimes out of crevices between the rocks of an inch wide. They grow out of rock walls and then turn upward as they form, and are frequently found high up in inaccessible places, growing luxuriantly out of some crevice in the rocks, with a most precarious hold. Yet they grow from twenty to fifty feet in height and probably average more than one foot and a half in diameter.

[16] From Conner's description it is impossible to determine the exact species of prickly pear he meant. The plant abounds in Arizona and the other southwestern states and is minutely described in Thomas H. Kearney and Robert Peebles, *Arizona Flora*, 579 ff. Lyman Benson, in *The Cacti of Arizona*, 55, Figure 12, says that the "Engelmann prickly pear, *Opuntia Engelmannii* [is] the commonest and largest prickly pear in Arizona."

[17] Conner probably is referring to the saguaro or giant cactus in this and the following paragraph. For exact descriptions see Benson, *Cacti of Arizona*.

The greater number of them have no limbs whatever, while some have one, two, and three, but I do not remember to have ever seen one with four boughs. They hold to the ground by one straight tap root which enters the ground, similar to the garden radish and stand very straight wherever they may be located. They have a skeleton composed of long slender poles oval in diameter and about the size of a large man's wrist and also about the same shape. These poles are more than a dozen in number and all grow out of the tap root in the ground and stand in a circle a little apart from each other, and thus extend to the full height of the tree, where they arch over and grow to each other in the center. If we would stand a number of such piles close together in a circle of eighteen inches in diameter and then take out every alternate one, we would leave the skeleton work of this curious growth, except that the standing poles all run into one root at the bottom and are connected and held firmly in position by small cross bars of the same material, growing from one pole to the other like cartilage at distances of four or five feet apart, all the way to the top of the tree. The cavity thus formed and the spaces between the poles are filled with a solid seamless and seedless white, watery, tasteless pulp, which is nearly as easily cut out as the pulp of an ordinary watermelon. The outside of this tree, if tree it is, is covered with an evergreen and tender skin, which is as easily scratched as that of the watermelon and presents a ridged surface, like the surface of an ordinary musk melon.

Each pole or rib forms a ridge from the foot of the tree to its top. Now draw a fine line on the center of each of those ridges the whole length of the trees upon which to plant thorns about the size of common sewing needles, only much longer and sharper, with their points directed in every conceivable direction except inward and to the full number that can be crowded on to the line, and the tree is nearly complete in appearance. Some of those trees or rather trunks cannot be touched with the finger without prickling it, so well are they protected by these thorns. What few limbs they have are of the same construction—usually four to five feet in length, and hold to the main trunk by the tough little tap root which seems to enter the body just like the root of the main trunk enters the ground.

A few small flowers of red, yellow, and white grow among the thistles upon the top of the different species of these trees, from which a delicious fruit is produced to the size and shape of small or half-grown pears. This fruit is filled with small black seeds like a fig and very sweet. The pulp in some of them is most exceedingly bitter to the taste, yet they all look alike, except perhaps the bitter ones may be of a shade darker green than the others. An ordinary gun rammer could be thrust through one of those trunks between the ribs which are tough and stout, and when seasoned and dry, very light. They hardly even fall down but can be easily curled about by placing a pole or gun against them. But when one does fall or is cut down it decomposes very rapidly, all except the skeleton pole, which retains its shape for a long time and might roll about the desert for years if not broken apart. Such is the character of this species of cactus, which botanists call pitahaya....[18]

It was one of these specimens upon which I went to work with my butcher knife on the night above referred to.

After trimming off all the thorns from a small place I cut a hole into the tree between two of its ribs, large enough to admit the hand, out of which I took enough of the watery pulp to fill every available place in my clothes, pockets, hat, and bosom. When I became pretty well loaded I took my journey on the trail—walked and ate pulp until I arrived at the party's fatigued and barren-looking camping place, which was silent and desolated in the extreme.

Men, mules, and dogs were all resigned to a famished and patient desperation that was painful to behold. But it was not long until day. When the sun arose we were within five miles of what could easily be seen to be barren mountains. We were off again at daylight and in due time reached the dry mouth of the

---

[18] The old name of the pipeorgan cactus was *pitahaya dulce*, denoting the sweetness of the pulp. Kearney and Peebles, *Arizona Flora*, 569–70.

creek that we were destined to follow, pronounced by the Indians "Haviamp," with a labored grunt on the "p." [19] This creek emptied its high waters upon this desert, but as this was a low water time we had to follow its dry, sandy bed quite a distance into the hills through a gorge-like channel before we reached the damp sand at a point to which the water had flown the day previously. This I thought was a singular freak, but I learned since that it is quite common in this dry country for the water to gradually cease to flow at night and then extend its distance as the sun rises. We kept up this creek as the sand became more damp as we proceeded, and finally we met the water coming and encamped just out of the banks, and in half an hour had quite a flood of running water at our feet. And we all did drink. At night the water again restrained itself to the extent that there was none to be had and again came afresh on the following morning and lasted all day.

There are a few who understand what real hunger means—such hunger as extends to the whole physical and mental system and of a nature that food alone cannot give immediate relief. But there are none who can understand and explain the cruel and murderous situation where extreme thirst is added. Placed in such a situation and under such circumstances—such as seem to defy and to mock all efforts for relief—the humane and Christian man become a resigned brute and as much a brute as any other brute. His suffering are those of disease and he is just as incapable of following any particular line of conduct while laboring under this species of madness as any other ferocious animal. The cry "water, water, water" had always been an old song set out in some of our childhood's school books and earliest lessons but they were never understood and maybe never will be. May heaven ordain that poor earthly creatures, one and all, now and hereafter may never be punished again by this species

[19] Hassayampa Creek bore a variety of names such as Assamp, Hassamp, and Hasiamp, besides the name Haviamp. The creek rises on the northern slope of Mount Union and flows south, entering the Gila River at Powers Butte in Maricopa County. McClintock said the name means "water that is hidden" or "water that is in a dry bed." Barnes, *Arizona Place Names*, 200.

of calamity which renders the human mind and form truly the objects of pity. I can never revert to that famous "Jornada" on the east side of the Rocky Mountains without a pang of horror because of the silent and unbending cruelty that it had dealt out to unfortunate flesh and blood so continuously for many years. ... We moved up stream and encamped within a few hundred yards of the subsequently discovered and famous gold lode known as the Vulture. For several hundred yards the croppings of this mine stood several feet high out of the ground within plain view of our party, who only observed it as we did any other ledge of rough rocks. But being black from the weather and time it was calculated to deceive any one as to its real character. Henry Wickenburg, a German, who with others followed our trail a year later, discovered that this ledge was quartz and it has since proved to be a rich mine upon which a large quartz mill has since been placed.[20]

The town of Wickenburg in Arizona, situated on this spot, takes its name from the discoverer of the lode. Although our party was exploring for gold it passed by this great deposit of that metal in haste to leave the bleak and inhospitable place as we did other barren wastes. Day by day we continued our journey up this stream which I thought in my soul that it was the roughest country to be composed of ordinary mountains and hills that I had yet seen in all my Rocky Mountain experiences. The creek was a narrow gorge-like cañon that could not be traced either direction with any degree of certainty as to its general course and it wound its crooked way amongst the mountains apparently down deep beneath the general level of the balance of the country. Numerous obstacles in its bed, such as falls, accumulated boulders, &c over which it was impossible to take the mules, frequently turned us out of the steep banks, where our

[20] The Vulture mine, located in Section 33, Township 6 North, Range 5 West, was discovered by Henry Wickenburg in 1863 and was named supposedly because of the hovering turkey buzzards. Wickenburg was an Austrian who came to Arizona with the Pauline Weaver party. The town of Wickenburg, located on the Hassayampa in northwest Maricopa County, is named after this early miner. Barnes, *Arizona Place Names*, 486; Lockwood, *Pioneer Days in Arizona*, 199.

route would become either up or down continuously on account of the numberless arroyos, gulches, and gorge-like hollows found to be pitching down the mountains into the main creek. This kept us in continual search for places to get up, down, or across these precipitous barriers. The only trees about were the sparse clumps of cottonwood in the bed of the stream and the pines in the distant heads of hollows against the summits of the main ranges on either side. This extensive uneven scope of ridges and hollows was liberally clothed with a slow, desert growth of stiff stunted chaparral mostly of oak and amansonito, three or four feet in height.[21] I doubt the orthography of the last, but it gives the proper sound, which is the best that I can do for now. It is a red-colored shrub, wood and bark, except the thin, sappy portion, which is white. The bark is fine, smooth, and as stated, a deep red, and the bush grows exceedingly branchy and crooked. It is very inflexible and . . . stout, snaps quickly when broken, has leaves the shape of mistletoe, but of large dimension. Altogether, the chaparral, composed of the entangled branches of this shrub and stunted oak, forms no ordinary barrier, even upon level ground. Buckskin pantaloons even fail to withstand the wear and tear of this brush very long. We found a liberal prospect of gold all along this creek and its tributary hollows.

We slowly proceeded up the stream until we came to quite a stretch where the water in the creek had sunk beneath the surface, leaving the bed dry and at the instance of Irotaba, we encamped under one of the half-dozen large cottonwood trees there on the sand in the creek. The Chief told us through our interpreter Charley that he had been signaled for a pow-wow by the natives. We were at a loss to know how he got his signal, for he and his associates were all the while with us, but as the slang phrase goes, "He got it all the same." Irotaba was the chief of the Mohaves whose territory was nearly confined to the Colorado and the southern border of California. His people had fought

[21] Scrub oaks comprise the most numerous parts of the chaparral on exposed mountainsides in southern and central Arizona. Kearney and Peebles, *Arizona Flora*, 216. The "amansonito" is undoubtedly manzanita. Kearney and Peebles, *Arizona Flora*, 633.

the Californians until they had become about helpless and they were friendly with the white man rather from necessity than from choice. Irotaba hesitated not to say so. He was a tall and large man with a careworn cast of countenance, knitted brow, and of a quiet, observant, and thoughtful demeanor. He was dressed upon this occasion in a cotton, checked shirt, thin blue cotton pants, and a chip or straw hat of Mexican manufacture, and was barefoot part of the time and wore moccasins a part of the time. None of the savage features that so distinctly stamped those of Mangus, whom we captured, was to be traced in the face of Irotaba. As before stated, he was acknowledged as a kind of protector over a small band of Apaches, who inhabited this immediate locality, who called themselves Apache-mohaves, but all the Apaches roamed this whole country at pleasure.[22] Irotaba has since visited Washington under the supervision of Captain John Moss and was said to have learned to speak English while on his trip thence, but I cannot say whether this is true or not as I never saw him but once after his return and then never spoke to him.[23] But at the time he was with us, he knew no English.

However, when we were all settled in camp in the shade of the cottonwood trees on the Haviamp, Irotaba delivered in a yell, a string of gutturals that resounded all through these cañons, gorges, and craggy mountain sides, and then stood looking up the rocky defiles, perfectly quiet. After quite a pause he raised one arm aloft and steadily held it there while his eyes were fixed steadily upon a high object up in the mountain.

He stood thus for some moments like some crazy practitioner in witchcraft and then quietly resumed his seat, upon a large

---

[22] These Indians are correctly called the Yavapai, a Yuman tribe, but are popularly known as the Apache-Mohave or Mohave-Apache. Before their removal they claimed the territory between the Verde River and Black Mesa and from the Salt River to Bill Williams Mountain. Hodge, *Handbook of American Indians*, II, 994; Poston described their condition in 1864 as follows: "They live along the roads from the Colorado river to the interior towns and mining camps, depending somewhat upon the subsistence they can obtain from travellers and trains of provisions." *Report of Commissioner of Indian Affairs, 1864*, 156.

[23] Poston refers to Captain John Moss as ". . . an amateur representative of the Americans . . ." among the Mohaves. *Report of the Commissioner of Indian Affairs, 1864*, 150–51.

rock in the edge of the creek on the same side and to the left hand of Capt. Walker, who was seated upon his blanket and saddle. Charley was lying in the sand in front of them and the black warrior, with long hair on his legs, and the humped-back squaw took rather a back seat. The members of our party who were not on guard all lay scattered around in the dry sand, patiently awaiting the result of Irotaba's vocal hieroglyphics. Although we were silently awaiting the arrival of the savages whom we had not seen nor heard anywhere in this apparently habitless country, we were all surprised to see thirty or forty of them, black and nearly naked, watchfully and stealthily emerge from the nearest rocks around our position nearly within ten paces and trepidatiously halt, as though they doubted the propriety of coming nearer. This was a sudden apparition to me, for a low hum of interjections from some of the "boys," caused me to look up and find this crowd of Indians all in sight without knowing how they came.

If Irotaba had never been with us, we should never have known, perhaps, that one of these savages were anywhere about us, unless we had been attacked by them.

After observing this phenomenon, some one of our party began to say irreverently that "Christ smote the rock and the water—." "D—n such impious comparisons," broke in another cutting short the remarks of the first speaker, and who continued with emphasis to say that "These naked, barbarous wretches sneak out of their holes as insidiously as so many rats, and are not entitled to a consideration more dignified than that which is accorded to the rats and mice about the city livery stable." He continued to insist that the rifle and the six-shooter were the proper implements with which to make such treaties and that the whole tribe of them would swear eternal friendship with the same breath in which they form a mental resolution to murder the objects of their devotion upon the first opportunity. All treaties with them, he considered, at an end, upon the formal recognition of their stipulations, and that nothing but a rifle treaty would stick. Here our old mountain captain put an end to all objections by quietly saying, "Be easy, be easy, for the more you become acquainted with these savages, the more you will respect their demands, and we will put off all rifle negotiations as long as possible, for I fear they may come too soon for us at best." Here he ended by saying, "Charley, tell Irotaba to tell these people that we are strangers and come to be as friends, and don't want to hurt or harm them." Charley shot off some gutturals at Irotaba, after which the latter arose from his seat and in a standing position, and delivered a little earnest speech to these naked creatures, who seemed not so well pleased with it, as they might have been.

Irotaba evidently did not want us to go further up that creek. He resumed his seat at the end of his speech with his brows more knitted than ever, and Capt. Walker did not believe that he had told the Indians what he had directed. The Captain continued, "Charley, tell Irotaba to ask these people whether or not they are going to be our friends." Charley got off some more of his Mohave gutturals, while he was evidently embarrassed. He employed himself as he lay on his elbow in the sand by picking little straws to pieces, as he talked. He gave great attention to the particles of grass in his fingers to avoid looking at any one as he talked. Charley evidently felt that he was in a tight place. Irotaba arose again and made a long speech with the gutturals he also seemed to make as he proceeded, and a number of savage glances by the natives, one to another, was the sequence. Irotaba again resumed his seat, evidently unable to restrain his feelings and was plainly dissatisfied about something. Our side made several similar attempts at learning their feelings toward us, as well as their intention, but without success. Irotaba grew more vigorous and loud in his speeches and looked more savage when he took his seat. The audience also showed great displeasure by their gesticulations, either at our language or that of Irotaba, the import of which we had no means of understanding. The surest means we had of understanding them was through their actions, which indicated more hostility than friendship and therefore we had no confidence in the treacherous, half-friendly replies which they gave us. We were probably trying to make the first treaty of peace with these natives ever attempted. Irotaba told us that we were the first white men ever so near the source of this creek and further informed us that one other party attempted to ascend it and perished.

I was lying just in front of Irotaba and had a good opportunity to observe him throughout this negotiation. He would look careworn and reflective after every speech. Once I caught him with puzzled air and knitted brows, thoughtfully and intently observing me. I felt that he was contemplating me inquisitively as to what business a "pale face" boy had there, anyway. "Actions speak louder than words," and especially words so little understood as were those. And sometimes actions constitute the best language, even within reach of our best grammar schools; therefore we felt justified in continuing our trusts in the language of actions rather than to depend upon such an impromptu beginning at learning a foreign language for such an occasion as this. The natural conclusion therefore was to take nature's interpretation for nature's language and our Captain made his last observation by directing Charley to tell Irotaba to tell his people that we came to hunt gold, of which they knew nothing, and for which they cared nothing, and that we wanted to be friends and would not hurt them. "But," he continued, "if they begin to steal our mules and to shoot our men, we will quit hunting gold and go to hunting Indians."

Charley began his rigamarole as he mechanically picked at his straws, to all of which Irotaba listened attentively to the end and then arose a little excitedly and made a furious speech which drew from his audience a few bursts of indignation. The savages would frequently, during this last speech, turn toward one another, overflowed with gutturals. Capt. Walker asked Charley what Irotaba was saying to the Indians. Charley replied, "Me don't know what he say when he talk Apache." "Well what does he say in your language to you." "He say, he no fight if you no go up Haviamp." That settled the matter, for we did intend to

Daniel Ellis Conner,
from a photograph made shortly after his Arizona adventures.
(From James H. McClintock, *Arizona: The Youngest State,* I.)

go on up the creek and therefore could no longer entertain the conditions of our friendly enemies.

But Irotaba didn't know that Charley had negligently given that little piece of information and still thought that he was cheating us as to his own real views. At the end of Irotaba's last speech the savages would look at the nearest friend and lean up toward him and deliver a number of "Ugh Ugh Ugh's." Irotoba dismissed his Indians who (excepting those who came with him) proceeded to scatter off into the rocks and disappear as easily as they had come. They were unarmed, but of course their arms were not far off. The old Chief tried hard to make us believe that there was no water above this point and that we would perish if we persisted in going further into the country and offered his services to pilot us across to the Colorado River to the border of California, all of which we respectfully declined. He now became morose and silent, and as night came on he declined to talk and after we all retired to sleep he and his associates of the royal family took *French* leave of us and also took all the smoking tobacco that the party possessed with them.

The tobacco was done up in one large package and they had learned which pack it was usually put into and profited by it. We were thus relieved of the company of our distinguished guide and guests without the formalities of a farewell address here in the wilderness and without even knowing when they had concluded to start. The tobacco was a sore loss to some of the smokers. But after all I did not consider Irotaba a bad man, for his habitual expression of contemplative care and anxiety rather gave him a gentle appearance. Unlike Mangus, whose oval-shaped face, bold expression, and total want of amiability stamped with resolution and firmness, proclaimed him a desperate character. There was more reckless cruelty expressed in one glance of his bloodshot eye than is discovered in the whole Mohave race. I felt for Irotaba. I felt that he considered his mission a failure, although he was accustomed to say that if he could he would make war on the whole white race. He well knew that a footing for the white man in central Arizona would

seal the fate of the Indians there. He mimicked the battle with
the soldiers in which his predecessor had lost his life, by picking
up a stick and thrusting with it like a soldier using his bayonet,
as the Indians charged them with their war clubs, such as the
Mohaves still use in battle. He gave us a detailed account of this
battle by his actions, assisted and interpreted by Charley.

We moved upstream about fifteen miles without finding
water in the bed of the creek or anywhere else, but encamped
at the end of the dry stretch. But now the continuous hardship
of desert travel began to tell their story. One man after another
began to get sick. F. G. G[illiland] became delirious and had to
be supported upon his mule for hours until we reached a camping place. Others became unable to travel and there were but
few who escaped. It always started by a sudden attack of vertigo,
which would rapidly increase to unconsciousness. The attack
would be sudden and render the victim deathly sick, which
lasted until unconsciousness resulted. My turn came just after
eating a hearty breakfast early on a pretty morning when feeling as hearty as I ever did in my whole life. We had encamped
the night before on a little upland flat just below what was
afterward known as the "big cañon" in the Haviamp. The party
had "packed up" and were in a line going to the lower end of the
cañon in which there were green cottonwood trees within its
walls for probably a mile of its length. Before descending the
river bank to get into the mouth of the cañon I felt the attack
of vertigo which rapidly increased to violence and vomiting.
Then a cold perspiration and deathly sickness followed, and by
the time we were fairly into the cañon, winding a devious way
between the cool walls and under the shady trees, delirious sen-
sations came flooding over my senses like an irresistible wave
to overwhelm me.

I just had sense enough left to remember the unavoidable
rough handling which some of the others had received while in
the same condition and therefore, without warning any one of
my condition, I dismounted, threw the bridle reins over the
saddle, and allowed my mule to keep its place in the line as

though I would walk awhile. So soon as the party had passed me I turned out into the shade of a large cottonwood and stretched myself upon the cool sand which had drifted deep around and under this tree. A little later and I would not have had time to have made any arrangement whatever, for I immediately swooned away into a delirious, horrible dream which seemed to last an age. I would now and then awake into a semi-consciousness, just to again sleep off into unconsciousness.

This flighty condition seemed to have lasted an indefinite length of time, as though I had always been there. But it began to subside as the cool sand allayed the fever and a clearheaded recognition of my surroundings confronted me. I did not remember anything whatever of what I did with my arms, but found my gun sitting against an old fallen trunk some distance away and my belt and two six-shooters lying loose and wallowed into the sand.

I quickly started on upon the fresh trail of the party which vividly brought to mind the fact of having once before followed that trail under trying circumstances more than a thousand miles away from this locality. An unsteady head and consequent unsteady step retarded my progress greatly, for the terrific effects still lingered and periodically threatened another spell, as I began to grow warm by the exertions of walking.

When I had traversed the cañon to the upper end where it opened out so that I could see the country, I was surprised to find myself within twenty paces of an Indian rancheria and attempted to draw back, but I was a little too late for the squaws and children who hid themselves from the party as it passed found that they were not to be molested, came jumping out toward me, each trying to rival the other in shouting for tobacco. "Bac, bac, bac," was vigorously howled by them, all at once. But their levity ceased and their faces quickly straightened into an evident disappointment, when I waved them back with my hand and passed on. I had not gone however more than a half-mile when I discovered two Indian braves off several hundred yards to my right hand, directing their course to my route ahead of me. We came together and I set my gun down and drew a pistol with my right hand, and took their proffered hands with my left hand. They smiled at this precaution but submitted to it. By signs I attempted to get them to go back, but in vain, every effort was made. I dared not allow them behind me and therefore could not proceed, for they followed me upon every attempt that I made to go. I was afraid to shoot them for fear that so soon as their war began, I would be charged with beginning it.

I started again and as they got into the trail behind me I raised the lock of my gun, which was now on my shoulder and sprung the trigger, and it failed to go off. I had suddenly taken a foolish notion that if they would walk behind me that they ought to have their brains blown out accidently, and half done purposely. They saw this little motion and became suspicious of me, whereupon they left me upon the trail and traveled ahead of my course. They saw that I would not trust them and seemed to give up gaining my confidence. I traveled along after them until they were out of sight, and then I turned out to the trail again and took another little flight into the dream lands under a little black thorn bush. This was the most grateful repose I ever experienced and I really became right happy as I lay stretched in the shade, half asleep and half awake. A total want of all inclinations to talk or to move seemed to be the distinguishing feature which marked the conduct of all who was thus attacked. It was very provoking to be even spoken to and altogether it was rather a singular piece of business and more especially as recovery within a few days became as speedy as the attack, without remedy or medicine. Our medicine supplies had long since been destroyed and we were without all such conveniences. I again after an apparent age of time stirred myself up with only a faint recollection of how I came there and made another feeble start, and had not gone far before meeting Sam Miller and M. Lewis in search of me. They had been encamped for hours some five or ten miles away. I mounted the animal which they were leading for me without saying a word, as I was afterward informed. The mules were already packed and only awaiting for our arrival when the line of march was taken up and continued until we reached a grove of little black walnut trees, where we again halted for supper. This is one of the prettiest points in Arizona and has since retained the name we gave it and still goes by the name of Walnutgrove.[24]

Here, while I was lying on a blanket, I became delirious and talked wildly and became conscious so suddenly as to catch myself at it. I asked S[am] Miller, who was reclining on his elbow, whether or not I was talking foolishly, and he quietly remarked, "Yes." From this time on, recovery was speedy. I have puzzled myself many times since this trying and never to be forgotten period of my existence, to contrive some reasonable speculation as to the cause and nature of this sort of ailment, but all in vain.

Here the Indians were hovering the summits and ridges of the neighborhood mountains. The "signs" were not quite right and our Captain ordered another "catch up" and only a few minutes after supper. Now came the tug of war. Bordering the upper edge of this pretty little valley upon both sides of the creek lay a terribly broken and chaparral country with a few scattering pines commingled. Just where the creek came out of this rugged country into the valley were a number of impassable falls, above which the creek was but little else than a gorge clear on to the distant pine woods, which we had seen in the distance for several days and were trying to reach. A woodland country began to look right pretty and inviting since we had seen so little of it for many months. About a half-mile to our right hand, facing up stream and therefore on the left of the stream, was a tall, sharp chaparral mountain peak. We left our little grove of trees and climbed that mountain and encamped upon its treeless summit among the chaparral all night. Upon examining those falls we found deep holes worn into the rocks were the water fell and therefore we called the place "The Tanks," which name it afterward retained, and I presume it still

[24] Walnut Grove was located on Hassayampa Creek west of Crown King and seventeen miles slightly west of south from Prescott.

does. . . .[25] We directed our course up stream quite a half-mile from the creek and therefore in crossing the numerous ridges and their intervening hollows that pitched into the creek we had a constant up and down hill route. One one occasion in descending one of those steep hillsides, the crupper of Captain Walker's saddle gave away and tossed him over the mule's head down the hill, where he landed upon his shoulders into a bunch of prickly pear bushes. He was not serious hurt, however, having had the force of his fall resisted by the chaparral which was standing dense all about there.

Upon arriving upon top of the next ridge we turned at right angles and followed this sharp back-bone down to the creek above the falls. Here we found the immediate bank of this gorge so precipitous as to have to push the mules down upon their haunches to the bed of the creek. We now turned up this narrow gorge a few hundred yards and encamped about dark at the mouth of another little creek which flowed (when it ran at all) in from the opposite side of the Haviamp on the west.

Upon making tea with the water from this creek it was found to be so strongly impregnated with copper that it could not be used, and we therefore named this stream Copper Creek, which name it retained.[26] I had gotten over my sick spell and went on guard at the mouth of Copper Creek in the fore part of the night and heard the first frogs croak of which I remembered of having heard since my enlistment into this wild stampede. As a slight indication of what may be expected sometimes in the way of information concerning adventures in the western country, I will stop here to remark merely a little incident which occurred at or near this place nearly four years later. I was riding down this creek and passed the mouth of Copper Creek with a party of men, none of whom I knew. One of them was entertaining

---

[25] Contemporary maps do not show such a place on the Hassayampa. The tanks do not show on a detailed sketch of the Hassayampa and Kirkland creeks' drainage basins in Eldred B. Wilson, *Arizona Gold Placers*, Arizona Bureau of Mines *Bulletin*, No. 132, 3rd ed., facing p. 32.

[26] Copper Creek flows from the northwest into the Hassayampa about fourteen miles north of Walnut Grove.

the others in a loud tone of voice as all of us passed down the Haviamp. The subject was of different explorations and that of the Walker Party especially. Everybody by this time had heard of the Walker Party. Men who never knew one of the members of this party only by reputation, would speak of it as if they knew everything that they did. It was just so with this fellow who was describing the route into this country made by our old party and located it upon the wrong side of the creek. He was evidently not aware of the presence of any member of that party while he was giving his grand discourse. As we came to the spur down which we had pushed our mules just below Copper Creek, as before stated, I noticed that the water from rains had washed a gully from the start that our trail had given, down the steep hill. I here called to the enthusiastic narrator and remarked to him, as I pointed to the gully, that that wash was started by Walker's trail made on first coming into the country. He turned in his saddle and looked back at me, and responded, "No sir, you are mistaken; Walker's Trail is away over on the west side of the Haviamp—the one made when he first came into central Arizona." I replied that I was not mistaken and knew that the said trail came down the hill which I had pointed out and was the cause of that washed gutter, which I had indicated. "Oh my dear sir," he responded as he looked back, "I was with that party and know that we came in on the west side of the creek." Here I passed the witness and said nothing more as he talked and explained, and I at last parted with that crowd of travelers without allowing any of them to know that I, too, was a member of that party that first came into this country, and had never seen this fellow before.

So it had been, since gold was first discovered in the Rocky Mountains. Men will lie about their exploits upon second-hand information. Casual passers through upon the old beaten routes, which may be a thousand miles apart, will borrow from any one they happen to see, who also borrowed again from some one else and so on until an event of the northern section of this train of mountains will become finally located a thousand miles south by some enterprising publication cheaply gotten up, for the digesting of just such materials. And occasionally they swindle some first-class papers and dailies, too.

But, however, when we left the mouth of Copper Creek on the following morning we went up the steep, sharp, and high spur formed by the junction of the two creeks. F. G. G[illiland]'s pack mule was one of the last to start up and when he scratched his way up about twenty paces, his pack over balanced him and he stumbled backward and rolled to the bottom of the hill from where he had started. I supposed that he was surely killed, but it was not at all the case, for that old mule arose from the ground and on his own accord made another vigorous charge at that hill and succeeded by a desperate scramble during which he seemed to put forth as much exertion as though his life depended upon climbing it. Upon the top of this hill we had an open view of the large woodland tract of country which looked beautiful and inviting. We descended into the creek again down from this steep mountain through dense chaparral and left the bed of the creek only once more to pass a blocked place and came into the edge of the woods and followed the creek a few hundred yards into the woods and encamped for the night upon a pretty and comparatively level situation near the creek. There was no undergrowth of any consequence and therefore the woods were just open enough to look pretty.

We considered our long journey at an end, for we were at last in the unexplored regions of central Arizona, the place of our destination, and located in the finest and largest woodland country by far to be found within the extensive limits of the whole Territory.

This, our first camp in these woods, has always since been a prominent place and will be alluded to frequently hereafter. It was within a few miles only of the extreme head of the Haviamp, whose mouth we had to cross deserts to find and whose whole course we had patiently followed, as we might follow a gorge through an uninviting, broken, craggy, and hot country, clothed by chaparral only. This woods we found to lay in a strip extending about twenty miles from southeast to northwest and was about six or eight miles in width. Our camp was located in the south edge of it. Out of the woods in all directions lay the desert country dried and parched. Toward the north was a grassy plain perhaps over twenty miles in extent, but it was dry and waterless. These woods were on the highest country between the Rocky Mountains and the Colorado River, except perhaps the San Francisco Mountains which stood toward the northeast about eighty miles away, but were distinctly seen from our "big woods." [27] Therefore, many creeks of which accounts will be hereafter given, have their sources in these woods and dry up in the distant deserts as they take their different courses north, south, east, and west. This fact, to some extent, explains the reason that this country was so long unknown and unvisited. The water courses having their rise in it, dried up before crossing the desert country which lies extensively all around it. There was never a finer location for a headquarters of a lawless banditti than these woods, previous to our visit there, so well were they fortified by formidable obstacles in the way of waterless deserts. So soon as we were encamped and a little before night L[ount] went back into the woods to shoot a deer for supper. He had not gone more than three hundred yards from the camp when he discovered some leaves freshly turned over and upon investigation found a deer recently killed, with its entrails taken out and covered with the leaves, probably done by a mountain lion. He stole the carcass and brought it to camp and thereby saved himself the further trouble of hunting one of his own. Not having heard the report of his gun, some one asked him how he got the deer and he replied that he had run it down and killed it with his knife.

. . . We spent the following day in a more thorough examination of the bed of the Haviamp to determine the character and extent of its gold production, and was pleased with the

[27] The San Francisco Mountains lie near Flagstaff, Arizona, with Humphrey's Peak having the highest elevation of 12,655 feet. Barnes, *Arizona Place Names*, 383–84.

prospect. One day after another added confidence and resulted in the final decision that there was gold in this creek in paying quantities and there was plenty deer and other game in the woods. This being settled, the next thing to be done was the building of a permanent corral with which to secure the mules at night and to do away with the necessity of standing around them all night continuously, as we had been doing constantly for the last nine months. We had but one axe and by first one and other, it was kept in constant use felling large pine trees one after another in the same direction, upon each other, and we had a long rectangular corral, constructed with whole trees, which were too large to be moved or broken through. This was the stoutest corral ever built in central Arizona and when the stock was once into it, they might be killed, but there was no such thing as storming them out of it.

The next move made was the holding of a miners' meeting. Being only twenty-six of us, there was not much discussion. The district was first defined by bounding it by the distant ridges and primary ranges of the country, without any trouble of any measurement. A mining claim was defined and declared to be one hundred yards of an ore vein or quartz-lode, and the same extent on a creek bed in surface or placer diggings. The claimant was to hold all the ground on either side of the creek in placer diggings and on either side of the vein if it was a quartz ledge for a distance of fifty yards, thereby constituting a claim of one hundred yards square, lying upon the "pay streak" whether of quartz or surface mines. The claimant was to own the possessory right and title to "all of the earth and minerals therein contained." It was further provided that each member of our party should be entitled to two claims each, upon all discoveries of any character of mines whatever—one by the right of discovery and the other by virtue of pre-emption.

I neglected to state that on permanent organization, Capt. Walker was declared by acclamation to be the Governor of the District and declined upon the grounds that a young man should be appointed. Whereupon the humble instrument of these notes, being the youngest of the party, was appointed and also declined on the grounds that he would not be there any longer than the first opportunity to get away presented itself. Then Thos J[ohnson] was appointed and accepted.[28] I was then elected secretary and recorder of claims for the District and declined, when Mr. W[heelhouse] was appointed, and accepted, and acted. This humble scribe was one of the committee appointed to draft the bylaws, and the writer of only a few resolutions, which were adopted and the meeting adjourned. Thus ended the first miners' meeting ever held in central Arizona.

One of the resolutions referred to provided for a committee to be appointed by the Governor, to measure, and stake off and number fifty-two claims upon this creek (Haviamp) which ran by our camp and to begin with No. 1, which was provided to be layed off just opposite camp and to number each way up and down the creek an equal distance.[29] Then it was further provided that the secretary should mark on bits of paper the numbers corresponding to the numbers on the stakes, both up and down stream, indicating—No. 2 up,—No. 5 down, &c. These scraps of paper, after due preparation as provided by the resolution of the meeting, was put into the soundest hat to be found in the party, from which each member drew one ticket twice around and thus settled the personal ownership of the respective mining claims, indicated by the stakes to the numbers of two apiece. The Governor held the hat while the drawing was going on, but I have forgotten whose hat got the premium and it makes

[28] In the manuscript "Journal of the Pioneer and Walker Mining Districts, 1863–1865," 5 (hereafter cited as "Journal of Pioneer and Walker Mining Districts"), a meeting of the "Walker Prospecting and Mining Company," held May 10, 1863, on the "Oolkilipava River," another name for the Hassayampa, elected J. T. Johnson president of the district. Johnson, however, is not listed in an enumeration of the original prospectors of the party, see p. 2. In his letter to Miss Hall, May 1, 1910, CONNER MANUSCRIPTS, Conner lists Johnson as being a member of the original party. The page citations given here and following to the "Journal of the Pioneer and Walker Mining Districts" are to the original journal in the custody of the Yavapai County Recorder, Prescott, Arizona, of which the editors have a microfilm copy.

[29] The "Journal of the Pioneer and Walker Mining Districts" contains original claims. Conner, listed as D. Ellis, had claims 23 above and 1 below from the point of the original discovery. See pp. 242–46 of the manuscript journal.

little difference, as there was no preceptible difference between the hats belonging to the party about this time. They were all patched nearly equally, but there might have been better sewing done on some than on others. Each man now began to hunt his claim by the numbers of his tickets and to mark them on the trees. This humble miner drew No. 1 opposite the camp, which proved to be the most worthless claim upon the creek. Mr. W[heelhouse], while arranging his records, remarked that he intended to give this creek a Spanish pronunciation and therefore entered the flat "Haviamp" as pronounced by the Indians with a strong accent upon the last syllable upon his records—spelled "Hassayampa," which has been sustained by our geographies, thereby rendering a pure Indian word, by the assistance of a Spanish dialect, obscure and uncertain. This seems to be one of the failings of all dominant powers. They engraft their own peculiar ideas upon a barbarous tongue and thereby add to the confusion of the latter's history. I shall hereafter call this creek—Hassayampa, but it is not the pronunciation of the Indians. Irotaba, while indicating the passage around the great bend in this creek, after Indian fashion in such explanations, would raise his hand high as he pointed at arm's length and with his fingers pointing toward the distant bend slowly and steadily follow its course around, repeating fast all the while the name of the creek. *Haviamp, Haviamp, Haviamp,* and *Haviamp* to the end of the course indicated by pointing. There was another creek that headed in those woods, which he called *Cumyam-muck,* with a strong accent on the second syllable, and whose course he indicated in the same way as he did *Haviamp.* I believe it to be the creek known as Walker, or Lynx Creek, which will be spoken of again.[30]

We all now felt at home as the different messes were located around our heavy corral, with our stock safe within its stout high and rugged walls, and our mining property all divided off.

---

[30] Lynx or Walker Creek rises near Walker, Arizona, and flows northeast to the Agua Fria River, entering that stream near Dewey, Arizona. Barnes, *Arizona Place Names,* 256–57.

There was no white population within hundreds of miles to be laying claims to our vast empire of deserts, whose capital was this camp in this splendid woods. . . . I felt that we were safe from everybody except the Apaches and Navajos. There were not many Irotabas to be found, who would point out the way across the deserts to be the mouths of those creeks which lead to these woods. We had now but one more duty to perform which appeared to me a hard and doubtful one. That was to return over the deserts to the Pima Indian Village to obtain some of their home-made flour and frijoles (beans) as we would soon be out. This was June, 1863, but we knew not what day of the month it was and we really dated our records as of that month at a venture. We dug a deep hole, off from the corral, on the opposite side of the creek, in which we buried all of the superfluous plunder, and then built a fire upon the grave to conceal the fresh dirt and then took our departure down the Hassayampa, bound for the Pimas again.

The members of the Walker Party were as follows: Capt. Jos. R. Walker, Jos. R. Walker jr., Martin Lewis, and Jacob Lynn of California. Geo. Blosser and Alford Shupp of Pa. J. J. Miller, Jacob Miller, S. C. Miller, and Solomon Shaw of Ill. Hyram Cummings, Hyram Mealman, —— Wheelhouse, and Doctor Coulter, N.Y. Johnny Bull, Geo. Lount, and Roderick McKinney, Can. Wm. Williams, and —— Benedict of Conn. A. French, Vt. Jacob Snider (Dutchman). J. H. Dixon, Miss. Frank Finney, La. —— Young, Ks. Jackson McCrackin, S. C. J. W. Swilling, Ga. —— Chase, Ohio. Chas. Noble, and Henry Miller, Mo. F. G. Gilliland, Felix Burton, Tom Johnson, Chas. Taylor, and this humble subscriber, D. E. Conner, both of Ky.[31] Some few of the above deserted us and went with the soldiers, and were not with us when we first located in the woods, but they came amongst the first immigration to the country after this date. Thirty was our number at the first arrival. We again

[31] Besides this list two other sources of the Walker Party are available. See "Journal of the Pioneer and Walker Mining Districts," 2, and letter from Conner to Miss Hall, May 1, 1910, written at Wilmington, California, CONNER MANUSCRIPTS.

reached the Maricopa Wells and encamped there, and did our trading and left letters with the Pimas to send to New Mexico and California by the first soldiery which might pass either way. These letters of course gave a full account of flattering prospects for the future of our New Eldorado. We were gone to the Pimas for supplies just 20 days. . . . We packed up and started across the desert just before night and about midnight we were surprised to learn that we were about meeting a body of mounted men on our trail and stopped under preparations for a conflict with the Apaches.

But the strangers proved to be a party of men from California, who had heard of the Walker Party strolling through Arizona for the last year, by messages to the military department, from the soldiers, which we had met before, as has been already referred to. These men had come into this desert from the Colorado River under the leadership of Pauline Weaver, an old trapper who was with them.[32] They continued on to the Pimas, after receiving the description of our New Eldorado and immediately returned on our trail as far as the mountains and began to prospect on their own hook, forty or fifty miles southwest of our woods. We continued our journey over our old trail a distance computed by us at the time of one hundred and fifty miles from the Pimas and arrived a second time in the woods safely after the usual hardships to those of the first trip. We had been absent just twenty days, during which we had done terrible and continuous work, but found our camp just as we had left it. We again settled back into our old and respective quarters around the corral and devoted our time to business. . . .

. . . After we had arrived at our corral in the woods again I mentally resolved I would never again cross the Gila Desert if I had to even go by the way of China to avoid it, and I have thus

[32] Pauline Weaver, born in Tennessee in 1800 and part Cherokee, came to Arizona in 1830 while in the service of the Hudson's Bay Company as a hunter and trapper. Later, he served as a guide to the Mormon Battalion under Philip St. George Cooke in 1846 and also discovered the placer mines at La Paz, Arizona, in 1861. He led another party of miners into the Hassayampa area in 1863, where the Weaver Diggings and Weaver Mining District were named after him. Lockwood, *Pioneer Days in Arizona*, 124–27.

far kept that resolve, for I never saw it again only at a distance. My three messmates and myself concluded to build a stout log house which would be convenient for a fort in case of necessity for self-defense. We finished one in about two weeks, built of logs three feet in diameter and covered with stout timbers upon which we put pine boughs and lastly a foot of dirt which rendered it fireproof, but if it ever became waterproof it was after I left the country. This was the first house built by any of our party and consequently the first ever built in central Arizona that we know of, by the Anglo-Saxon.

We now devoted our time to hunting and prospecting when not at work upon our claims. Trees were felled, out of which the ordinary rocker was constructed for washing gold. Rude planks which were split out with an axe had to serve our purpose and such implements as could be made out of such materials for mining purposes were pretty soon in operation. The diggings did not yield near our expectations, but it was enough to convince us that we were in a gold region where the best of mines might be found. The Apaches began to visit us. They seemed not to know anything of our efforts to make a treaty with Irotaba. They importuned us by long and senseless speeches to go with them upon a "big" bear hunt. They were troublesome only for a short time, for they went to war with us and that ended their visits. One of our party imprudently kicked one of them out of his way while cooking his supper after a tiresome day's tramp and the whole batch of them immediately left the camp in great indignation and never returned again.

A Solitary Journey from Prescott to the Colorado River

SO MUCH HAS been said and written about the proper mode of conduct that ought to be adopted for the sake of reciprocity with the Indians, it might be well to refer to an incident of fair average to illustrate the difficulties to be surmounted before their love and undoubted confidence can be secured.

On passing the cañon on the Hassayampa en route for the diggings the second time, some of the natives who belonged to the rancheria where I found the women and children concluded that as the party did not disturb them upon that occasion that it was safe to venture into our camp.

Although when we came by the head of the cañon the second time the rancheria was gone. They couldn't think of staying after the pale face had been at their headquarters. However, about a half-dozen of these "braves" came into our camp and they were treated so friendly that one of them became very generous. His generosity arose from seeing members of the party distribute bread and meat amongst them. This fellow was not to be outdone in liberality and he therefore unrolled a package of two or three pounds of roasted and dried mescal, from which he would pinch a piece about the size of an ordinary chew of tobacco and hand it to a member of our party with a gesture and air of bestowing a great favor.[1] He thus passed from one man to another with the roll of goods in one arm and with the other hand pinching off and giving each a piece in the style and manner that a king might condescend to adopt in the distribution of alms. But now came the reciprocity part of the transaction. After he had given all around and smiled his recognition of having served us all, he wanted a mule for thus throwing himself away by his generosity. And he evidently became greatly disappointed and angered when he learned that the mule was not to be forthcoming promptly, and yet the chews of mescal were gone beyond the hope of restitution because each recipient of the valuable gift had put the precious morsel into his mouth immediately upon its reception. This was a dilemma. We tried to rectify the blunder by being right liberal sure enough, but all to no purpose for they could not see why the "pale face" could not just as easily give a mule as an Indian could give mescal, especially as we had forty or fifty of them. This fellow now became solid and demanded ammunition to be given them. This was peremptorily forbidden by Capt. Walker, which was unnecessary, however, for we would have had to become quite as liberal as poor "Lo" in demanding the mule before furnishing them with ammunition with which to shoot us. They persisted in leaving us without becoming mollified, and that was the end of it. As stated, they soon after took the war party, which they continued for years. This was a fair specimen of an effort and its results, at living in peace with the Indians. The longest-faced preacher in the New England states would fail to do any better

[1] Mescal was produced by the Apache, Mohave, Yuma, Pima, Ute, Paiute, and practically every other tribe located in a region which was the habitat of agave. The fleshy base leaves and trunks of the various species of agave became a sweet and nutritious food when roasted in pit ovens. Mescal was extensively used in commerce between the above Indians and outlying tribes, such as the Hopi and other Pueblo groups. Hodge, *Handbook of American Indians*, I, 845-46.

with them, nine times out of ten, than we did on this occasion, and so continue to fail until he divided his property amongst them and put on the breech-cloth and feasted on snakes and lizards with them jovially, as becomes a good friend.

One morning as the sun shone pretty, I strolled down the creek from our cabin and corral until I passed out of the woods into the chaparral country. I wandered about prospecting the different arroyos until I came suddenly upon a lone Indian some twenty paces from me. He was peeping under some rocks and in a stooping position when I first saw him. He was prompted to run when he first discovered me but desisted after thinking better of the short distance which lay between us, and stood until I came up to him. My very soul seemed to sink within me, as I looked in silence upon this silent fellow. Although our little party was unprotected by any force except our arms, far away from civilized assistance and to some extent at the mercy of these most implacable of all cruel savages and in the heart of their own native wilds. This specimen enlisted my sympathy, rather than fear, and that too to an unusual degree. He had the head of an antelope secured to the small of his back, in such a position that he could stoop down and look backward between his legs and thus bring the animal's head to an upright position, so as to appear in the distance to be a *bona-fide* antelope. These Indians by this means enticed herds of these timid animals near enough to kill them by shooting backward from between the legs while in this stooping posture.

But this was not the fact which invited the most particular attention. He also had a belt composed of many circles of a small cord around his waist behind which he had stuffed as many rats, mice, frogs, and lizards of various kinds as there was room for, and all of which were squeezed tightly against the naked skin. Some of them appeared to be so warmed by the heat of the sun and pressed so hard by the narrow belt, that they looked as though they were about to burst. But they were all good food for poor "Lo," either raw or cooked, "feathers" and all. . . . A nastier looking display of undressed edibles I never had seen. And perhaps never will again see such a spectacle outside of a fashionable city restaurant. This fellow probably had all the property he possessed with him, and had not even a scalpel with which he might dress his game for eating. He carried besides his bow and arrows a short stick similar to that of a shepherd's crook with which to hook rats, &c out of their holes and dens. I made him show me all about it and stoop to throw up the antelope head, all of which he did promptly when he understood what was expected of him. . . . I left this fellow profoundly impressed with the idea that we were imposing upon his race. . . .

It began to get late in the fall when the members of the party were prospecting about the different tributaries nearest our camp in small squads to find better diggings. Pursuant to this object a number of us followed the Hassayampa to its source and passed over a range lying at right angles to it and out of our organized district. On reaching the eastern foot of this range we found another creek and encamped near its head. We found here the best diggings yet discovered. While prospecting about a mile upon its course S[am] C. M[iller] came across a lynx and shot and wounded it. Instead of trying to escape, the vicious little animal made a charge upon its assailant who had to use a six-shooter vigorously before it was subdued. This incident gave this creek the name of Lynx Creek, which it retained.[2] We now passed out of the head of Lynx Creek toward the southwest and over another range and thence descended into another creek whose course lay about east. Here we found some gold, but the prospect was not flattering. After traversing this creek a few miles down its course we came nearly to the edge of the woods which bordered on the rough chaparral country, where we found a large covey of wild turkeys, some of which we shot and ate for

[2] Lynx Creek is traditionally said to have been explored in the winter of 1863–64, and the Lynx Creek mining district lay east of Prescott. Richard Hinton, *The Handbook to Arizona*, 103.

supper. This incident gave this the name of Turkey Creek, upon which many important scenes were subsequently enacted.[3]

We turned at right angles with this creek and passed out of it and over the adjoining range north into a chaparral country and thence into another creek nearly parallel with Turkey Creek. We were now about twenty-five or thirty miles from our camp. We encamped in this creek and dispersed the individual members of a very large convention of wolves. For what purpose all of these wolves were assembled on this creek I could never surmise. But there were enough of them to give this creek the name of Wolfe Creek, which it ever after retained.[4] We found no gold here at all. On the following morning we continued our course north and found another creek in a chaparral country, but not far from our woods, and it really headed in the edge and ran east, as did the other creek just passed over. This creek subsequently became the center of a fine mining district, whose mines will continue to be worked probably for fifty years yet to come. Here were found gold in what we supposed paying quantities. Before we left this creek, J[ohn] D[ixon], a large goodnatured, noisy fellow came into our temporary camp, carrying between two sticks the largest bug that ever grew even there, and the largest that I ever saw. He laughed and yelled over it until every one of our party had to examine the wonder. This creek became Big Bug Creek in consequence, and a Big Bug District has been since organized here.[5] We left this creek and passed northwest over the range and into Lynx Creek lower down than where we passed it in going east. We kept our north-

[3] Turkey Creek is southeast of Prescott, heading some nineteen or twenty miles on the eastern side of the Bradshaw Mountains in Yavapai County and is a tributary of the Agua Fria. Later a mining district took the name of the Turkey Creek Mining District. Barnes, *Arizona Place Names,* 458; Hinton, *Handbook to Arizona,* 101–102.

[4] Barnes, *Arizona Place Names,* does not cite this creek, but the official map of Arizona Territory drawn by E. A. Eckhoff and P. Riecker, dated 1880, shows a Wolf Creek about five miles south of Prescott.

[5] The bugs referred to here were probably skippers. Big Bug was a mining camp about fifteen miles southeast of Prescott, and later a mining district bearing that name came into existence. Barnes, *Arizona Place Names,* 45; Hinton, *Handbook to Arizona,* 101.

west course for probably ten or twelve miles along the edge of the woods and the border of the grassy prairie lying north of these woods already referred to until we reached another creek which flows out of the woods and takes its course across this grassy plain for thirty miles in a northern direction. Here we encamped for about two days on the bank of this creek in the edge of the woods. We called it Granite Creek, in consideration of the amount of granite boulders found upon it, and scattered in the woods near it.[6] I will here remark that our camp here is covered now by the City of Prescott, which has been the capital of Arizona. We encamped on the right side of the creek in the mouth of a little valley probably twenty paces wide and about three or four hundred yards above the present public square of the city. Upon the opposite side of Granite Creek in the flat woods was located an Indian rancheria. We had a little conflict with them before we were through, but when we first came up they were hostile and savage, but still came over to our camp in very ugly humor and one very black and painted warrior made a savage speech to them. The weather was getting quite cool and we had fires built. One brave came walking up to the fire, as though he didn't see some cooking utensils near by and at his feet and Capt. Walker seized him by his long hair and pushed him back with a little petulant order to stay out of the way. He leaned toward the Captain and brought a deep prolonged "ugh" as though he was much insulted.

When we arrived here these Indians were engaged in breaking a young horse on the other side of the creek, over which they were having a merry time. Every time the colt would toss one of them over its head, a storm of shouting and laughing arose upon the air and made the woods sing. But they were prepared for war—they were all hideously painted and looked vicious. In the mêlée Capt. Walker's mule broke loose and ran down stream affrightedly. I overtook him on the present site of the

[6] Granite Creek was named by miners in 1864, according to Barnes, *Arizona Place Names,* 187, but Conner here indicated they were on Granite Creek in the fall of 1863. The creek rises southwest of Prescott, flowing generally north through that town and joining Chino Creek near Del Rio.

plaza of Prescott City, where he had stopped and was quietly grazing.

We decamped and traveled across the woods south for about the distance of six miles to our place of beginning and found our house, corral &c just as we had left it. So we were at home again after quite a tour of observation. By this trip we became better acquainted with our woods and its surroundings. We had been to the western end of this tract of timbered land and therefore had a pretty good idea of our situation. This woodland tract we found comparatively unobstructed by undergrowth and in this respect unlike the broken, pitched, and upheaved country which lay all around it and covered with numberless crags and chaparral. But these woods were very uneven and the ground lay in all sorts of irregularity, liberally sprinkled with ridges, knolls, and clumps of rocks. But the rough surface of the woods was nothing to compare with the lower country out of them on the southeast and west, which reached as far as the eyesight could penetrate. Yet the woods were so much higher that I have seen the snow two feet deep upon some of its ridges, when it only fell eight inches at the edge, where Prescott City now stands. The contrast was so great between this woodland tract and the country we had so lately and continuously traversed, that we were daily becoming more attached to our Eden. . . . Capt. Walker, who had been roaming the mountains for thirty years, remarked that this was the only unknown section of the United States possessions and that this was his probable last expedition, and therefore we had better stay here, as it might be the best region now to be found. The only fears he had was that we might fail to hold out against the Apaches until we had assistance from immigration.

And it was feared that we would have to hold out for nearly a year before we were found by enterprising gold hunters. But, however, we had possession, and for the time at least what other spot would we exchange for this? We could see all the ledges of rocks, of hills, valley and dale covered with new born verdure, the varied beauty of the shrubs and trees, and wild flowers just scarce enough to make them rare and more precious—bedecked by nature, with the double charm of perfume and color. . . .

We had occupied our encampment with only one house and one corral for several weeks and until we found that our claims on this creek were not going to *pan out* as liberally as we supposed and therefore began to prepare for a change. We made preparations over on Lynx Creek for a new home. The heads of these two creeks lay within less than a mile of each other, but flowed at right angles with each other near their sources. We bade farewell to our old camp and soon had a new headquarters established on the head of Lynx Creek in a new field of activity. The placer diggings opened up flatteringly and proved worth all of the trouble it cost in the exchange. We now considered the question of residence finally settled and respective "messes" divided their cooking utensils amongst the individual members of each. They cast lots for first, second, and third choice, etc. All I remember about the result is that I got one tin cup and a tin platter for my share. But it was satisfactory all around and entirely so with me, for I knew but little about cooking anyhow. We all had a sheath-knife apiece to begin with. The Indians had not yet given us much trouble, but were preparing themselves well before striking any heavy blow. Stragglers couldn't refrain from throwing random shots into our camp now and then.

As soon as I got my cup and platter allotted to me I went upon the mountain range toward the head of Big Bug Creek to hunt a deer to cook in them. I was not over a half a mile from the camp and upon the top of a ridge when an Indian fired at me not over thirty steps distant from a clump of rocks and threw his bullet through my hat rim without touching me. He was evidently alone or else more shots would have been fired to make a sure job of it. I therefore went to this place of concealment without giving him time to reload and he escaped into some larger clumps of granite beyond. This fellow lost his game on this occasion because he was afraid that if he shot me through the body that I might escape to camp, so that he would miss getting my arms. I turned my course north, however, and in proceeding another half-mile, I sat down on the ground upon the top of one of the numerous ridges pitching down the mountain toward the creek. I here discovered two deer that had evidently been disturbed, coming toward me crossing these ravines and ridges in trepidatious watchfulness. When within probably a hundred paces, they stopped in doubt whether to take up the ridge they were on to the top of the main range. When they made a motion to go that direction and leave me, I fired at them and missed. At the report of the gun they quickly turned on their original direction and ran toward me, and stopped within ten paces of me, still sitting upon the ground. They were so confused now, that while they were watching back, I killed them both from my sitting posture with a pistol. I immediately went to camp for assistance to take care of all this venison and to get somebody to cook it on shares. Two of us caught up a mule and pack-saddled it and went for the deer, and on arriving at the place we found that the Indians had come and slaughtered the deer and carried away the flesh to the top of the mountains, where they stood peering down at us, mimicking the wolves and owls in howling and hooting at us. We knew from the airs they were putting on that there was no fighting force up there of which they gave additional proof by firing scattering shots at us. But we were afraid if we went up there that we could not take care of ourselves and the other mule too, and therefore returned to camp, where I was threatened with a suit for breach of contract in failing to furnish venison to be cooked on the shares.

When we first arrived in these woods the deer would not retreat at the report of a gun, but would startle by thunder strokes. This creek was entirely dry and we therefore used rockers of home manufacture with which some of the men would wash out as high as fifty dollars in a day, some days. I again made another raid upon the deer with better success, and on returning to camp I crossed the creek quite a distance from camp at a lonely and lonesome place where the bed-rock was bare and clean. I stooped and chipped off a small fragment of the shattered *bed-rock* with my knife, under which I found a particle of gold of about the amount of a dollar. I then laid aside my gun and searched the little crevices until I had obtained an ounce of gold, and all in less than an hour. I began to feel that I was giving too close attention to gold-gathering to be safe and that I might be shot without knowing how it was done. I therefore located a claim here and left for camp.

We began to find gold enough for the present use, but could buy nothing with it and it therefore appeared worthless at least. No one but he who has experienced this sort of a situation can properly appreciate how little riches are coveted. Food appeared to be of immense value beside that of gold. When I returned to camp on this occasion, my dinner consisted of hard bread made of unbolted flour alone. It was amusing to see my messmate eating his simple meal. He would chew so carefully that I asked him why he was so particular in the mastication of his food. He quietly replied that "This bread is about half sand." "Well, that ought to take that much more force to grind it," I rejoined. "The gravel is harder than my teeth and I shall not try to eat it."

I could not help but reflect upon the dainty appetites which were at that very instant being fed and coaxed into the reception even of sweetmeats in all the cities. But the process of mastication on this occasion was aided by breaking the bread into small bits and putting it into a cup upon which water was poured until it was of the consistency of soup, and after all made a pretty fair meal, if it did look like feeding upon grindstones. But it is not intended to be understood that we lived this way all of the time on this creek, for when we captured a deer or bear we generally made up for these fasting spells. . . .

It seemed marvelous that the Indians of central Arizona lived at all, except the portion inhabiting our "big woods."

These had plenty of wild game, including rats, lizards, and snakes. But in the desert portion they subsisted mostly upon mescal, prickly pears, and grass seeds—on the larger water courses, mesquite beans of which there are several varieties. I might describe mescal, the botanical name of which is agave, as being about three feet in diameter, broad leaves, armed with teeth like a shark, the leaves arranged in concentric circles and terminating in the middle of the plant in a perfect cone. These leaves terminate at the point by a black thorn like that of the black locust and seem always in the way of the man on guard, on a dark night. It is the root which is used by the Indians for food and which might be described as being of a spherical, bulbous growth, usually six or eight inches in diameter and located in the ground, similar to the position and appearance of an inverted cabbage head, with the stock projecting upward, upon which the broad thick leaves grow. Some of these have stocks growing from the center nearly or quite fifteen feet in height, which, when dry, are straight and have tapering, graceful proportions and are used by the Indians for lance stocks. These spherical roots or bulbs peel off like cabbage, but is more compact, solid and white. The Indians roast them in kilns of rocks to a soft red color, when they become clammy and very sweet, and are said to be very nutritious. It was of this material that the liberal Indian desired to swap a few pinches for a mule. The Mexicans also distill from this bulb the celebrated aguardiente, a white fiery brandy which is noted for its "body" and strength of character. Clear, white, and full of fire and "business." It sparkles, beams, and beads constantly for the want of something to do, and never fails to take stock in all enterprises whatsoever, when invited.

Upon one occasion when I was right hungry I concluded to try the edible qualities of one of this plant's thick leaves. Cutting a fine heavy head I peeled the bark or skin off of it, leaving a soft fungus, watery substance that looked delicious. I was now satisfied that I had made a discovery. I rather thought that I was becoming a little more acute than my friends, and more ingenious in providing way and means for food. I took a "bite," as I smiled over the stupidity of my comrades for having never thought of it, while the plant grew in profusion all over the country. Never did confidence become so crestfallen in so short a time before, when all the merits of the old fashioned Indian turnip began to shoot fine needles through my tongue and lips, with a lively energy that discounted the best model of Grover & Baker that ever reached the patent office. I thought that I was being killed fast. There was no water near and I put dirt in my mouth to draw some of the lightning out, and then tried chewing oak leaves—tasted some gun powder &c. . . . The final effects wore away very gradually and deliberately, but did come to an end at least. This is the only time I ever tasted a mescal leaf, just the same number of times that I ever tasted Indian turnip. . . . Thereafter I stuck to the old habit of trusting such food as I could get that had already given satisfaction. This was not my first experiment, for I well remembered of having found and ate some wild mustard while I was in Colorado Territory, which sickened and vomited me worse than any "three black crows" ever did anybody. And I also witnessed one of our party F. G. G[illiland] partake of the carcass of a scrawny coyote, which he had shot and cooked, with about the same results. At any rate I considered these experiments of my own quite sufficient for any common man and therefore never acquired the habit of eating unknown things to a great extent. But I afterward became instrumental in getting one of my comrades to try the mescal leaf, which made him very wroth, but upon learning that I meant that it should be cooked before eating, he reluctantly forgave me, but still objected to me teasing him about taking it raw. There is evidently about as many snakes and vipers in the raw leaf as there is in the distilled brandy from the bulb.

We enjoyed this loneliness as long as there could be any enjoyment to be found in it and I began to think seriously of leaving the country at all hazards. My patience was worn threadbare and the more I thought of it the more my impatience hurried me. I therefore approached some of my companions upon the subject, from some of whom I received such replies as "goodbye; wait until morning, &c." Others said that there was not enough of us to stay where we were easily to do the best we might.

I knew that the Colorado River was about two hundred miles

away on a due west course and I therefore prepared some pinole, & started about dark on a calm quiet evening alone, without warning any one. . . .[7] I soon discovered the necessity of continuous attention, substantially given, to the direct course before me and that all depended upon keeping a direct course in spite of the continuous presence of insurmountable obstacles, some of which required hours, sometimes, to get around. In the midst of thus wading through brush and darkness I sometimes found myself going a direction at right angles with the course of my selected star, on awaking from a reverie into which I became frequently settled, without being aware of it. I would hence become confounded at the great change of place assumed by my start and with difficulty get my consent to resume its direction again and again. But reason prevailed and I kept after the star with implicit confidence.

Before the sun was up on the following morning I had found a brushy hollow and cut grass enough for my horse. It was in a sand bed against a high perpendicular rock where I located myself for the day's nap. The water had collected the sand deep at this point, it being a little crooked place in the gorge-like dry creek. I was lying upon my elbow with my back to the wall and my head resting on my hand. My horse was at the far edge of the sand directly in my front some ten paces away, eating the grass which lay before him.

I must have been about half asleep when I descried plainly the outlines of a wolf, which had the effect to bring me wide awake, although I kept quiet and still. Sure enough, upon becoming wholly awake, I saw the wolf standing at the horse's head, with one fore foot raised off of the ground, as though he was afraid to let it down again. He was cautiously scanning the ground all about him and occasionally stole a glance to see what

---

[7] Conner overestimates the distances because of the lack of well-defined trails at this time to the Colorado River. Hinton, *Handbook to Arizona*, Appendix *xxiii*, gives the distances from Camp Mohave to Prescott as 165 miles and Ehrenberg to Prescott as 190 miles. The legislature of Arizona Territory paid mileages on the basis of 180 miles from Prescott to La Paz and 160 miles from Prescott to Fort Mohave. *The Arizona Miner* (Prescott), November 23, 1864.

the horse was eating. The horse would back his ears at the wolf, as the latter would take another stand within three or four feet. I thought it strange that with all his apparent prudence, watchfulness, and cunning, he failed to see me lying in plain view, looking at him. Knowing his habits, I was at a loss to decide what to do with him. I knew if he discovered me that he would run off to a position out of my reach and howl at me as long as I remained there, and also draw associates to help him. They would thereby become a standing signal by which to direct the Indians to the place of my concealment, who would know as well or better than myself that an unusual cause was the occasion of such howling. On the other hand the report of my rifle would be heard farther and create a greater certainty of an enemy's hearing it. But upon reflection, I knew that the report of a gun would die away quickly and that of the wolves would be continuous and prolonged. So I settled the quandary by shooting the wolf dead within a few feet of the horse's head. I was suffering greatly for the want of water and therefore had to risk daylight some portion of the time, in order to find it.

For this reason I started an hour before night this time, which was unquestionably safer than the morning, for escape is always easier under cover of night than in daytime anywhere. But I failed to find water and traveled all night again and encamped for the day as usual. Becoming intensely thirsty I again started earlier than usual in the evening.

I had learned to travel old Indian trails when they ran any way near my course. The sun was an hour high in the evening when I came to a country where the low rocky and broken hills bordered a low flat, ashy desert to my left, sprinkled over the bunches of sage-brush. The trail which I was following along an edge of the solid highland passed between a high bare peak on my right hand and a long, low rocky ridge on the left and bordering the ashy sage-brush land. When I became opposite the peak I discovered that it was composed nearly wholly of black volcanic rocks and that it had split across the center and one part had fallen down the hill, scattering its debris for two hundred paces thick upon the ground. At the foot of this perpendicular wall thus left standing high, I discovered some green bushes. I could not ride to it for the scattering rocks and therefore I quickly dismounted, dropped the lariat on the ground and hastened through and over the rocks to the bushes at the foot of the wall. There was a little water trickling out of the wall which appeared so loose and threatening that it looked fearful and dangerous. I held my canteen under the trickling water for a while and then I would drink awhile, as I turned my back to the wall and looked everywhere but at the water. I was afraid of the Indians arising out of those rocks and I was afraid of the wall tumbling down. The water ran excruciatingly slow, but I had a drink and some in my canteen, when I noticed my horse cease browsing and look forward. I remembered that he had failed to become affrighted at a wolf and therefore felt certain that the horse saw Indians and that too in the direction I had to go. I say had to go, for there is no experienced man who will in the face of danger, leave an old well-marked Indian trail to hunt a new route, where he may be hemmed up when he is least expecting it.

When I saw this disturbed action of the horse, I made my way quickly out of the rocks and ran for him, where I arrived just in time to see three Indians, one after another, pass rapidly around the farther end of the rocky ridge on the left of the trail already referred to. I quickly decided not to give them time to get up into the rocks and arrange themselves satisfactorily, for I had to pass the trail along by the ridge within easy gunshot of them and knew not their probable number. On reaching my horse, I therefore threw myself upon him, hung my carbine to the saddle and took a six-shooter in my hand, and spurred him into his best speed and dashed through the gap in less time than it takes to tell it. A volley was fired at me as I passed, without even wounding my apparel, but one ball passed through the upper edge of my horse's neck, which subsequently gave me some annoyance. I kept on a full run until I reached the point in the trail where it left the hard ground and went into the ashy, flat desert nearly two hundred paces away, when the bulk of their forces fired after me without effect. The most of their bullets striking the ground behind me and bounding harmlessly past to the front. As soon as this second volley was fired I knew that all of their guns were unloaded and I stopped and turned broadside to them, put up my pistol and fired with my carbine at the black crowd which had arisen from the rocks in plain view. This single shot scattered them back behind their rocks instantly. I rode on into the flat desert country which now appeared to extend for twenty miles ahead, to some distant mountains, which I could distinctly see. The sun was about setting and we were all soon lost to view and I had to entrust my horse with the task of keeping the trail, so dim it had become on the dusty surface. And right well did my poor famished horse keep to the trail. Sometimes he would mistake it in the darkness and on some occasions he would stop of his own accord and get right again.

He had followed trails for many a weary mile, but this seemed to be the hardest of all to follow on account of the light, ashy substance drifting by the action of the wind like snow. I had guessed the enemy aright, for if I had waited an instant to reflect on a proper course to pursue and thereby given them time to have gotten over their surprise at seeing the first intruder perhaps ever known to visit their watering place, and otherwise to prepare, the result might have been different. Their war-whoop after the delivery of their second volley, sounded strangely upon the deathly silent air and came near throwing my affrighted horse into a panic, but he quickly became calm upon hearing my familiar voice. . . .

This was the first and last time that I ever saw this watering place, but I can see it with my mind's eye any day. After passing over this level land to the distant hills above referred to, I was struck with the unusual formation of this mountainous region. There were no ranges or spurs. They were high barren mountains and had no connection with each other, but presented just such a region as a great plain would with artificial peaks built here and there all over it. They looking like imposing obstacles in the distance, before reaching them. I found that I could keep the same level and go all around and between them without ascending any of them. On going in between two steep mountains a third stands in front, giving the appearance of an abrupt termination of the trail, but to continue, a passage is found winding around first one and another, keeping the same level for miles. Had the waters of the ocean rolled around amongst these hills and leveled the ground between them, was a question continuously presenting itself for solution. If so, it left a multitude of separate hills standing. I passed, day after day, and night after night after this fashion, for about ten days, without getting into any further conflict with the Indians, whose campfires I frequently saw and of which I had a great dread of accidentally approaching too close to escape without arousing them.

One morning after the sun arose in all of its splendor and after I had secreted myself for the day, I ventured out upon a little spur hard by and to my inexpressible joy had a full view of the long looked for and eagerly sought valley of the Rio Colorado. I knew that no other river than the "Mississippi of the West" could present so grand a display of cottonwood trees and undergrowth as this. My impatience started me out before night, and after a few hours travel, I found myself encamped on the bank of the river within twenty feet of the water's edge. I immediately put my hungry and fagged horse out in the small brush to browse upon the young cottonwoods, as there was no grass about, but that grown from an alkaline soil, which all kinds of animals refuse to eat. The question upon which I slept that night was how I was to get across the river. It looked so low that I began to hope that I could ford it. I was quite happy, for California came to the water's edge upon the other side of the river and I was about to tread the soil of a state. I do not remember to have ever been better satisfied or to have experienced more buoyant hope than I did on this occasion, all on account of the apparent prospect of getting again into civilization, although

Courtesy Sharlot Hall Museum, Prescott, Arizona

King Woolsey, the Arizona Indian fighter.

three hundred miles of desert country lay between me and the frontier settlements of California.[8]

I continued to puzzle what little brains I had left about the best way of crossing the river. The sun again arose beautiful and bright upon the following morning and I again put my horse out into the brush some ten or twenty paces away to browse. After having a good look at the river by daylight, I found myself undecided still as to whether to drive the horse across and swim it myself, or to ride across and swim or ford, as necessity compelled. While having this matter under consideration, my loneliness was broken by the appearance of an old squaw walking confidently toward me, followed by a little squaw perhaps twelve years of age. I thought that now the question was solved, for I would get that old squaw to tell where to find a ford and I would reach the opposite bank before any warriors knew that I was about.

She came up to me with a frown upon her face and began to complain about my intrusion and waving her hand low over the ground to indicate the destruction of their grass, where there was none sufficient to graze a goose for an hour. A continuation of all sorts of gutturals and signs rolled out of the old hag, who could not hush long enough to answer a single question. They were both nearly entirely nude, the greater part of their dress consisting of strings of beads.

I gave the old one a piece of chewing tobacco, thinking that to coax her into a good humor might prompt her to tell me something of the river. But she was inexorable and refused to listen with any patience, although she accepted the tobacco. All this time the little squaw was standing behind me, attempting to steal one of my pistols from the scabbard. I could feel my belt lighten up as she would steathily raise the pistol. I looked around at her and she let it drop back into the scabbard. I had no coat on and none to put on. She began to prank again with my pistol

---

[8] Here Conner again overestimates distances. Although there were few, if any, trails at this time, La Paz was about 160 to 170 miles from San Bernardino, and Fort Mohave a slightly lesser distance.

and I turned and made an ugly face at her, for I was afraid to make the old squaw mad before she told me of a crossing. But I made up my mind that she would tell me nothing, and on the third attempt the little squaw made to lift my pistol out I made a catch behind me and caught her wrist, which she gave a twist and broke her string of beads, which came off in my hand and some of them wasted on the ground. The black old hag became thunder-struck by this misfortune and began to groan in great distress and aimed a blow at my face with her open hand which fell upon my shoulder. I stepped back from her and pretentiously drew my pistols as though I would shoot her. Without a moment's hesitation she started off the direction she came, followed by her cub. I looked after her departure for some time with unrestrained amusement, to think that the poor old creature was afraid of me shooting her. But my amusement was cut short for upon looking after the old squaw, I described through a little neck of cottonwoods some warriors peering through the bushes at me. One fellow was in a stooping position with his hands resting upon his knees.

I quickly picked up my gun and started in the opposite direction to get my horse, with my mind suddenly made up to mount and plunge into the river right away. But my anxiety was now raised to the highest pitch when my horse had moved from where I left him a few moments since. And it bordered on horror when I discovered some of the horse's footprints in the alkaline dust, half blotted out by moccasin prints. The cold perspiration began to stand upon my face as I hurried after the departing footprints of my horse and found them joined by other moccasin tracks farther off. The crushing reality now flashed over me that my horse was gone beyond recovery. These Indians were not prepared to fight and had sent their lady commissioner to me to be interviewed while they stole my horse. I was well enough acquainted with the Indians to know that a regiment of soldiers could not give these wretches five minutes the start and ever get that horse back alive in such a country as this, known comparatively only to themselves.

It was all now plain to me, but too late. There was not another horse nearer to me perhaps than Capt. Walker's camp, that I had left, and which was about two hundred and twenty miles away. I knew that it was impossible for me to walk and carry enough food and water to sustain me while crossing the desert on the California side. Never was disappointment felt so keenly as this. Ten thousand dollars would not have hired me to have taken the back track which now appeared inevitably necessary, even to survive at all. The cruel shock affected me to the extent that produced reckless feelings. I turned and hurried back, hoping to find the squaws that I might throw them into the river and drown them. I visited the spot where I had seen the "braves" peering through the brush at me. Not one of them could be seen anywhere, male or female. All was silent and I was alone to enjoy it. All of my fruitless and determined meanness were compelled to meet and surrender to helplessness under the keenest misfortune I ever felt. I am afraid, but do not think that there are those living today, who, if subjected to the same test, would openly rebel against their God—the perfection of all criminal acts together in one. I returned to the spot of my encampment and sat down upon my saddle and reflected with a cold nervousness upon past facts and future probabilities. I went down to the water and refilled my canteen and came back and my decision was completed. I gathered up my saddle by stirrup strap and threw it into the river, together with everything else I had, not indispensably necessary to existence alone, and started on the back trail in broad daylight. Of course I didn't pretend to follow the same trails &c which I came, but took the direction merely. All feelings of insecurity had vanished while the idea of those two squaws and drowning them in the river still possessed me.

The more I thought over it the stronger the matter presented itself to me as a splendid idea. I traveled up the river bottom nearly all day, diverging from the stream and converging toward the foothills of the high land or desert country. Late in the evening I looked for water in all available nooks and corners in vain. I came across a deep, inclined hole in the sandy bottom which had been evidently scratched out by some wild animal in search of water. At the sharp pointed bottom of this hole several feet deep there was about a pint of standing water. I could not dip it out with my canteen, therefore I concluded to crawl down head foremost and drink it out. But my hands, while ascending, pushed enough loose sand ahead of me to cover the water before I reached it. And to add to my discomfiture, the sides and top caved in upon me, compelling me to reverse action and back out like a crawfish. When I got out, the hole was filled up with the loose caving sand and I left it and proceeded on my journey without a drink or further effort to get one. Weary fatigue began to soften my chronic hard reflections as the day slowly wore away. I came to some freshly used Indian trails meandering among the stunted, scattering mesquite trees, on the wide bottom land. I was not much alarmed however, for night was drawing near with its generous protection. The nearer night approached the more carelessly I followed these freshly beaten paths until I came face to face with an Apache, who was just turning a sharp corner around a small mesquite tree, meeting me. He halted as quickly as if he had discovered a ghost, and leaned forward a little with his vacant stare fixed hard upon me, he fetched a deep labored "Wooh!" and stood like he was glued to the ground. I do not think that this "customer" could have turned and fled to have saved his life, so great was his surprise at the discovery of such an apparition within ten paces of him. I had the advantage of this Indian because I was expecting to meet some of them and this fellow perhaps was not conscious of the presence of a white man within a distance of hundreds of miles. I followed his "big wooh" by quickly lowering my gun and marching up to him for fear that he right run, and I just then had more use for a live Indian than a dead one. If I ever saw surprise and terror depicted in the human countenance, this was the instance. He evidently was not prepared for such an adventure and looked me in the face steadily, with eyes expressionless as stone.

He became greatly relieved when I turned my canteen upside down to show him that it was water that I wanted, and he quickly pointed ahead on the course which I was going. I bade him to lead off, which he promptly did, while I followed. After following him longer than I had expected necessary I spoke to him and he wheeled around facing me in an instant. I cocked a six-shooter and placed it to his head, accompanying the act with other signs to the effect that if he took me to where any other Indians were, I would blow out his brains first. He understood me easily and protested earnestly by gutturals and lateral shakes of his head. I wondered if all barbarians and civilized people on earth had adopted alike the lateral shake of the head to express a dumb negative. I bade him start again, which he promptly did and doubtlessly was expecting to be shot all the while as we both marched vigorously along in silence. Presently he walked up to a small lagoon of light colored, translucent water, and pointed down to it. There were some mesquite trees standing around it. I promptly passed my guide and stepped down a few feet to the water into which I submerged my canteen and then looked up to keep an eye on poor "Lo," but "Lo," he was gone.

I bothered no more about him, for I knew that I would never see him again on that occasion. He made what he deemed a lucky escape. This Indian showed me water and I felt that I could not harm him, although I felt like killing the whole breed.

I intended at least to take him with me far enough to prevent him from arousing his neighbors to the fact that I was present, before I had time to get beyond their reach. I also had meditated using him in some way to force them to return my horse, but my fighting force was not strong enough even for protection during negotiations. I went into the desert hills of this bottom, and when night came on I changed my course and traveled all night and on the following morning crept into some brush, worn and weary, and slept until nearly night. When I aroused myself from this stupor the first thing that drew my attention was a rattlesnake a little way from me. The sudden buzzing of his rattles showed that I had just aroused him, as well as myself. I sat and looked at the serpent crawl off, feeling that if it could enjoy this desert home, it was entitled to do it. Before starting I was unluckily discovered by a wolf. These annoying animals seem to have been invented for nothing else but to discover everything that is going on and to make noise about it. This little coyote howled at me as long as it could howl its breath and continued its lonesome, piteous notes long after I had left the place. I could hear its sad and melancholy strain as it came floating upon the still night air until it gradually died out in the distance and ceased.

To get water was the greatest trouble. I now found that I needed more than I did when I was mounted upon my poor unfortunate horse, whose flesh probably made a roast for a whole picnic of these wretches before two days had expired after his capture. Two nights after leaving this rattlesnake lair, I saw a light that seemed to be a mile off. I looked good at it and the more I looked the nearer it seemed to be. I never was so deceived. When I moved a little I soon had it located within a hundred yards of me. I began to feel my way around it when the distance appeared still nearer. But I succeeded in getting around it without any disturbance. It was no doubt an Indian rancheria, but it was all quiet and I saw no one or anything whatever except the light shining against the rocks, and chaparral. Again I saw a firelight and this time I could see the inhabitants between me and the light, but it was quite a distance away. One night I heard them sing and of all the unearthly tones to call music I ever listened to, these came the nearest to being "fit" for "treason, stratagems, and spoils" of any I ever heard. Over and over, the same thing, all the while, without any variations, change, or pause. . . . I was more than a mile from them probably on my way when I heard them yelping and howling, which I supposed was the ending of their hymn.

This night wore away and on the break of day I found myself in sight of the woods which now appeared more than ever like a Garden of Eden. Another stretch brought me to camp after an absence of twenty days or probably more. I still had no date to go by. When I met my stammering friend and gave him a syllabus of my failure to get away, he remarked that "you m-m-must think that y-y-you'r d-d-d—n pack of fools." That ended it, for I felt like a pack of something. I fell back into my usual train of business but had no horse to go anywhere with, as usual. The music of that Apache melody, however, never deserted me and probably never will. For it so frequently flashed across my mind that it is still fixed in my memory with all of of its volcanic respirations breathed into it by its authors and was of the probable style from whence Dante drew his inspiration for his Inferno. While I was absent some of the Apaches made a raid upon the "boys" and left some scalps, but I don't mean to say that they were taken off of the head, for I can say in truth that I never knew any of our party scalping an Indian.

It was not long after my return when some of the men who were out hunting came in at night and reported that they had seen from the mountain top some white objects like tents or lodges off toward the north on the grassy prairie some ten miles away. Capt. Walker said that he guessed that the imagination had helped the picture which he rather supposed were probably rocks in some of the departing creeks from our woods. But they were confident that it was somebody and therefore arrangements were made to investigate the strangers on the following morning. When morning came all were impatient about "yesterday's" phenomenon, but Capt. Walker, whose prudence was always on guard, suggested that care and caution should have the first consideration. He said that the Navajos roamed in this direction and that they were to be feared.[9] He sent a little party up the mountain with the telescope, who came back and reported that the objects were in the same position that they were the day before and that they were United States government mule teams. They appeared to be swamped from some cause or other. We

---

[9] During the summer and fall of 1863, troops under Kit Carson campaigned against the Navajos and invaded their stronghold of Chelly Canyon. By the spring of 1864, 2,400 Navajo prisoners were sent to Bosque Rendondo. Walker was apprised of this campaign in a letter from General Carleton, June 22, 1863. Keleher, *Turmoil in New Mexico*, 340.

took our usual dinner of unbolted flour and gravel and had hardly finished, when we discovered a half company of United States soldiers coming riding down the creek, single file, from the opposite direction of that of the wagons. They were within a hundred paces of us before we saw them. Because their clothes were not patched all over, I thought that they were the finest dressed set of men I ever saw. We had not seen any white people for so long that we were delighted to see them.

They had passed our camp and gone entirely through the woods to the south edge and turned back and found our encampment on their return. That accounted for them coming to our camp from the south. The squad was under the command of the surveyor general of New Mexico—Gen. [John A.] Clark. He informed us that our letters, written from the Pima Indian Village on the Rio Gila, had found their way to New Mexico, and upon their reception Gen. Carleton commanding that Dist., immediately sent this command to search for us until we were found. They had been out some months and found us by accident at last.[10]

While on this prairie one of their wagons had broken down and while delayed there, they saw the smoke arising from our woods, differing altogether from the Indian signal smokes seen on their route. They also heard the distant reports of fire arms more regularly in these woods than elsewhere and therefore determined that they would investigate our Eden. They said that the locality had been so well indicated in the letters that they traveled five hundred and twenty five miles without varying from the true course but twenty five miles, and that was to the west of our position. The General examined our mines, panned out some gold of some rich dirt prepared for him and he pronounced the diggings rich. He said that we had a romantic

[10] General Carleton instructed Captain Nathaniel J. Pishon, First Cavalry, California Volunteers, then stationed at Fort Craig, New Mexico, to escort John A. Clark, surveyor general of New Mexico, to "The Walker Mines, Arizona." He was also ordered to obtain specimens from the mines and return via the Whipple route to Albuquerque. Keleher, *Turmoil in New Mexico*, 341.

situation and pretty woods, if the lower region of desert country did effectually corral it. The soldiers stayed with us and rested a few days and took their leave of us back upon the same route which they came. Their route lay by the Zuni Village, thence to Albuquerque in New Mexico. They deserted their wagons, which they left standing in the plain north of our woods where we had previously discovered them. Soon after the departure of General Clark, the old trapper, Pauline Weaver and party already referred to, discovered rich diggings about forty miles southwest of us. The creek in which the gold was found took the name of "Weaver," after the name of the old trapper and still retains it.[11] There was a pretty grassy prairie near this creek of several hundred acres, one hundred and sixty, of which was located by one "Peoples" of Weaver's party, and subsequently bore the sobriquet of "People's Ranch." [12] The owner thereof upon the arrival of the party into an encampment there, chanced to kill a couple of antelope on this ranch which gave the large hill standing in the angle of the creek and ranch the name of Antelope Hill.[13] In a little arroyo on the summit of this hill was discovered the richest *placer* diggings found in central Arizona. This little party located at Antelope or Weaver or both and maintained themselves as possessors until immigration came and made a permanent settlement of it. The first immigration to arrive and come to our assistance was Van Smith and party

---

[11] Weaver left his name on a number of sites in Arizona. The town of Weaver was founded in 1863 by Pauline Weaver and was located fifteen miles north of Wickenburg. Similarly, Weaver Mountains, twenty miles north of Wickenburg, Weaver Peak on the north end of these mountains, and Weaver Pass, twenty miles southeast of Ehrenberg, all carry the old trapper and prospector's name. A mining district, the center of which lay fifty miles southwest of Prescott, was known as the Weaver Mining District. Barnes, *Arizona Place Names*, 477-78; Hinton, *Handbook to Arizona*, 97-98.

[12] Peeples Valley, named after A. H. Peeples, who with Weaver discovered the Rich Hill mine, is located about twenty-five miles southwest of Prescott. Barnes, *Arizona Place Names*, 324.

[13] Antelope Hill was located in the Weaver Mining District and was named by A. H. Peeples. It was also the name for a stage station, store, and hotel, three miles north of Weaver, which served the mining population concentrated in that district. Barnes, *Arizona Place Names*, 19; Hinton, *Handbook to Arizona*, 97.

from California.[14] It was late in the fall of 1863. They located on Granite Creek at the north edge of our woods, where we had previously seen the Indians breaking the young horse upon the present townsite of the City of Prescott. Geo. L[ount] of our party, built the first house ever erected there.[15] Smith located a ranch there, built a cabin and corral, and accepted the stock of immigrants to graze and to care for at one dollar and fifty cents per head per month and the place thus became a general headquarters for the incoming immigration.

[14] Van C. Smith, one of the first immigrants from California, was also one of the committee which laid out the townsite of Prescott. Robert L. Swor, *The Development of Prescott*, 7.

[15] Traditionally, the first permanent building located on Goose Flat was constructed by a woman called "Virgin Mary" and became known as Old Fort Misery. Swor, *Development of Prescott*, 8.

6

The Apaches Begin Rifle Negotiations

SMITH'S PARTY was followed by another and another until arrivals were numerous. Strangers were seen daily coming in large and lesser parties. I purchased another horse of a party from Los Angeles upon which to feed my musical countrymen. Parties of men soon took possession of all the mines which we had previously deserted on the Hassayampa, the first and oldest of all the camps, became the headquarters of all the immigration that came from the Gila on our old original trail.

Lynx Creek was soon claimed up, from one end to the other, and cabins built upon its course every hundred yards upon that portion which lay in the woods. Every prospect for a speedy population of the country about these woods now was considered good.

The Indians discovered that there was not a Capt. Walker at the head of all of this immigration and profited by that discovery, for they began to succeed at killing and capturing stock on every hand. They killed seven men on the Hassayampa at one swoop and drove off their horses. This was the first killing of white men about these woods, but the example was followed up promptly and every day saw some unlucky one bite the earth.

Men located claims one day and abandoned them the next. Cabins would be built and deserted in four or five days. Parties of men would arrive and take their leave from the states without investigation of the cause of the excitement, as though they had expected on their arrival to load up with gold and return to their home. Many expressions of surprise were indulged as to the merits of what was called "this God-forsaken country, where the grass even had thorns in it." I heard one fellow say that he had no doubt but there was plenty of gold in this New Eldorado, but that it had too much dirt mixed with it and he therefore considered life too short to begin to pan out a desert to obtain it. Another declared that if he could load his pack animal with gold and start immediately, it would not bear transportation over the route to California. Many of these new immigrants lost their animals and many lost their comrades and animals both, on the route, while others who were more lucky would sell out their surplus outfit and immediately take their departure for home, whether they ever reached it or not. Of course many of them failed, for the Apaches were having a glorious picnic during the continuance of which they quit hunting rats and lizards and the cooking of mescal and lived on horseflesh, like the French. The first inquiry always made by the immigrant on this arrival was, "Where is the Walker Party?" They seemed to be deceived because they had expected to find that the Walker Party had failed. Of course the identity of the old party, as a body, soon became lost in the tide of immigration and the individual membership thereof scattered. But the query always brought forth a falsehood from some pretender, who could tell all that was necessary to convince the questioner that he was a member of that body. I was many times greatly amused, while being one of the auditors, of a total stranger, at listening to some of the exploits of the Walker Party detailed by him as an active member of that organization. What a great power it is, to possess a sufficiency of self-control, to smile a conscious falsehood, from an earnest countenance all decorated with brilliant sun-beams, and honest complacency.... Smith agreed to give a portion of his ranch for a town site and a military post, on condition that it was accepted and occupied promptly.[1]

Pursuant to this understanding, arrangements were made to survey and set apart a site for a town and a site for a fort, to be prosecuted at an early day. From this time on myself and J[ohn] [H.] D[ixon] concluded to keep an account of the reported lost stock, which we did for nearly eight months succeeding, and it footed up to exceeding seventeen hundred head. The Indians of course captured many little squads of horses and their riders with them, who were never heard from at all. A party of us, consisting of some newcomers and some of our old party, took a trip east probably fifty or seventy-five miles in search of better mines.[2] We had been gone several days out when we pitched camp in a little flat woodland neck. Fourteen of us repaired to a gorge-like creek that had no name and began to prospect in its bed for gold. The opposite side of this creek from our camp was bordered by a steep cliff twenty or thirty feet high, from whence the hill slanted back and up to the main ridge. This hillside above the cliff was thickly covered by rough, black, volcanic rocks fringed with stunted chaparral. The hill opposite was steep and high, but comparatively smooth.

We were all busily picking away amongst the boulders in the bed of the creek when a sudden blast of rifle shots came from the volcanic rocks up the hill, whizzing among us like hail. Everyone now dropped the implement of labor and caught up that of war. But there was no enemy in sight to shoot at—they were all behind the rocks away up the hill. Upon the explosion, my friend of the old party, F[rank] F[inney], on turning around quickly to pick up his gun, which reclined against a boulder, fell over the stone and blundered considerably on the ground amongst the boulders. The Apaches thought that he was killed

---

[1] Smith undoubtedly possessed squatter's rights on the land at this time but little else. A United States Land Office was opened at Prescott on November 3, 1868, where the first pre-emption claim was filed on May 26, 1871, and the first homestead entry registered on November 10, 1871. Wyllys, *Arizona*, 237.

[2] This distance would have placed them east of the Verde River and in the country occupied by the Tonto Apaches.

and raised a terribly hilarious shouting and triumphant yelling. But F[rank] F[inney] arose from the ground unhurt. Hyram M[ealman] of our old party, made more demonstrations than anyone else. Upon the explosion of the volley he went hopping around on one foot, badly shot, but on further examination, the leaden mark across the instep of his boot showed that the ball had glanced and did not go through as he supposed. This discovery soon enabled him to walk again on both feet, which was none too soon, as we had to beat a retreat from this trap up the opposite hillside in the face of the enemy behind the rocks just across on the other side. We kept up a regular fire upon them however, to keep them behind their rocks until we were at a safe distance where we sat down to consider.

While sitting here, a lone shot from the opposite side sent a ball of large caliber in our midst, which however did no harm. It was replied to by one of our party without any known effect. After defying each other a little while, we took our final departure and saw them no more. These Indians made the worst job of this that I ever knew them to make. A fair, steady shot by at least twenty of them all at once, a distance not exceeding thirty paces, and hurt no one. This result was the merest of accidents, but still it does not go far to prove the generally acceded, splendid marksmanship of the Indians, poetically claim[ed] by the usual popular style of modern writers. We learned before leaving that these savages had cunningly stationed a greater portion of their number in the gorge below in ambush, expecting our party to retreat down the creek into the trap when fired on. Our party we considered too weak to enforce our company upon the natives of this section and therefore retraced our steps and arrived safely into the camps of our woods again. Upon our arrival we found some visitors of the Antelope Hills diggings already described, who had the day previously come into our woods, and as they were passing over the high and steep boulder hill at the west end of our woods they were attacked by the Apaches and some of them killed and all wounded. Among the latter was Pauline Weaver, the old trapper and the leader of their party, who, when finding himself wounded, saved himself by quietly taking a seat upon a rock and chanting some Indian gutturals, without farther noticing them.

The Apaches became superstitious by this conduct and left the old man to his ghostly incantations. After the Apaches had gone, the clever old sibylistic male performer crept into concealment, from whence he made good his escape to some of the mining camps after dark. The old man died about one year after this incident.[3] This circumstance had been passed about six months when I witnessed the operation of cutting out of the chest of a man wounded on this occasion a section of an arrow shaft, about three or four inches in length. The arrow, with which he had been wounded, had broken and this large piece had healed over and remained until extracted by this surgical operation.

Shortly after the attack made upon the Weaver Party there came some refugees from the border of Sonora and from Ft. Yuma, California, who had enlisted in a party of men to go to join the Rebellion at the South.

The leader of the party, whose name was Sumners, previously a resident of Nicholas County, Ky., had recruited his party near Los Angeles, Cal., in 1861, and passed the Colorado River about Ft. Yuma. They turned south and took up their line of march on or about the line between Sonora and Arizona so as to avoid capture by the Mexicans or Americans by crossing and recrossing the line, as necessity dictated. They were betrayed by the Mexicans and compelled to surrender, which they all did except the refugees referred to, three in number, who made their escape. Those who were surrendered were shot, including Sumners. These refugees claimed that it was done by the order of the Governor of Sonora, and laid to the credit of the Apaches. But however that may have been, Sumners and his party were known to have perished violently and those things purporting to have

---

[3] Pauline Weaver died a natural death while acting as a scout for troops stationed at Camp Lincoln on the Verde River in 1867. Lockwood, *Pioneer Days in Arizona*, 124–27.

been the fact published in California, placed the charge upon the Indians, which was doubtless false. The story of these refugees, one of whom subsequently became the recorder of claims in the Walker District on Lynx Creek, was corroborated partly by a gentleman from Los Angeles, who knew that Sumner's party had hidden their arms in a hay stack near Los Angeles while perfecting their organization.[4] I only mention this incident because there had been so many Americans lost upon the border of Mexico that it became a common remark that the greasers were more treacherous toward the Americans than the Indians.

However, the new settlement worried through the winter of 1863, in a mild climate. The snow fell deep on the higher mountains and ridges in the woods, but from three inches to one foot was about the usual depth of it at the north edge of the woods on Granite Creek. I have never spoken of the snows which the Walker Party encountered the winter previously, while constantly moving, because we had but little to contend with, and what there was of it was shallow. In the gaps and valleys the snow hardly ever remained on the ground more than three or four days at a time and seldom fell at all in low localities. But I can safely say that I experienced severely cold weather in central Arizona in the winter of 1863-4, and that the ground froze as I have seen it do in the Western states on the Atlantic side. The winter of 1863 broke early into spring—gentle spring, which began promptly to send along her soft and balmy signal waves, the remembrances of childhood's happy peace—gentle peace, birds, and flowers.

Excepting the storm cloud's crash of thunder and lightning

[4] During December of 1861, Union officers in California watched the reported small parties being organized there which intended to go to Texas and fight for the Confederacy. One of the leaders was an individual named Dan Showalter, a native of Greene County, Pennsylvania, who was arrested and later released at Fort Yuma when he took the oath of allegiance. Later he made his way to Texas, where he organized a regiment which participated in the campaigns in Arkansas and Indian Territory. One of Showalter's party was listed as E. B. Sumner of Perquimans County, North Carolina, who gave his age as thirty-four and his occupation as a miner. *Official Records of the Union and Confederate Armies*, Series I, Vol. L, Part 1, 728-29, 839; Part 2, 33 ff., 39.

and the scorching animated heat of the summer's sun, the natural elements assigned to central Arizona are mostly kind and conservative. Her atmosphere is exceedingly light and clear—her breezes mellow and soft, and the rosy freshness of her spring mornings is only enhanced by the fruitful brightness of her earliest eastern ray. It might almost be said that her sky is forever pure and blue and that her stars forever twinkle. But then there are so few flowers, and it might almost again be said that there are no birds. My reflections were painfully quickened once upon staggering upon this subject. I was sitting on an old fallen tree. It was a pine tree sufficiently seasoned for the bark to have all fallen off. It was clear of the ground and supported across some granite rocks. There seemed to be not one square inch of the surface of that tree for more than twenty feet which had not an acorn in it. Woodpeckers had patiently picked out holes just large enough in which to bury an acorn just below the surface. Each hole had one acorn driven into it exceedingly tight, giving the log the appearance of having been shot all over with bullets that just entered deep enough to stick fast. I wondered where the birds were, for I had not seen any of them, and I also wondered where they had found the acorns, as I really thought there were more of them sticking in this old tree than I had ever seen elsewhere in the country altogether. I once saw some martins in those woods where Prescott City now stands, and made a box to invite them to stay, but they refused to notice me or the box put up for their benefit. Ravens and buzzards are found in Arizona and the blue quail abounds. The latter have a plumage slender and heavier at the top and probably two inches or more in height. They can lower this little plumage forward, which gives the bird the appearance of having a long beak in which it is holding a bug or other substance. This quail chatters, but does not sing anything like the ordinary quail in the Atlantic states.[5]

There were none of them about our woods, but they inhabit

---

[5] If one substitutes the word "crest" for "plumage," which is the meaning of Conner, the description given fits Gambel's Quail, but the blue quail is an entirely different bird.

the low warm valleys. I have seen published descriptions of this bird, giving them the same habits of our quail in the Atlantic states, as roosting upon the ground for instance, but this is not true altogether, for I have seen them fly up into mesquite trees at night to roost as regularly as do the domestic chickens of the barn yard. I have noticed a whole covey raise together and all settle into one bush, to roost. This is about the most I can say of the birds of Arizona, and if our woods have them now to any noticeable extent, they have either increased wonderfully or else immigrated thither. I know that I have been in those woods and their surroundings for more than a month without seeing a bird, and have no recollection of ever seeing a dozen altogether save the kinds mentioned. Their companionship is a much greater relief and of much more consideration than is generally supposed by those who have always been accustomed to them. Their absence is greatly felt and their room cannot be filled satisfactorily with anything else, but birds.[6]

As before stated, Smith gave a portion of his ranch of one hundred and sixty acres for a town site and a location for a fort. Pursuant to this arrangement, a public square or *plaza* was located in the north edge of the woods and upon the right hand side of Granite Creek. With reference to this square, a plat for a town was drawn by Henry C[?] of Ky., and the ground surveyed by R[obert] W. G[room] of the same state, but then a resident of California. He was assisted by a number of persons among whom was this humble relator.[7] While we were surveying this plat, the Apaches attacked one of Smith's herders and shot him through the temple before the unfortunate man knew anything of a hostile presence. Crasthgrove was his name and I think Joseph was his Christian name, and I never knew what

[6] Elliott Coues, *Lists of Birds of Fort Whipple, Arizona, Proceedings* of the Academy of Natural Sciences, Vol. XVIII, 39–100, describes some 244 species which were present in the vicinity of Prescott as of 1866.

[7] Prescott was organized on May 30, 1864, at a meeting held at Fort Whipple. The townsite was selected on the east bank of Granite Creek, containing two quarter-sections of land. The town was platted by a committee composed of Judge H. Brooks, Van C. Smith, and Robert W. Groom. Swor, *Development of Prescott*, 6–7.

state he was from, but the Indians succeeded in stampeding the herd of one hundred and twenty horses and mules. In their wild flight they came across our surveying party.[8] The Indian that led the affrighted herd failed to see us in time to gradually lead them off from us and therefore, in order to save himself, turned at a shorter angle than practical for the herd, the effect of which was to leave the herd to charge immediately toward us, without a leader. Our little party of a half-dozen now dropped the surveying instruments and began promptly to wield those of war. The result of this quick and unexpected fight, as far as known, was that the herd of flying horses split about equally, one half circling around and back to Smith's ranch and the other half turned eastward, followed by thirty or forty crazy looking savages and were therefore lost. They were soon out of sight in the direction of Lynx Creek, leaving everything about us calm as they found it. We could only congratulate ourselves in saving about sixty head, for we soon learned that poor Crasthgrove had died without knowing how.

He was the first white man to die in the vicinity of Prescott City. The most exciting of this same chase came off on or near Lynx Creek some ten miles away eastward. S. C. Miller of our old party, Dr. Alsop,[9] and an old gentleman named Moore had previously left our locality, passing the usual trail around the north edge of the woods. They stopped to cut bunch grass for their mules, which they intended to take with them to the mining camp originally established by our party on that creek up towards its head.

While they were engaged in cutting grass, this herd of captured horses came suddenly over a little ridge toward them, still on a wild run, closely followed by the mounted Indians, all of whom dropped off their respective animals at the sight of the

[8] Joseph Cosgrove was shot March 16, 1864, at Sheldon's Ranch, twenty-five miles south of Fort Whipple, in what is reportedly the first attack in the vicinity of Prescott. Thomas E. Farish, *History of Arizona*, III, 199; *The Arizona Miner* (Fort Whipple), March 23, 1864.

[9] John T. Alsop is listed as a native of Kentucky, aged thirty-four, and as a physician in *The 1864 Census of the Territory of Arizona*, 171–72

"pale faces." The three men had not time to mount their own mules, which suddenly broke away from their hitching and joined the loose passing herd, leaving their riders to do battle with the overpowering numbers of the enemy, flushed with success. The creek was four or five hundred yards off, at its nearest point in the direction the herd was going. These three white men retreated in the same direction, with the herd's course, closely followed by the Indians, who fired on them constantly as they ran. The savages were so exhausted by their own stampede, that it seemed impossible for them to hit the whites, who were now dodging and fighting from tree to tree, as they were pressed and hurried toward the creek. The exhausted Indians flanked them on each side to within ten paces and still failed to stop them. The running fight continued thus until the white men reached an old deserted miner's cabin on the creek. The rude puncheon door was firmly closed from the inside. This necessitated another delay and conflict, during which M[oore] ascended the corner of the cabin and descended the chimney and opened the door, through which the outsiders quickly entered. The Indians now gave vent to their disappointment by a parting war-whoop, avoided the cabin as though there was evil in it, and went on their way in haste. By this adventure they obtained three more mules and the Doctor's bullet pouch, which he had hung on a little oak post while cutting grass for his mule. The three white men found themselves slightly wounded, except M[oore] who was shot rather seriously. A ball passed through his leg near the knee, which necessitated the sending of assistance to him. The following day I passed up the same creek and over the same battle ground, where I saw the piles of grass already cut, and dismounted and procured the grass, with which I fed my own animal.

This incident was soon forgotten and lost in the confusion of other and fresher ones. The survey was however completed and a town started, which ultimately grew into the present city of Prescott. It remained some months however, liken unto the celebrated city of "Duluth," as described by one of our witty congressmen—a "city all staked off." John M. Boggs was the new citizen who suggested the name of Prescott, after the historian Wm. H. Prescott, as a proper title to give the new town, which was adopted. The Indians were now full of animosity and their sudden raids and incursions were constant. They paid little or no attention to the greasers, who began to come in numbers from the northern states of Mexico, without arms or provisions. If the Apaches ever killed one of them, they did it for fun, or probably for the want of something else to do, for they had no fear of them whatever. Numbers of these greasers found their way to "Weaver Diggings," which place became their headquarters subsequently. They began to work up the Hassayampa and form settlements upon this stream and the miners of that section held a meeting and decided that the Mexicans should retrace their steps. Pursuant to this edict thirty or forty well-armed Americans marched down the Hassayampa from our old original camp and corral and ordered the Mexicans to depart hence, instantly. The order was vigorously enforced and the creek was speedily cleared of this Mexican population.[10] This act was subsequently regarded by conservative men as ungenerous and uncalled for, especially as this class of Mexicans was very poor and had no means of transportation except their donkeys. These diminutive animals are inseparable from the greaser interest and usually all the property they possess. They always abuse and overtask these little docile and harmless animals to the extent of cruelty.

I never knew or heard of one of these sleepy little animals kicking their owner in my life, as badly as I have known some of them to need it. The Mexican addresses it by the name of "burro" as though he was commanding a person and halts the

[10] Mexicans and other foreigners were discriminated against in the western mining camps. Charles Howard Shinn, *Mining Camps: A Study in American Frontier Government*, 203-208. At the first meeting held by the Walker party on May 10, 1863, a resolution was passed which stated that ". . . no Mexican shall have the right to buy, take up, or pre-empt a claim on this River [Hassayampa] for a Term of Six Months to date from the first day of June, 1863 to Dec. 1st, 1863." A month later Chinese were excluded from working any portion of the district. "Journal of the Pioneer and Walker Mining Districts," 5, 6.

animals by a prolonged "Sh-e-e-e" like one frightening away fowls. The *burro* is a mischievous animal about a camp. The carnivorous little brute will steal bacon or other meat to eat like a dog and will almost starve lounging about the camp, in quest of bacon-rinds and other *debris* in the way of bones &c.

If he ventures away from the camp and becomes frightened he will hasten back for protection and usually when he gets there, he will wallow in the dying embers of the campfire like a lazy negro, until he is scorched all over. When he gets half of the hair burned off of him, he will stand over the fire with his nose to the smoke and his eyes shut, perfectly still, sleepy and happy, for hours at a time or until he is awakened by some one. I was once alone on Lynx Creek after the desertion of its mines, and met two adventurers who had a donkey for a pack animal. They stopped in a deserted cabin and I put up for the night with them. They turned the little burro loose to shift for itself and moved the load into the house. After partaking of the usual luncheon the two men lit up the house with a pine knot, straddling a split board, face to face, and began a game of euchre, with an old greasy pack of cards, which they had with them. They played quietly thus until quite late in the night. Suddenly an unusual noise out in the dark, accompanied by the sound of horses' feet rapidly approaching the cabin, fixed the attention of this hitherto silent little party. I quickly clamped the door by its rude but stout fastenings. In another moment the door was burst wide open and in came the little donkey and jumped over the board between the players and the fire and stopped still. We of course were now all in a standing position with drawn six-shooters, looking for the cause of the animal's conduct. But everything had just as quickly become quiet as the noise had begun. Upon observing the affrighted little animal more closely, the hindmost thigh joint was found to be badly torn and mangled. This discovery explained the matter instantly. A panther or lion pursued the donkey to the door and caught it behind, and the little creature made a desperate effort, which tore loose the savage grasp and at the same time butted the door to pieces and came in. It was a wonder that the lion had not followed the donkey into the house and probably it would have done so if there had been no light. We stepped out of the door with our rifles ready, thinking that we might "shine his eyes" and kill him, but we made no discovery whatever—"darkness and nothing more."

The old original Walker Party, having now lost its identity as an organization, the individual members were only units amongst the multitude of the constantly arriving immigration. So our old Captain conceived the idea of collecting another little party for a short expedition northeast of Prescott, about a hundred miles or more. Therefore, a number of us were soon ready and took our leave of the settlements toward what is known as Bill William's mountain some forty miles northerly from Prescott.[11] When we became about twenty or thirty miles northeast of this mountain it became necessary to further progress, to cross what appeared to be a rough and lofty range of mountains.[12]

We saw signal smokes in different directions all day, but now we discovered some of them immediately in our front and on the top of this range. A number of spurs fell down from the main range to the comparatively level country like the ribs from a gigantic vertebra, all of which were heavily studded with granite boulders intermingled with scrubby chaparral.

It was at the foot of one of these spurs that we halted to prepare and arrange the mode of ascending it. Capt. Walker called for volunteers to the number of nine men, just the half of our party, to take possession of this rib to its terminus, where it joined the main spine, its highest point. The required number started and on arriving about a half-mile up the spur the Apaches disputed all further progress by sending a volley of rifle balls at us, which rattled and sung amongst the rocks harmlessly. This timely warning put each one upon his own individual guard and the progress became slow and cautious. The savages began to

[11] Bill Williams Mountain lies northeast of Prescott a little more than forty miles.
[12] If Conner's distances are correct, the party would have been in the vicinity of the San Francisco Mountains.

dodge from rock to rock as they slowly but steadily gave away, backward and upward. We just as steadily advanced by the same means. A scramble from one rock to another sometimes became difficult upon this steep hillside, and especially where the chaparral intervened. But this mode of ascending the hill continued for possibly an hour, during the whole of which time both parties were gradually working up the ridge in a silence unbroken only by the sporadic shots from either side of the contest. Presently Dr. W[?], a physician from Georgia, received a rifle ball through the thigh and sat down. This caused a halt and it required two of our men to help him down the mountain, leaving only six of us to hold the distance gained until their return. They were met however, by two men who remained with the mules and were relieved of the care of the Doctor and returned, when the forward and upward move was again resumed. It had not been continued, however, only a few moments when the savages followed one of their rifle volleys by a shower of rocks. One of these rocks alighted upon the top of "one of our heads," which temporarily killed a man and laid him out in the chaparral. He looked like a beautiful corpse, for a while, but awakened up again, when a "big brave" came pitching headlong down the hill and fell on his face in the chaparral near him. We were now getting into close quarters when the killed or wounded of the enemy would fall down the hill into our ranks. But the blood-stained ground began to show us that all the wounded had not fallen down the hill.

    The savages began to throw arrows with amazing rapidity that broke into fragments against the granite rocks and occasionally would strike fire sparks with the flint points as they struck the boulders. One of these pretty missiles struck one of our men in the fleshy part of the jaw and passed through, leaving an ugly and ghastly wound. Following closely upon this another "brave" sprang from behind his rock and came leaping down the hill and suddenly halted in a bunch of chaparral. Upon peeping over his rock he raised his head too high above it. They now began to give signs of weakness, which gradually grew into a total desertion of the contest. We gradually and prudently made our now unobstructed way to the top from whence we could see in all directions and all over the country. The other half of our party were still at the foot in charge of the mules and looking on with great interest to see the result of the little conflict, which was in progress so high above them. But we could see them distinctly from the top where we stood in comparative safety. What a transition in so short a space of time! Only a few minutes had passed since this ridge and hill was defiantly held by thirty or forty Indians. But now deserted and as silent as though no human creature had ever been there. Not a sound or a sign of anybody or anything indicated the presence of aught but the rocks and their lonely deserted surroundings. By signals from headquarters we were ordered to retrace our steps, which we did immediately and arrived at the foot to learn that Capt. Walker had decided to return to the settlements, because he thought that the party was not strong enough to proceed further and more especially as we were unlucky enough to have some of our men wounded and to care for. This was a disappointment indeed, but we, however, had quite a famous precedent for just marching up the hill and then marching down again and therefore philosophically considered that the best-laid plans of mice and men sometimes go awry.

We returned to the settlements immediately and this ended my experiments in the way of explorations in company with Capt. Walker, although I was with him afterward under some minor difficulties, which might be mentioned in the proper place. Upon arriving again in the settlements I had occasion to visit a little party of new comers on the Hassayampa, above our old camp and corral where the first miner's meeting was held.

I found quite a number of men there, among whom were four young men fresh from the states with all of whom I made a slight acquaintance. But it is to be understood that it was not necessary in the early settlement of Arizona to know a man's name to be acquainted with him. I knew many men whose names I never knew. It was the case with those young men I knew one of them was named Geo. Goodhue, who was a native of Lexington, Missouri. Another was called Charley and the fourth was addressed by the expressive sobriquet of Sugarfoot Jack, which was frequently abbreviated into the more convenient "Sugarfoot."

I left these four young men occupying an old deserted cabin not far above the original one at the corral. On the following morning three of this party decided to accompany four other passers-by over our old trail across the woods to Prescott. But Sugarfoot Jack refused to go and concluded to stop alone at the cabin and accompany the first prospecting party coming his way. The three young men packed their blankets &c, joined the other four strangers and they were therefore soon strung out single file upon the trail leading across the woods to the city, so-called. When they were about half mile on their journey and where the trail leads through a rocky rough place, the Indians arose from their ambush and fired upon the party, killing George Goodhue, who fell with the single exclamation that "I am killed," and wounding some others slightly. The whole party, after firing promiscuously, dropped all of their goods and chattels and stampeded, leaving the body of Goodhue only. The Indians quietly proceeded to strip and mangle the body of Goodhue and to gather up the spoils of their victory.

But each of the flying white men thought that the other was an Indian after him, and therefore continued to run each other nearly to death before the true state of things was discovered. Being several miles ahead of them yet to travel they were badly scattered along the line, each being located in accordance with his speed and bottom. Charley followed by George, who was a large overgrown clumsy fellow. Charley was small, quick and active, but George seemed to have the best wind, and began to overtake Charley, who had run off from them all at the beginning. But Charley had on when he started a bright red shirt figured by small black dots and no coat. He thought as he ran that the Indians would exert themselves much stronger to obtain that shirt and therefore he began to tear it off by handfuls as he traveled. He thought that George, who was also stripped and hatless, was an Indian gaining upon him, while George knew Charley but thought that the Indians had torn his shirt off of him. Thus they both ran until both were about to fall on account of sheer exhaustion, when Charley in the last agony of despair on being overtaken by the supposed Indian stopped and snatched up a stone and turned upon George to kill him with it. About the same instant George gasped out, "Let us stop, Charley, they ain't coming." Charley now threatened to strike George with the stone for running him down. All of them made good their escape except poor Geo. Goodhue, who had to receive all of the butchering alone.

But what became of Sugarfoot, who was left behind alone armed with one old fashioned dragoon six-shooter? When he heard the rapid and consecutive reports of fire arms, he was convinced that the men had been attacked. He started on a run for the scene of the action, guided by the sound of arms and quickly arrived in the vicinity. All was silent. He cautiously walked up a little rocky ridge with revolver in hand, watchfully scanning his surroundings and caught the first sight of the enemy. The Indians had dissected Goodhue and loaded themselves with the lost plunder and were coming single file down the ridge meeting Sugarfoot some fifteen in number.

He cautiously knelt behind a large rock unseen and waited until the foremost Indian was within ten paces of him, when his deliberate aim and calm shot killed the leading Indian dead, and passing through the body, the same bullet wounded another. It was now the Indians' turn to stampede, which they did by dropping their plunder and rushing pell mell down the side of the ridge in confusion. But Sugarfoot did not stop, but killed another before they got entirely off of the ridge and wounded still another before they got out of his reach. The Indians probably thought that the woods were full of white men, when they became so unlucky on their retreat as to come within gunshot of an old man named England, who killed another of their number. England had been out in the woods hunting deer and like

Sugarfoot had turned his course toward the battleground upon hearing the attack and arrived in time to make a parting, fatal shot. The Indians finally cleared themselves, leaving these two men in possession of the field, and their dead.

Sugarfoot and the old gentleman discovered amongst the blankets &c captured upon this occasion, the property of other white men who had fallen without knowing how or where. They gathered up on this occasion sixteen pairs of blankets and many other articles of wearing apparel doubtlessly stripped from the dead bodies of their victims. Goodhue's clothing was amongst the lot thus obtained and his body was found stripped naked except that his shoes were left on his feet. He was mangled and cut to pieces. His remains were buried about ten paces from and back of our old first cabin at the corral on the Hassayampa. The name of Sugarfoot Jack, who is dead, will be mentioned again in its proper place. He was about twenty-two years of age and one of the handsomest young men I ever saw. As a dare-devil he proved that he had but few equals—brave, reckless and cruel to the last extent.[13]

As an Indian fighter, Charley was not a success, but as a vocalist he had but few equals and was the first to introduce into the early settlements of central Arizona all of the Rebel songs of the war, which he would sing with a gusto. He learned an anecdote upon this occasion, which he told frequently and laughed heartily on becoming acquainted with the condition of the country. He said that when they first met this narrator upon the Hassayampa, one of their party began to propound to me pompous interrogations after the following order of conversational language. "Where is the Walker Party?" "The members of it are scattered about the different settlements," I replied.

---

[13] Another account which conflicts in some details with that of Conner's is given in Albert F. Banta, "Albert Franklin Banta: Arizona Pioneer," (ed.) Frank D. Reeves, *New Mexico Historical Review*, Vol. XXVII, No. 2 (April, 1952), 101. In his memoir, Banta gives the following description of Sugarfoot Jack. "Sugarfoot was an English convict from Van Diemen's Land [Tasmania]. He had escaped and made his way to California where he enlisted in the California Volunteers, but was discharged for thievery. Jack came out as a bullwacker. The rascal was as brave as a lion even if he was a notorious thief."

"What has become of all the hostile Indians we hear so much talk about?" "They too are scattered about the wilderness and seem to have no particular place to reside." "Well, I 'spose you are not on visiting terms with them, and that is about all that's the matter, is it not?"

"Oh no, we don't visit, but they are fashionable like all other pagans and merely make calls." "Well, they have not called upon us, but perhaps they are aristocratic and don't like new comers." "Not at all the case, they generally show a preference in this respect for new comers, but in no case do they ever send their card in advance." "Well, we would like to see a few of them to learn what kind of neighbors we are to have." "They will not be likely to ignore you altogether."

Charley would laugh and repeat this conversation, as he frequently reminded me of it, and mimic the speaker's pompous manner and speech to perfection. He said it was the first thing he thought of when the Indians attacked them on the following day. But the loss of Geo. Goodhue on that occasion cast a gloom over Charley, who stated that Goodhue had been wounded in Price's army and that on recovering, his widowed mother had prevailed upon him to leave the dangers of the war and go to Arizona where he had not more than arrived before he died at the hands of the Apaches....[14]

Quite a number of stragglers passed up the Hassayampa a few days after the above circumstance and of course they all had their respective packs of Apaches on their trails. I descended the creek and stopped near the Tanks or Falls, previously described as being located just above Walnut Grove. Mr. P[?] seemed to be the leader of this little party. About noon on the next day we missed our horses which were grazing a little way from us in the chaparral and hillside gorges. Upon investigating the cause

---

[14] Sterling Price, governor of Missouri from 1852 to 1856, was a Confederate general who campaigned in Missouri, Arkansas, and Mississippi before being forced to retreat into Texas in 1864–65. After the Civil War he went to Mexico, but returned in 1866 following the collapse of Maximilian's empire. Jay Monaghan, *Civil War on the Western Border, 1854–1865*; H. Edward Nettles, "Sterling Price," *Dictionary of American Biography*, XV, 216–17.

we found that the Indians had very recently borrowed them and their trail indicated that they had gone eastward with them. Four of us about noon started upon their track which we followed without difficulty. Our greatest fear was of being ambushed. For he who knows the character of the country directly east of these Falls for miles, wants no pretended description, for the attempt would be useless. The steepest and most precipitous gorges lying the deepest into the ground and clothes the heaviest with chaparral on the sides to the bottom with the most abrupt beginnings or headings of all the rolling country in Arizona, lay in this section. I have thought that the wild deer had to pick their way ever to successfully traverse it and I know that no man can do it unless he follow the narrow lands that nature had kindly left here and there, which sometimes bisect each other at angles of all degrees. A journey through it would naturally lay in all possible directions, horizontal, perpendicular, diagonal, north, east, south, and west. We cautiously wended our devious way fearfully. When we came in sight of a smoke arising out of the chaparral our further progress was necessarily more uncertain, but we hung on to the trail for our four horses were the stakes put up as a possible forfeit in the result of this game, to say nothing of our own lives.

The sun was getting low and warned us that night was not far off. We were silently following a trough-like, brushy gorge, which led into another not far off at right angles with it. We were so low into the ground that we could no longer see the smoke but believed that we were close to it and when we came to the intersection, we passed into the other hollow and suddenly within ten paces of the savages standing around the dead horse, which they were roasting. We were ourselves surprised at being so close and attempted to draw back to prepare the attack, but we were too late, for we were seen. We therefore unhesitatingly fired quickly and fast and kept it up as long as there was a live Indian in the hollow. They had selected this place at which to barbecue the horse, directly in the deep precipitous head of the hollow. The most of the Indians, numbering perhaps nearly a dozen, had laid aside their arms and our presence was so unexpected and near that they had but little time to get their arms and indeed but few of them succeeded at all, and then failed to get to use them. Only two or three random shots were fired at us, altogether. I noticed one old "brave" make a grab at his bow, which was hanging upon the leaning chaparral, and caught it, but the troublesome weapon hung to the bush and refused to let loose until poor "Lo" at last fell and expired without ever getting the bow off the bush. One of them attempted to fight some before his retreat began and was therefore so long getting over the hill that he fell and crawled out of sight across a little naked place on the top of the ridge. A number of them were wounded in getting up the hill, but only three were killed outright. But if all of them had gotten their arms in time they could have beaten us from the top of the ridge. Their fire was built of small, dead chaparral, but it was sufficient to burn all their plunder and arms, which we put into it. One of the guns we captured was a small, single barrel shotgun, brass mounted, and of English manufacture, and it was loaded with a ball that looked as though it had been beaten into its spherical shape by hand.

We took our other three horses and started back and we became so badly entangled in the dense chaparral that we could not travel at all. The darkness was as dense as the chaparral and we therefore stayed quietly in this brush until daylight and finished our journey to the camp before noon on the following day. I was amused at Mr. P[?] who wore buckskin pantaloons upon this occasion. After the fight was over, he was walking about with an arrow dragging after him. The arrow had passed through the pants near the foot and hung by the feathers on it, which failed to get entirely through. When his attention was drawn to it, he was surprised to see it, without having any idea as to when it got there. He remarked that if there had been any squaws along that he would have been convinced that there was some reality in witchcraft. This is only a sample of the numerous incidents of this kind which were constantly transpiring during this year of 1864. . . .

I shall now leave the Indians and gold-seekers for a little while to fight and scuffle all over central Arizona, while I invite the reader to join me in a brief welcome of the United States authorities who have just arrived for the purpose of establishing a civil government for the Territory of Arizona. . . .

Lead or Strychnine—the Pinole Treaty

THEY CAME OVER Surveyor Gen. Clark's route by the way of the Zuni villages and arrived on the headwaters of the Verde River about twenty miles north of Prescott with bugles, soldiers, and camp followers. They established a post of tents, and called it Ft. Whipple and remained there a few weeks, then moved up to within one and a half miles of Prescott on Granite Creek below the town.[1] The name and all was moved for they established a permanent fort which bore the name of Lieut. Whipple of the United States army and it still goes by that name.[2] The dignitaries escorted upon that occasion into these wilds for the purpose of forming a civil government for Arizona was done under an act of Congress approved Feb. 24, 1863. The officers appointed under the act must have been

[1] Fort Whipple was first located on December 21, 1863, at Postle's ranch in Chino Valley, which was about twenty-two miles northeast of Prescott. On May 18, 1864, the post was moved to Granite Creek about a mile or a mile and a half northeast of Prescott, McClintock, *Arizona*, I, 155.

[2] Amiel Weeks Whipple (1813–63) surveyed in 1853–54, the thirty-fifth parallel railroad route, which passed north of the Prescott area proceeding west from the region of Bill Williams Mountain. David E. Conrad, "Explorations and Railway Survey of the Whipple Expedition," M. A. Thesis, University of Oklahoma, (1955), 20–24.

either very slow to act or late getting their commissions, if their destination was settled, because until June, 1863, these woods and their locality were as silent as the grave so far as civilization was concerned. For it will be remembered that it was in June, 1863, when the original party first entered these woods and many a weary month passed before any company came to help break the monotony even after that date. However, the government was established during this year by the following named officers to wit: John N. Goodwin of Maine, governor; R. C. McCormick of New York, secretary; Wm. F. Turner of Iowa, chief justice; Wm. T. Howell of Michigan, associate justice; Joseph P. Allen of Connecticut, associate justice; Almon Gage of New York, district attorney; Levi Bashford of Wisconsin, surveyor general; Milton B. Duffield of California, marshal; and Chas. D. Poston of Kentucky, superintendent of Indian affairs.[3] These names constitute a full corps of the United States officials necessary to the task in hand.

The conduct of those officials at first seemed to be very cautious and prudent and even a little suspicious. But this was to a great extent justifiable, for the whole American citizenship seemed to be at war with itself, and it was reasonable to suppose that this impromptu and decisive new population of this wilderness was composed of refugees and bold adventurers from every class of society. The Union was trembling in the scales and here subjects were confronting each other in deadly conflict upon the recent fields of fertile agriculture. There were no women and children here to prompt considerations of peace and safety. Every man was armed from necessity and disappointed as a natural consequence of his existence, anywhere. The new and constantly increasing population knew not even how to hunt gold without assistance from experienced leaders and there were not teachers enough to take charge of them as they arrived. The consequence was that the country was filled to overflowing

[3] Lincoln's original appointee as governor of Arizona Territory was John A. Gurley, who died on August 18, 1863, and Goodwin, who had been chief justice of Arizona Territory, was appointed in his place. Associate Justice Allen's name is correctly spelled in official records as Allyn. Wyllys, *Arizona*, 166.

with a powerful and armed idleness. Everybody wanted employment but there were no employers, and no hope of any.

Deserts had to be recrossed with all the attendant hardships and deprivations before the glimmering probability of a cheap job at low wages presented itself. Men in physical health suffer long before they will renounce the folly that created the situation, desert their principles, politics, and religion in their violent search for relief. . . .

One thousand men, free of the care and charge of women and children in Arizona, would have necessitated the cost and attention of twenty thousand at the time if they were hostile to the Union. But however that may be, I shall dismiss the subject by saying of the founders of the present government of Arizona that their cautious suspicions were well founded and that their foresight and wisdom was only equaled by their generous patriotism and firmness of purpose. Their success at establishing a government without halt or mistake will always remain their best eulogium in the face of its correct story. I have therefore no complaint to make against these men, although a frequent recipient of material disadvantages, arising from their suspicious jealousy. . . .

If the camp followers on this occasion were to be credited with ordinary veracity after being corroborated by all subsequent official records, the Governor halted somewhere on his route in the wilderness and delivered his proclamation, setting forth his authority and his intentions to establish a government over this wild and broad domain of Arizona, the lands of Montezuma, the Aztecs, and Toltecs. The boundary lines of Arizona had not been surveyed and those of New Mexico in that quarter had never been marked. It may be possible that the Government of Arizona is not a legal one because there will always rest grave doubts about the exact locality of the Governor's camp when he formally proclaimed his authority and ordered elections. Some of the citizens of Prescott claimed that he was not in Arizona, but in New Mexico. The act of Congress under which he was acting provided that the officials should do all of their official acts within the boundaries of the Territory, as prescribed and embodied in the organic act.[4]

Neither the Governor or any of his party could tell just where they were located when the proclamation was announced to the world, and it was finally agreed that they themselves could not find it again, even with Kit Carson to assist them. The subsequently printed copies thereof solemnly warned all good citizens against unlawful acts and treasonable practices under severe penalties, &c, and they were further reminded that Arizona had already been claimed by a so-called Southern Confederacy &c. At the same time that this formal speech was being delivered by the authority of this portable government in chrysalis, the agents thereof were lost in the wilderness and surrounded by the silent atmosphere of a boundless desert either in Arizona, New Mexico, or somewhere else. But, however, the authorities arrived in the settlements and executed the instrument, whether it was legally served or not.

They were gentlemen and earnestly did a patriotic duty, the result of which are this day enjoyed by an industrious and intelligent population. . . . In accordance with the organic act the authorities aforesaid divided the Territory of Arizona into three legislative districts, from which there were nine councilmen and eighteen representatives elected to compose the legislature. The legislature thus organized pursuant to the Governor's proclamation, convened at Prescott on Monday, September 26th, 1864. The first bill introduced, for the appointment of a commissioner to report a Code of Laws. This bill was introduced on Saturday Oct. 1st, by R[obert] W. G[room] of the

[4] There seems to be little doubt that Governor Goodwin delivered the proclamation at a site known as Navajo Springs. According to a contemporary report the site was located about forty miles west of the Zuñi pueblo. A map compiled by the Bureau of Topographical Engineers entitled "The Old Territory and Military Department of New Mexico," dated 1859 and corrected and revised to 1867, places Navajo Springs about eighteen miles west of the Arizona–New Mexico boundary and about thirty-five miles west of the Zuñi pueblo. A United States Land Office map, dated 1883, places Navajo Spring about twenty-eight miles west of the Arizona–New Mexico boundary.

Council and passed and was approved and signed by the Governor Oct. 4th, 1864.[5]

In pursuance of the provisions of this act, the Governor appointed Hon. W[illiam] T. Howell as the commissioner, who accepted the task. The commissioner reported the Code, as required by the first act of this, the first legislature of Arizona, under the date of June 10th, 1864, which shows that the Code was already prepared before the meeting of the legislature. In the report the commissioner speaks of having arrived in Arizona in 1863 &c. If he did it was at some other point than Prescott. It may have been at the point where the original proclamation was issued. However, this Code was adopted by the First Legislature of Arizona and at this term of September, 1864. This was the beginning of the civil law in Arizona, if indeed, the first miners' meeting, held by the Walker Party in June, 1863, at the old camp on the Hassayampa was [not] considered Civil Law.[6] The Governor took up his residence at Prescott as the Capital of the Territory and Chas. D. Poston became the first delegate to the Congress of the United States from Arizona. Now as the authorities are all settled, I shall go on with some of the affairs of the people in their struggle with Indians and their next greatest enemy, to wit: Poverty. Before the civil government was organized and even before a beginning, excitements arising from newly reported discoveries began to become numerous from all quarters. One of these reports came to Prescott, that a man by the name of Bradshaw was at the head of fifty men from the Weaver Diggings and en route eastward to a point about fifty miles distant where it was reported rich mines had been

[5] Council Bill No. 1 was introduced by Robert W. Groom in the Council on October 1, 1864, and upon suspension of the rules was given the second and third readings and passed. Associate Justice William T. Howell was appointed on the same day to prepare the code of laws which when adopted became known as Howell's Code. The legislature convened on Monday, September 26, 1864, but attempted no business as several members of the legislature had not as yet arrived. *Journals of the Legislative Assembly of the Territory of Arizona, First Session, 1864*, 17, 57, 59. Hereafter cited as *Journals of the Territory of Arizona*.

[6] Typically, throughout the western territories and states the regulations of mining camps were validated by later legislative acts and therefore could be called civil law. Shinn, *Mining Camps*, 266 ff.

discovered. I started with a small party from the vicinity of Prescott, to join Bradshaw. We had to pass through our woods and therefore our party being constantly increased, pretty soon amounted also to nearly fifty souls.

Upon passing down Turkey Creek we struck the fresh trail of Bradshaw's party and followed it until we caught up with it. But we were nearly at the locality sought, when we found this party. We all arrived at our destination about noon the next day and found the whole matter a myth. A more disgusted set of men never before sent on a fool's errand. This was a new land and looked at though it had never contained any human souls. . . .

These old hills and rocks echoed back that day the first horrible oaths expressed in the English language that ever graced this hitherto sterile and graceless quarter. This trip served only to name a mountain near Turkey Creek. Bradshaw Mountain retains its name.[7] These disappointed men soon scattered away in squads and left the region as we found it. . . . [Later] I fell in with a little squad of thirteen, some of whom were members of our old original party. We concluded not to be outdone so easily and took a northeast course, which we followed for nearly or quite fifty miles, with the intent to reach some huge mountains that we saw in that direction. We were soon out of hearing of our last company and had a large country to ourselves. We crossed the Agua Frio at a steep rock wall, upon which many hieroglyphics were marked.[8] There were two cuts among them intended to represent deer. One of them was a pretty neat representation, while the other was a poor effect. There were many different figures represented, but it all appeared to be modern and some of them were just such characters as a child might draw on a slate. The Agua Frio ran, here, through level table land

[7] The Bradshaw or Silver Mountains lay south of Prescott and are named after William D. Bradshaw who, with two brothers Ben and Ike, came to Arizona in 1863. Barnes, *Arizona Place Names*, 60.

[8] The Agua Fria rises on the west side of the Mingus Mountain, flowing south and drying up in the desert near Beardsley station on the Santa Fe Railroad. If Conner's distances are accurate and his observations correct, the party was likely in the valley of the Verde River where it flows through or near the Black Hills.

covered with grass amongst which was hidden fragments of
black volcanic rocks, thickly strewn. We could not see the creek
or any appearance of it until we were within a hundred yards of
its banks, between which the creek lay apparently a thousand
feet deep. It appeared singular to see a large water course flowing through a high table land for miles. We only found the one
crossing which was a wash apparently a mile and a half long
falling into the creek at right angles. The banks of the wash were
also abrupt, necessitating quite a trip back on its course even
to get into it so as to descend to the creek to cross. It is at this
crossing, commanding both the approach to the river and the
wash that I counted the rooms of the old fortifications previously
referred to, to the number of fifty-four.[9] This was an exceedingly singular section of Arizona. We passed on northeast from
this crossing toward the large mountains referred to and came
to a high rolling country liberally clothed with short, stunted
chaparral. Many little shallow ravines traversed it which had
their courses slightly marked by little clumps of small-growth
willow. Some of these willow bushes bore prolific crops of long
slender beans probably fifteen inches in length and similar to
the beans of the catalpa tree. Some of this same species of willow
also grew southwest of Prescott twenty or thirty miles.[10] The
most of these ravines were dry. On ascending one of those flat,
waterless ravines we discovered in the distance ahead of us two
Indian squaws who ran into a little neck of small willows. An
old Indian warrior slowly arose from his sitting posture on the
ground. He was greatly bent with age and began to turn around
and around in one place continuously with a stooped posture,
with his long hair falling forward on his shoulders.

All the while he was slapping backward with his open hands
in an agitated manner. We rode up and stopped, but he never

[9] Contemporary maps show ruins scattered along the Verde but not the Agua
Fria River.
[10] The desert willow bears fruit from seven to twelve inches long when
matured. Charles E. Faxon and Mary W. Gill, *Manual of the Trees of North
America*, 869.

did stop his constant turning around and slapping backward, as long as we were in sight. We found on coming up that he was totally blind and was whining all the while, like the low feeble moan of an animal. He was nearly naked and did not even wear moccasins. He was evidently very old but his long hair was not much gray. I saw two *ollas* of earthenware of the probable capacity of two gallons each sitting near with water in them, and I dismounted and took a drink from one of them. The two squaws that we had seen I now noticed peering through some little tufts of grass on the creek bank a few steps of me. Their eyes shined in the grass like those of rabbits and they held equally as still. They were little girls. Some of the men pointed a gun at them, but they kept so still without "batting" an eye, that we concluded that they knew not the meaning of pointing a gun more than any other animal. The *ollas* were all the furniture about the camp of any kind. They were spherical and of a reddish cast as if made of poor material, and unpainted or ornamented.

The ground was worn smooth like this had been a camp for many years, and probably had been the home of this old "brave" a long while. We departed, leaving them as we found them, and the poor old warrior, whose wrinkled skin hung upon him as loose as that of a rhinoceros, still turned around, motioning backward, as long as we could see him, and for that matter, may be still at it. But he didn't look as though he could last much longer. I never saw the place nor its inhabitants again. We proceeded a few miles farther on and bivouacked for the night upon a high scrubby ridge and slept until morning without further incident than the annoyance of howling wolves. We only proceeded a short distance on the following morning toward the mountains which we were attempting to reach when we found a large stream lying between us and the mountains. We now knew that we were standing upon the bluffs overlooking the San Francisco River and for the first time calculated our dangerous locality, because we were so much farther from assistance than we had intended going.[11] We were in the most dangerous locality in the Territory and therefore beat a retreat immediately.

We turned down a stream which ran nearly in the direction home, beginning at its head. We were afraid to take a direct course through the hills and gorges, for fear of becoming hemmed in, so as to be entrapped. We preferred seeing more Indians as we would be sure to do on a creek, to the doubtful progress of an air line.

We traveled right hastily and soon saw a rancheria ahead of us. We knew that the safest way to get by was to dash right at it and throw the natives into confusion by surprise and the impetuosity of the attack, which we did successfully and passed on some distance before they rallied sufficiently to fire after us. Further on a few miles we came to another rancheria on a little oak flat. This one seemed to be a more extensive settlement, but we knew that if we attempted to avoid them by going around that we would be discovered and followed and perhaps entrapped in some impassable gorge. Therefore the same policy of quickly settling the matter was promptly pursued and succesfully carried out. Upon being charged so unhesitatingly the Apaches, after some random firing, retreated both ways to either foothill amongst the rocks from whence they discharged all of their arms at us, while we were in the midst of their camp, wounding a man and a mule. There was no shelter of any kind about this camp nor indeed any of them, but the little stunted live oak trees, ten or fifteen feet in height, and upon which there could be no straight limb or branch found exceeding three feet in length. These trees are not the regular live oak but they are ever green and their leaves fade a little during the winter.[12]

I saw small piles of grass seed on the ground here and there

---

[11] Conner here becomes confused and perhaps loses his sense of direction. If they had proceeded in a northeasterly direction from the Verde River toward the San Francisco Mountains, they could not have been checked by a river for none exists in this region and direction.

[12] Conner here could have been referring to any one of several species of live oak which grow in this region.

and a sheet-iron camp kettle boiling on the fire. A number of half-dressed deer skins lay about promiscuously where they had been hastily dropped upon our approach. I noticed too a gorgeously trimmed headdress on the cap order, hanging high up a little oak and attempted to poke it off with my carbine, but I was only just able to reach it enough to stir it a little. I was afraid to dismount and knock it down for fear that the mule which I was riding would break away from me in the confusion as the balance of the party hurried on. This cap was ornamented by a compact row of white feathers standing all around its edge perpendicularly.

I hurried on after the constantly retreating form of our men who continued to move down this creek until we came to another rancheria, which we again charged and saluted with arms in the same manner. We would only have to shoot three or four times each before they scattered and deserted their respective camps to the hillsides.

But we came to a fourth where the "braves" only retreated a little distance and rallied. We turn upon one squad and charged them in a hurry to the foothills, but upon turning upon another little batch of them on the opposite side of our camp they stood their ground and together with their shooting, fixed lances, and war-whoops, hurled back our mules and sent them into an unmanageable stampede with us after approaching to within fifteen paces of them; two of our men were wounded here and several of the mules carried off arrows sticking in them. These Indians were smart enough to know that we could not ride them down if they stood their ground and fired upon us, while they war-whooped our mules into frenzy. This "brave" little band of perhaps twenty, wavered a little upon our next charge, but they saw that we could not manage the mules amongst their war-whoops, and they took advantage of the situation and thus encouraged the first demoralized squad on the other side of the creek to come to them. There were now nearly forty of them together, ready for the fray and refusing to get out of our way, although the rocks were but a little way off. They seemed determined to command the trail over which we had to go. We now changed our tactics and instead of charging them with the six-shooter, we sat upon our mules where we were and played upon them with rifles, which we knew were heavier guns than they had and we had more ammunition to spare. They refused, however, to stand that process long and stubbornly retired to the rock. We now again secured our guns to the saddles and drawing a pistol each, we started suddenly like we were going to charge upon them in the edge of the rocks, but when we reached the trail we quit the charge and suddenly wheeled to the right hand, followed the trail, and made our escape through this narrow point and went our way hastily. We thought that they were attempting to detain us long enough to have this gap manned, which they would have done immediately if they had had men enough to have it done without deserting the children and squaws in those rocks. I don't know how many of these "braves" got hurt, but there was quite a number carried off into the rocks, all of which was unnecessary, for all they had to do was to let us pass, when all would have been well with them, as well as with ourselves. Signal smokes now began to arise in different directions. We came to a fifth and sixth rancheria. These were the last of them that we attacked in the same manner, and successfully passed, but nearly every mule in the party was more or less wounded, as were also nearly half of the men.

But this lucky narrator had like Caesar wounded vestments but no drop of blood ever came from the "dumb mouths" of such ones. Some of the "boys" were awkward enough to catch such complaints on this occasion, and growled over the same considerably. We left the creek and traveled over a rolling country, all of the afternoon and until dark and encamped on a creek bottom after crossing the dry sand bed where the water was supposed to run, when there was any to flow at all. We were out of provisions and had nothing to do but to roll up in a blanket each and go to sleep, which was soon done. Upon waking in the morning we discovered that the long low ridge upon the opposite side of the creek, which we had passed the previous evening, was lined with the savages who had collected and followed us. The greatest danger found in fighting them is being surprised by them. I would rather make the attack and fight five to one than to receive their attack and fight two to one, or really one to one. When we saw this array of prepared savages on the ridge we knew that we either had to fight or leave and that quickly.

We had no use for Apache scalps and could not well spare our own, therefore we took the latter course and were off in a few minutes. They saw the movement and bid us good morning with a surprisingly heavy volley of rifle shots, but they were not near enough to accomplish anything but to warn us of their overpowering numbers. As we mounted and started I was attacked with a sudden acute pain in the edge of the hair above the temple which I really thought would become unbearable. I was sure that I had been bitten by a centipede or tarantula. But as we were so energetically pressed through the next gap, the sting died away and I forgot all about [it] until the sore temple was pressed by my hat. I concluded that the sting must have been that of a red ant, one of the pests of Arizona. These industrious insects build little mounds of sand all over the country and their bite is equal if not more painful than the sting of a hornet. The centipede and tarantula abound in Arizona and are said to be very poisonous.

I have many times encountered little settlements of tarantulas. Upon being disturbed they will rush to the front of their little caves in the attitude of defense and it would be hard to imagine concentrated in so small a space, so much expression of defiance and rage and ability to do mischief as these spiders present. Some of them are more than an inch across the back, which is coated with long hair. It is common in Arizona to meet them traveling in the bare trails in the months of October and November. Stamp the foot at them or toss a little stick at them, and they will immediately assume a hostile attitude and stretch up high upon all fours and come sidewise to the attack, with all the confidence necessary to attack a locomotive. If the enemy backs off, the little animal in great rage makes a leap to catch the intruder anyhow, even if it should be a grizzly bear. They, however, seem to be perfectly useless and of no benefit for any purpose and are unlike the red ant above described in this respect, for the latter are said to be noble little animals to strip a careless miner's garment of vermin, when spread over one of their little knolls. One fellow having been caught thus imposing upon the ants, was taken to task about it by his friends who came with him, and who asked, "Why, John, now what would your friends in the States think of that?" "Oh, I don't know," replied John, "but I reckon they would think about the same that they did of you for turning your wife's turkey into the tobacco patch to worm it."

We came into a desert country and distanced the Indians, who pretty soon began to drop back, one by one, until there was none to be seen. We had considered a good run better than a bad stand and profited by it. That night we pitched camp in a desert of alkaline dust, amongst the scattering bunches of sage-brush where the rattlesnakes never cease to rattle all night long. One got into the sage-brush bunch at my head and that of my friend F[rank] D[ixon] the Louisianan. He raised his head off of his saddle and asked me if I heard the snake at our heads, to which I made no reply. Thinking that I was asleep he nestled back to his position, muttering that "maybe the d—n thing won't bite a man when asleep."

We arose early on the following morning and recrossed the Agua Frio and on ascending it we saw an Indian rancheria ahead of us. They saw us, but never moved nor made a demonstration. Upon arriving at a point to within a hundred paces we discovered that a deep and impassible washed-out gorge lay between the two parties. When we stopped an old "brave" came forward with a white rag for a flag and in all ways expressed friendship for us. There was not over a dozen of them and their encampment was a pretty, green, grassy flat, studded sparsely with large and low black walnut trees with long horizontal limbs not higher than five feet from the ground. These trees bore nuts not more than half the size, if that large, of the same growth in the States. The old Indian directed us by pointing around the head of the gorge, the route into his camp which we followed and were soon amongst them. They desired to test their friendship by guarding and grazing our mules for us, but of course this kindly proffer was declined. We could not trust them to care for our mules but made amends for this apparent want of confidence by trusting them to gather and carry walnuts to us. I noticed a warrior with a cord of human hair wound around his waist many times to serve as a belt. He gave me to understand that it was made of his victims' and he seemed to be very proud of this reminder of his cruelties. I attempted to trade for it but he would not listen to any proposition. About two hours later I chanced to put a little piece of rocksalt into my mouth of which I had about a gill. This fellow saw me and held his hand for a piece, which I gave him. He put it in his mouth and cracked it like he was eating parched corn and immediately began to unwind the cord from his waist, which he completed and bundled it into a hank and tossed it to me, and again held out his hand toward me for salt. I gave him all that I had and no mans' eyes ever sparkled with a greater brilliancy at the sudden and unexpected prospect of a fortune than did this Indian's eyes upon finding himself in the possession of a spoonful or two of this salt. All of his associates crowded around him for a taste, for which they all, old and young alike, became clamorous. It was really a pitying spectacle to see this fellow who would so earnestly and so cautiously select a very small particle and place it carefully into the open palm of an importuning old Indian's hand. Then, the recipient would so carefully handle the little grain until he got it into his mouth for fear of dropping it, that it looked painful. But when he got it safely deposited his care and trepidation ceased and his face became all smiles and full of roses. Salt was at a premium in this market. I never saw anything of the fabulous salt fields which I have heard existing in Arizona and I am rather inclined to guess that no one else ever did either.

I sat and ate walnuts for an hour and it was the first food I had tasted for more than two days.

A boy carried them to me and kept me supplied the whole time and I had some left. This was the handsomest Indian I ever saw, male or female. He appeared to be about fifteen years of age with dimples in his chin and cheeks, large full eyes, and exceedingly bright and pleasant face. The high cheek bones were wanting and a straight intellectual nose with arched brows gave him a fine appearance.

He was nearly nude like the rest of them except that his shoulders and body was nearly concealed by his luxurious suit of long black hair. He was proud of the broad leather band upon his wrist, which he had lately put on to keep the bowstring from cutting the wrist, while shooting. He informed me by signs that the strap showed that the wearer had ceased to be a boy and indicated that he had become a warrior. I thought that I would like to see that boy in school, to see what could be made of him. He certainly was a manly fellow, as well as handsome. We left these natives expressing friendship for the whites, but there was no knowing when to trust any of them.

Our party arrived in the settlement safely and as we rode up the hollow to the edge of the woods one of the "boys" called to mind a little incident which took place more than a year before in the Walker Party, as it was first approaching the woods by the way of the Hassayampa. While it was strung out single file plodding the lonely way in silence, one of the members, who seemed to be studying about the war, broke the silence by saying in a loud voice like he was talking to the whole line, that when the war ended Abe Lincoln would be a dictator. Another one near the rear, who didn't pretend to like airs much, and who failed to catch the import of the remark, quickly responded in good-humored appreciation and triumph, that "Old Abe will be d—n lucky to have any taters to dig, time he is done fighting."

This ludicrous mistake and innocent air of earnestness brought forth a general hearty and mirthful laugh that made these silent old woods ring. We learned on our arrival that five men were killed on the Hassayampa in our absence, and several others on the route from the Colorado River to Prescott. . . . After becoming settled at Prescott again provisions gave out and I determined to go in search of some. For this purpose I obtained two mules and went over the direct trails to Antelope or Weaver and arrived at the place at daylight.

It was forty miles from Prescott and when I started back I took day-time for it, because it was very dark going and I became confused and lost my way. But before starting I learned that a little party was going after the Apaches east of Prescott to attempt to retake forty or fifty head of stock recently taken from a ranch on the Gila above Ft. Yuma, called Agua Caliente, which had been claimed and occupied by K[ing] S. W[oolsey].[13] I further learned that the owner of the ranch and the stock would be along in a day or two and would attempt to get some followers from the mines about our woods. I concluded to accompany the party if I could get back in time. So I procured my flour of Mexican manufacture and therefore consisted of ground and unbolted wheat and sand and started. Another party of stragglers had just started around the mountains the long route for Prescott and I thought as the Indians would be likely to follow them that it would be safer for me to take the direct route, through the mountain trails. I traveled all day and until after dark when it began to grow too dark to see anything, and I halted for the night. After building the packs around my bed of blankets to secure me from being shot from a distance, I went to sleep. My position was a naked spot amongst the low chaparral. About midnight I was aroused by the snorting and agitation of the

---

[13] King S. Woolsey, born in Alabama but reared in Louisiana, came to Arizona in 1860, locating a ranch at Agua Caliente on the Gila some eighty miles above Yuma. In 1863, Woolsey established a ranch near Prescott and was a member of the first legislature of Arizona Territory in 1864. A noted Indian fighter, Woolsey led several expeditions against the Apaches, one of which culminated in the "Massacre at Bloody Tanks," to which Conner here refers. This same incident, which took place in January of 1864, was also called the Pinole Treaty because some authorities allege that the Apaches were fed poisoned pinole by the Americans. McClintock, *Arizona*, I, 185–86; Lockwood, *Pioneer Days in Arizona*, 138–40; Browne, *Tour through Arizona, 1864*, 120–24.

Iretaba, chief of the Mohaves, and some of his subjects, from a painting by H. B. Möllhausen.
(Reproduced from Lieut. Joseph C. Ives, *Colorado River of the West.*)

mules that charged up to my bed as far as their picket ropes would permit. Such actions by mules was always regarded as a sure sign of the presence of Indians. I stealthily crawled out of my blankets and into the neighboring chaparral and sat up in a concealed position until daylight and kept quiet until the sun arose. My expectations of a certain conflict at the break of day was not supported, for I never saw or heard more of the matter. I arrived in Prescott on the following day and learned that the party preceeding me did have a conflict and lost all their stock. This party had seen Indians behind the rocks on their route, a mile ahead of them, with a telescope, and at last, let the wily savages outwit them, kill a man, and wound several and capture all of their animals and supplies.

Woolsey came sure enough, and quite a number of men from the upper Hassayampa joined his party, in all amounting to nearly forty men. This was the first party organized to go after the Indians, both to recapture stock and to chastise them for taking it. This party took the trail of the stock and followed it at least a hundred miles into the Apache strongholds of central Arizona, directly east of our woods.[14] Signal smokes warned them that they were followed, and therefore the wily savages scattered the stock so that they could not be trailed any farther without [making us] take separate tracks, and we could not divide our party. The threatening attitude of their sentinels and other skulking Indians convinced us that there was a force of them not far away. We had been out nearly two weeks on the alert in this pursuit, when one pretty sunny morning, while we were having a quiet single file march around the foot of a smooth, treeless mountain, we were surprised by a sudden appearance of a horde of Apaches filing around the mountain above us. They came from the opposite direction, meeting us. At the foot where we were, the hill arose very slightly as it extended back steeper and steeper, toward its summit. They were all done up in paint and feathers and kept ominously silent.

[14] This would have placed the party in the vicinity of the Mogollon Mesa and Tonto Basin.

They filed across the foot of the mountain about one hundred paces from us and a little above us, leaving the mountain behind them. Some of our men guessed their number at three hundred and others put it at five hundred, but I thought either figure was a little high. I thought that they might number about two hundred and fifty. We dismounted and quickly side lined our animals so as to prevent them from a stampede, and prepared for the worst. One of our party, who didn't like the prospect any better than the rest of us, remarked in a suspicious tone, that "Now we have found the stock and more of it than we want." Quite an expression about the probable results took place amongst our "boys" in sotto voice. One suggested that we had better make a treaty with them. "No," responded another, "they are all too much primped up with paint and feathers to come for a treaty." "They are all devilish quiet, ain't they?" says another. "Yes, and they won't stay that way long either." At this moment Woolsey bid them good morning in Spanish. This salutation was promptly answered in broken Spanish, which now bid fair to become the diplomatic language of the negotiation, at least, until that of arms became substituted. The ice was now broken and quite a talk took place, all of which resulted in an agreement to have a regular pow-wow.[15]

They evidently intended that no men of our party should ever escape and their preparation to carry out that intent was complete. But the difficulty with them was that they wanted to succeed with little or no loss and they felt certain that in an open and bold conflict these "pale faces" would do much damage. So they were not adverse to a pretended treaty pow-wow during which they expected to get the advantage. According to agreement six of their chiefs met five of ours about halfway between the two forces. W[oolsey] acted as chief on our side and warned us to be constantly on the watch and that he would raise his hat with his left hand for a signal by which to begin the attack, and which must be made with all the force and determination possi-

---

[15] The "treaty" and resulting conflict took place near the present town of Miami, Arizona. Wyllys, *Arizona*, 154.

ble. One volley from them to begin with would kill or cripple every man in our ranks. If we attempted to leave them, that volley would have been delivered and there was not a man in our party who was not satisfied of that fact. Our commissioners pleaded for mercy and only asked to be permitted to leave the country. As W[oolsey] thus talked to their six chiefs, they would proclaim it to all of their warriors along the hillside, who would laugh heartily in their triumph. The whole hill seemed to laugh as the naked wretches stood strewn along the hill as thick as blackbirds.

The eleven commissioners were engaged together midway between the hostile forces for an hour. Woolsey sent down to us for a red blanket for the two "biggest braves" to be seated upon and he succeeded in getting them to sit upon it, while he kept upon his feet, himself. He selected each of his companions [an] Indian to kill and warned them in good-humored English which the chiefs could not understand, not to let one chief escape to rally the privates and the battle would be thus already half won. Laughingly telling his men to be ready and telling Lenon to take the Indian who was leaning upon his lance, he raised his hat with one hand and drew his six-shooter with the other, and in an instant every chief was killed, except the one with the lance. Lenon shot him twice through his body with a six-shooter, but the old "brave" drew back his long eight-foot shaft pointed with a Mexican sabre blade and thrust it through the body of Lenon in the twinkling of an eye. Lenon fell forward, thus bracing the blade in his body, so that the old chief had to rear around the backward vigorously before he could pull his lance out of the body.[16] But the rest of us had come upon the double quick and came by these combatants in time to kill the chief, who was so determined to have his lance, and passed on against the main body. Our party was armed with repeating rifles mostly and two six-

[16] Several varients of Lenon's name appear, but the most likely correct spelling is Lennan. Cyrus Lennan was a partner of Ammi White, the Indian trader to the Pima and Maricopa Indians. His death is reported in *Official Records of the Union and Confederate Armies*, Series I, Vol. XLVIII, Part 1, 901; Series O, Vol. L, Part 2, 74; and in Browne, *Tour through Arizona 1864*, 121.

shooters apiece. The rifle was used until we came within fifteen paces of them, as they still stubbornly held their ground and shooting fast, but it was a little down hill and they overshot us in their surprise and excitement. When we got to within fifteen paces of them and still approaching, someone in our party loudly exclaimed, "Take the six-shooter to them." This was obeyed immediately and everyone quickly "whipped" out a six-shooter, which increased the rapidity of shots so much that the Indian line gave away. Then they all wanted to go the same way and the hill behind prevented them from backing backward and in pressing their line endwise they became confused and in a crowded knot at the point of attack twenty-four of them fell without being enabled to retreat. The pistol thus became the weapon of wicked effect in the midst of this accidental entanglement where the savages were so crowded for a moment that every shot must have either killed or wounded. They were so confused by the sudden and unexpected loss of their captains that they seemed to be paralyzed and hopelessly stupid.

They began by discharging their rifles in excitement and at random without effect, and were not given time to reload when if they had given us a well-directed volley from all their guns in the beginning, their success would have been certain for such a volley would have killed or disabled every man of our party. When they gave way they became totally demoralized and fled in confusion around the foot of the mountain and up a narrow hollow, where the rocks had been rolling down the mountain for ages and formed a roof of them along the foot. This created a desperately wicked running fight, for the distance of a half-mile and until the savages scattered and disappeared. One very athletic man among them was attempting by determined and desperate exertions to carry his wounded comrade on the retreat. He would lay down his burden and fight and suddenly snatch up the crippled "brave" and run again. He continued this for some time and successfully kept beyond the reach of our men who were also becoming scattered. This devoted man had just picked up his wounded friend and started again, when he was fired at. The ball either hit him or came so close as to suddenly prompt his resistance, and he quickly laid his man down, brought his rifle from over his head as he turned facing us, and lowering his gun. At this moment and while his arm was up sustaining the descending gun and just before reaching a level, the gun of my companion at my side cracked and the Indian's gun descended harmlessly to the ground, while he turned and fell upon his face in the opposite direction with the low and single exclamation, "Wah." He was dead. My friend's leaden messenger had found poor "Lo's" heart, while his arm was lifted high, as directly as if it had been placed in the right place with the fingers. We examined this body as we returned. He was a tremendously large man and bloody all over from carrying his wounded friend, which still lay beside him and still alive. He had died for his friend who outlived him and for whom he made desperate efforts to no purpose. And for this devotion this dead "brave" had my sympathy as he lay there motionless beneath the skies of his nativity and in the shades of the gloomy old mountain peaks, which he had loved for so long and so well. . . .

As we passed on back to our animals, some of the men discovered an old gray blanket stretched over a recess in the rocky reef referred to. Several shots were fired at the blanket under the impression that some of the fleeing warriors had taken refuge in the rocks and concealed themselves behind this blanket. The blanket was of a salt and pepper color and therefore looked like these old granite rocks. Shrieks of agony and distress behind the blanket responded to the sharp crack of the rifles, which continued to play upon it until silence was restored. Upon taking the blanket down the unfortunate inmates were found to consist of three young and likely squaws, all dead. They were probably of the royal family, which fact accounted for the privilege they had to be present at the proposed massacre, which had just miscarried. However, these poor creatures would never have been harmed if they had only showed themselves so as to be known. Their concealment was fatal.

We never knew how many Indians were killed upon this

occasion and never waited to count them, but hurriedly prepared to leave this unholy place.[17] We had several wounded, but only one man killed. We tied Lenon's body on a pack and carried it for nearly twenty miles southerly and buried it on the Gila River bottom in a lonely and wild place where I have never been since nor heard of any one else ever being there. I doubt whether any of the party could ever find his grave again after leaving it. Our apparent treachery in thus taking the advantage of the Indians to make this attack was justified because the men who composed the party were experienced in Indian fighting and they had learned this tricky lesson from the Apaches, who upon this occasion intended to do the same thing. . . . This bit of experience convinced us that so small a party could not go into the Apache country with impunity, and after burying poor Lenon, we concluded to return to the settlements. The most painful duty of all was to wrap Lenon's body in his blanket and put him into the ground in this lonely and silent country and leave him, the associate of the wild wolves, Indians, and animals. . . .[18]

We learned upon our arrival in the vicinity of Prescott that what few soldiers there were at Ft. Whipple, one and a half miles below the town, were constantly annoyed by the enemy skulking in the neighborhood and prevented them from going to any one's assistance. The consequence was that another citizen party of one hundred men started eastward again to chastise the Indians into keeping the peace. This party passed toward the Rio Gila not far from where we buried Lenon, from whence it took a northerly direction beyond the late battle ground. It soon became apparent that this party was too large to fight Indians successfully and therefore was divided into two forces, which were to meet again within four or five days. The wing

[17] A report of Major Edward B. Willis commanding Fort Whipple, dated February 11, 1864, gives the number of Indians killed at this action as twenty-four. *Official Records of the Union and Confederate Armies*, Series I, Vol. XXXIV, Part 1, 121.

[18] McClintock, *Arizona*, I, 186, maintains that Woolsey learned of the intended Apache treachery from a young Apache captive who accompanied the party, resulting in Woolsey's determination to kill the leaders of the Indians at the council.

which I accompanied took the inside track of the circular course laid out, hence we had more leisure time. I cannot point out our locality because there was no known landmarks by which to indicate it, but it was little over one hundred miles probably. We would remain in camp a whole day and keep out sentinels to discover the campfires of the other party.

During these periods of inaction, a dozen or fifteen members of the party would take little jaunts for several miles away and sometimes remain all night and a whole day. A small party could travel so much faster that it could easily overtake a larger one. Upon one of these short visits we were caught in a pretty heavy shower of rain and the party took refuge under a rocky cliff located in a steep hillside. One of the party wore a pair of buckskin pants and was an older miner of years standing. He called himself Smith and he took quite a pride in being rough and ready. Always in good humor, with fine health and good appetite, usually quite noisy, and had a wide mouth, from which he was capable of throwing a hearty laugh for a mile. Smith was a short heavy fellow and loved the rain but didn't like buckskin pants when they were wet. He said that wet buckskin pants next to the skin was abominable and he therefore took his pants off and buried them in the ground with a small prospecting shovel which some one had carried with the party, to keep them dry. He was thus left nearly nude and seemed to enjoy the rain hugely. As he stepped ten or twenty paces down the hill away from the cliff where the rest of the party were crouched, in order to keep dry, the "boys" now and then would start a large rock rolling down the hill and Smith would stand and wait the coming of the stone to see how close he could allow it to approach without it being necessary for him to move. Again and again he would stand until the stone would look as though it would roll over him. Presently one of the men knocked the underpinning from under a large loose rock in the cliff, which, as it rolled away on its journey down the hill for Smith to dodge, enlarged and opened a crevasse in the cliff next the ground that had not as yet been seen.

Smith had his eyes upon the approach of the huge stone and failed to notice a large bear that tumbled out of the hole pretty soon after the rock left it. As soon as the rock passed him, he threw himself into a parrying position for what he supposed on the moment to be another rock coming. Just then the bear, as it followed the stone with loose waddling jumps, fetching an affrighted, hoarse growl and seemed to be puzzled as to what course to run. Smith in his astonishment brought out a war-whoop that would have done honor to the loudest Apache "brave" in the land, as the no less astonished animal made a ferocious lunge at him with a mixture of growl and whine that sounded more like a squall than anything else. Smith accompanied his Apache yell with a terrific leap and landed into a bunch of stunted chaparral as the bear passed him at a headlong gait, down the hill. The affrighted animal never stopped to look back but continued its long awkward jumps down the hill, snuffling its nose like a scared hog does under surprise until it was lost to view. Smith as he "scrambled" up, looking after the retreating bear, exclaimed in his subsiding excitement, "Go it, d—n you, go it." He was evidently the worse surprised man that ever beheld a wild bear, and after delivering a number of hearty laughs, he boasted that he was the only man in the party who would throw himself into a hollow square to receive a bear, without having breeches on. "And the only one who would jump into a thorny chaparral without 'em on," added someone. "Well, jest look at my hide sure enough, how it's scratched." He was pretty badly scratched, but he was not the man to complain about trifles.

The rain ceased and the party moved and encamped for the night in the vicinity of our friends. On the following morning some of the party discovered that they had vermin on them and began to arrange matters to rid themselves of this humiliating and annoying pest. Nobody had more than the clothes they wore. Therefore each man wrapped his blanket about him while he dipped his apparel in a camp kettle of boiling water to kill the insects. After the goods were thus dipped and wrung, they were hung out in the sun to dry some ten or fifteen paces away. While this crowd of old-squawish looking people sat about cracking jokes and teasing Smith about trying to frighten the bear to death by yelling at it, with their serapes drawn over their shoulders, we heard firing in the distance. Someone suggested that we would make a pretty picture now, if the Indians should make an attack from an ambush. The speaker arose from his sitting posture and walked out to the laundry, felt his clothes, and reported them entirely dry, and dressed himself.

All of the men followed the example except Smith, [who] was never particular whether he had clothes on or not while he was in camp. But upon being hurried preparatory for starting he reluctantly went for his clothes. When he became dressed with all except his pants, he lazily stopped to pick them up. He had one hand on his knee as though he was contemplating them. Still keeping his position like he was in a deep study he raised his buckskins a little height and let them fall and they rattled like a dry gourd. Here without taking his eye off of them he musingly remarked to himself "The water was too hot fur 'em." His pants being made of buckskin had drawn up to about the dimensions of eighteen inches in length and had become fixed and as hard as wood. Some of the "boys" caught the situation at a glance and remarked Smith's quandary, which elicited a burst of levity and laughter, not often enjoyed on such tedious journeys. Smith still leaning over his pants lying upon the ground, like he was afraid to touch them, with one hand resting upon his knee for support, walled his eyes up the hill at the merry fellows, without a smile and without a word. This brought another storm of hearty laughing.

Smith looked hard and contemptuously at them until that burst was about over, still in a stooping position, then mocked them as he emphasized it with petulant nods of the head. . . . However, he soon got to work upon a blanket out of which he cut a pair of pants with his sheath knife and was tendered and received all of the assistance in the camp to sew them together. After they were done he said they were no beauties, but anything would do to stop a foolish sniggle. When he got them on they proved to be tights and burst in several places, and this fact only proved to him that he had made a splendid fit. He looked like he had been melted and poured into them "and made him feel," he said, "like he walked like a turkey." We, however, joined our party and moved on toward a woodland table land some miles distant and still heard nothing of the other party. Upon ascending the mountain to the timber we passed up long chaparral ridges. There were many of them pitching down from the high woods clear to the creek, which was dry. From the signal smokes we were convinced that we would have resistance in the ascent, which we did have, although it was feeble, considering the advantages the savages had. The top of this mountainous ridge proved to be a level, flat, and narrow country covered with a liberal growth of pine and post oak with a limited sprinkling of large old juniper trunks with dead or dying boughs.

We approached this table at its side and consequently it was only a few hundred yards across it to the opposite side, where it again changed into a long descent of chaparral ridges to a dry creek at the foot, nearly a half-mile away.

But upon first reaching the brow of the hill in the edge of this table land, the Indians made a stubborn resistance from the trees as they slowly fell back from one to another. Smith was charged with playing the role of Daniel Boone by taking up all of his time poking his hat out from behind the trees on [the] end of his gun, for the Indians to shoot at. But he insisted that it was better and safer for all of us to have the savages waste their ammunition by shooting at his hat than at his head, and he continued to insist that the proper mode of fighting Indians was for each man to do it his own way like he did, and therefore he would attend to his own business. As we approached a point nearly midway of the strip of woods the rapidity of the shooting upon both sides became a little furious. It was a calm day and the smoke from the guns slowly curled and settled about the ground and amongst the trees as the savages withdrew from the contest and disappeared.

While the shooting was at its most angry height, there was distinctly seen away through the level woods a diminutive nude, human form, facing us and jumping from tree to tree directly in front of our guns. It cautiously kept up the approach until it came up to us looking like a ghost in the smoke, darting from one tree to another in the face of danger. The shooting ceased as the savages gave way on a final retreat and left the men standing here and there by the respective trees reloading. This little dark and tanned specimen of anatomy came directly up to us and stood with its feet crossed, gazing from one man to another, as if at a loss to know what step to take next. It was the poorest, starved, anthropological sample I ever saw, as it stood there, a mere naked skeleton dressed like Eve before she sinned. Our friend who had such a chase by the grizzly bear in Colorado laughingly pointed the little creature out to one of the good-humored old jokers of the party, who was quietly standing near his tree engaged in reloading his gun, and asked him what he would call that little animal. The interrogated good naturedly replied that it was a "D—ed little, old, dried up, Ingin squaw," thus creating some levity at the unfortunate little creature's expense. But now the miracle understood the "squaw" and quickly proceeded to relate in Spanish language the whole story, and said, "I am no Indian squaw, but a Mexican girl," and proceeded, "I was captured in Sonora, —two years ago by the Apaches."

This broke up all the levity toward the little skeleton and Lewis asked, "How old are you?" "I am now about fourteen and was about twelve when they caught me." "Well," prompted Lewis, "tell all about it."

This poor unfortunate girl proceeded to relate a most heart-rending tale of woe and despair in a straight forward manner that left no doubt of the truth of her statement. When she saw that her story was listened to kindly she burst into tears and proceeded with difficulty and began to show signs of being ashamed of her nude person. She said that her sister was engaged in teaching school in Sonora when she herself was captured by the Indians—that the savages starved her purposely and had always refused to allow her to go any distance away from their rancheria alone for fear that she would escape. But she said that she never intended to try to make an escape for she knew that she was too far away to ever be able to cross the desert alone. And that when she heard the loud reports of our guns she was sure that they were the arms of white people and waited purposely for the Indians to be driven away while she ran toward our party. She wept profusely when she found that she was not to be left again. She was nothing but skin and bones and thus presented a fair insight of the character and heartless cruelty of "poor Lo" whose pure and single devotion to savage rage and pitiless bloodshed is as patent in one age as another wherever he is found. This girl gave her name, but it was so long and of such a liberal mixture with Spanish that I soon lost it, and more especially because the men gave her the name of Lucy by which she was always known and addressed subsequently. "Oh hell, call her Lucy," said Gilliland.

We passed across this woodland neck and down the chaparrel ridges upon the opposite side of the dry creek without further resistance. We followed down this creek until we came to water and camped early in the evening. We never knew the extent of the damage we did the savages on the hill for there was but one of their bodies left on the ground and might have been all the harm done for aught I know. Mr. Lewis and others of the party gave Lucy some empty cotton flour sacks and a needle and thread with which to make some clothes. After eating her first hearty meal for so long a period as two years she began a dress and completed it before the camp was deserted on the following morning. She showed a handy aptness in the construction of this dress that surprised us all and when she got it on there was never a poor mortal who looked prouder and happier than this unfortunate girl.

She gained in flesh so rapidly that in two weeks she became a good looking girl and appeared to be at least forty-five years younger. The dark wrinkled skin became smooth and light, her confidence increased daily until her hearty laughs were quite interesting and amusing. Our camp duty was soon materially lightened, for Lucy's industry increased with her pride; and she kept at work about the camp as long as she could find anything to do, and she learned to speak English with amazing progress. But she still had her troubles, for she became a fine picture of despair when she thought preparations were being made for a fight with the Indians and sometimes cried with terror at the prospect of our getting whipped.

But our party altogether was too large to do good and after meeting the other wing, the whole body returned to Prescott pretty badly worn out, not accomplishing anything in the way of conquering a peace with the Indians.

The first wedding that ever took place occurred in central Arizona and in Prescott brought together in holy wedlock the two souls that constituted the family John Dixon and Mary Ehle—in which we placed Lucy for a servant girl, and a good servant she proved to be.[19]

In after years when female immigration graced the streets of Prescott City, Lucy was a grown young lady and was admitted to be as neat and as pretty as any of them, and spoke about as good English. She really grew to be handsome. She always called the party that captured her, her soldiers, and when she heard of one of them being in town, she always sought them out. Two years later I saw her waiting upon one of "her sick soldiers," and it was impossible for me to realize that she was the same little wretched and nude, wrinkled creature that I had seen in the wild woods of central Arizona. She was still at Prescott when I left the country and not one syllable have I heard of her since. But I have often in my reflections felt that if this hard and tedious expedition against the Indians was fruitless in conquering a peace, the hardships and time lost were to some extent compensated for by the timely and accidental relief of this wretched girl, whose gratitude never wore out, but was lavished upon her deliverers at every opportunity. There was a remarkable coin-

[19] Others spell Dixon's name as John H. Dickson or Dickinson. He married Mary J. Ehle on November 17, 1864, at Prescott. Swor, *Development of Prescott*, 11.

cidence with the above [which] transpired at Prescott upon our return.

At least it was nearly contemporaneous and similar in effect. A Mexican boy who had also been a captive amongst the Apaches, came into Prescott, reported his escape the night before, and proffered to go and show where the band of Indians that he escaped from had hidden their superfluous goods on Granite Creek, a few miles below the town. A party of men accompanied him and he led the way directly to the spot where they found and robbed the commissariat and returned into town with the stolen property. He appeared to be about fifteen years of age and said that he had been with the Indians for several years, and that this was the first instance of them ever allowing him to accompany them upon a raid near the settlements. This boy became also a useful hand in the first blacksmith's shop ever established in Prescott, which was owned and operated by Wm. Crump, Esqr. This boy was still working at the blacksmith's trade when I last saw him and in the same shop.

A Visit to the Mohaves with Joe Walker

NORTHWEST OF PRESCOTT about eight miles there is an imposing rocky spur lying along the west border of the grassy prairie, already described as lying north of Prescott. There is a high point in this spur called Granite Mountain.[1] There is a creek which sometimes flows along against the eastern foot of the spur, but nearly always dry. The new road established by immigration coming from California by the way of the also new town of Hardyville on the Colorado River to Prescott ran along near the foot of this spur on the edge of the grassy prairie referred to.[2]

Quite a basin which was sometimes a lake lay on the edge of the rolling prairie opposite and adjacent to Granite Mountain and extended nearly to the dry creek which ran at the foot. At the east edge of this basin or lake ran the road from Prescott

---

[1] Granite Peak is about six miles northwest of Prescott and was once called Mount Gurley for the first governor of Arizona Territory. Barnes, *Arizona Place Names*, 187.

[2] Hardyville was founded by Captain William H. Hardy as a trading post, ferry, and steamboat landing on the Colorado River 10 miles north of Fort Mohave and about 350 miles above Yuma in 1864. For many years it was the head of the steamboat transportation on the Colorado River. Lockwood, *Pioneer Days in Arizona*, 315–16; Barnes, *Arizona Place Names*, 197.

to the Colorado at Hardyville. This lake became quite a prominent place for immigration to camp upon.

Granite Mountain is one huge mass of boulders and it therefore became a prominent point from whence the Indians watched immigration. The consequence was that there were many incidents connected with this place, a few of which will be mentioned. I had previously encamped upon this little lake some time before any road ran by it and remembered that the water in it was quite deep, for I had waded into it in search of bird eggs and gathered my hat full. Although when I got out with them they proved to be unfit for food as they were nearly hatched. The birds were a kind of waterfowl called the Walloons. These were the only ones I ever saw in Arizona, and they built their nests on top of the water and tied them to a few rushes so that they could not float to the shore. The floating nests had from a dozen to eighteen eggs each in them.[3] It was to this lake that I concluded to make another visit upon my return from the last Indian campaign already related. There was a wagon train going from Prescott over that route to California, and therefore myself and a friend took passage with the train as far as the lake with the intention of returning on foot, so as to explore the country for game. We found the lake nearly dry and located it for a ranch seat and stuck up written notices to that effect, claiming one hundred and sixty acres, which more than covered the basin. This being done we started up the dry creek at the foot of the spur and searched along the route for a drink of water. We came to a place where the creek ran through a gorge which began in a low little valley farther ahead of us.

Upon descending into the little valley we noticed fresh moccasin prints and therefore became cautious. Presently we caught a glimpse of an Indian's black hair as he slid behind the rocks of a little spur that extended down from a bench on the side of Granite Mountain. We first thought that it was a raven that sailed behind the rocks. My friend J. M[iller ?] took his

[3] This was probably not a species of the loon but rather a Fulvous Tree Duck, which lays approximately this number of eggs in its nest.

stand as a sentinel while I approached the dry creek . . . in search for water. As I got pretty close to the steep wall my friend told me suddenly to "look out." Quickly casting a glance up to the bench thirty or forty feet above me I saw a smoke from which I cringed under the impulse that it was a gun just going off. But I soon discovered that it was a signal smoke which had just been so suddenly started probably by the fellow whose hair we had seen pass behind the rocks. As I backed off from it poor "Lo" stuck his head over the cliff and exclaimed as he looked down at me, "Apache-Mohave" in a low tone. I kept backing off until I was thirty yards away and to where my friend stood. We tried to coax him down by offering him tobacco. Directly we discovered another way up in the rocks among the boulders at least a hundred yards higher up. Still another stood behind a little stunted pine which grew out of a crevice in the rocks, whom I tried to show to my companion but never succeeded until he moved. This one who kindled the smoke now started down the little spur as though he would come after the tobacco, but as he passed from rock to rock he eyed us constantly and held two arrows with his bow, to show that he was ready for emergencies. He continued to thus slowly descend until a voice arose out of the side of the mountain, higher up stream, that fairly made this old range ring. This voice evidently told the fellow to stop, or at least he did stop, and refused to come any further. My friend told me that if I could see the one behind the bush to shoot at him, while he thought I was aiming at the one with the arrows in his hand. Upon raising my gun quickly he darted from the bush behind a rock as quickly as a cat could have done it. We began to think that those fellows were entertaining us, so that we would stay until the signal smoke called in a sufficient number to deal with us, and we left.

Only a few minutes was requisite to teach us that we had not left too soon, for as we ascended the bluffs that bordered the little valley toward Prescott, we saw them descend from their camp to the number of twenty or more and start for us, like a pack of hounds. We passed over the bluffs out of their sight and beat a hasty retreat and by taking a circuitous route, we eluded them entirely and arrived safely in Prescott.

A party of men started after them upon the following day and found their rancheria on the bench of the mountain, but the birds had flown. This fact now convinced me that it would be safer to return right away to the lake and build a little shanty upon the land, which I had located. This was necessary to hold my claim to the land. Pursuant to this . . . , I procured the consent of another friend to accompany me. This friend and myself started as soon as the party returned, who had gone to surprise the rancheria and failed.

Upon approaching the lake through some little arroyos from the east, we suddenly came upon a lone Indian, who when he discovered our near presence, dropped his arms &c, like they burned his finger. He came walking promptly forward as though he had important business to transact and unfolding a piece of white paper, which proved to be a fragment of an envelope, with a part of the address upon it. Doubtlessly he considered the hieroglyphics on the paper which he had picked up of some charmed importance that would protect him in emergencies. As this fellow was nearly to us, my friend of peculiar pronunciation exclaimed, "Shoot um, shoot um, d—n um, shoot um, don't wait for um to beg off."

Now it was the rigid rule all over the country to shoot these savages upon sight and I had drawn a heavy revolver for the purpose as soon as he came near me. Having the pistol in one hand, I reached to take the paper with the other and he handed it to me. I knew the pretense of handing a piece of paper was a very common trick with them by which to obtain a hearing in a close place. But as this fellow handed me the paper he accompanied the act with a remark or so in gutturals, which drew my attention to his voice, which appeared very feeble, and fine in tone. The first impulse, created by his tone, was that he was a woman. But upon looking at this fellow for a moment it was plain that he was either sick or starved nearly to death. The latter might have been the case, for when we first saw him, he was walking about kicking up the leaves under a little black walnut tree, hunting nuts.

His physical condition was a good counterpart to that of the starved girl already described, for he was a mere skeleton and had as small limbs as any I ever saw a human stand upon. He was a pitiful sight and whined like a subdued and helpless animal, as he looked from one to the other of us to detect the meaning of our conversation. J. Y[oung], my friend, who was a native of Philadelphia, insisting that poor "Lo" was only a little sick and would soon be well enough if we let him go, to kill many white men yet. I walked to where he had dropped his bow and arrows and saw that he had plenty of venison left, but it was alive with maggots and green flies. I didn't wonder at him hunting such delicacies as walnuts after an examination of his commissariat. When I returned my friend asked me if I was going to kill this specimen, to which I replied that I would not. But he insisted that it ought to be done. I insisted that if he desired to do so, his right was unobstructed, but that I had made up my mind to the effect that I could not get my own consent to kill such a looking creature as that, and this much was settled. After quite an argument over this pagan's fate I desired my friend to either kill him, or let him go at once, for the poor creature was standing impatiently awaiting the result of the pow-wow, of which he seemed to understand the purport. I at last motioned toward Granite Mountain for him to leave. He wheeled and started immediately and after going ten paces, I called to him and he quickly turned again, evidently expecting to receive a rifle ball, at the proper distance.

And then my friend also helped my fears a little by his dark prognostication as to the *finale* of our imprudent liberality. But we soon got to work, dug a little trench in the ground, and planted short poles in it, forming a little square shanty, which we covered with brush and called a house. The work of building upon this ranch was thus finished. But we concluded to dig for a drink of water in the dry bed of the lake, which was prosecuted several feet before we reached water. After thus getting a drink we left the place and arrived again in safety at Prescott. I will state here that I afterward dug a large ditch from the lake into a dry creek at the foot of Granite Mountain, by which it was kept drained until it was plowed and planted by a man by the name of Lee, who first built a substantial house at this point.[4] It was built of adobes and the Indians burned the roof off of it. I plowed a day on this original breaking of the turf on this ranch, the first work of this kind that I had done since early boyhood. My friend said upon our return to safety that we should keep our part on the Indian's life a secret if we didn't want the community to call us dupes and fools, to all of which I demurred. For all the experiences that I ever had in the wilderness this came the nearest to have been regretted. I should never have been justified in my own estimation, for killing this humble and pitiful savage, whose face and features I can yet see, and upon which the silent and helpless appeal for mercy was visibly stamped. I have lived and learned, up to the present time, that my sympathy for the unfortunate creature has rather increased instead of fading and I feel grateful for it. Upon this account, sure enough, an old gentleman took me to task for having let this Indian off with his life. He took the occasion to say that if I didn't want my "Inguns killed," that I had better keep them out of his way. I responded that there were yet very many stout and hearty "braves" in these mountains that he had never killed. He became quite angry and quickly retorted that it was only for the want of an opportunity. The old gentleman thought that a member of the original party who settled the country should have been better trained by desperate experience than this, and that the example of setting free an Indian, once in custody from such a source, was a bad one. . . .

It was only a few days after his bitter complaints of my loose conduct when he became one of four persons who had a misunderstanding with the Apaches. Northwest of Prescott about

[4] Later this was called Lee's Ranch and was a stopping place on the Prescott stage road about eleven miles from Prescott. Who Lee was, is unknown, but Orick Jackson, *White Conquest of Arizona*, 16, lists the Lee party reaching Prescott from the East in 1864. See also Hinton, *Handbook to Arizona*, Appendix, *xxviii*.

one and a half miles, a small creek runs down the edge of our woods and empties into Granite Creek below Prescott. This creek is bordered on the opposite bank from the woods by a rolling prairie. Between Prescott and this creek lays almost a solid mass of Granite boulders so that a roundabout road is the only pass between the two points. At the edge of this little prairie not far from the woodland some parties had built a log house fronting the prairie and a corral adjoining the house on the rear side in which to secure the stock that they were grazing there for different persons. It was quite a romantic situation, as it opened toward the west, prairie and all and having for a background a terribly rugged country of undulating fields of rocks, ridges, low hills, and undergrowth that extended nearly to the town. The house was new and had not one room as yet, unchinked.

Having taken a stroll down Granite Creek below Prescott, early one morning, I struck this creek and followed it up until I came to this house. I came by the corral and around to the front, for it faced up stream, and stopped at the door a moment. I saw quite a herd of horses and mules quietly grazing a few hundred paces in front of the house near the edge of the woods, and was really admiring the location for a stock-ranch. Upon stepping into the door I found the old gentleman above referred to, and two other men, all of whom I knew. . . .

Upon looking out of the door, we discovered the Apaches after the mules and horses, to the apparent number of thirty or forty. Each of us seized our guns and went out, but as we saw the main body of them coming for the house upon a full run . . . while a small party were driving off the stock we halted in the front of the door. . . . We hurled rifle balls at them, as fast as four men, with repeating rifles, could do it, and still they came, with demoniac yells, firing as they ran. But our lively work began to cool them a little and their party split into two bodies and each took a little circle around in opposite courses and closed in on each end of the house, at the same time, while two or three jumped over into the corral to shoot in through the cracks of the house from the rear side. We therefore took refuge in the house and finished the battle from the inside, mostly with six-shooters. But it took quick work and lively vigilance to watch all the cracks and dodge their lances as they were occasionally shot through the cracks. They came in earnest to take the house, but as they began to get their faces spoiled by exploding six-shooters, as they peeped in, they became more cautious and less unlucky. The old gentleman after unloading his six-shooter, reached up to one of the joists and pulled down a pair of saddle-pockets from which he drew an old fashioned wide-mouthed horse pistol loaded with buckshot, with which he blunder-bussed an Indian full in the face as he peeped in a crack from the corral. The battle was begun, fought, and ended in a very few minutes.

The savages departed leaving their dead, amounting to seven in number, and of course had more wounded than killed, and when they were all gone before we could realize their absence. We cautiously crept out and examined all around and found peace and silence, profound and perfect. The battle was over, the enemy routed, and the old gentleman had killed his Indian or two, and was therefore happy. . . . The Indians took every head of those horses and mules and made good their escape with them. They were a total loss. None of our inmates were hurt seriously in this impromptu conflict. Before I left the country this house was occupied by some Dutchmen who manufactured two neat mill-stones and placed them in running order in this house, with which they ground meal of the first crops of corn raised in the country. They turned the upper stone by hand and could grind several bushels per day. This was the first grist mill put in operation in central Arizona. All of my experience with the Indians convinced me that it was a highly colored old fable that persisted in teaching the public mind that they were a grateful people and never forgot a favor. The books and periodicals of the last decade teem with these gratuitous and fictitious representations of the character of the American Indian. They are evidently written either by blind men or an over philanthropic enthusiasm. While we are in the limits of an Indian country the only favor that we can possibly do them is to leave it. Every other act performed within their boundary for their benefit is regarded by them as our duty merely, and merely theirs to receive it, as they would any other benefit or right they claim, without thanks to anyone. He is a conceited, proud man and believes that any act of kindness toward him is simply a recognition upon the donor's part that it was due him as of right and consequently accepts it thus, without feeling under any obligation whatever for it. . . .

Although the circumstances was of a later chronology than the above incidents, I will risk giving it here and claim the liberality usually awarded digressions—by those who make them—perhaps. Provisions frequently gave out about Prescott and I accompanied Capt. Walker to a little supply post on the Colorado River about two hundred miles distant, which was newly started, and called La Paz.[5]

Upon reaching the Colorado after a two-hundred-mile wandering through crags, gorges, and chaparral, we found quite a number of supply stores and a population of white people, and greasers to the number of twenty or thirty perhaps. I saw a little light-draught steamboat here, the first I had seen for years. The Mohave Indians were seen lounging about the place night and day. Although I believe one or two of the merchants had their wives here with them, the Indian in the nude condition had the freedom of the place. They were friendly ostensibly, but not lovingly so, and were regarded by the sparse settlers with suspicion and doubt. I noticed two "bucks," so called by both men and women of Arizona, playing a singular or rather a senseless game of something, as they trotted lazily side by side for an hour or more. Each had a slender pole six or eight feet in length like

[5] La Paz was a mining town established in Yuma County in 1862 on the Colorado River about ten miles above Ehrenberg. It was probably named by Pauline Weaver, whose party discovered placer mines seven miles east of La Paz in January, 1862. By 1863 there were about 5,000 men at work in these placers, but the boom town faded quickly as the placers ran out in 1864. Hinton, *Handbook to Arizona*, 156; Barnes, *Arizona Place Names*, 238.

a fishing rod, which they would pitch little end foremost, at a small hoop eight inches or less in diameter as it rolled from them, after being tossed forward by one of them. The hoop was wrapped well with ligaments as though it was intended to last permanently and the rods were straight and neatly finished. The men wore breech-cloths merely, but the squaws wore a kind of dress made of narrow strips of cottonwood bark. The upper end of these strips, probably an inch or less in width, were fastened in a roll around the waist and hung in loose profusion and pendant to a little below the knees. This constituted all of a female's attire, and altogether the tastiest, neatest-looking style that I ever saw amongst the Indian anywhere.

The Indians here employed themselves in carrying large rolls of grass from a distance to this settlement, to sell to the passing immigration with which to feed their animals here on this desert town site. They sold each roll of grass thus brought for miles for fifty cents, which was considered cheap by strangers, who failed to find grass for their stock in any quantity whatever. One Indian came with a bundle of grass and sold it to Captain Walker, who, through mistake, gave him a twenty-dollar piece for a half-dollar in silver, the price of the grass. When the old gentleman discovered the mistake he went in quest of the "brave," whom he soon found in another trading house and asked the Indian to let him see the money which he had given him. The Mohave pulled the twenty-dollar piece out of his breech-cloth somewhere and promptly handed it to the old Captain and remarked "Me know it, too much-e—me no steal—me no want to steal." This fellow drew Capt. Walker's attention on account of speaking a little English, who now observed him a moment and queried "Is this Charley?" "Yes, yes, me am Charley." "Well, Charley, you know me." "Yes, yes, me know Capt. Walker." "Well, Charley, I thought you said that you didn't steal. I suppose you have forgotten that you and Irotaba and the black warrior and squaw stole our smoking tobacco on the night you all slipped off from us on the Haviamp about two years ago." "No, no, me no steal tobacco."

A VISIT TO THE MOHAVES WITH JOE WALKER

Charley proved to be our old interpreter, when we had attempted to make the first treaty with Irotaba and his Apache-Mohaves, when our party was alone in the wilds of central Arizona. At this date Irotaba was on his visit to Washington City, accompanied by Capt. John M[oss], while these Indians were distressed about his long absence and mistrusting that something [was] wrong about it.... The white people were continuously under apprehension, for the discontented Indians felt that their chief was gone forever and their treachery might at any time surprise this weak settlement by an uprising of the savages. I heard many expressions to the effect that some one ought to be dispatched to California to see if Irotaba had arrived and if he had, to hurry him on to his tribe.[6]

To add to the apprehension of danger, an unfortunate incident occurred while I was there. Although it was modified a little by a most amusing termination before my departure.... There was one lone and very black Negro, who had by some unaccountable and stray breeze been wafted into this inhospitable port and engaged as a *roust a bout* in the store houses. This Negro, like they are everywhere—just a Negro, improvident, happy, and free from care or consequences. This Negro, like the rest of the immigration thence, considered it a free country and, in the absence of law, exercised just such rights as he deemed his own, with but little consideration of their extent or results. He had but little respect for the savages, if any, and whilst he was annoying a small Indian boy, under the facetious impulse, thrust the small blade of a jack knife into the naked little wretch and laughed heartily over his act. The Indians at once arose in excitement and great indignation and drew off from the town, if it was a town. They were the Mohave Indians and the people of Irotaba, our old guide, whose absence was already distressing the natives as before stated, and they were only quasi-friendly at best. The people had been trying hard to pacify friends of the

---

[6] *Reports of the Commissioner of Indian Affairs, 1864*, 150–51, mentions the visit of Iretaba and Antonio Azul to Washington accompanied by Captain John Moss.

Mohaves, for some time, but they refused to overlook this breach of friendship and act of perfidy under any consideration. They wanted the Negro to put him to death. A committee of whites waited upon them in a very friendly way and informed them that it was against our laws to kill Negroes; but it was our custom to whip them.

The committee first proposed to whip the Negro for them, but the proposition was rejected promptly. After quite a pow-wow it was finally agreed that the Indians themselves should whip him until they were satisfied that he was hurt as badly as the papoose. Pursuant to this arrangement the Indians were invited to come up before the stores and get the offender. They came up, men, women, and children, all in a promiscuous crowd, and collected on the level ground, out some distance in front of the stores. The Negro now became alarmed, when he was called by some of the white men and told to step out there. But when he was formally given over to three of four savage looking old "braves," without explanation, his eyes were rivited upon the white men, with a wondrous puzzled expression. He knew something was to be done, but what is was, was the all important question, and he began to grow ashy in the face, as the Indians began to form a circle around him large enough to give a place to all of them who were present, even the children.

Two of the old warriors stepped forward into the ring with knitted brows and in a business-like way began to strip the clothes off of the Negro, with as much nonchalance as if they were ungearing a horse. The Indians all, little and big, observed the strictest decorum, for there was no laughing even by the children, who all looked on in silence. I began to think that the solemn importance of the occasion would really frighten the Negro to death, before the preliminaries were through with him. The darky made no resistance by word or action. After he was stripped they put him down upon the ground and began to tie him, hard and fast. All being thus completed, the circle of Indians joined hands and began to revolve around the Negro as a center and dance and chant with long serious faces and unearthly gutturals which brought harsh reminiscences forcibly to mind of my own entertainment by such music sung by the Apaches on a dreary and solitary occasion in the night and a night that I shall long remember. Upon a single guttural expressed by the officiator in the center, with the darky, all the chanting, dancing Indians would cease and stand deathly still, and start again by another grunt just as orderly.

This was a tremendously prodigious occasion, anyhow. Finally, after the poor Negro was nearly frightened into listless stupor, the acting "brave" was handed a bundle of good-sized switches. The weight of these scourgers rather seemed to relieve the prisoner a little, as they were not necessarily the weapons of death. The old warrior selected three from the bundle very leisurely, as though there was plenty of time, and at the end of his examination of them, without further ceremony but that of a grunt to start the dancers, commenced on the Negro, with measured strokes. The offender rolled and tumbled about the ground under the infliction, as though his life was really being taken, while the ring of Indians kept up their grunts and dancing without being guilty of grinning a single smile. The operator would occasionally stop to enjoy it. Sometimes he would cease a moment without a word to adjust his weapons. The Negro looked hard at the old warrior and as he seemed to hold his breath on one occasion, he gave way with a big boo at the old Indian, who only kept up his strokes the more regularly. After giving the darky about fifty lashes, a few of which brought blood, the old warrior ceased and expressed satisfaction in grunts, gutturals, and all other languages, and promptly unharnessed the Negro and tossed his clothes to him. He turned now to the Indians and gruntingly dismissed them, who immediately broke their orderly ranks, with shouts of laughter and frolicsome confusion, pointing their fingers with great mirth at the darky. The Negro failed to notice them as he dressed in silence, walked off, and entered a store. The Indians dispersed and that was the last heard of the boy being stabbed. But I can imagine that horror-stricken countenance of that surprised darkey is still petrified in the landscape there, as he rolled his eyes to assist a demeanor which bespoke the full and desperate consciousness of his approaching end of an ill-spent life. . . .

During the whipping of this Negro I saw quite a number of Indians at a distance, who were not prepared to go into company. They had just such white looking heads as I had often seen fleeing from our approach on very many occasions in their mountain fastnesses. These light colored, solid looking heads are the result of besmearing soft mud into the hair upon which coat after coat is put until the surface of the hair is covered and plastered over sleek. Then it is left to dry hard and when it becomes of a light color. When the hair is worn in this condition I presume as long as in the judgment of the wearer it is necessary for the destruction of the creeping, crawling, and kicking *humor* in the scalp, the clay mud is dampened and washed out again, and thus he or she becomes ready for the picnic or to receive company again. Before we got off I was again bantered by an Indian for a test shooting match between the bow and arrow on the one side and the six-shooter on the other. A small wager was put up against a piece of tobacco, as usual. The "brave" beat me all the time at short distances amid the plaudits of his friends, but when we moved the target off fifty paces he backed out of the match, this time amid the jeers of his friends, and actually became so ashamed of himself that he slunk off and failed to put in appearance again. When the Indian shoots even on unobstructed ground, he leans away over and becomes balanced upon one foot before he lets the arrow fly, thus showing that his best practice is from behind obstacles where he first conceals himself either from game or an enemy.

The old Captain and myself started for Prescott, and in the night of our first day's travel my mule broke away and left me with only my pack animal, which was loaded with supplies. It was one of the mules that we had nearly two years previously captured from the Apaches, which accounted for this Indian trick.

He kept to the trail which we were following and I was compelled to walk, which I did until noon, when we unpacked the animal at a lagoon amongst some mesquite trees to rest. Upon hastily unpacking the mule, a sharp new axe, which we had bought from the supply store on the river fell from the pack upon my instep, inflicting a dangerous and wicked wound. This was the most helpless condition imaginable to be placed in. Capt. Walker's eyes were failing so fast that he could not see far enough to hunt the mule and I couldn't walk. The wound was dressed as well as could be expected and I immediately mounted a pack mule and followed the trail rapidly for about ten miles, when I met two Mexicans with four animals, which they had stolen on the credit of the Indians, from immigrants, and were making their way through these bytrails to Sonora to sell them. They had met my mule and one of them was riding it, and I lost no time in claiming it, but they rode on and I turned into the trail behind them and followed until about dark, when I thought I was about opposite to the lagoon where I had left Capt. Walker. Here I rode up to the side of the fellow upon my mule and caught the mule's bridle, and he attempted to draw his revolver, but I had one already in my hand, and they stopped and wanted to talk it over. Thus we stood, all watching each other, for some moments, when I told them that my party of men was at the lagoon a few hundred yards away and that they would never reach Mexico with their stolen stock if in a conflict with me, one or both of them got crippled, to start on. They denied that the stock was stolen, all of which I refused to believe, and told them that I knew it to be the fact, as soon as I saw them.

The fellow dismounted upon the opposite side of the mule and I was afraid of him shooting me from behind the animal, so I vigorously jerked it back by the bridle behind me. They told me now that I had my mule and to go on yonder to my party of men. I tried to get them to go on, and they refused to budge an inch, and I was afraid to start or to turn my back upon them. I hurriedly told them if they didn't go on that I would give my party a signal to come after them. One of them told me to do it and suffixed the injunction with an oath. I kept my eye upon the worst looking of them and fired my revolver off toward where Capt. Walker was, one shot. Capt. Walker, believing it to be me and that I was lost, quickly answered my shot by discharging his pistol. This convinced them that I was no imposter and they turned their horses about and left instantly. They evidently wanted my mule badly and intended to have it, but they knew it to be true that they had too much desert country to pass over to run any great risk of being wounded even if they didn't get killed in a conflict over one mule.

I soon arrived in camp and found Captain Walker, who said he thought it strange that I would get lost so near and in sight of the mesquite trees. I told him that I was compelled to play the bluff on the Mexicans and his timely shot was all that saved me. He was agreeably surprised at my early and speedy return, for I had taken provisions with me and a blanket so that I was prepared to follow the mule until I did find it.

Capt. Walker, who was my friend in fact as well as in name, afterward told me that this little incident had caused him more trouble for a short time than any other one had for years. To send me upon so uncertain an errand with such an ugly wound to start with and yet unable to go himself, he considered a very unsatisfactory state of affairs. But necessity is inexorable and the future, unfathomable. This was the kindest man I ever knew, considering the desperate chances which he had been constantly taking for thirty years amongst the savages, burning deserts, and bleak snow of the Rocky Mountains. But, however, we continued our tedious way back to Prescott and my wounded foot gave much trouble and apprehension of unlucky results, but came all right in the end. Soon after this Capt. Walker returned to California and I never saw him again. His eyes failed entirely and I learned not long afterward by indirect information that he was dead.[7] I was with him two years of his last explorations of our mountain country under the most desperate hardship and

[7] Joe Walker reputedly left Arizona in 1867, returning to California, where he spent the remainder of his life. He died October 27, 1876, at the home of his nephew, James Walker, and was buried at Alhambra, California. Watson, *West Wind*, 106–109.

still I could never see any change in him. Always cool, firm, and dignified.

I never heard him tell any wonderful story. He was too reticent about his certainly bleak and wild experiences and he was never given to saying foolish things under any circumstance. Brave, truthful, he was as kindly as a child, yet occasionally he was even austere. I was but a boy and he kept me out of dangerous places without letting me know it or even know how it was done. He is now gone and it may be that I should say but little of him. . . . But knowing him as I did and under constant and the severest tests, from the moment that I first saw him upon overtaking his party, to the last time I ever saw him still in the wilderness of Arizona, I feel constrained to say that he was very nearly the best friend I ever had and certainly as true and by nature as well fitted for that delicate and pure relationship as any man.

I fully confess my weakness, if weakness it is, to the effect that my greatest concern is the fear that his character will never be known as well as it ought to be. His services have been great and unostentatious, unremunerated and but little understood. Modesty was his greatest fault. . . .

In a few days after returning to Prescott I was riding through the woods west of the town one morning and met quite a number of mounted men, among whom there was a number of our old party. Upon learning that their destination was Lynx Creek, I turned back with them. They were taking this circuitous route to make a general survey of the character of the country. The party moved on in single file through the rolling woodland region quite leisurely. At a point about two and a half miles west of town the party surprised an Indian, who was doubtlessly a spy and who had been posted in that locality. He sprang from a clump of rocks and darted into a little hollow like a wild animal and meandered the gorges about three hundred paces through the woods from us and began to cut all sorts of antics at us. He applied the Spanish language to his numerous epithets, one of which he called us a herd of she-goats, then he would pucker his mouth, howl, slap his lips rapidly with the palm of his hand, producing a loud quivering sound. Restless impudence seemed to be the height of his energetic impulses. But as the party leisurely kept on this course, quietly observing his fun, crossing little ridges, and their intermediate hollows on the unbroken single file, poor "Lo" failed to notice that two of the party stopped in a little hollow and fell back down stream to meander to his position the same way he did himself. I stood sentinel at the mouth of this hollow, while S[am] C. M[iller] dismounted and stole up the ravine to a position nearly opposite to the Indian and peered over the brow of the ridge and found the unconscious savage within twenty steps, looking after the moving party, gesticulating all sorts of meanness. A deliberate shot from M[iller]'s rifle surprised the poor fellow so greatly that he ran, yelling vociferously, for a hundred paces, when he fell and expired. . . .

We turned our course and bisected the Hassayampa at the old camp and corral and thence up stream to its head and passed over the mountain range and down upon the waters of Lynx Creek to the mining settlements and halted and scattered, each going his own way, to attend to his own affairs. Myself and friend of the old party from Louisiana followed down the creek a few miles toward the edge of the woods to obtain some venison, as the deer had been pretty well frightened away from the vicinity of the mining camps, and our supply was out. When we came to a selected place for a temporary camp at which we left our pack animal, and necessaries, we separated and each took his own course to search for a deer or other wild game, alone. It was late in the afternoon while I was quietly following along the side of a long, low, chaparral ridge probably a hundred paces from the top, when I heard the sharp crack of a rifle upon the ridge, followed by the half-surprised whine and hoarse growl of a grizzly bear. I immediately turned directly up the hill toward the locality and when I arrived upon the top of the ridge, where the noise proceeded from, I found everything quiet and silent. I became suspicious that I had mistaken the shot of an Indian

Courtesy Sharlot Hall Museum, Prescott, Arizona

Ed Peck, who fought Indians for his gold.

for that of my friend and began to believe that the savage or savages had concealed themselves near about me. All of this was quickly considered and feeling that I had been probably entrapped (for an Indian can mimic a bear to perfection) I sprang into a clump of rocks near by.

But just at the moment I glanced toward the woods from whence the ridge emanated, and saw my friend on a full run approaching the woods and occasionally glancing back. I arose and stood upon the rocks so that he could see me, which he did and hurried back and showed me where the bear had been engaged in digging up a yellow jacket's nest. There was a flat bone clinging to some flesh hanging upon the weeds where the ball had left it, showing that bruin has been pretty badly wounded before he retreated one direction, leaving his assailant to take the other, both of which seemed to have been promptly done immediately upon the discharge of the rifle. We trailed the bear by its blood until about dark and into a jungle where we could not venture, especially at that time of day, and therefore we deserted the chase and returned to the mining camp with only a small venison.

I have often wondered why there were no squirrels in Arizona. If I ever saw one during an experience of over four years there, I have now no recollection of it. But they would have to burrow in the ground or rocks like some of them do in Colorado, and I presume that all the cavities in Arizona are in the possession of rattlesnakes, centipedes, and tarantulas. We became industrious and began to delve into the bed of the creek for gold and succeeded about like miners usually do. Enough gold would be found in one day to encourage us to continuous efforts from day to day and to inspire a hope that was never realized. Men thus dug, delved, and labored from day to day to find a fortune, by mere chance.

This was about the state of affairs when one morning early a couple of miners arrived from the Big Bug District just over the mountain five miles east of us, learning the tiding that one hundred Indians had just before daylight corralled six men in their close quarters and still had them surrounded and would succeed in taking them if they failed to get speedy assistance. About fifteen miners crawled out of their respective pits and were strung out on the double-quick in less than twenty minutes, bound for Big Bug. This small party crossed the range nearly at the edge of woods toward the north. This circuitous route was taken with the view of having the benefit of a concealment, so as to surprise the savages. As soon as we were across the range we could easily see the little ridge in the low country upon the opposite side of which the six men were housed in an excavation on the hillside, about eight square feet. They had been engaged in sinking a shaft to a quartz vein and had cut this little pit into the side of the ridge for the express purpose for which they were now using it. But they had failed to cover it securely and the Indians threw heavy stones from the upper side of the hill upon it to break it in, in such profusion that the men were compelled to take the little poles composing their "bunk," with which to prop up the weak roof. There was a house built of logs down at the creek about a quarter of a mile away, but they had no opportunity of escape to it. When our party came to within two hundred paces of the ridge, its members promptly formed into line and thus pushed rapidly to the top of the ridge and halted. We could look down upon the rock-laden roof of the cellar-like room in the hillside, but could see no living thing nor hear anything. We saw a smoke arising from the chaparral down the ridge a few hundred yards. The men kept their places and in readiness, while two of them were detailed to examine the premises. They soon found an Indian lying dead just below the cellar, with a bullet hole at the corner of his mouth.

The platform and windlass used for drawing dirt and stone out of the shaft were thrown down into it and the large rope which was used upon the windlass was cut into short pieces with the axe which lay near by the fragments scattered about the ground. The little underground house was deserted. We made our way to the cabin on the creek and found on the route where a portion of the savages had been concealed to cut off the escape of the men in case they attempted to reach the cabin. It was from this cabin that the two men escaped to bring the alarm over the range to the miners on Lynx Creek. Upon our arrival at the cabin we found the men all safe in it. They told us that they had not been in this cabin five minutes before they saw our party arranged along upon the ridge overlooking the quarters which they had just left. The savages had seen that relief was near at hand and departed hence. They succeeded in killing five of the Indians. The one below the house caught the bullet at the corner of his mouth from a half-ounce rifle while attempting to look up the hill into the front of this little establishment. There was some little dead oak chaparral thrown upon his head, together with his bow and arrows (which were broken), and fired. But the fire had gone out without consuming the wood or body. I noticed that it had melted some of the beads upon the neck, the balance of which were taken off. I have now one of them, but I am unable to determine the nature of the material of which it is composed. We visited the smoke on the ridge, previously referred to, and found that it came from the fire that burned their dead. And just here I made a discovery, for which I cannot account and therefore cannot relate it with any degree of satisfaction to the incredulous minds now so abundant in the land, for fear of being charged with imposition. But, however, I shall relate it and whosoever charges to read it may make out of it just what suits them the best. Upon scratching in the ashes of this fire the carbon of the consumed bones and a few small fragments of them charred were found. The heart only was found whole and soft, and from which the blood trickled. In short, the whole body was consumed while the heart did not even appear to have been cooked in the ordinary acceptation of that term. The victim must have fallen early in the action, for the men said that the smoke had been arising from that spot continuously since daylight.

The savages had been flustrated to begin with by a small puppy, which some of the men were rearing for a watch dog. When they retired to bed on that night, some of them took their quarters under an old wagon sheet which had been previously stretched across a pile as a substitute for a tent outside of the little excavation. The savages at the break of day were stealthily crawling to this tent, when they aroused the puppy that gave the alarm. The savages immediately fired upon the tent, riddling it with bullets, all of which passed harmlessly above the sleepers and only served to awaken and hurry them quickly into safety. They fired too prematurely to effect much, but if they had waited until the men were aroused the same volley would have killed all four of them who were sleeping in the tent.

But repairs were made and safety again established, at least for a short time, and our party took its leave for Lynx Creek and the six beseiged men remained at this post, determined to prosecute their work and did it. The mine proved rich and a quartz mill was built upon it. The wolves ate the dead brave, whom his friends could not get to cremate, and I saw tufts of his long hair lying about the place six months afterward, while passing that way. The Apaches' superstition forbids him ever touching or otherwise attending to one of their dead who fell in battle and remained in the enemy's line long enough for the enemy to have possession of the body. They never return to the field to obtain the bodies while the battle is in progress.

The fine and fertile valley situated twenty miles west of Prescott and known as "Skull Valley," took its name from the abundance of human bones scattered about it, when our party first saw it.[8] While lying under a shady tree in that valley I used a human skull for a pillow for some time before I noticed what it was. After looking about a little I saw a little pyramid built of them. Doubtlessly this profusion of human bones lying upon

---

[8] Various explanations for the name of Skull Valley exist. Barnes, *Arizona Place Names*, 410, approves the tradition which has Major E. B. Willis naming the site following a skirmish between United States troops and Mohaves and Tonto Apaches. Skull Valley could also have achieved its name for skulls found there during 1863–64, the remains of some intertribal battle. The main road from Prescott to Ehrenberg ran through Skull Valley, where at least fifty white men were killed during the early Indian conflicts. Patrick Hamilton, *The Resources of Arizona*, 387.

the top of the ground was the result of superstition. It was only a few days after our return from assisting the men on Big Bug, when I was asked to go back again and a little beyond toward the Agua Frio to assist in gathering up the scraps, the remains of Leroy Jay, one of my acquaintances, who had been slaughtered over there on a trail. We went and found his body and that of another man, literally cut to pieces. Their moustaches were picked with the lip and all, as it had been trimmed from off the teeth. Their arms and fingers were cut off and they were really disjointed all over. Seventeen arrows were sticking into one of the trunks. They were otherwise mutilated in a manner too shocking to relate. I only mention this case in particular, because I knew one of the men. But there were many such cases coming under my personal observation, which I will not speak of for want of space and very many others which I know of, but never saw, that cannot be mentioned for the same reason. Then there were again many such incidents and calamities of this nature, whose victims' names have escaped me, leaving only the time and locality where they were perpetrated. . . . After burying all of these two men that we could find, five of our number rode on to the Agua Frio and encamped for the night a few hundred yards above the fall. Just above the fall the country is open and there was a large tract of level, grassy soil where Lynx Creek circled around and spread over the country and about where it loses itself and irrigates and keeps moist a large tract of arable land. At the lower edge of this tract it pitches off into a deep gorge, and thus the water from it course through the narrow gorge, which really is the beginning of the Agua Frio and which opens below and again forms into a gorge. It will be remembered that this creek had been before spoken of as coursing down deep through a level table land covered with grass and volcanic rocks. This cut is the second gorge below the fall and indeed this fall is the abrupt beginning of the Agua Frio.

There was no settlement about this place upon the evening we encamped there. It was very windy that night and we cut small brush enough to build a half-circle around our little camp to break the western winds a little during the night. We were encamped just at the mouth of a dry, flat little valley that headed west of us in the rolling chaparral hills. There was no timber near, but over on the east side of Agua Frio stood a high chaparral mountain fortified upon the summit. This mountain stood against the creek and was high enough to frown down upon the surrounding country. We slept in peace and picketed our animals near a little knoll which stood by the foothills between the little valley and the main creek early at daylight on the following morning to graze, while we ate breakfast. As I had completed my morning's meal I left the rest of the men and stepped out of the little brush corral and very naturally cast a glance toward the horses. I looked just in time to see an Indian shoot an arrow from behind the knoll at my horse, which caused the affrighted animal to pull up his picket pin and flee up the little valley, dragging the long rope with the picket pin bounding hither and thither after him.

The first chaparral reached, the picket pin became fast in it and thus stopped the horse securely. The Indian also ran parallel with the animal's course and kept out of sight behind the ridge bordering the south side of the little valley until the horse stopped, when he ran over the ridge and down into the valley and caught it. But when I saw the beginnings of the rascal's operations I gave the alarm, caught my gun, and followed the horse at my best speed, and was within less than a hundred and fifty paces of the naked wretch, when he darted down the hill to the horse. I well knew that no one could ever ride that horse without a saddle and that it might have been a peculiar notion of that animal, but it was nevertheless true. I had seen it tried and the contrary brute would risk breaking its own neck first. So I kept running to get as near as possible as the savage could not lead the animal off as fast as I could travel, and I knew that he would always keep the horse between me and himself, at least until I could pass the animal. The horse baffled every attempt of the savage made to mount him, and he saw that I was coming pretty close and he left the horse and fled, keeping the horse between us. I never halted a moment until I passed the horse. Then I stopped and leveled my gun and "poor Lo" leaped a zig-zag line and baffled every effort to catch a sight upon him. I lowered my gun and ran again until he began to travel straight when I suddenly halted and tried again to get a sight upon him, but he zig-zagged it again and baffled me again. I was becoming tired so that I could hardly hold up my gun upon a level at all. But I tried it a third and fourth time by running each time to get him, leveled down to a straight line before trying to catch a sight upon him. It was all in vain for he at last got into the thick chaparral and escaped without a scratch and without even being fired at. I had run too far to begin with, but this was the cunningest rascal that I ever met. He was as naked as the day he was born and had not even a breech-cloth. I could not conceive what he did with his bow and arrows, but he had left them on the route somewhere. The other men were following but they never did catch up. I went leisurely back and when I came up to my horse, it was standing with one fore foot a little raised. Upon examining for the cause, I found a very small wound high upon the shoulder. It looked as though it had been made by a small knife-thrust. The blood trickled from it very sparingly, and I thought no more of it, thinking that it was made by the arrow, which the savage shot to stampede the horses at the beginning.

I led the horse back to camp by the picket rope and on getting ready to start in the afternoon he was too lame to travel at all. We laid over until morning on account of it, but instead of improving the animal laid down and refused to get up. We laid over until the following morning and he died. Then I wanted that Indian worse than ever and would have freely given my horse for him. That was the second time "poor Lo" had relieved me of my riding horse and I began to resolve to never excuse another one of them under any circumstances. I told Capt. Walker about it and he laughed and said that it was an old trick of the Indians to stab a horse high up where the shoulder blade was thin and easily cut through, when they wanted to kill him. The inflammation sets in behind the bone, and it can never be gotten into the exact position that it was, when the wound was inflicted, so it is thus closed effectually and is certain death. He told me of another trick that the Indians had successfully practiced upon the soldiery in the early contests upon the frontier. He said that when the soldiers were in pursuit and began to press the savages too closely, one of them would slip stealthily in amongst the horses after dark, pat, caress, and quiet their fears until he succeeded in putting a few fine shots into the ears of each horse. The horses would shake their heads in vain for relief while their owners were ignorant of the cause and could not get the shots out if they were not and hence the horses would die in numbers. He wound up the explanation by saying that that was the only use that the savages had for the fine shot that they captured.

While at this point I will state that long after this date, K. S. Woolsey claimed and located the arable land above described and built upon it a substantial dwelling. He also erected an over-shot water-wheel fifty feet in diameter at the fall below the house in Agua Frio to which he attached a quartz mill of nine stamps, and again subsequently attached a grist mill to the same machinery. The stones used in this grist mill were the first ever imported into central Arizona. This became a prominent point and many conflicts with the Indians occurred at and in its vicinity. It was about twenty-five miles around the plain to Prescott from this point of the Agua Frio along an old Indian trail, which was continued to be used by the white man. An amusing little incident occurred at this mill, which was long after I had the race with the Indian for taking my horse. I accompanied an acquaintance to this mill, which had not been running for some time, and was taken care of by some persons who lived there. Upon our arrival we found a Dutchman in charge and his associates had deserted him and had not been heard of for several days and he thought that they had become victims of the Apaches.

We took dinner with him and after it was over we proposed to hunt a deer for supper. I had on this occasion a double-barrelled shotgun charged with buckshot, and therefore left it with the Dutchman and borrowed his rifle to go hunting with. Myself and friend loitered through the chaparral hills east of the Agua Frio half of the evening and became tired of it, and on returning toward the mill we came upon top of the high peak overlooking it, above spoken of has having been fortified. We sat around amongst the old ruins I presume something after the manner of Gaius Marius amongst those of Carthage (of course) and saw no enemy. We enjoyed the inspiration of triumphal possession by thus associating our bilious appetites with the monstrous achievement which culminated the catastrophe. Upon ascending the ladder to headquarters we saw a host of shadowy victors, and "smote them with our eyes," like Romans of the first water.... But in midst of thus concocting a scheme for imaginary glory, a charge of buckshot came whistling about us, *spatting* the rocks and singing above the old fortifications, wickedly. Before we could draw a good breath and get back into the ordinary affairs of life again, another similar charge came likewise, only that two of the buckshot whistled through my friend's vestments, while one only struck my gun stock. These two shots came quick—one after the other, and were followed by the reports of the gun, bang, bang! down at the mill. The Dutchman had seen us on the old ruins and thought we were Apaches and proceeded to use my own gun upon us. We quickly vanished like our ghostly victors behind the rocks and dismissed all of our poetical considerations, to let the Dutchman know that the battle had long since been over and the fort in ruins. After testing the capacity of our pistols for long ranges by shooting at a little bush a few hundred yards across the Agua Frio, we descended the mountain to the mill and found the Dutchman still mad for having frightened him into war measures.

Upon being shown the bullet holes in my comrade's clothes, he said, "I don't gif a tam ef I kill you both; does tam Indians come dare effery dime I here alone and I got to choot efferybody dat go dare." We succeeded in getting our host into a good humor, and departed for a temporary encampment near the foot of the range westward, where we arrived and remained over night.

On the following morning some of the inmates of this camp took my gun off on a short hunting tour, but I mounted a mule and started around the edge of the plain bordering the woods on the north armed with my brace of six-shooters only. It was a distance of over twenty miles to Prescott; my destination and my mule became worried a little. There is an impassable reef of rocks stretching across this prairie about five miles below Prescott and crossing Granite Creek at right angles. The reef terminates in a point west of the creek in a rolling chaparral country. Through the scattering rocks in a little basin at this terminus, the road passed. This place became known as "The Point of Rocks," and a famous point for being attacked by the Apaches.[9] On my trip to Prescott on this occasion I came through this treacherous gap and when I came to about the middle of it, my mule suddenly halted, giving a short vigorous snort, and stubbornly refused to proceed for some moments. In my alarm I raised my pistol above my head, for I didn't know from which side to expect an attack, and kicked my mule vigorously to stir him into action again. But mule-like, he took his time for starting, but went rapidly after getting his machinery off the center. Upon reaching an elevation twenty paces away from this trap I halted, turned broadside, and took a good survey of the surroundings and the closest scrutiny failed to detect the movement of a single thing. False alarm, was my final determination, and I rode on. But upon reaching a distance of two hundred paces and out of sight of this point, I heard the rapid explosion of fire arms back there, and halted again. Presently I saw a man coming on horseback at the top of his speed, who only checked up a little, when he saw me waiting for him. It proved to be an acquaintance by the name of Johnson. His first observation was, "Did I see any Indians as I passed through the Point of Rocks?" to which of course I gave a negative answer. "Why," he said in

[9] The Point of Rocks referred to here is about ten miles north of Prescott in Yavapai County. Barnes, *Arizona Place Names*, 341.

surprise, "I saw several slipping farther back into the rocks, and we fired several shots apiece at each other." This was true and Johnson killed one of them, whose bones from some cause or other were left to bleach in the weather and in the sun up to the time I left the country. He couldn't imagine why the savage failed to shoot at me, while they were so prompt in firing at him. I charged that it was because he was riding a horse and I came near convincing him of such a probability by citing the fact that my mule had stopped and dared them to shoot, when he knew that they were present and stood stubbornly until he backed them down.

But the Indian is a very suspicious man and the only explanation for his conduct upon this occasion may be found at the bottom of that fact. They probably prepared the ambush for me because they could see my approach for a mile, and as they aways have a previous understanding, so that they can all shoot together and thus make sure of their game, it is almost certain that the action of the mule and my sudden demonstration with the pistol confused their signal. . . . After I had passed out of reach they concluded to steal further back into the rocks where they could look out for another opportunity; when Johnson unexpectedly came along, having emerged from a trail into the road and discovered them moving away. Thus being discovered, their plans of concealment were at an end and they boldly fired upon him with the above results. A horse, when frightened, will flee, but it seems to take a mule a week to lay out his plans when once he finds himself in danger, and if much frightened, will plant himself to stay. Therefore, the man who rides a mule into danger and expects that mule to do anything but the opposite of what is desired, he will be as badly mistaken as the Negro who went to sleep on one and was thrown into the dust and left. . . .

In the fall of this year of 1864, I took occasion to again visit Walnut Grove, previously referred to on the Hassayampa below the Tanks. Just above it there were about a half-dozen men encamped from whence they prospected the surrounding country for gold. While I was at their camp, a young man by the name of Harvey Twaddle, who claimed to be a native of South Hanover, Indiana, being one of their number, went to hunt their two mules which seemed to have strayed away out of sight.

Upon striking their footprints he followed the tracks for some miles and found them browsing quietly amongst some chaparral and large rocks. He approached within twenty paces of the animals, when an Indian fired at him from behind a rock in the chaparral and missed him. Harvey immediately raised his gun and thus hurrying the savage, who had resorted to his quiver for an arrow, and shot the same instant that Harvey did. He killed the Indian dead and the arrow struck him immediately over the heart and penetrated. Now the first thing a man invariably does when shot with an arrow is to pull it out or to break it off. Harvey pulled this arrow out and threw it down, to attend to some other savages who were also shooting at him. One of them mounted one of the mules to escape, but upon receiving a ball from Harvey's repeating rifle, he too fell off of the mule on his way to his "happy hunting ground." After wounding a third, he started the mules homeward and picked up the arrow that had wounded him. He frightened the mules into a run and followed them by running himself. As he went along he examined the arrow and discovered that it had no flint point on it and never did have, so he felt that the flint point had not pulled off and remained in the wound as they usually do. The Indians carry some of the arrows in their quivers for shooting rabbits and other small game and these they never point with flint, but just sharpen the shaft to a point and harden it in the fire. This savage was pressed too closely to select his arrow and he happened to get one which was not pointed for shooting large game. However, Twaddle came with the mules to camp, but he was entirely unconscious and showed that his acts were all mechanical and only laid down his gun and took off his six-shooters as a matter of habit.

He was evidently wild and delirious and looked strangely about, and spoke to no one. The men took charge of him and found the wound over the heart and that it was the only one. The wounded man made no resistance nor explanation and everything that was done, had necessarily to be guessed at.

Everything that could be suggested was done by the party and all other passers-by during the night. He kept unconscious all night, but wide awake. On the following morning he became conscious and as clear headed as he ever was, and quietly told all about his adventure, even to the most minute detail, and in a few hours became unconscious and lingered along toward evening and died. Some fellow on the order of Robt. Burn's doctor, opened his chest and found that the arrow had cut the outer coating of his heart merely.

Harvey as before stated was a native of South Hanover, Indiana, where this humble recorder had spent many happy days at school. I wrote letters there, detailing the unhappy fate of Twaddle, but never received any reply. He was buried at Walnut Grove as decently as circumstances would permit. . . .

The Perils of Prospecting

THE SCARCITY OF BIRDS in Arizona has been previously remarked, but I remember of having seen a humming-bird near the Pima Village in Arizona in the fall of 1863. I discovered its nest built upon a leaning willow which was nearly horizontal over the water in the Rio Gila. This nest had four tiny white eggs in it and was the first and only one I ever saw. I also remember of having seen two or more mockingbirds in central Arizona the following year. One of them was on Date Creek forty or fifty miles west of present Prescott City. . . .[1] There was only two of us who had previously deserted the main exploring party in order to return to the Prescott by way of Antelope Hill diggings 80 miles distant.[2] We expected to encamp at a ranch recently located and established on or near the head of Date Creek by some Mexicans. Upon arriving there as

---

[1] The source of Date Greek rises on the west side of the Weaver Mountains in Yavapai County and is a tributary of the Santa Maria River. Barnes, *Arizona Place Names*, 122.

[2] The Antelope Diggings were in the vicinity of Antelope Peak in the Weaver Mining District on the north side of Weaver Creek about twenty-five miles southwest of Prescott. Hinton, *Handbook to Arizona*, 97–98; Barnes, *Arizona Place Names*, 19.

THE PERILS OF PROSPECTING

the sun was setting, we found that the inmates had all been massacred the day before by the Apaches and the log cabin plundered. The night was coming on and we were compelled to halt until morning....

We awoke on the following morning and our bird departed first, but we lost no time in leaving the melancholy place. As we departed, we saw some mountain goats on a low rocky ridge overlooking the narrow valley, but passed on our way without halting, and arrived at Antelope Hill Diggings just in time to see some men bring to their camp the mangled body of an Irishman whom everybody called Tommy. I had seen Tommy alive but should never have recognized this mutilated form as his. He and a friend by the name of Roberts, it seemed, had gone a half-mile from the camp to cut grass for their animals and the savages fired upon them and shot the Irishman down, and Roberts, being very fleet of foot, made his escape by running.

This was the only escape ever made about these early settlements by sheer speed, and this was said to be quite a miracle and would have failed had the distance been a trifle greater. We continued our journey on to Prescott, with a little fear and trepidation, and camped at Smith's ranch below the town site. This was still the headquarters of this section, where strangers could be daily seen and the most of whom left their animals in the care of the ranchmen here. This was in the fall of 1864, and campfires were built under some pines near the ranch cabin, around which many stragglers were seated upon the ground. Night cast her shades on the country and the campfires looked cheerful. Quite a discussion was going on about the peculiar talents of the Indian. One man wanted to know why an Indian could so thoroughly mimic an owl or a wolf as to deceive the most experienced mountain man. Another wanted to know why a wolf could and frequently would mimic an Indian so nearly that a white man was always in doubt as to which it was.

Some pretended to know and some had no idea at all about it. Now and then they would compare opinions and listen to the distant war-whoops to settle them. For the Apaches were making night hideous west of the ranch, which appeared to be a half-mile or more away.

One war-whoop after another would die out, with a peculiar guttural finish, more like an animal than man, and frequently with the tone of the wolf. Then the speculating exchange of views would begin again and be renewed upon every burst of savage music in the adjacent country which finally ceased at a late hour. It was finally agreed that all of us should sleep around the corral for fear that an attack would be made at daylight, as the Apaches appeared to be unusually restless. In the midst of this discussion a storm of voices suddenly broke loose out in the dark, fifty or a hundred paces away, sufficient to stampede a mule itself. Such another scattering of men from around the fire would never occur in a briefer space of time—an explosion of artillery could not have been more sudden and unexpected. The surprise was complete. It proved to be a serenade of a band of wolves, and judging from their tones, there must have been amongst them quite a number of all ages, sizes, and conditions. . . .

The winter of 1864 now began to set in and the Apaches began to increase their desperate warfare by every effort possible.[8] Again and again men organized in bodies of from twenty-five to a hundred to chastise them into peace. Upon reaching their strong-holds, they would scatter so that they could not be found. Then they would follow the party back to the settlements where they would rob a ranch, murder straggling miners, and plunder the country, through which they would sweep like a hurricane and escape eastward into the heart of their wild country and scatter the stock thus taken, into so many localities that it did no good to follow them. One party of white men organized and obtained the services of a Maricopa Indian (whose tribe are neighbors of the Pimas) as a guide. We gave this fellow the name of Jack and a good guide he proved to be, faithful to every trust;

[8] Although the Apaches continued to attack the miners about Prescott, it is apparent that their raids were in addition to attacks by the Colorado River Indians, such as the Hualapais and Yavapais. Lockwood, *Apache Indians*, 156–57; *Report of the Commissioner of Indian Affairs, 1865*, 128 ff.

he looked upon everything the white man told him to do as right of course. Jack knew exactly where to find the Apaches, who were the ancient and mortal enemies of his tribe and also of the Pimas. The Pimas have a tradition handed down from their ancestry, which makes it an imperative duty to go at least once a year on the war party against the Apaches.

A party of about forty-five men from the different mining camps came together and started with Jack as the guide. Several days were passed in reaching the San Francisco River, during which we saw signal smokes all about the country, showing that the wily Apaches were not asleep.[4] We passed through a large rancheria which showed recent signs of occupation. Jack thought that they had deserted it upon our approach. But there was one circumstance which served to deceive their own friends, and one another, as to what kind of an enemy they had to deal with. We reached a kind of open plain and saw a finely armed and mounted band of Indians in the distance emerge from some rough hills and stop. There seemed to be a hundred of them. We concluded they were Navajos and prepared to receive them. They were a very dangerous and bold enemy during the early settlement of Arizona. They seemed to be feeling their cautious way up the brow of a chaparral ridge and very slowly. Finally they halted and sent a rider forward, who dashed confidently up to us and stated that he was a Pima and that the band we saw were Pimas and Maricopas on the warpath after the Apaches, and that they desired to join us to fight the common enemy. He was told to bring up his warriors, which was soon done. They came up and recognized some of us as having been at the Pima Village and therefore the utmost confidence was immediately established. Doubtless the Apaches had misunderstood their own signals, as there were two parties coming from different directions after them.

We told them to lead the way and we would follow, and the

---

[4] Conner here is probably referring to the Verde River again. Although directions were never given by Conner, there also is the possibility that the parties traversed the area between the Salt and Gila rivers.

first rancheria sought was surprised and cleared out quickly. Our party took the gap which the enemy were likely to retreat through and thus took the bulk of the burden, while our allies brought up the rear on the hillside and cut off retreat over the mountain. We thus came to the close quarters near the gap where the principal part of the destructon took place. The Pimas and Maricopas were afraid to come far to the front, mistrusting that our men might mistake them for Apaches. But when the battle began to wax warm and earnest our allies acted right bravely, but their war-whoops commingled with the shooting was the most important part of their work.

Their howls were quite sufficient to frighten the Apaches out of their wits, especially when connected with heavy rifles, and such assistance as our party were able and willing to give them. The battle ended and the enemy was badly defeated, with a serious loss, and all that could get away of course left as soon as possible. Now it is not my purpose to give the details of all the skirmishes we had in the company with these Indians against the Apaches, for that properly belongs to the province of history. It is considered sufficient merely to give the characteristic outlines of the raid. We were together for a week, during which time we destroyed three very considerable rancherias and several lesser ones. After this battle was over I noticed our allies going around killing the wounded and all that we could say failed to deter them from their joyful pastime. It was their custom, handed down from their ancestry, and it must be done, and they did it in the most shocking manner. They would raise a stone that they could scarcely carry above their heads and totter under it until they could get astride of a wounded, fallen foe, then hold hard and steady look down into the victim's face and begin with "You stealum Americana's *mula*, Pimas papoose &c; *pickimi pi yah.*" Upon the last syllable expressed with a strong emphasis, the stone would descend with a crash and crush the poor creatures head to atoms. Some of them would take pains to provide a good flat stone upon which to pillow the head of the unfortunate enemy so as to make a splendid job of it, and smash the skull and brains to smithereens.

I saw these barbarous friends of ours thus smash Apache heads until I was heartily sick of their enthusiastic brutality.... I never have fully justified myself in my own estimation for even being compelled to recognize the wicked and vicious bloodthirsty conduct of my friends the Pimas and Maricopas on the occasion above referred to.... As stated, the Pimas were our allies and friends but they would cut off a victim's hand, punch a hole through it, and hang it at their girdle with as much apparent warmth of appreciation and satisfaction as a school girl displays over a fresh-culled bouquet.

And I was perfectly conscious of the truth that a very slight change or places might be all that was necessary to induce them to take off mine, to put to the same ornamental use, with equally as great satisfaction. Yet I saw some men look on full of satisfaction, like the fabled god of wickedness infinitely higher in rank, or lower ... than any member of the royal family of satan claiming a name on earth or in this country. For savage civilized men are the most monstrous of all monsters. I saw a deal of this delicate pastime before I was done with this party and became gratified when it was over and I got back to the settlements. I mentally resolved never to go on the war party again with this sort of soldiery, however greatly the Apaches needed scourging. I took up my residence on Lynx Creek in the mines on my return, but many other parties sent after the Indians took Jack for a guide. He gained quite a reputation for bravery amongst his own people and the everlasting hatred of the Apaches, who could have made a fine roast of him if they could have only caught him.

After accompanying all of the expeditions which went for a while, Jack was sent to Lynx Creek in charge of a gentleman to me, to see him safely through the mines on his way home to his people. The miners mostly knew him by reputation, but personally they did not know him from an Apache. I started with him up the creek and I was annoyed greatly by men getting out of their pits to kill Jack, swearing that no prisoners should be made of an Apache. Jack observed this vigorous displeasure with quite a concerned countenance occasionally. We passed them all, however, in safety and followed Lynx Creek to its head and on the ridges beyond. After cautioning him to avoid all the creeks and all white men to whom he could not identify himself, I left him to look out for himself. He was an athletic young fellow and tolerably black. He became the idol of his tribe for having been selected by the "pale faces" for a guide. He had one hundred and fifty miles to go alone through the Apache country before reaching his people on the Gila, but he succeeded in arriving in safety at the Pima Village.[5] He bade me an affectionate farewell, because he remembered that I was looking on at some of his most wonderful feats of smashing Apache heads, after they were wounded to helplessness. I turned back to Lynx Creek and never saw our guide again.

Lynx Creek was now becoming deserted because of the failure of the surface diggings there. The miners also began to find better mines on different creeks at a distance. In short, the population began to spread over a larger scope of country, prospecting for both placer diggings and quartz mines. This pulling up of the Lynx Creek miners soon left the stream marked by a string of old deserted cabins along the creek for the distance of three or four miles. I don't believe the Apaches ever approached the old cabins after their desertion, for reasons if they had any, which were only known to themselves. I believe a Georgian and two or three others were about the last to leave it for newly discovered diggings. But they first undertook to stay alone and work a quartz mine which was on a hill overlooking the creek but one morning P[?], the Georgian, walked up the hill to the mine alone and was ambushed and shot down by two or three rifle balls passing through him, so they were compelled to leave. This left the creek again to its silent wilderness and calm, for

[5] Here Conner's distances are too great. If Jack followed the Hassayampa, the distances would have been close to 120 miles, and if he took a more direct route, it would have been about 80 miles.

many months and until quartz mines were sought nearly altogether. The Hassayampa in the vicinity of our old camp and corral was also deserted for months at a time and was only known to be inhabited occasionally by straggling new comers who would take temporary quarters in the old deserted cabin along the creek, while engaged in prospecting the neighboring hills for quartz mines. On one of those occasions I was with a party of three or four persons engaged in the same pursuit. The cabins roofs were badly out of repair and it rained continuously for three or four days, and I started for Prescott alone, wet, and sleepy. Before I was half way, what was subsequently known as Groom's Dale, an Indian snapped his gun at me and it failed to fire.[6]

Owing to the rain he was discouraged as well as myself, and however many there may have been of them, they made no further effort and allowed men to walk backward for fifty paces without ever budging out of the reef of rocks where they were concealed. I traveled briskly on and pretty soon met two acquaintances who warned me that the woods were full of Indians and that traveling alone was bad business. But while I was relating to them the above fact, to caution them, a frightened deer came dashing toward us from the suspicious direction, watching backward until it came within ten paces of us, standing in plain view. This convinced us that the savages were in sneaking pursuit and the miners turned back with me and we all proceeded to town together. The Apache does love to shoot a "pale face" from a concealed place, but he will not risk an open combat for small stakes. Upon our arrival in Prescott we saw twelve or fifteen Mexican soldiers who volunteered in the United States army and who had just fled from an encounter with the Apaches at Skull Valley, twenty miles west of Prescott. They were escorting a ten-mule team which was being driven by Joseph F[?], a mere boy. It seemed that the Indians had attacked the team and

[6] "Groomdale" was about eight miles south of Prescott, being named after R. W. Groom who surveyed the townsite of Prescott, discovered the Sterling mine near Prescott, and served in the Arizona Territorial legislatures. Barnes, *Arizona Place Names*, 192.

soldiers just as they arose out of the valley on to the highlands of rolling chaparral country and at the first volley, one soldier fell and the remainder stampeded without halting until they arrived in Prescott with wonderful stories of the destruction of wagons, goods, and all.

They were speedily reinforced and the cavalcade arrived at the scene of action in due time and found Joe in amongst the dead mules, safe and sound. It appeared that when the attack was begun the driver sprang from his wagon, ran to the leading mules of the team, and led them around and back to the foremost wheel of the wagon, and there secured them strong and fast. After this was done, he hurried in amongst his mules with his arms, and by keeping thus concealed, he successfully defended himself and the load of goods until the arrival of assistance. The savages shot the mules down, but the plucky driver still took shelter behind their carcasses, from whence he dealt death of several of his assailants before they deserted the contest upon the approach of aid. The new road laid out to La Paz on the Colorado ran through Skull Valley and this team had brought the goods from the former place. The Apaches subsequently halted two or three wagons loaded with supplies in this valley. The escort was weak and agreed to give them a certain amount of provisions to spare them. But in the meantime they sent runners to the settlements for assistance, which was speedily sent. A party of citizen soldiers surrounded them and killed over forty of their number before they were enabled to escape. Their bones lay scattered about the valley when I left the country, thus strengthening the expressive name of Skull Valley.[7]

It is said that this battle was directed upon the part of the savages by a white man—then a little distance in the hills overlooking the valley. And this man, whose name was known, was said to have had a hand in the famous "Mountain Meadows Massacre," in Utah.[8] But it is certain that I saw a man and be-

[7] See footnote 8, Chapter VIII, above.

[8] The Mountain Meadows Massacre took place on September 11, 1857, when 140 emigrants from Arkansas and Missouri were attacked in southern Utah by Indians and Mormons, who killed all but seventeen children of the party. John D.

came acquainted with him, who claimed to have lived with the Indians and I presume according to his own word that he actually wore the breech-cloth and ate horse flesh with them. In my opinion this man did have something to do with this Indian war and should have been held accountable for his savage cruelty. I saw an Irishman with them on one occasion and he looked funny enough, with his breech-cloth barely large enough for a papoose and long, red hair streaming in the wind. His sun burned red hide looked as rough and scaly as if he had had the leprosy and I thought that he needed killing much worse than old Irotaba, with whom he was keeping company. I will merely mention one important fact here without explanation, or attempt at one, which probably had more to do with the continuous efforts of the savages than was supposed. That is, that there were men roaming these wilds who stripped and went naked with them awhile and then dressed themselves and deported themselves like civilized people awhile.

A few days after the attack on the soldiers and the teamster, I joined a little party to go and examine the country on and about the Verde River. This river heads about twenty or twenty-five miles north of Prescott and abruptly pitches into a gorge from off of a valley like the Agua Frio. This gorge divides the plain from the mountains, which are distinctly visible from Prescott. The first encampment of the United States troops was located about half a mile above the beginning of this gorge, which it will be remembered by the reader of these notes, was called Ft. Whipple, previously to the removal of the military post nearer town. The gorge continues rough, craggy, and abrupt for quite a distance, when it debouches into a respectable looking stream with small valleys here and there along its course.[9]

It was probably five or ten miles below this rough beginning

Lee led the Mormon militia in this attack, and after confessing participation as leader, he was executed March 23, 1877, by a firing squad at the site of the massacre. Lee, while avoiding authorities, lived with the Indians in northern Arizona. Juanita Brooks, *The Mountain Meadows Massacre*, 48, 151; Wyllys, *Arizona*, 216.

[9] Conner correctly places the Verde River here, but, as seen in previous notes, confuses it with the San Francisco River.

of a river where our little party of six souls intersected it. After wandering around the adjacent hills and through their rugged defiles for a day or two, we started up stream. We saw no signs of the wily savage anywhere and therefore felt easy and contented. After spending the afternoon replenishing our commissariat with fresh venison, we encamped in the midst of a little treeless valley on the river bottom near a place where the meandering stream had cut straight across the valley nearly from hill to hill. Our camp was on clear ground about midway between the rock foothills on the one side and the creek bank on the other. We had Munk with us. Munk was a famous hunting dog for large game and very reliable and as black as a Negro and a native of Prescott. . . . He growled about camp and complained throughout the night. There was evidently something wrong and it was therefore determined to arise early on the approach of daylight, in order to get to die standing, as it was said that Caesar ought to have done. Accordingly, one of the party arose before it was entirely light and struck a fire with some slight fuel prepared the evening before. Pretty soon all of the party crawled out of their blankets and went to the fire to stand and comment upon Munk's fretful attitude, who was still sullenly standing around with his bristles raised and continued to do so until broad daylight. With all of this warning we were surprised at last, for a volley from rifles flashed from the rocks in the foothills, to which our attention was drawn just in time to receive another volley at right angles with the line of the first, from a point under the creek bank.

All transpiring in the twinkling of an eye. Some of the savages, thinking that we were going to stampede, which would have been fatal, sprang out of the creek upon the level ground, ready for the expectant race, when a volley from our crowd killed two of them too dead to fight more. When they caught the idea that we were going to stay, they quickly took shelter again and kept quiet for a few moments. A boyish young fellow of our party had left his brace of revolvers lying on his blankets and quickly leaped out of his bed a little distance to get them, when an Indian sprang from behind his rock and knelt on one knee, rested his elbow upon the other and took a fair shot at Johny, as he was familiarly called, and missed. He sprang back to us in great mirth, like it tickled him to be shot at. One of our men was severely wounded, but one of them only slightly. We were thus disabled so that we had to stay and do the best we could. But presently one "brave" concluded to make a bold run across the level bottom from one of their regiments to the other, and a volley from our camp killed him deader than Hector before he got halfway. Notwithstanding this dangerous proximity, G. S[wain] of our party ran through a storm of bullets to the body of the fallen savage, robbed it of some trinkets, and brought the scalp of "poor Lo" back with him, in the face of the attacking parties, some of whom were shooting at him all the while.

His clothes had several bullet holes in them but no drop of blood was drawn to pay the penalty of the reckless venture. I will venture to say that this Indian was killed, robbed, and scalped in less number of minutes than any other had ever been in the Rocky Mountains. After a few more random shots were fired, the savages disappeared as stealthily as they came, leaving us to enjoy our wounds and their defeat.

H. C[?] was worse wounded than any of the rest; one ball having passed through his thigh above the knee and another ball from the other party passed at right angles to the first, about an inch above the other wound through the thigh, while a third passed through his wrist. The skirt of his coat was riddled. He thus drew the greater part of the fire, because of having on a fanciful, nicety, buckskin suit fringed with strings and trimmed around and about with beaver fur and the enemy thought that he was the "big chief" of the party. George Adams, the next seriously wounded, had a wicked wound through the side of the leg above the ankle. This man and a friend subsequently became engaged with the savages and were both killed, but it was supposed that he killed himself with his last charge when he found himself overpowered, to escape being burned at the stake. He was found sitting behind a little temporary fortification which he had built of loose stones as he fought, with a bullet hole in his forehead.

This accounted for the Indians deserting his body without mutilating or disturbing it. They had been after the savages with a party of men, which they left and concluded to return to their camp and met a body of the Indians following the party that they had just deserted, resulting as above. The bands of them that fired upon us on this occasion, shot too low, for their bullets cut the surface of the ground at our feet like hail and bounded past. We were compelled to desert our deer and use our pack animals for the conveyance of our wounded to Prescott, which we succeeded in doing in safety. G. Swain, who took the scalp so quickly, was also subsequently killed by the Apaches, and his body was horribly mutilated. But that scalp had fallen into someone's hands who tacked it on the outside and the center of the printing office door in Prescott, where it remained with its long black hair streaming down as long as I remained in the country. G. G[?] at the same time obtained from the body of that savage a small silver canteen finely finished, most like the result of pillaging and murdering some Mexican nabob, who used these pocket canteens in which to carry smoking tobacco with which to make cigarettes. The printing office door referred to, belonged to the office of the *Arizona Miner,* the first newspaper ever published in Arizona. Mr. Bently was the superintendent and publisher and came hither with the press in the company of the officials who came to establish a Territorial Government for Arizona. Mr. B[ently] in a conflict with the Apaches received a severe wound from which he subsequently died, leaving the paper to be conducted by J. M. Esq. [?], who was still publishing it when I left the country. The *Arizona Miner* became a substantial factor in aid of permanent settlements in central Arizona.[10]

[10] Originally this paper was owned by Richard C. McCormick, the first secretary of state and the third governor of Arizona Territory, and edited by T. A. Hand. The first issue of the *Arizona Miner* appeared March 9, 1864, but it was not

THE PERILS OF PROSPECTING

It was during the winter months of this year [1864] that city life in Prescott became irksome after our little breeze before mentioned, and I found myself in Big Bug District again. Upon learning that a new party would start in a few days to hunt better diggings across Agua Frio, I concluded to accompany it. There was absolutely no employment but that of mining, prospecting, and fighting Indians. I learned that a friend whom I desired to go if I did myself, in company with others, would pass by the old camps on Lynx Creek en route for Turkey Creek, and I concluded to cross the range of mountains lying between and cut him off. I left the camp on Big Bug bright and early. I took it afoot because of the rugged trail across the mountain and was soon meandering the serpentine path amongst the lofty crags of the mountain side. Upon arriving on top, the trail wound its way through the woods on a gradual and easy descent. Whilst I was thus tripping my lonely way through the woods at a lively gait, a glance ahead halted me as suddenly as if I had been shot at. I looked again and again to assure myself that I was not mistaken. The more I looked and thought the more I felt panic stricken. But I could not be mistaken; there they were; a pair of old shoes which had been carefully placed side by side as if put there by the painstaking care of an old antiquated compounder of water-gruel and catnip tea before retiring to bed. But why become frightened at a pair of old shoes sitting in the trail was the question.

The answer would force itself on my reflections to the effect, that shoes were an exceedingly scarce article in central Arizona, and it was plain that no sane man would ever throw aside as good a pair as these in that country, for they appeared to be sound at a distance, but I didn't approach them. I still stood fearfully agitated and was really afraid to move, as I glanced hastily and repeatedly at all available places there, for ambushing the trail. I absolutely refused to believe that those shoes

---

the first paper ever published in Arizona, for that distinction belongs to *The Weekly Arizonian* of Tubac, which appeared in March, 1859. Lockwood, *Pioneer Days in Arizona*, 345, 348.

were put there for other purpose than for me or someone else to be shot, while examining them. I was equally confident that the real owner had gone on to his happy hunting ground or to some other friendly port.

But what bothered me worse was my singular nervous condition, for I never before had experienced such a trepidation and I felt suddenly helpless. I thought that I must be sick and felt that I was surely lost if I should be attacked under such a spell. I acknowledged to myself that I was totally unfit for self-defense and so forcibly was I thus impressed that I determined not to invite attack by passing those old shoes until I got over my nervousness, if it took me a week. So I stepped out of the trail and took my seat upon an old log, wondering what was the matter with me for my usual lively confidence was totally gone and I was ready to surrender then and there. I must have remained seated upon this log for a half-hour before I began to feel that my own arms were effective too. But finally I felt myself growing into myself again and I boldly arose and circled around the old shoes and went my way cautiously until I was out of sight of the ghastly objects. I came to a deep ravine in the woods and descended it to get a drink of water, but just as I laid down my gun a limb fell off a tree near by and I snatched my gun up and sprang out of there on short notice, without my drink, and never ventured back again. I missed the connection by this delay, for the fresh tracks of horses showed that the men had passed on and I returned to Big Bug over another point of the range in feverish condition. Of all my experiences in the Rocky Mountains, this one incident caused me more fear and trepidation than all the rest put together and puzzled me until I told everybody I met about it, some of whom tried to convince me that I was sick, but I felt that my health was good. But not long afterward I had a terrible spell of fever. This strange and unaccountable disability, however, left me entirely and I proceeded with the party across the Agua Frio in quest of employment and forgot all about the old shoes. But still there was never any doubt in my mind about the fate of the owner of the shoes nor any doubt of the presence of savages when I left them.

There was about twenty-five of our party on this occasion and we found gold in small quantities in several of the tributaries of the Agua Frio on its east side, but none in sufficient quantities to justify a halt and thorough test. The portion of country not covered by chaparral was composed of rocks and cliffs of every shape, character, and position. The country was really worthless for everything except for mineral, if there was any in it. In traversing a gorge-like cañon with high rough cliffs, we came to an Indian rancheria. At first we thought that there was nobody at home, but on a more thorough examination we found that we were mistaken. Some of the boys peered into a horizontal crevasse about five feet from the ground and in the rugged craggy wall of the cliff and discovered three little black, naked brats about a foot and a half long and hauled them out, like pulling rabbits from a hollow log, by the hind legs. Someone called out that the carrion crows had flown, but left their nest of young ones. These poor, friendless creatures were as naked just exactly as they were when born, and looked as expressionless as so much stone. They would not attempt to move a muscle, but just remained in the position that they were last turned, perfectly still. Their nest of grass, leaves, and sticks were just such a lair as any other brute would be likely to provide for its young and precious offspring. We would motion like slapping them in the face without any effect whatever, they would never bat an eye. They made no noise or exertion whatever until we put them to the front of the crack in the cliff and then they crawled into the nest and sidled around so that they could see out at us. They seemed to know when we were done with them, and settled down silently into the leaves like they were when we found them. It was quite cold, but they didn't seem to mind it and creeped back into the rocks without a shiver. I have seen very many papooses and have seen them under very different circumstances, but I never saw one cry. I don't know whether they can or do shed tears or not, but I will venture to say if they do, it is very seldom. The eyes of these children were as motionless as their bodies. . . . We left those creatures of the wilderness to enjoy in the name of Heaven all that could be found about the bleak and dreary place to live for. Yet we were ready to kill the old rats at a moment's notice and would do it if possible, and what then would become of these three helpless, diminutive cubs. They would perish like other animals in the same situation.

When we left this place I felt that we ought to leave the country and them to the God who made them and leave them immediately. It appeared to be a wild, serious and sad situation for the human form. Piteous strife and melancholy submission to its cruel results seemed of more consideration than the country they inhabited. . . .

Seeing these children reminded me of previously witnessing some citizens and soldiers fire upon an old squaw with a child on her back, in the distance, not knowing that it was a squaw. Upon approaching the body it was found that the ball that killed the squaw broke the papoose's leg and the men killed it to put it out of its misery. Another occasion offered nearly the same disgusting spectacle at a different time. A squaw was killed while running with the child upon her back and the ball that killed her wounded the child's leg and someone in the party took charge of it and took it to Prescott and placed it in charge of a kindly wife of an immigrant, A. G. Dunn, who was raising it when I left the country. It was a little girl and it would sit upon the floor in the position the lady put it, all day, and until it was removed by her. This child was like the rest of their kind. I never heard it cry at any time although I saw it frequently.

But the worst case of brutality occurring up to 1864 was the act of one of a party in taking off the scalp of an old gray-headed squaw after she had been killed by himself. This fellow speedily became the subject of a drumhead court martial, but was excused after he was found to be a demented specimen of humanity, and had been treated for insanity, but he was never afterward permitted to take part in the raids after the Indians. We turned back toward the Agua Frio under the impression that there was no gold in this volcanic, black, basaltic-looking land. But we found on reaching the crossing that we had quite an army of "braves" handing upon our rear, to guide into the settlements. Their signal smokes were becoming monstrously common and we also ceased to pay any attention to them. We made our way back to the Big Bug and remained in camp a few days and looked at the snow fall in the woods on the high ranges while we were observing it from the locality of sunshine. One morning R. Snow (who was subsequently killed by the Apaches) and myself, passed over the range by the locality where I became so frightened at the old shoes and encamped on Lynx Creek in an old deserted cabin alone. The next morning we concluded to continue our journey over the next range on to the head of the Hassayampa and thence down that stream past our old camp and corral to the edge of the woods and prospect for quartz. When we started up the steep mountain out of Lynx Creek, it was snowing furiously.

We had but one animal upon which all of our stores and bedding were packed. After a hard struggle up the hill through the increasing depth of snow, we arrived upon top and found the snow falling so thick and fast that we could not see ten paces ahead. We kept the direction confidently and began the descent in good spirits, down, down, and continuously down a steep hollow which we had no doubt of being one of the heading cañons of the Hassayampa. Then the snow's depth upon the ground gradually and materially lessened the fatigue of wading through this pure element.

We came to where the water was rippling and only a little farther and found a well-known landmark which convinced us that we were again on Lynx Creek and but a little distance about our late point of departure. This was discouraging to say the least of it, but we proceeded without delay to our original point of departure and again energetically renewed our efforts to ascend the snowy mountain and in very few places found our tracks on the original ascent. A second time our arrival upon top of the mountain was accomplished and still confident that we could walk right on down the opposite side on to the waters of the Hassayampa we pushed on through the blinding snow and followed the same treacherous gorge down the wrong side of Lynx Creek again. My now thoroughly disgusted comrade peevishly exclaimed that a member of the Walker Party ought to be able to find the way over this range to the Hassayampa blindfolded. This stirred up my conceit a little and I insisted that we could go, snow or no snow. My friend suggested that we had better stay for the night in an old deserted cabin not far away and try the ascent on the following morning, when perhaps the snow would have ceased to fall so densely. I persisted that the snow was already deep enough upon the top of the mountain and it might become impassable. We started again to wearily climb this treacherous old range and again after a long and worrying struggle reached the top, pretty well worn out, horse and all. Night was approaching and the snow still falling and loading down the boughs of the tall pines heavily and shutting off the power of sight nearly completely. We ventured another start down the mountain but had gone but a little way when we straggled into the boughs of a fallen tree and it became so dark while making exertions to extricate ourselves that we unpacked the horse and hitched him to one of the boughs and built a fire. We had the remnant of an old wagon sheet which we used for covering the pack and which we now stretched over a horizontal bough for a tent. We laid down quite a comfortable bed under this tent at the entrance of which was located the fire. My comrade proposed to have a cup of coffee as we had some of that article with us, already parched, and he agreed to make the coffee if I would melt snow enough in a quart tin cup (which served us as a coffee pot) from which to get the water. It was a long tedious task, but nearly a quart of water was obtained from the snow and my friend proceeded to make the coffee.

But he could find no rocks for the deep snow and darkness,

Courtesy Sharlot Hall Museum, Prescott, Arizona

Governor Richard C. McCormick, friend of the miners.

with which to crack the grains of the coffee and he therefore became impatient and put the grains into the water hole, and boiled the ingredient thoroughly and then sat the cup off the fire for the contents to become cool enough to drink. The coffee even failed to stain the water, for which my friend could not account and he therefore gave it another boiling, all of which resulted about the same and therefore making coffee without breaking the grains was abandoned as a waste of time and talents. My companion, however, consoled himself for the disappointment by the gratifying triumph of doubling the amount of coffee by the process, for he said that each grain had swollen to twice its original size, all of which he dried again for subsequent use.

We retired to sleep and awoke on the morning of the brightest of days. We crawled out of our low and completely snowed in tent and found ourselves still on the top of the mountains, where we could see a world of wonderfully broken and snow shrouded country, picturesque, bleak, and bright. Habitless lands of the Montezumas! ...

Myself and friend descended the mountain to the Hassayampa and followed it to where it leaves the woods and meanders the chaparral country. Just at the great bend below the woods we encamped and were not there but a few days before we had the company of two others who came to search for quartz lodes. We united our forces and built a log cabin on an island in the creek, or rather a sand bar, for our mutual protection. We spent weeks here without molestation from the Indians. The snow never fell deep here and generally left the ground rapidly, especially as the springtime was approaching. It was within about five miles of Prescott, but we seldom ever saw anyone except our own household. Prospecting (so called) is the miner's holiday in the Rocky Mountains; and if he fails to find a good lode for a certainty, he easily consoles himself by locating and claiming two or three at a venture and then considers them rich, which answers all purposes anyhow, for he would have to wait for capitalists to come and buy them or assist in opening them, whether rich or worthless. The simple process of locating can be easier understood by giving one of the notices of claiming possession in full, which is written, folded, and placed in a little pyramid of rocks built upon the place of discovery to attract attention and show that the ledge had been claimed. Although these notices vary frequently in their wording, they usually serve their purpose. I find two of these documents now in my possession, the true copy of one of which is in the following words and characters, to wit:

TERRITORY OF ARIZONA

   WALKER'S QUARTZ MINING DISTRICT

    Recorders Office
            March 12th 1866
This is to certify that M. P. Parsons, J. J. Bachas, and Dan Ellington are the owners of (800) Eight hundred feet in the lode known as the "Rough and Ready" lode in this district.
          J. J. Bachas, 300 feet

The same being recorded in book No. 2 (two) Page 91 of the records of this district. April 26th 1866 at 2 o'clock P.M.
          F. D. Cole, Recorder.

 This notice is copied by the claimant when he located the claim and presents the copy to the Recorder, who makes the above entry and the work is done, after paying the usual fee therefore.

 When a prospector fails to find a lode to this claim, he saves his time by hunting game. Thousands of men roam over one year's end to another, thus in search of an accidental fortune. They struggle over hundreds of miles of craggy mountains, each year for many years, passing their lives with tenacious patience and fortitude, determined to have a fortune or nothing. . . . Nine out of every ten who assume the role of prospectors and are industrious and tenacious of purpose, are doomed to this nomadic wandering just so long as their physical manhood will endure it and a result of poverty as a finale. They finally end with a deep consciousness of having been the victims of the profitless though hardest struggles and hardships experienced in this life. A deceptive train of imaginary probabilities is constantly flowing through the brain of the prospector, by which he is seduced into abandoning the usual arts of peace, ease, and comfort and the finer impulses of useful citizenship. It was into this profession that our party of four concluded to plunge on the waters of the Hassayampa and for the prosecution of which we built a cabin on the sand bar. We succeeded in finding one lode and succeeded in making it cost some capitalists quite a fortune to convince us that it was worthless.[11] They sunk a shaft upon it subsequently to the depth of a hundred feet and went to enormous expense of erecting a fine quartz mill thereon, and by dint of expending much money and doing a world of work, succeeded in proving that the mine was not worth the paper upon which the fact of its existence was recorded. But however, we are not that far along, for we had not been here two weeks when the lode was found and it was many months before the mighty work began. . . .

I heard that there was a prospecting party on Turkey Creek about thirty miles away, and I determined to take the short route thither by way of the head of Lynx Creek. I had previously obtained my mule from a ranch, where it was being cared for. I was ready to start on the morning of the slight snow referred to. I mounted and took my route up the creek which lay in the bed of the stream nearly up to the edge of the woods. The creek bottom was covered with boulders, amongst which the water was standing partially concealed by the snow. My mule blundered through the snow-capped boulders until I feared that he would fall and I therefore dismounted and led the way, stepping from one boulder to another. I continued to slip off of the boulders into the water until I became quite wet

[11] In the *Organization of the Walker Mining District*, 102, 151, several lode claims made by Conner are recorded under the name of D. Ellis. On December 8, 1864, Conner, J. Young, and E. B. Bradford claimed eight hundred feet of the Big Bug Lode in the Walker Mining District.

before reaching *terra firma* at the edge of the woods, where I mounted and went my lonely and tedious way. This wetting of my feet I believe to have culminated the sickness which probably made its first step on the occasion of seeing the old shoes in the trail and which resulted in the most desperate experience I ever had in the mountains. I rode on, following the course of the Hassayampa up stream nearly to the divide between it and Lynx Creek.

Upon arriving on the top of this range I again felt the same old symptoms of trepidations felt on the occasion of discovering the shoes, but not near to the same extent. On descending the mountain toward Lynx Creek I became deathly sick and delirious and I halted for the purpose of lying under a tree. It was a hard struggle that reason had to overcome my inclination to dismount and had I have done so the fatal result would have only been a question of time. I rode with difficulty and had just memory enough barely to know that direction through the woods to an old deserted cabin near the head of Lynx Creek, where I directed my way until I came to it, dismounted, hitched my mule to a tree before the door, took off my saddle, blankets &c, entered it, and lay down.

With my saddle for a pillow and a pair of blankets spread out upon the split slab floor for my bed, I put in the day. Night came and the morning followed without finding me in any better condition. At intervals my reason fled and on its return, I only felt listless, stupid, and happy. To get my consent to move became a hard struggle. I alternately dreamed and awoke all day. And at each time I awoke I thought of the mule standing hitched to the tree for so long without food and each time mentally resolved to get up and turn it loose to browse, but postponed it continuously until the darkness of another day warned me of the length of time I had been there. I arose and slipped the bridle from the mule's head and returned to my couch. I now regretted exceedingly that I had not gone on or returned at all hazards. But I could not remember distinctly; how hard it was to think, for when I forgot about the cabin, even while en route to it, I would frequently have to arouse myself up with desperate energy to remember where I was going. But I was located and there was no helping the matter. There was a little ditch of water passing the door, it having been turned out of the creek the year before for mining purposes. For several days I would make tea in a quart cup and mix a little *pinole* in the water for food, but all to no benefit, for I was bound to be sick and gave up all other considerations.

Ten days passed and the killing effects of a high fever of the intermittent character bent all of its malignant energies upon me with an effect truly horrible. I wondered in desperate despair if no one was ever again going to pass that locality. I tried to keep the number of days that I was there, by marking on the floor with my sheath knife. On one occasion while attempting to make the mark, being delirious and partially demented, I seized one of my six-shooters, which was lying in reach, and raked it on the floor and discharged it some way. The report of the pistol brought me to my senses and I instantly knew what I had attempted to do, and laid the pistol back and took the knife to make the mark, as usual. The fever resolved itself into a regular and orderly tormentor. For nearly two weeks my head was perfectly clear early in the morning, after which it gradually grew dizzy until unconsciousness was complete and I could know nothing more until the afternoon, when I came conscious under a full perspiration toward the last. My mental faculties would become cloudless in the afternoon and remain so until all the excruciating pains I ever felt in all my bones had exhausted themselves, and punished me into a frightful and exhausted sleep. Day after day did this frightful condition last until about twelve days had passed, at which time I had thus been prostrated a little over twenty days. Conscious in the morning, lost in oblivion until the afternoon, then become conscious again, only to be punished into sleep by the most cruel and constant infliction I ever experienced. . . .

In a few days more I began to get hungry and ate my *pinole* with a relish. I even became stout enough during the following week to venture out of the house with a pistol to shoot a bird. But I didn't go further than ten paces before the exertion overcame me and I sat on a log and became so faint that I began to fear that I could not get into the cabin again. I slipped off of the log onto the ground and leaned back against it and wished in vain that I was only back in the cabin. It was some time before I got back, but I did and the trip out of it and back only served to discourage me again, for I thought that I should not be able to walk soon. This was a case in which the disease was worn out and defeated without medicine or any assistance whatever. I don't know the exact number of days that I was prostrated thus in this old cabin, I know that it was over thirty-five days and know that it was not forty. . . .

On my last day alone I was lying on my side quietly looking out of the door (for it had no shutter) at the bright sun of a pretty spring morning, when I heard the sounds of horse's feet, I thought. I held my breath to listen and could not be mistaken. It was surely the footstep of an animal approaching nearer and nearer. I reached for a six-shooter and lay still in the same position.

Presently a mule passed the door with a deer tied on it across the saddle. It was being followed by a man whose familiar face I knew at a glance, and who stopped, turned to the door with his rifle on his shoulder, laid his hand on the logs of the door, and put one foot on the door sill.

He stood thus and looked at me in silence for several moments, as I, too, lay quietly without saying a word. "The Lord J— C—t," he drawled out slowly and at full length. He wanted to know if I had been "here" alone every since I had been missing. Upon being informed that it was quite probable, he said that my mule had been found about twenty miles below on Lynx Creek by some prospectors and taken to Prescott a month since and that I was reputed to have been massacred.

He threw off his deer, broiled some of it for me, and mounted the mule and left for Prescott and never stopped traveling until he returned with a companion after me. It was fifteen miles to

THE PERILS OF PROSPECTING

Prescott, making a round trip thirty. After having proper nourishment I rapidly regained sufficient strength to ride a mule, which I did in a few days and arrived safely once more to the settlements. I presume most all Arizonians know E. G. Peck, if he is still alive, and many remember him if he is dead. He was the man who thus came to my final assistance and who, when I last saw him, was a guide for the United States troops in that country.[12] The one who came with him was J. B. Slack, who was afterward a member of the Arizona legislature, and has since been prominently known in the Atlantic states. It is more than useless to express any obligations here toward these two men. . . . The mountain fever (so called) was my disease, and I have thus said so much of it to give those who may read this, an idea of its character from a personal experience, and the trials which may prove to be of some benefit to those who may read and understand for themselves. . . .

[12] Edmond G. Peck was listed as twenty-nine years of age, a native of Canada in the *1864 Census of Arizona,* 169–70.

The Fight at Battle Flat

THE SPRING OF this year [1865] opened up with many stirring events. I neglected to say that a steam sawmill had been established on Granite Creek about a mile above Prescott in the woods, by Lount, Norris & Co., the first ever brought to the country, and it furnished lumber with which to build up the town rapidly. Planks took the place of split boards of which the first house ever built of framework order, was weatherboarded. It was built and boarded with split boards of four feet in length by Bowers and Co., and was located on Granite Street in Prescott. The Legislature had convened the fall previously on Sept. 26th and adjourned Nov. 10th, a little over one year from the discovery of the country by the Walker Party. I neglected to state that after the first legislature of Arizona adjourned on the said 10th day of Nov. 1864, and the members thereof adjourned to the Governor's Mansion for refreshment, that a third house convened in the huge old State House, by the people. They kept up the revel all night and laid the Governor's two houses in the shade for frolic and fun. They ridiculed the pretended authority of the Governor and Legislature by passing many bills in an orderly manner, upon which fine speeches were made in profusion.

One old dissipated fellow whom they called Tat offered a resolution upon which he made a furious speech. "What," he says, "do these two houses of the Governor mean, by *Bill Engrassments*. Do they want the laws written in Spanish? Bill Engrassment! That sounds like Mexican. I wonder," he says "where they git em! Do they come in boxes or bottles? Tell me, Mr. Speaker, for I want to know." Tat was here interrupted with, "Take him out, take him out." The old fellow turned and pointed his finger warningly toward the lobby and exclaimed, "Be quiet thar, be quiet I tell you, for the gentleman from *Sonoma* will be heard, and yer had better keep quiet thar, if ye don't want to hear the harmonious click of a six-shooter." They all kept "quiet thar" until Tat exhausted himself and sat down. This third house, as it was called, adjourned about daylight.

As an illustration of the reckless character displayed in the settlement of this country, I will mention here a subsequent circumstance. Tat, whose speech (I presume was taken from an incident in a California Legislature) is partially reported above, took occasion to drop into a drinking saloon to steam up a little. As the bartender placed before him a tumbler and a bottle, two soldiers stepped in for the same purpose. Tat was just ready to drink, but pushed his glass back and looked at the soldiers in affected surprise and remarked that he never drank at the same bar with "Niggers." One of the soldiers replied that they were not Negroes, but as white as anybody. Tat, without further parley demanded that they go to the foot of the counter, and pull off their hats and drink like "Niggers all ought to do." They still gave no attention, but proceeded to drink or motioned that way. Tat repeated his demand with a warning not to trifle with him. The soldiers still paid no heed to him, and he drew a heavy pistol and shot one of them dead on the spot. The other escaped by running. Tat left and I heard nothing from him for a long time. But when I did hear of him again, it was when he was found shot to death in the vicinity of Tucson, Arizona. It was believed that the soldiery killed him but no inquiries were ever made about the matter any farther than was dictated by curiosity. Thus ended the famous speaker of the third house of the First Legislature of Arizona. . . .

Prescott had a town site but no town by a large majority. But as stated the winter of 1864 gave a decided impetus to city improvements. Drinking saloons, the first enterprises to flourish in new mining settlements, soon outnumbered all other establishments and soon became very popular, although their first stock in trade was made from imported drugs from which experts compounded all varieties of chained lightning, which quite frequently broke its thongs to signal a storm under a clear sky. At first they were the most expensive and capacious buildings erected in Prescott. All other sorts of necessary buildings, however, arose rapidly.

One of the first was a hotel built of logs erected by a man by the name of Orsburn, who brought his family with him, consisting of his wife and three daughters.[1] They were the first white females to arrive in central Arizona. The family of Mr. Ehle were the second. That of Mr. Roundtree were the third, and perhaps the family of Mr. Banghart was the fourth.

This was the beginning of the female population, but the spring and summer of 1865 it was very materially increased by other arrivals of the fair sex.

But all the time that the town was increasing both in population and residences so rapidly, there were miners in the different camps of the country at distances of five to thirty miles, who were not about Prescott once in six months, although it became the central depot for supplies. Men coming from a distance were frequently surprised to see a town where they had left their horses in the care of ranchmen on Granite Creek. It was just such an instance of surprise that "Buckskin Smith" enjoyed after a long absence. . . .

Smith was the same stout, noisy, and rollicking rough everywhere he was found, and he came walking down Granite Street

[1] The name of the individual in question here was John P. Osburn.

in Prescott one morning in a great humor. He declared that he began to believe he was entering San Francisco and made many burlesquing inquiries about where to find the theatre, and that hotel and the Academy of Music &c. He was unshaven—wore moccasins and a full dress of his own style, made of buckskin, rawhide &c. Heavily armed, he wore a bullet-pouch the size of a hunter's game bag. . . .

But it was not long [until] it was not so rare a sight to see a lady on the streets of Prescott. Even ball rooms were prepared before the year was out and the arts of Terpsichore were cultivated extensively. But there was a great drawback for the want of ball room gear, and the officers of the army became about the only lady's men in the country and there were but few of them. The ragged miners considered it the height of impudence to go where a lady was without having on two pair of moccasins.

And while attempting to bring incidents from the very important period marked by the first arrivals of the fair sex in those wilds, to where we left off in the spring of 1865, it would seem quite appropriate to compare this sudden change of respectful demeanor to that preceeding it. . . .

Nomadic adventures varies of course to suit the emergency over differing journeys through the mountain glens and plains, and especially in such cases where the communication is closed up behind every move forward. It is quite natural to imagine correctly the external appearance of a party of adventurers thus isolated for a year or so, without the opportunity to refit, a little. Such a set of ragamuffins as were the "Walker Party," when it arrived in central Arizona is not seen or imagined often in one lifetime—patched, sewed, tied, strapped, and ribboned off like a Kentucky Bluegrass horse show in all patterns, fancies, and designs. Each individual member had his own fashion and sustained it. All of them again differed from the style of the Apache, who dressed in regular uniform, the same which was generously bequeathed by Nature. Their suits were however relieved and improved somewhat by the trimmings which consisted of breech-cloths (in the common parlance of the day pronounced britch clouts) and moccasins, and in rare instances, a string of beads. This usually constituted their toilet, under which they would strut as proudly as do all other princes, who take much pride in wearing fine feathers upon their beautiful persons. A pair of spurs and ear rings was considered a full summer's dress for an Indian in southern Arizona on our Mexican border. But let us go on with the white man's dress of those days, and occasions. The member of our party who was prudent enough to save all the exhausted flour sacks he had for future use for patching and mending, was accounted the most provident and solvent man in camp. Patched hats, patched shirts, trousers, and moccasins all were patched, and I remember but little about the coats, for toward the last there were none in the party. But the stockings, I had like to have forgotten, as it was the fashion to make those out and out, because of being more economical than repairing. The prevailing style was much more convenient than the old fashioned cut adhered to in the States, more simple in the general makeup, and less costly.

The pattern was of a rectangular shape and of the dimensions of twelve or fifteen inches in width by fifteen or eighteen in length and of the material of an exhausted cotton flour sack. The mode of putting it on was first to spread it on the ground and place the foot to be benefitted, upon it a little quarteringly, with the heel in the neighborhood of the southwest corner, while the toes were directed toward the northeast. Then draw the sides up over the instep and fold the projecting extremity at the front back over the toes and it was all ready for the moccasin, which was slipped over all very neatly. It seemed to be a simple arrangement, but it took some practice to do it quickly and comfortably. The style became well established in central Arizona and continued in great favor long after the Legislature first convened at Prescott, and especially did it flourish after its adoption by the Governor, members of the Legislature, and other high officials, who browsed about his camp. There was only one objection to the style to be made, even by the ladies. That was, that the heels were left exposed. This had never been regarded as any particular objection until the ladies came with their whims of what it took to constitute true politeness, and their never ending theories of decorum. But they, however, modified their demands a little, as they became accustomed to the ways of the country, and only objected to gentlemen attending the balls in this rear, lowcut style. That was one of the reasons that the miners didn't dance as above stated.

The good old customs which had obtained for so long prior to the immigration of the ladies thither, seemed in imminent danger to being destroyed forever. There were no ladies present at the first celebration of the Fourth of July ever enjoyed in central Arizona, which was in 1864, at Prescott. The Governor and other officers of the Territorial Government were present. The platform erected for the speakers and musicians was all in one and was located under and against a tall pine about twenty yards south of the south boundary of the public square (plaza) in Prescott City. It was also about opposite the point midway of that line and hence the place of the platform was nearly directly behind the store house built by Wormser & Co., subsequently fronting the plaza. The reason that the ladies were not present was that there were none in the country. There were no seats arranged about the rostum for the audience which consisted of about thirty or forty persons, most of whom were miners dressed in all sorts of costumes. The music was drawn out of two violins and picked out of one banjo, all at the same time. These were pioneer musical instruments of these early settlements. L. B. J[?] brought the fiddles along with the Government Officials and W. D[?] brought the banjo from California. Their feeble tones were pleasing enough in the open air, but appeared strangely lost on this occasion. The whole proceedings were conducted with proper dignity, but a glance at the audience scattered and lying about in little clumps here and there upon the ground gave the whole affair burlesquing color. There was no town there—only the woods. The rough men lying upon the almost grass-less ground, quietly whittling sticks and looking thoughtful—all appeared to be thinking of something else than a Fourth of July celebration.

The officers were dressed ordinarily, while the citizens, miners, or adventurers, whichever would be their proper name, for the most part were dressed most any way. None of them had coats. Some had moccasins on, while others wore old shoe tops alternately half-soled and worn out, probably a dozen times previously. The patent hose, already described, were in the height of fashion on this occasion, while the wearers had patched trousers, and one I remember in particular, wore only his under pantaloons of white cotton, because he had no trousers to put on. All of them had the remains of a check shirt and what was left of what was once a felt hat that had been mended so often that it was of "many colors." This happy family laid all around there on the ground with pistols and butcher knives, buckled around them, quite indifferent about the Fourth of July.

But when the speakers began the solid work, they aroused these old woods for the first time since the beginning, perhaps, with Roman story through and by means of imported Roman oratory. This became very interesting from this fact alone, for it sounded monstrous new, because it was new in this new land. One of the speakers had met in London, England, some years previously three distinguished American citizens and drank together the health of the Union of our states on that occasion. He mentioned their names and little did he then think that the party so loyal and so patriotic would be equally divided, for and against the Union when the test came. "But alas, such was the truth." He himself was loyal he said, and one of the others, who was at that moment commanding an army in the Union cause, also was loyal to the toast which they had drunk in a foreign land. The other two were traitors, one of them a refugee in Canada and the other had stepped out of the Presidential chair, after turning over the Government to the Rebellion. Little did he think, he repeated, while in a foreign land, so far removed from his own native country that it was ordained from on High that he was to return to his dear, dear native land and participate in bearing the Stars and Stripes through an unexplored waste and plant them finally and permanently amongst the boulders in the midst of the vast, unexplored wilderness of the ancient Montezumas. "But such was the case," he said, and that the unscrutable Providence of God could not be fathomed and that the sacrilegious impiety, which would suggest it, was of sufficient reality to him to drop the subject. The speaker, after dwelling upon these miraculous events to some extent, he agreed to finally content himself with the consoling reflection that "We were here."

Some careless wag in the audience remarked slyly that if "being here" was any great consolation, he had comfort for sale. The speaker ended and the violins and banjo struck up Hail Columbia in a feeble, but rather sweet and innocent tone, for the audience wanted the Devil's Dream or Sugar in the Gourd. Other speeches were made about in the same strain and followed by music in various styles and the meeting broke up.

After the usual formalities were completed, the highly and lowly—the *noble* and the *vulgar* orderly repaired to their several and respective places of habitation under the trees and behind the rocks, to put on a pot of *frijoles* to cook for a late dinner. And while the cooking was going on, to meditate upon the many blessings showered upon Republican Institutions in a land so far removed from the baleful influences of kings and princes. This was the freest country on earth at that time. No civilization, laws, or books. No restriction nor anything to eat. Democracy was in her prime. Thus ended the first celebration of the Fourth of July ever had in central Arizona, and it was a success and pleased all the attendants. I remember that a light shower of rain fell after it was over on that day, the first of the season. I also remember that the first rains which fell on the two following years, fell on the Fourth of July at Prescott, although the rainy season proper usually began, at least for several consecutive years, about the first of September each year and lasted until about the last of October. When it ceased, it never began or rained for any amount again until the usual time the next year.

But now I shall leave the incidents of 1864 and go begin where we stopped in the spring of 1865, for they all cannot be related, nor the tenth part of them. But Prescott, being quite a headquarters, I will have to be in and out of it frequently, just as I really was.

During this year an incident occurred on Turkey Creek which will be considered one of the most important circumstances transacted in the early settlements of the country. Turkey Creek had not yet a single settlement upon it and only one settlement could be said to be within twenty miles of the spot were the circumstances came off. It occurred about as follows. It was in this year of stirring events that five young men came into the country and made a temporary stop at Walnut Grove on the Hassayampa, with which place the reader is already acquainted. They were accustomed to Indian warfare and therefore negligent, but brave to the last necessity. I remember only two of their names, having lost my notes of the event. Mr. Binkley and Frederic Henry are the two referred to. The five concluded to go prospecting, as hunting gold was called, and directed their course toward Turkey Creek. They leisurely moved from place to place and encamped wherever night found them and finally they passed over the mountain range above Bradshaw Mountain and down on to the bottom of Turkey Creek and encamped for the night. They were ignorant of the fact that they had selected their camping place near a famous point that the Indians passed, going from mountain to mountain on their way east. The valley of Turkey was very narrow and quite rocky, with a streak of timber in it. The woodland only reached the foothills at this point on the north, which arose from the creek bottom gradually and was very slightly clothed with chaparral. The men picketed their horses on grass, spread their blankets, and slept without a sentinel near the trail, constantly traveled by the wily savage. During the night the Indians discovered them asleep and their camp silent and therefore had ample time to prepare thoroughly for the catastrophe at daylight.

The first thing they did was to silently lead the horses over the mountains some half-mile distant, where they slaughtered enough of them for a grand feast. While the feast was being prepared by some of them, the remainder stealthily surrounded the sleeping and unconscious men by forming a circle of nearly one hundred paces in diameter.

It was never definitely known what their number was, but it was supposed that there were more than fifty of them. They silently threw up fortifications of loose stone into short ridges at short distances of each other all around the circle and thus completely enclosed the men. Thus prepared they just manned the fortifications, constantly taking time about with each other, as they alternately watched and feasted. Just before they came it rained a little, just enough to make the sleepers, who were still unconscious of danger, draw their blankets more securely over their heads. At the approach of day the savages all took their places around the circle behind their respective fortifications, ready for action, and an easy prey. They had appointed a committee of "braves," who were to stealthily crawl upon the sleeping men and to slaughter them, if possible, in their blankets and thus save even the risk and uncertainty of an open conflict, in which some of their number would almost be certain to die.

The crawling approach began just as day was breaking and successfully prosecuted within twenty feet of the men, when one of the sleepers intuitively felt something was wrong and suddenly threw the blankets from over his head with both hands and sprang to his feet in the twinkling of an eye. It was all such quick work that the surprised man never thought of arousing his friends, but snapped his wet rifle at the would be assassins, who quickly gave back. The rifle failing to fire, he dropped it and caught up a six-shooter and fired. All of this having been done in an instant, the men all sprang to their feet and the crouching savages gave way toward their fortifications out of the way just in time for the whole circle of savages to send forth a solid volley, which wounded the whole five of the unfortunate men at the beginning. They saw at a glance that they were surrounded by the concealed savages. It took them but an instant to decide that they had to cover themselves in some way, and therefore they hurriedly threw all of their blankets, saddles, and packs into a circle around them and began to dig with a small shovel and their sheath-knives. But they were not given much time to prepare, for the Indians made a charge upon them, which they resisted with their guns to begin with, and their six-shooters finally, and hurled the savages back with a heavy loss. The lucky result of this charge gave the men new hope and inspired them to desperation, while it cooled the ardor of the Apaches very materially. This gave them more time to prepare, reload &c.

The savages now began to throw volley after volley from behind their fortifications at these unfortunate men, who crouched as close to the ground as possible, to avoid the constantly flying, leaden messengers. Wound after wound was thus received. But the savages began to believe that they were only wasting their ammunition or else the men would not take the constant fire so patiently and therefore determined on another charge. They therefore arose from their fortifications and again came with a war-whoop. But the men being already wounded badly and therefore rendered more desperate, they arose to a sitting posture and poured into the savage ranks a steady and well-directed fire, which they finished at a distance of ten paces with six-shooters, resulting disastrously to the savages, and in again hurling them back to their fortifications. However, this charge wounded all of the men anew and broke the thigh of one of them. They began to despair of ultimate success and to believe that it was only a question of time when they would all be disabled, one by one, and finally perish. Another charge was made and more Indians killed and more new wounds received and two of the men could not get up from the ground at all—one from a broken thigh and the loss of blood, and the other from the loss of blood. But they still assisted, by loading the guns and pistols as they lay on the ground. Each charge of the Apaches seemed to grow more determined, but their effort [was] less effective because they used their fire arms less and began to use arrows more.

The men attributed this to their want of ammunition, but still the battle went on and they broke every arrow that lodged within their reach. The number of Indians along toward 10 o'clock A.M., began to perceptibly decrease, but this was of course attributable to its correct cause—that of caring for the wounded. The Apaches are good calculators and they knew that it was not impossible for a straggling party of prospectors to hear the guns and call to learn the cause, and therefore the wounded were sent off constantly for safe localities. The white men on the other hand felt that their only hope was to defend themselves and depend for final aid upon the accidental assistance of any stragglers who might be in hearing of their guns. Vain hope, they were alone, and at least twenty miles from assistance.

The savages ceased their charging, for they generally lost as many on the retreat back to their fortifications, as they did on the advance, and therefore contented themselves to keep in safety and shoot leisurely.

This was destruction to all the hope left the besieged and they began to calculate the plan of making their way up a little chaparral ridge at the foothills beyond the fortifications. There was a small knoll on the ridge, from whence they thought that they could successfully defend themselves if they could only get there. But upon starting they found that they were all too weak to make much progress. Henry and Binkley took the man with the broken leg between them, and the party started under difficulties. The savages gave away from the fortifications in front of them and charged several times, compelling them to lay down the wounded man often to fight them off. They thus tediously and slowly made their way to the little ridge and up it a distance to a point within twenty yards of the knoll sought to be reached, when they were charged again by the savages with terrible effect. More wounds and more resistance and more dead savages.

This volley threw a rifle ball through the chest of Henry, while another cut through Binkley's nose, carrying away the ball of one of his eyes, entirely. These were now the only two who were left stout enough to do anything. Still they kept upon their feet and resisted to the last. They started again with their wounded man and persuaded the other two to crawl as they could no longer get up from the ground, and still before reaching the knoll one of the men on the ground refused to crawl farther, or to try. They were thus compelled to stop again. The man who refused to notice them farther than to beg them to go on and leave him, now gave it up. He said that he would die anyhow and insisted on them going on, all of which they refused to do. Henry and Binkley then undertook to carry them, but from the loss of blood, found themselves too weak to do it and they were all compelled to remain perched on the little ridge where they were. Here was a dilemma. They coaxed the men to try again to move a little further, but all in vain. They refused to move again. During this deadlock, Binkley squatted down upon his feet with his back against a little bush for support. He hung his head a little while he employed his idle time in gathering the coagulated blood out of the socket, where he had lately had an eye. After obtaining some of the clotted blood in his hand, he would hold it out to Henry without raising his head, and say, "Fred, look and see if that ain't my brains." Henry would reply, "No, you fool, you wouldn't be talking if that was your brains." Following this, Henry would call to Binkley to "get up quick—here they come again."

And they did come again and again until their ammunition gave entirely out, and then they began throwing rocks, by which they failed to do much execution. Binkley received a glancing shot from his blind side in the socket of his eye, by an arrow, which he said was more painful than the original shot, which carried the eye away. Every rock which the savages threw they would accompany the act with "How, how." Thus ridiculing the white man's salutation of how do you do &c. The savages after this began to dwindle away, one by one, until none could be seen. They evidently thought that this was the hardest crowd to kill that they had ever undertaken. It was about 2 o'clock P.M. when these men, cut to pieces, it might be said, were deserted and left by all the savages save one, who tenaciously hung around until he got an opportunity to die and did it in a manner and form as shall be presently stated. Not one of these men had less than a dozen wounds and yet they all lived through the fight to its end. And it was the most miraculous instance of the kind which had occurred in the early settlements of central Arizona.[2]

Some of the men would say now and then, "Great God, if only a party of miners would happen along." But it was in vain, no one happened along and the grave question after the battle was ended was how assistance was to be had. It was finally settled that the only hope left was for Henry and Binkley to attempt to reach the settlements and that a very precarious one, for both of them was shot through and through more than once and very weak from loss of blood. The nearest point to any settlement was Walnut Grove, which was thought then to be about twenty miles over a mountainous chaparral country. Their ammunition was nearly exhausted, but they recharged all the arms and made two of the men promise to defend themselves until assistance came. The third was unconscious and they dragged him down the side of the ridge under a cedar tree in some thick chaparral. They now helped the other two to roll and tumble also into the chaparral under the cedar. When they all were concealed thus, Henry and Binkley gave the stoutest of them a double-barreled shotgun loaded with six-shooter balls, with which to defend them all—bade them good bye and departed

After they had been some time gone, the Indian who persisted in examining the place came close to the chaparral and as he casually whistled and peered down the hill into the brush to see the position of the men he became greatly pleased to see

[2] Henry Fish, "Manuscript History of Arizona," quoted in Barnes, *Arizona Place Names*, 39, lists Fred Henry, Samuel Herron, Steward Hall, Frank Binkley, and De Morgan Scott as the five men engaged in the fight. After the skirmish, the site was known as Battle Flat. Hamilton, *Resources of Arizona*, dates the conflict as May, 1864. In the Prescott *Arizona Miner*, July 6, 1864, is found the following news item: "S. M. Wall, Fred. Henry, Frank Binkley, and D. Scott, four of five men who fought the Indians so bravely near Turkey Creek, some weeks since, have nearly recovered from their wounds. We regret to report the death of Samuel Herron, the other member of the party."

the unconscious one's head plainly. He gathered up a huge stone and made an effort to land it on the dying man's head, but missed his aim and the rock fell before the face of the unfortunate man and almost covered it with leaves and trash, all of which the unconscious man failed to know of or to notice. But this served to draw the attention of the man with the shotgun who leveled it from his lying position and fired. It proved a lucky shot and poor "Lo" came crashing down the hill through the brush and fell dead upon his face in the little hollow only a few feet from the men. That was the last shot of the battle. The men remained until night, crawling about the little hollow, in search of water, but without success. The one that was unconscious of course never moved. Henry and Binkley by marvelous exertions arrived at Walnut Grove about noon the following day, where their story was heard and where they were regarded as splendid examples of courage and distress. It is needless to say that they were well cared for, and in twenty minutes thereafter, fifteen armed and mounted men were under the direction of J. W. S[willing?] hurrying over the hills toward Turkey Creek. The direction given by Henry and Binkley was a good one, for this party found the battle ground and traced the wounded men by the dead bodies of the Apaches and the blood from both parties, which plainly stained the ground all about the field.

These men found fourteen dead bodies in one pile, put there preparatory for burning. The Apaches are the only cremators as a nation on our continent perhaps. I mean those who cremate their own dead, for there are many nations of the savages that cremate all enemies living or dead, if once in their power.

This party soon found the wounded men under the cedar, two of whom were totally unconscious. The other had crawled into the hollow after water and was lying upon his face, beside the body of the last Indian killed by himself. But he was not conscious of the presence of "poor Lo." The three men were taken to Walnut Grove, where one of them died and all the rest recovered. This was considered the most desperately contested conflict which had been fought since the discovery of these new settlements, and a most miraculous event that any of the men escaped at all. Henry told me afterward that he began to feel toward the last of the fight that the Indians could not kill him at all. I afterward met Binkley at San Bernardino, California. He expressed himself entirely satisfied with the wilderness country. His eye was of course gone, but he had fully recovered otherwise. But he had however participated, before leaving Arizona, in the battle fought at Skull Valley, already referred to. It was hard to conceive how so many wounds could be inflicted with arms, without more fatal consequence, but, however, it was done in the midst of the hardest struggle for life that ever happened in central Arizona. An old darkey is reputed to have said that it was hard to know a man until you've hoed corn with him awhile, and it might be said that it is equally hard to know who will defend themselves after cruel inflictions are received until they fight Indians awhile. Nearly two years later I was on the battle ground above described and saw a skull with a bullet hole in it near the temple, still marking the locality of the lonely and desperate conflict. Turkey Creek afterwards became the scene of the most lively and animated mining operations in central Arizona and also of incidents of Indian warfare, some of which will be remarked in the proper place as we proceed. But the savages were plying their avocation of theft, robbery, and massacre all over the country. The soldiery at Ft. Whipple was reinforced, but this fact had but little or no influence upon the ever wakeful and eternal vigilance of the Apache. The soldier was always under the command of officers who knew nothing of fighting Indians and therefore their very orderly efforts only served to encourage the Apaches and amaze them by the easy and agreeable tasks set them by stupidity.

It became the surest plan which could be adopted by the miners who wanted to be attacked to put a few soldiers dressed in uniform in the ranks with them.

The Apache depredations were constantly on the increase while his wits and animosity grew with the country. The soldiery cared but little whether the Apache was punished or not and therefore very indifferent about the matter, and the Indians knew it. One thing was absolutely certain and that was that the necessary perseverance and privations for successful Indian fighting was the worst part of the business. The final battle was not what was avoided by the soldiery, but the preliminary hard work and hardships necessary to get the opportunity to fight them. If the savages could have been persuaded to draw in line and fight the troops, the result would have soon settled all the Indian wars.

This was the drawback that the country labored under while the miners had not the supplies to live on and therefore their efforts up to this period were mainly confined to accidental attacks about the camps of the country and on the trails between and upon prospecting parties. And sometimes, when the Apache failed to get a good long start ahead, after killing someone or capturing some stock, the miners would follow them and they very generally inflicted some punishment before returning. Hence the savages became as fearful of a party of miners as they were indifferent of the presence of soldiers.

About this period another unnecessary and unlooked for source of constant annoyance arose amongst these infant settlements to breed discord and endanger their final success. I have reference to the poisonous venom of reasonless faction.

We were nearly four thousand miles from the seat of the war in the states, but on the arrival of a respectable showing of troops, good and conservative citizens of previous high standing became too patriotic and demanding in their deportment to be of further use as citizens. They became a fair sample of the good Christian who got too much religion and sin resulted from the excess. Many of the previous good citizens of central Arizona, on the arrival of a sufficiently imposing array of soldiers, fell from grace through and by means of infecting an overcharge of loyalty. It is hard to conceive how a man can become too loyal to his country indeed, but it was accomplished. The unnecessary cultivation of a war spirit in time of war has never yet been known to fail to produce what is known as public informers, whose fetid breath poisons everything. These insects have overturned some of the best governments in the world, and when fully recognized by those in power, become wonderfully prolific and as destructive as the grasshoppers in Kansas. They are much worse because they flourish at any time of the year and in any country on the globe. I am truly sorry to say that these enemies of the peace, good order, and prosperity first made their appearance upon the establishment of a provost guard in the City of Prescott. The ghostly shadow of this mischievous brute is everywhere; it infests the headquarters of all political parties, religious associations, and domestic relations. They have no religion—no political party nor conscience of their own, and are the common enemy of all. The gentlemanly officers and soldiers of Arizona were not acquainted with these creatures; it was the politicians who laid the eggs and their flunkies sat on them and the first viper hatched was a public informer. His growth is rapid in the darkness or in the light, both of which are all the same to him. He lurks about the fireside in every presence, continually seeking employment and constantly finding it. These were the vampires who came into existence, from whence God only knows, to feed upon the weak and half-starved settlements of central Arizona.

Shiftless men, who were quiet, orderly citizens before employment became easy and lucrative, sought the first opportunity afforded for a fat and lazy livelihood in the profession of public informer. They were neither Democrats or Republicans, Union men nor war horses; they were public informers, whose business it was to whisper into trepidatious ears all sorts of probable schemes of disloyalty of a poverty stricken little colony, already in a death struggle with the savage Indians, over three thousand miles from the seat of the war, and that, too, in the midst of a hitherto unexplored wilderness. All, all transpired while the Flag of the Union and of the United States was being defended by more than a million of volunteer American soldiers, actually in arms.[3]

This class of American reptiles, fresh from the back alley, mudcat hatcheries of political adventurers, were for a time as thick as the locusts were once said to have been in Egypt. But like the 'hoppers referred to, they began to decrease of vegetation or commissions, until they, too, disappeared. Then comes the query: where do they go? Where do the locusts and 'hoppers go? It is hard to say, but when the usefulness of the public informer ceases, he is pretty certain to be found close around a pulpit and officiating in religious matters, having concluded that the ordinary affairs of men are all vanity and vexation anyhow. Having thus fled to the mountains of "Hepsidam," where the whangdoodle mourneth for its first born, he looks down from his lofty perch with pity upon the masses of erring humanity.

He looks like a pretty good fellow after all. Let us be pardoned if we tell too much truth, but those who began this unenviable profession in our little sparse settlements, were not aware that their secret was well known by all the miners in the country. They were not aware that one of the soldiers, who had every opportunity to know the facts, had betrayed them from the beginning. He was not a disloyal soldier but a disgusted one. It was owing to the good sense and conservative good will of the United States officers, both civil and military, that these new settlements were not checked, blighted, and broken up finally. The animosity thus kindled by those private individuals had its effects and an evil and dangerous one it was, for many times preparations were made to meet it unknown to them. Things stood thus all through the winter of 1864, and suspicion

---

[3] Union officials kept a watchful eye on the miners about Prescott despite their protests of loyalty. Gustav Brown, a government detective, wrote from San Juan, California, on October 16, 1864, that "There are men going daily from Los Angeles by twos and threes who represent themselves as miners going to Colorado. I learned from a man who came from the Walker Diggings District that there was a man by the name of Woolsey who has organized a company for the purpose of fighting Indians, but his real motive is to commence a war in Arizona as soon as they can get help from Texas. . . ." *Official Records of the Union and Confederate Armies*, Series I, Vol. L, Part 2, 1019.

was aroused and it was hard to settle. The result came near being culminated by a little difficulty occurring in the streets of Prescott between two prominent citizens representing both sides of the war policy. One was struck across the head with a rifle used as a bludgeon. The one suspected of disloyalty left the town in company with a number of associates and established a temporary camp on Turkey Creek to prospect for quartz. A disloyal motive had been attached to the difficulty, which was really a mistake, and consequently a demand was made by the military that this man accused by public informers should surrender himself to the authorities and give bond in the sum of five thousand dollars for his good behavior in the future. He was a member of the first Arizona Legislature, as well as the second subsequently, and he agreed to give the bond for the sake of quieting the bad feeling which was thought to be growing, but refused to come to Prescott to do it. Governor Mc[Cormick] had succeeded Governor G[oodwin], who had gone to Congress from Arizona.[4]

The Governor agreed to meet him in the woods between Hassayampa and Prescott at an old deserted cabin situated on a little creek in a locality which afterward went by the sobriquet of Groom's Dale, after its founder, and take a bond and go on it himself. The accused accepted the proposal against many dissenting friends, who were certain that it was only a plan laid to capture and imprison him. But he persisted that he would go on the day set, anyhow, and give the bond, because if a conflict should ever ensue between the soldiers and citizens he did not want to be the occasion for it. He accordingly made his way in company of three or four friends, as surety against Indians, from Turkey Creek to the old cabin at Groom's Dale in the woods. The Governor arrived promptly with an escort of twenty sol-

---

[4] Richard C. McCormick did not become governor until appointed by President Andrew Johnson in 1866. John N. Goodwin, the previous governor of Arizona Territory, was elected delegate to Congress September, 1864, over Charles D. Poston and Joseph P. Allyn. George H. Kelley, *Legislative History—Arizona, 1864–1912*, 17, 19; Wyllys, *Arizona*, 174. The individual giving the bond was Robert W. Groom.

diers, and took the bond, and all parties separated satisfied, and retraced their steps respectively. Good faith marked every act and it was the end of the growing danger, for the present at any rate. I really expect that the Governor is to this day ignorant of the fact that there was a strong party of miners who volunteered and went on their own responsibility, within two hundred paces of that old cabin on that occasion and kept concealed behind a hill to await the result of taking this bond. There were men in that party who felt disappointed because the soldiery escort failed to arrest the accused, so as to give an excuse for opening hostilities at once. The Governor was very popular and I never knew a man in all that country whom I believe would injure him. But ill feelings had been unnecessarily aroused and there was danger of a collision at any time. The Governor was a conservative man and knew the real position better than any other officer in the land, and did more to reconcile these conflicting elements than any other one man in the country. In reality, but for him, there would have been war other than that with the Apaches. The mortal chilliness of war always begins like most other diseases at the extremities. . . .[5]

That ends the anxiety generally and we finally agreed to submit the points in controversy without argument and praise the Lord for the result, whatever it may be. There was enough excitement constantly emanating from numerous conflicts with the Indians to temper almost any appetite for bloodshed. . . .

[5] A good deal of confidence placed in Governor McCormick by the miners stems from the fact that he was deeply interested in mining and is often found as a member or part-owner with other parties of claims in the Walker Mining District. See "Journals of the Pioneer and Walker Mining Districts."

The Last Campaign of Sugarfoot Jack

AGAIN AND AGAIN means were adopted and put into execution for the suppression of inroads and incursions of the Apache, whose strong-holds and headquarters were moved back from the settlements toward the east. When the savages now succeeded in capturing a herd of stock, they would take it upon a flying trip eastward without halting in less than a hundred miles.

Men and adventurers having nothing particular to do, would frequently follow them for a week at a time and nearly always fail to find them and return after they were half worn out, disgusted with their efforts. It became evident that the whites had to go after them and not wait until stock was taken or a massacre occurred in order to follow them when they were of all time most alert and watchful. The greatest science in fighting these Indians was the art of finding them at all and then catching them off of their guard. To simply defeat them in a battle was the least part of the undertaking. The Apache was not a warrior, he was just a murderer. His disposition to kill and slay was never excelled, but at the same time his first and most important consideration in all of his calculations was to do it totally without loss and without any risk whatever, if that be possible. But when he is once entrapped he will fight in desperation unto death, and if one bone is broken he uses all the powers of the others to make amends for the inconvenience. When he makes up his mind to take desperate chances he does it by a sudden, bold onslaught and terminates the risk as quickly and as desperately as possible. Under the constant necessity thus presented, another party was raised and proceeded on the warpath against the "Unknown tribes of the East."

This party too was as usual, when the spirit ran high, too large to fight Indians, for it numbered quite a hundred. A Pima guide had been previously obtained and the party crossed the Agua Frio and the San Francisco River into the heart of the enemy's country.[1] This party was doomed to disappointment as far as any very considerable achievement was concerned. In the first place, it was too badly mixed. There were many, old experienced hands amongst the members, who knew the *modus operandi,* but the greatest drawback was that there were many more who was never a participant in an Indian battle, who knew much more and wanted commissions for their want of proper information on the subject. In short, petty ambitions arose for the naked want of experience. Such individual members as this, each became surprised at himself for having found his individual self a general upon such short notice. This state of things embodying, as it were, so much useful information, served only to cramp and burden the work before this party and to materially lessen its probable results. But notwithstanding, its course was directed toward a strong-hold of the Apaches known by the Pimas as the "Big Rump" Valley. "Big Rump" was a famous Apache chief, who kept his headquarters at this valley, according to the story of the Pima guide of this occasion. We finally came to a long, brown, grassy mountain ridge bordering the famous valley and halted a little scatteringly along its brow in a position overlooking the low undulating valley for several miles to its opposite side. This was pronounced by our

[1] The San Francisco River here again is either the Verde or the Salt River.

guide to be the almost fabled valley of "Big Rump."[2] Instead of a valley it was rather a low rolling and knobby desert country sparsely studded with low stunted mesquite trees. From amongst these trees all over the valley arose the smoke curling like incense away from the numerous kilns in which the Apaches roast mescal bulbs into a jelly. From the number of these arising smokes, it appeared indeed that we were really at the door of the Apache capitol and our party of one hundred was not too large at all. While thus standing overlooking the dangerous prospect, one of our "generals" was noticed to be standing meek and thoughtful, without a single suggestion, for a wonder, and had one foot extended in an easy and graceful position, toward the front, while his full weight was thrown back stolidly upon the other. While he was thus standing silent and meditative, a comrade standing near, nodded his head very slightly to a friend to observe the slight tremor which had so ungenerously taken charge of the general's extended limb. This comrade leaned over a little and whispered, "By the gods, did you see how it did shake." That was ungenerous, but this was one of the generals who had previously been suffering from a commission.

This general quit commanding after that day and became a quiet, orderly private as he started out to be, without further annoyance to anyone. It did look to be a doubtful undertaking and presented itself thus to more men than the general. But there was one man there who was not frightened. It was our old acquaintance, Sugarfoot Jack, whose recklessness has been previously remarked.

The party concluded to descend the mountain into the val-

[2] The location of Big Rump Valley cannot be ascertained with any exactness except that it might be found in southeastern Arizona near the upper reaches of the Salt River. It is evident that several of King Woolsey's expeditions had that valley as their objective, and Big Rump, or Wah-poo-eta, was an Apache chief, perhaps of the Pinal band. See Fort Whipple, *Arizona Miner*, April 6, 20, May 25, 1864. Colonel Edwin A. Rigg reported from Fort Craig, New Mexico, September 14, 1864 that ". . . another month in the field would have resulted in clearing the Indians from the Prieto to Big Rump. As it is, Indians have for a time (except in small parties) left for Big Rump Valley, the Mogollon, and Sierra Blanco. . . ." *Official Records of the Union and Confederate Armies*, Series I, Vol. L, Part 1, 369.

ley and on reaching the foot a rapid forward march was taken up and on arriving at the first smoke the camp was found to be deserted. This fact indicated that our presence has been discovered and a double quick was taken up and became so rapid that the savages already on the move were overtaken, and a short conflict ensued. They couldn't travel so fast as when they came on a raid into the settlements without their women and children. They undertook to concentrate their power, but without success and were scattered, leaving their camps to our disposal, which were destroyed completely. Their light and frail *jacals* of wicker work, thatched with grass and twigs, were fired and quickly consumed. Their kilns of mescal were also destroyed by scattering the contents to the winds. The whole procedure was comparatively a failure for their were but few savages killed. Our guide was not the right man in the right place, or he would have conducted the party into the valley by a concealed route. He knew that his own tribe would not venture into this valley, and he concluded that it was best to conduct the whites to the high ridge so that they could adjudge for themselves whether it was safe to venture into it or not. The Apaches were thus warned in time to escape by seeing the strangers descend the mountain. The fracas ended and the men began to gather together back at the point where the pack animals were left preparatory to moving out again.

While thus straggling back and occasionally touching a match to the frail residences on the route, Sugarfoot was noticed to have thrown a papoose into the flames of a burning *jacal* and was quietly standing to observe the result. But he soon passed on as though in search of another living, human creature to cremate alive. The persons who discovered his cruel and brutal act, went to the remains of the consumed *jacal,* and discovered the little, black, crisped body of the murdered child, lying upon its side with its little hands and knees drawn up nearly to its chin, dead. They undertook to take the body out of the ashes, but the skin peeling off every time it was touched made the "boys" sick and they left it in the ashes, and passed on down the valley toward the mules in quite a savage humor. When the fact became generally known, there was much dissatisfaction expressed over the occurrence. But while these murmurs were boiling a little, Sugarfoot had discovered another papoose and had taken his seat upon a large stone and was engaged in playing with it. He would dance it upon his knee and tickle it under the chin and handle the babe in the manner of a playful mother, and seemed to be enjoying himself splendidly.

But he got done playing with the child finally and drew from his scabbard a heavy dragoon six-shooter, placed the muzzle to the child's head as it sat upon his knee turned his own face away and fired. He thus bespattered his clothes and face with infant brains to the disgust and indignation of every one who happened to be looking his direction. Sugarfoot thus defied the murmurs and complaints for the burning of one by blowing the brains out of another. But with all of his bold and brave recklessness he discovered in an instant that his time was at hand, without an accident, and for once in his life precipitately fled. He knew too well the character of the men who turned to pick up their guns, to believe that they were capable of making false motions. He escaped to the brush and remained away long enough for their foolish passions to subside a little. This matter threw the apple of discord into our ranks. Some thought that it was no harm to kill an Indian of any age, size, or sex. Others declared that they could not nor would not support such brutality nor countenance any war party that did. And that if such a war as that was to be carried on against the Indians, that their part was ended immediately.

To hush all controversy, those who refused to recognize such warfare split off from the main body and prepared to return to the settlements. Seventeen started and prosecuted the homeward tramp in peace until reaching the Agua Frio, where the savages disputed the crossing with us for an hour, but at last gave way after getting two of their "braves" killed, and as many crippled; it was not known how many. The seventeen arrived in the settlements safely. About three days afterward an old soldier of the United States Regular Army became disgusted and left the party and traveled alone in the night until he too arrived safely in Prescott. In about four weeks the main body of the party returned to the settlements, after having lost a few of their men, but Sugarfoot came in with the rest all right as he always did. Sugarfoot Jack subsequently died. Peace to his ashes. But still, he was the oddest man I ever met. He was said to have died at a Mexican Fandango on the Rio Grande, and in the common parlance of the day, "died with his boots on." A Mexican grandee stabbed him to death—so reported, "unwept, unhonored, and unsung." But these are only samples of Sugarfoot's exploits. He was always ready for any emergency. He was said to have been court-martialed out of the army for knocking his Colonel down with a bludgeon. In all of my experience amongst the rough and reckless population to be found about the mining camps of the Rocky Mountains, I considered Sugarfoot Jack the most hardened, indifferent wretch I ever met. With one who knew him, his easy and pleasant address on all ordinary occasions, together with his handsome youthful appearance, only served to affright charity from her generous commiseration.

The first Legislature defined a quartz claim to be the dimensions of one hundred yards square. "Pertinencia" was the statutory name adopted by that body. The claimant who recorded it had the possessory right to "all the earth and mineral therein contained." The bottom was not defined, therefore the boundary in that direction was left to the option of the owner. In all cases he could claim as deep as he pleased, without running any risks of subjecting the propriety of his pretensions to the decision of miners' meeting.[3] Chapter fifty of the "Howell Code"

[3] By Mexican mining law a *pertenencia* was defined as a claim 200 *varas* (a *vara* equaling 32.99 inches) upon the course of a lode to which a title was acquired by denunciation. The breadth of the claim varied according to the width of the vein from 112.50 to 200 *varas*. The area of the *pertenencia*, however, in the Arizona law was 200 yards square. It was the custom of many of the western legislatures to adopt the mining laws of the mining camps or districts as the laws of the territory or state regulating mines and miners. The fifty-three sections of the Howell Code referring to mining in Arizona Territory are reproduced in J. Ross Browne, *A Report upon the Mineral Resources of the States and Territories West of the*

was devoted to the mining laws and was the first instance of a Legislature taking the liberty of framing a mining law for gold and silver mines on the Pacific Coast, perhaps the Legislature of Oregon excepted. It met with but little favor amongst the miners because of its loose, speculative intent. It was liberal enough to have gorged Wall Street with speculative privileges. There was no limit to the number of claims which one man could possess, nor to the number of acres of ground, if he only had them recorded in "Pertinencias." Under that law one man could thave owned and exercised control over millions of acres, provided there was enough cloth from which to take such a pattern. Everybody had claimed all they wanted, consequently everybody was rich in "feet," as the claims were reckoned by that unit. But the mere holding and owning a claim on a ledge of rocks from year to year became quite monotonous and this fact quickened the pulses of ingenuity in aid of more practical results, on shorter time and better terms.

The sleek-handed adventurer, who came on general principles and didn't want to stay long, soon discovered a plan of success much more certain and speedy than the single-handed operation of owning and working the mine. He became agent for as many miners as would entrust him with business—provided himself with certificates of ownership from the real owners, with whom he was to divide—selected some of the richest specimens of ore found from any convenient mine and would go East to sell them. After arriving in New York or Philadelphia, he would raise a company, give it a heavy sounding name, issue and sell stocks as long as he could find a purchaser. After he has operated as long as practicable, he closes doors, loses the archives of the company's office, and goes his way rejoicing. The miners of Arizona wonder when he will return, but he at last is gone so long that they give the same mines and certificates of ownership to someone else in succession, who wants to raise a com-

---

Rocky Mountains," 39 Cong., 2 sess., *House Exec. Doc. No. 29.* See also Hinton, *Handbook to Arizona,* Appendix, lxxxiii; Charles Howard Shinn, *Land Laws of Mining Districts,* 41.

pany, to repeat the speculation just described over and over again. The middle man swindles at both ends of the line and retires to private life and is lost sight of. But the same mines are still good to sell if they are even worthless for anything else, which is the case of ninety-nine times in a hundred, numerously multiplied. Such schemes as this by unscrupulous adventurers very materially retarded the development of the mines of central Arizona. Sometimes these men would carry with them a bona-fide charter fresh from the moulds in the Arizona Legislature claiming a capital stock of millions of dollars, when the swindlers could hardly raise the means with which to pay their passage to New York and could not do it without the assistance of the miners, who sent them finally and forever.

These speculators made this profession nearly as profitable as the bogus Rail Road companies were once in the habit of doing through their agents, who would visit a state with a flaming show bill bearing the seductive "$5,000,000 cash Capital Stock and no poor kin," swindle and induce the prominent men of a county who are generally numerous, to carry the vote for a Rail Road tax greater than the people could pay, and then sue for a breach of contract, get a judgment, and go home. All that was left to do afterward was only to issue bonds in default of the money, and to pay interest on the same at leisure.[4] Our mining claim speculators received no interest, but they got all the principal to begin with. But this mining law was repealed by the Third Legislature.[5] There was no mail connecting central Arizona with the outside world for a long time and when it became established, it was only provided for two mails per month. The people never got them for the riders would only last about one month each on the average, therefore the Apaches received about half or three-quarters of the mails perhaps. This fact

---

[4] Robert E. Riegel, *The Story of the Western Railroad*, 20 ff., provides an interesting account of the railroad boom and promotion.

[5] Chapter 50 of the Howell Code containing the mining law was repealed by the third Territorial legislature. This repeal was unanimously approved by the lower house, of which Conner was a member. *Journals of the Third Legislative Assembly of the Territory of Arizona*, 178.

clogged the connection between the speculators and it was without remedy. One morning when the mail rider was reported killed, a man by the name of Alexander determined to go with an investigating party and pursuant to that object, he stepped out into the woods back of the Governor's Mansion to get his horse, which he had recently picketed to graze, and was slaughtered by the Apaches in sight of town. He made desperate efforts to escape in plain view of the Governor's residence, and failed. The following day a man who had located a ranch five miles below Prescott came to town to get ammunition. Stevens was his name and he had left two horses grazing near his house. Two or three Indians undertook to capture them when the owner's wife attacked them with a doubled-barreled shotgun so promptly that they were defeated and retreated, while the lady mounted one of the horses and escaped into Prescott. She rode one horse and the other followed and she thus saved them both. . . . I built a cabin also in Prescott and became a citizen of the town, but was not at home much of my time. But about the time I got ready to keep house, my provisions gave out, and I was therefore compelled to visit or starve. There was a pack train regularly plying between California and Prescott, but it sometimes fell behind. It was established by Messrs. Miller & Blasser, and made about one trip per month. To remedy the evil of famine I started in company with my old friend "Young," who had been an old Mexican War soldier from Kansas, in search of provisions.

We traveled in the night on the first part of our trip to escape the Apaches. We had two animals each and directed our course to La Paz, Arizona, on the Colorado River, a distance of two hundred and twenty miles. The reader will remember this as the same trading post on the river previously described as the place where the Mohaves whipped the Negro for stabbing a papoose. We had only a scanty supply of provisions to start with, and in reality, not enough to last for half the distance, but we were rather depending upon replenishing our light store from the pack train above referred to, which we expected to meet.

The desert country necessary to be traversed was wonderfully sterile and fruitless; therefore no wild game was to be or really could be depended on for food.

We missed the train, so numerous were the different trails through the country and ran out of provisions before we were half way. We wearily plodded the lonely way through the heated sand for three days without food, and the weather was extremely warm or rather extremely hot. We were traveling in the daytime, having passed the most dangerous Apache strong-holds from Prescott westward. In this desert and at this period the danger from Apaches decreased with the distance as progress was made from Prescott to the Colorado River. So when we reached half the distance we ceased traveling in the night and journeyed throughout the day to make better progress.

My old friend mourned now and then and declared that marching in Capt. Knight's company in the deserts during his experience in the Mexican War and following Jim Lane's regiment was real sport compared to this starvation and fatigue.[6] He would sometimes declare that he could not stand it much longer and that the burning heat exhausted him almost completely. I would attempt to arouse his pluck by laughing at him, for which he shamed me and remarked to me that I had forgotten that he was getting to be an old man and unable to bear all that a young man could. This fact had not previously entered sufficiently into my considerations, and I began to think more seriously of it, which to some extent made me disregard my own sufferings. Upon coming to William's Fork, a tributary of the Colorado, I frequently halted and filled my canteen with water and persuaded the old man to pour it under his clothes around the collar to cool him off and set the example myself by getting

[6] James Henry Lane (1814–66) served as a colonel of the 3rd Indiana Regiment and latter commanded the 5th Indiana Regiment which he led into Mexico City during the Mexican War. Upon moving to Kansas, he became a leader of the Free-State movement, and in 1861 he was elected to the Senate of the United States on the Republican ticket. Abraham Lincoln appointed Lane a brigadier general and he led the Kansas Brigade against the Confederate forces commanded by Sterling Price. W. H. Stephenson, "James Henry Lane," *Dictionary of American Biography*, X, 576–78.

into the water with my clothes on.⁷ I would crawl out of the water and give a hearty shake like a Newfoundland dog making his toilet after bathing in a mill pond, and the old man would tell me that in a few minutes I would be "hotter" than if I had not gone into the water.

We journeyed thus until one afternoon we stopped at a great bend in William's Fork to rest the animals. I saw some wild geese and immediately undertook to capture one. The old man said that he was willing to give fifty dollars for one of them. On seeking a concealed route toward them behind some foliage, I came across two new made graves in this wild and uninviting place. I was as much surprised as if I had discovered a ghost, and could hardly believe that I was in my right mind. Upon examination, I found a small stake not larger than an ordinary walking cane planted at the end of each grave, with one side flattened by trimming with a knife. There was something written with a lead pencil on the flat surface of each, but it was so illegible that I could not make it out, but presumed that the writing was intended for the names of the deceased. Many months afterwards I learned that they were the graves of California horse thieves who had started with their stolen stock en route for Arizona and after traveling such a long distance over a habitless desert they thought that they were nearly to Prescott and one killed the other two so as to possess all the horses himself. The living thief buried his comrades in the sands of this lonely place and proceeded in the darkness with his very costly property. But he made one grave mistake in believing that he was in the vicinity of Prescott, for that town was more than a hundred miles away, and he made another by getting drunk and entrusting his secret to a friend, who in turn entrusted it to others, which resulted in his violent death while resisting arrest, legally ordered, in consideration of those offenses. I failed to kill a goose, which fact immediately suggested an evil omen to the petulant fore-

⁷ Williams Fork is formed by the juncture of the Big Sandy and Santa Maria rivers. It flows west into the Colorado River and is named after the old mountain man Bill Williams. Accounts state that the river was named by Joseph R. Walker in 1840. Barnes, *Arizona Place Names*, 48.

bodings of my old comrade, who said that we had just as well give it up because he said, "that when people get so weak that a goose could outwit them, the end was not far."

We started on and pretty soon came across four men, the leading character of whom seemed to be a Frenchman. They were afoot and had their provisions packed upon two little Mexican burros and the little animals had been cruelly over-tasked and consequently were given out. They had their goods in a pile on the ground and were engaged in taking a lunch. "Saved at last," plaintively remarked the old man, and we rode up and halted. The old man's enthusiastic exertions in immediate explanation of our starved condition came near affrighting these inexperienced specimens into despair. He continuously poured out his woeful story of starvation until these men felt sure that they would perish before being able to return to civilization and consequently refused to let us have any provisions to any amount for any price. They declared that they would rather for us to perish in this desert country than to perish themselves.

The old man became thunder-stricken at this unlooked for turn of affairs. He pulled out several hundred dollars with which to tempt them, but all was in vain, for it was evident that they didn't intend to perish to save us. He now attempted to convince them that there was no danger of starvation in the mines, but only on the road, and that a heavily laden pack train with provisions had gone on ahead for the settlements at Prescott. This was all true, but these men totally ignorant of the country could not be made to believe it and only asked why we had not gotten provisions from that pack train ourselves. My old friend tried to explain that by telling them how we had depended on this train, and how we came to miss its route and so on. But it was all futile, for they thought that we were taking our final leave of the country and only telling them a falsehood about going after provisions. The old soldier had given them too much affright to begin with to ever rectify the mistake, and as a last alternative he turned to me and said, "Let us take it from them."

This remark evidently frightened these men worse, although they were four, and we only two. The result of that remark only convinced me at a glance that all I had to do was to draw a six-shooter and help myself. But reflecting that we were in the gorge of William's Fork, outside of which there could be no other route in that section, I felt sure that we would meet other immigrants. I succeeded by remarking this probability in appeasing or rather mollifying the old man's wrath a little. But he had become very impatient and rather furious at the heartless conduct of these men. As we started on he gratified himself to some extent by warning them that if he ever caught them in a situation like ours, he would give them food, but that in the meantime, he would take all their money—all their mules—a lien on their farms in the states, and make their wives and daughters his servants. . . .

The old man now began to despair in reality and began to insist that he would never get out of this "scrape," as he called it. But upon going a half-mile we espied a man walking rapidly to meet us. He carried a double-barreled shotgun on his shoulder and a wild duck in his hand. Upon coming near he asked without halting if we had met some men lately, and if so, how far back. The old man quickly replied to the interrogation by saying, "Young man, sell me that duck, for I'm mighty hungry." The fellow halted long enough to hastily toss the duck to my old comrade with the remark, "Why yes, I'll give it to you if you are mighty hungry." I told the hasty fellow that four men were only a short distance ahead of him and he passed rapidly on. The old man examined the duck a moment and he looked after the departing form of the young man and as though talking to himself, remarked that "That man didn't belong to that crowd of brutes, back yonder." Night was near and we encamped, cooked, and ate the duck and also a blue quail which I accidentally succeeded in killing with a six-shooter. This was a great feast and we were therefore all right for the time. On the following day we made a journey through the sand beds of William's Fork of probably twenty or thirty miles and a little before night, came to a camp of about a half-dozen men who were en route for the mines of central Arizona. They made many inquiries about the mines and the road ahead of them and particularly of the Indians. Of course we could only tell them that there was no road but simply a meandering trail for nearly two hundred miles through the chaparral rocks and mountain deserts, and that in some places there were many different trails and they all came together again at different points.

It was agreed that I should make the next application for food because the old soldier said that I had boasted of being able to do it without frightening the importuned into paroxysms to begin with. I approached this party's camp and was plied with such a constant flow of interrogations that I found it down right difficult to get an answer to anything. But an Irishman of the party discovered the difficulty and furnished me with the necessaries of life and deported himself in a manner indicating that he was proud to do it. . . . We kept up our journey until we were a reasonable distance away from that camp, when we halted and took supper and thereby brightened our prospects for the work of the following day, very materially. My old soldier friend boasted of becoming twenty years younger within the space of one night. I don't know when I ever became so aggrieved as I did at seeing this stout old man grow so feeble in so short a time from hunger and heat combined. However we arrived safely in La Paz in the midst of plenty and found a great increase in population and additional improvements.

The Indians too were contented, for their favorite Chief Irotaba had returned from his visit to the "Great Father" at Washington in safety. He was said to have made on his return the usual speech to his people by comparing the number of pale faces he met to the leaves of the trees and the sands of the desert. He informed them that New York was the greatest rancheria in the world, and that all the soldiers dressed just alike and that their guns in Washington were just like the guns used by them in Arizona. He was thus convinced that they were all the same people and that it was no use to fight them more. But some of his warriors doubted his sincerity, because his tale was too wonderful to be believed and thought that their Chief had gone over to the enemy, thus showing that several of their tribe should have been taken together, so as to corroborate each other to the satisfaction of their people. Irotaba refused to fight the whites again or to entertain such a question, but he consented however to fight the tribe of Yumas and began a campaign and led his "braves" in person. But he made a fatal mistake of putting on a flashy military suit (sword and all) which some officer gave him while on this visit to Washington, thus convincing some of his braves that he was indeed a traitor. The consequence was that he was defeated by the Yumas and himself taken prisoner.

But the Yumas, being desirous of keeping on good terms with the whites, and believing Irotaba to be in good favor with them, contented themselves with relieving the great Chief of his pretty uniform and trimmings. They thus stripped their distinguished prisoner to nakedness and set him at liberty and unharmed otherwise, though the loss of his uniform came near killing him, according to my informant. Of course, I was not with them to see these transactions, but was near enough to gather facts from sources which I considered trustworthy.

He was said to become greatly depressed and humiliated by his defeat and its results and he was finally stripped of his noble commission of Chief as completely as he had been of his uniform, from whence he sank gradually into insignificance. During the war a young man [John Moss] who was both a Rebel and a Federal alternately, as policy dictated, taught Irotaba to shout "Hurrah for Dixie" as a polite salutation, necessary for good breeding. [He] was the same young man who accompanied Irotaba to Washington.

He accompanied Irotaba on one occasion to Ft. Mohave on the Colorado and was much chagrined and surprised when he introduced Irotaba to some of the dignified old Union officers, to see the old Chief vigorously throw up his hat and repeatedly shout, "Hurrah for Dixie," at a war-whoop pitch. He continued to shout "Hurrah for Dixie," and its president, until his young friend hastened to quiet him. . . .

Myself and friend obtained our supplies and started our long and weary way on the return trip across the desert country to Prescott, without particular incident. When we arrived within fifty miles of headquarters we again adopted the safest plan of traveling in the night. . . .

John Moss, who taught the Chief Irotaba how to articulate treason, took a notion to come to central Arizona.

He had made several fortunes by living with the Indians and thus having the opportunity to find quartz lodes, which he sold to capitalists for very considerable sums on different occasions. On leaving the Colorado for the interior of Arizona he obtained the consent of several others to accompany him, amongst whom was Capt. Knight, a correspondent of the *California Alta*, a newspaper published in San Francisco. It was quite a long and tedious journey and somewhere on the route the correspondent straggled and became confused and lost. He could not be found and on a trip like that there is hardly ever sufficient preparation made to permit a long halt to hunt lost or straggling members of a party, and I was under the impression that there was but little effort made to find this missing man at the time. But it is very evident, however, that he who goes into that country to depend altogether on others for his safety must necessarily become the recipient of miraculous and favorable accidents to ever get out again. Just so with the correspondent, while he was wildly and excitedly following each Indian trail he came across, the party of which he was a member was quietly moving on to the settlements in the county of Yavapai at Prescott. The correspondent kept traveling on foot hither and thither like a mad man until night came on and found him exhausted. He slept in the chaparral and again began his efforts in the morning to find himself, and continued his extraordinary exertions throughout the day only to find himself in a similar situation at night. He put in a third day without finding any part of the world which was not all lost. A fourth followed and he began to eat grass, twigs, and cedar berries. On the sixth day he began to lose his reason, having failed to find a drink of water for the whole time, only what he sucked from his handkerchief after pressing it upon the dewy grass in the morning. I can testify to the precariousness of such a mode of obtaining a drink of water in Arizona, for there was but little dew ever fell there. His tongue became so swollen that there was not room enough in his mouth for it and hence he began to choke.

He finally at the end of the eight days wandered into an Indian rancheria, whose inmates considered him a crazy man and furnished him water and an abundance of cedar berries. It was a remarkable fact about the Apaches, that they were superstitiously fearful of a demented person. They have more than once been known to treat kindly those whom they believe to be unsound of mind. They thus treated our correspondent but refused to go with him anywhere and directed him toward the settlements of the whites fifty miles away. He wandered for six more days and finally and accidentally staggered over a little ridge into the woods of Lynx Creek one evening and came suddenly in sight and within thirty paces of a miner's cabin and saw a man standing in the creek, leaning upon a long handled shovel. He was so feeble and so overcome by the unlooked for occurrence of seeing a friendly white man that he swooned and sank unconscious to the ground, where he might have perished had the man failed to have seen him fall. But he was seen to sink down and the men, who were some prospectors lately established in one of the old deserted cabins before referred to, went to his assistance, and carried him into the house and gave him all the aid at their disposal for his recovery. . . .

He appeared to be much of a gentleman and the remnants of his apparel indicated that he was well dressed when he started on his wild goose chase. Capt. Walker had previously visited Arizona and on his return to California I accompanied him as far as the Colorado River and we took the correspondent with us, as he was quite anxious to return to California after his truly miserable experience. I traveled with him several days and thus had an opportunity to hear a full detail of his helpless situation. . . . I returned from the Colorado, where I separated from the unlucky correspondent and Capt. Walker and I have never seen either of them since. I came back to Prescott where my cabin was considered my home and rested for a spell and enjoyed a short, safe, and quiet retreat free from the eternal trepidation, the consequence of worrying, exhaustive vigilance.[8]

One evening I was sitting before my little cabin door, which was not over two hundred paces from the Public Square of the town, and southwest of it, just in front of a well-known reef of granite boulders there, which borders the little valley of Granite Creek. I had borrowed a book from the Territorial Library and was trying to read.[9] The meandering creek ran a little way in front of me, as I sat facing the town. The current of the stream ran slow; though very shallow, it was calm and placid. . . . From the various incidents that were going on about me and the varying features of the scene through which I had been struggling constantly for five long years, my mind turned unbidden to the great hopes and fiery aspirations which prompted my every move to get ready for the doubtful venture, beginning with the preparations first made by laying in supplies at the store of Henry and Garret in Leavenworth City.

. . . I was finally aroused by a visitor who came to know if I was in a good mood to take a little party and cut off the retreat of the Apaches who had just captured some Jew merchants' pack train about five miles west of Prescott, and who had to pass not a great way from the town on their usual direction east. They had slaughtered all of those in charge and were going like the wind with the booty.

[8] Watson, *West Wind*, 106, states, however, that Walker remained in Arizona until 1867, which would have Walker leaving Arizona several years later than the account given here by Conner.

[9] Conner here is referring to the Territorial Library established from the books brought from the East by Richard C. McCormick. The report of the Territorial Librarian contains a list of the holdings of the library which varied from literature to law to science. *Journals of the Third Legislative Assembly of the Territory of Arizona*, 255 ff.

THE LAST CAMPAIGN OF SUGARFOOT JACK

I well knew that the savages had traveled as fast as the news of the capture had in coming to Prescott and therefore in all probability they were already past the town. So I declined to go so soon on another wild goose chase for a hundred miles east, just for the privilege of coming back again. But he said that quite a number of men were now ready to start. I tried to persuade him to go on a fast horse to some of the mining districts further east and to warn the miners of the fact who were already ahead of the savages and who had nothing to do but to get in front of them.

No; that suggestion he said wouldn't do, but we must cut them off before they had passed Prescott. I finally agreed that the goods taken were only dry goods anyhow, and would be but little loss. "Oh," he says, "don't you mistake yourself, for Miss Nettie Orsburn's wedding dress was amongst the plunder taken."

That was a stunner. I had forgotten that a wedding was to come off soon and that the necessary gear had been ordered by the Jew merchants three months previously from California. I could not dissuade them from going to cut off the savages as they passed the town, when I was perfectly satisfied that they had already passed and that they had done it rapidly because of having the mules of the pack train to ride. But I accompanied the party south about two miles and found the fresh trail of the Indians, who had gone by the place for hours. We returned to the town in the dark and upon our arrival, we found several persons down from the mines, amongst whom were three prospectors who had seen the flying savages. They were ignorant of the massacre and robbery and gave an excited account of an extraordinary band of Indians with whom they had exchanged a few shots and retreated to the nearest mining camp. They said that it was the finest dressed set of Indians they had ever seen. They declared that all of them were bedecked all over with ribbons streaming back behind them for ten feet in the breeze and concluded that it must have been a tribe from some new quarter.

The Jews had ordered a supply of female rigging to meet the demands of a growing market. But the wedding dress was gone to ornament the squaw of some of those "braves," and the wedding in consequence was postponed another three months to give the merchants time to repair the great loss. But the nuptials were celebrated upon the next pass without failure and it counted No. 2 of the weddings transpiring in central Arizona. The first young lady, Mary Ehle, was married to her spouse, John Dixon, by Governor Goodwin, and she was a member of the second family to arrive in the wilderness. This young lady who lost her "preparations" belonged to the first family to arrive and was the second to marry. Our old wag of the Walker Party was present and heard the story of the finely dressed savages directly from the lips of the excited narrators. After the recitation was through with, he confessed that he was at a loss to know how an Indian or any other man could dress himself with shoe-strings....

I have seen strangers observe with comical expression the ludicrous styles of miners, as they stalked about, dressed in their buckskin trousers, moccasins, and untanned deer-skin hats. Amusement and pity commingled would sometimes beam on the face of the uninitiated; but it would all clear away upon better acquaintance. The proceedings had at miners meetings were most generally a test of cultivated ability wholly unexpected by new comers and who nearly always thought that they were amongst ruffians. A little acquaintance convinced many immigrants of their own want of judgment in such matters. Those mines have supported many educated men in the garb of clowns. Again it might be truthfully said that the nomadic symptoms displayed more or less by all of our Rocky Mountain adventurers, smacks more of Nature than of ignorance and barbarism. Yet such inclinations are usually subjected to aspersions and most generally from the most ignorant classes, who, when a little pretentious, are always prominently prompt in substituting their votes for a school tax in the stead of the education that the fund is supposed to secure....

Mining the Quartz Lodes

THE CITIZEN WHO gave the bond, R. W. G[room], in the sum of five thousand dollars, had subsequently retired to Turkey Creek and established a prospecting camp only a little distance above the desperate battlefield of Henry Binkley and company, and succeeded in finding a rich quartz lode upon the south side of the creek upon a high, sharp chaparral spur, which lay at right angles with the stream. Upon breaking some of the blossom rocks into fragments, he discovered a generous display of gold adhering to the fresh break of the quartz and excitedly exclaimed *"Bully Bueano."* From this incident the *"Bully Bueano"* gold lode took its name and by that name was known all over the country and was subsequently bought by a Philadelphia Company, who soon after erected upon it a quartz mill which was said to have cost one hundred and fifty thousand dollars by the time it was finished.[1] This was the first quartz mill

[1] The Bully Bueno mine was located about fifteen miles southeast of Prescott. Barnes, *Arizona Place Names*, 66. Hinton, *Handbook to Arizona*, 102, has a sketch showing the location of the mine. The Prescott *Arizona Miner*, August 8, 1866, reported that ". . . [Robert W.] Groom and E. M. Smith interest in this mine, nine hundred feet, have been sold to the Philadelphia company, represented by Major Coffin, and formerly represented by Mr. Vickory, for ten dollars a foot, and that the mill sent out by said company will be put upon it."

ever imported to central Arizona and it was done by what was termed the Walnut Grove Mining Company, of which George Burnham of Philadelphia was president and Mr. Hoops of the same city was secretary, both of North Broad Street in Philadelphia, where the company was organized. The mill was taken from Chicago by G. H. Vickory, the company's agent, and it required sixteen mule teams to transport it from the Missouri River to Arizona, and the train was on the road over three months. It reached the "Point of Rocks" five miles below Prescott late in the summer of 1865 and proceeded thence to Turkey Creek around by the way of Agua Frio and erected on that stream opposite to the Bully Bueno lode, upon which work was also immediately begun.

Bueano in Spanish means good; but I presume that the prefix Bully is a pure Anglo-Saxon abbreviation from Latin; but, however, altogether it might be considered very good Spanish. At any rate it answered the purpose and became the object for the expenditure of money, it was said, to nearly the amount of a quarter of a million dollars. A tunnel was run into the base of a spur two hundred feet, which failed to reach the vein, and the company became disgusted and refused to furnish money and there it ended. Twenty thousand dollars would have tested the value of the lode thoroughly. The company failed and refused to pay its enormous and unnecessary debts, and the mill was burned to the ground without ever being put in motion. The agents of the company knew nothing whatever and were too smart to take advice. This lode dropped out of the center of the spur, and all the formations of the country about it dipped to the west. Still the agents persisted in beginning their tunnel on the east side of the ridge so as to necessitate tunnelling three-quarters of the distance through the spur to reach the vein; whereas one-quarter of the way from the west side would have probably sufficed. Yet in the fact of this plain proposition they were sure of reaching the vein at the center of the spur directly under the croppings at the top, nearly three hundred feet above, and became discouraged because they failed to do it.

The lode still stands untested, only what was done by the owners before the arrival of the mill. They had selected quartz from the croppings and ground it by means of *arrastres,* the cheapest of all quartz mills, and found the ore after testing it thus, by the ton. The *arrastre* is constructed by first planting a stout post firmly into the ground to extend out of the surface about two feet for a pivot. A curbstone set into the ground in a circle of about eight feet in diameter around this pivot as a center is the next step. Then the surface of this circle from the curbstone to the post in the center is neatly paved with flagstones. The curbstone stands eight inches or a foot above the pavement. A stout beam for the mules or horses to pull by is balanced across the pivot in the center and extended a considerable distance outside of the curbing where the power is attached, so that the animals can walk around and around in a circular path.

Two large boulders weighing several hundred pounds are placed on the pavement and by means of drilling holes into them, in which to insert a pin to tie to, they are geared to the beam on either side of the post in the center. The quartz to be ground is thrown into this circular bed over which these large boulders are dragged by the animals as they go around and around all day, like they do when hitched to an old fashioned grist mill. This was the substitute for the quartz mill in Arizona and it was by this means that the *Bully Bueano* was first tested. And I might add, the last, for the mill never crushed a pound of quartz. Thus ended the first great mining scheme undertaken in central Arizona without even cutting the vein intended to be worked.

The company was swindled every way, the details of which is unnecessary to state here. The agents had located and claimed for farming purposes quite a quantity of arable land several miles eastward on the Agua Frio and to the amazement of all mountain men about there, they built cabins on the land and sent all the fine mules of the company which drew the mill machinery to the country out there to be grazed and cared for.

The new ranch was in charge of four hands of the company, who knew nothing of Indian warfare and were located beyond the extreme border of the settlements and the country toward the east, in the direction of the Apache strong-holds. I heard an old miner tell the agent that he had better give that fine herd of mules to the miners of the country, who would take care of them, than to thus use them to tempt the Indians, who would be feasting upon their carcasses in less than two weeks after sending them to that ranch. He smiled confidently at the miner as he stated that he knew what he was doing. But in common parlance, the Indians took the mules, all the same, and did in less than three weeks, every one of them, and killed one of the hands and crippled another to do it, and got away safely with them for their own use, behoof, and benefit forever.

This busy headquarters of a hundred men was thus nearly deserted and broken up. Only about half a dozen men remaining to protect the property of this company. But as long as the camp was busy building, cutting wood and sawing lumber, the Indians kept their distance. The screaming of the steam whistle sounded odd enough in those woods so lately the wilderness loneliness, which had never perhaps been awakened by other sounds than that of the savage rifle and war-whoop and the howls of wild animals. The Indians who saw those great boilers, as they came over the road, thought that they were great guns which the "pale faces" were going to locate on Turkey Creek. I was one of the surveyors of the road through these mountains, by which to bring this machinery into the creek. Well do I remember of having camped in this little clump of woods a mile or two north of Turkey Creek then known as "Pine Flat," through which the road was to come.

My old friend, who relieved me at the cabin after a spell of sickness, was with me and we were alone, excepting that the hunting dog Munk was along. We concealed [ourselves] in some brush in this little circular woodland of fifty acres perhaps, and listened at the Mexican *Lobos* howl at us all night. These howls were answered by the imitations of Indians northeast of us in the direction where the train with machinery had halted. Upon arriving at the encampment of the train on the following day about noon the crack of a rifle on the side of a high hill overlooking the camp drew our attention. We hurried around the brow of an adjacent hill just in time to see some Apaches taking one of their wounded into some rocks. In spite of all of our efforts, they escaped. They had been stealthily espying out the situation of the mules and had failed to discover one of the guards who was seated up in some rocks above them and who greeted their presence with a rifle ball without previous warning.

But without serious incident or accident the train made its way over these rough mountains to its destination. However there were many amusing incidents transpired, for it did seem that the hands who worked the road and cleared the way as we proceeded could not turn over a stone without stirring up either a wasp's or yellow jacket's nest. These little bees would be constantly getting amongst the hands and mules and raised a greater excitement than the Indians. Their sting is much more painful in that climate than in the Atlantic states, and the bees themselves much more vicious.

Before the arrival of this quartz mill and before the news of the surrender of the Southern Confederacy reached Arizona, a paper had been founded on Turkey Creek with preamble and resolutions of a hostile and treasonable character and variously signed and delivered to the commanding officer at Ft. Whipple. This humble subscriber's name was said to have been signed to that dangerous paper, but if it was, it was a forgery. The officer who became very reasonably alarmed, if it imported what it was said to have done, ordered out the artillery and doubled the guard at the post, and made preparations generally for war. A sergeant and twenty-five soldiers started on their own account to "clean out" Lynx Creek, as they expressed it. This creek had begun to be populated again. The soldiers at the lower edge of these woods chanced to meet the Governor and his escort coming from Lynx Creek and expressed great surprise that he had entrusted his safety amongst the miners. The Governor replied that he could sleep perfectly soundly in any miner's cabin in the mountains, and that if they were going up to the mining settlements with hostile intent, they might be lucky to be able to get back again.

They turned back, but of course they were heard from by the miners, who in turn were provoked to indiscretions as a natural consequence. The Governor thus constantly became the main support to peace and safety and good government in the Territory. Many acts of this kind came to pass, but on this occasion messengers carried the news of the preparations at the Post to the different mining camps and some of them prepared for war and actually selected leaders, preparatory to storming the Fort. Committees were secretly sent to Prescott to learn what was the matter. Many men who cared nothing for the country took advantage of this excitement to stir up the country to resistance, to bring about an excuse to take and pillage the fort, for the want of something else to do. As for the paper reported to have been found on Turkey Creek and delivered to the commandant of the post, it was a forgery to raise a conflict, which it came near accomplishing. There was little thought of rebellion there, as there was at the time in Boston. It was all the concoction of the Government's friendly enemies, the public informers. But to the gratification of all good citizens, the fictitious ghosts all passed away without harm and laws were enforced and respected.

Pretty soon the news of the surrender of the Southern armies came and the causes of distraction died out and the subject dismissed, but the old animosity would sometimes crop out a little, as will be seen as we proceed.

But the constant arrivals of new immigration gave quite an orderly balance to good order and business inclinations. There was also a public school established in Prescott and in successful operation. It appeared strange to me to see the little ones going to school in this isolated town, whose site I had seen two years before resting in the calm repose and heavy silence of changeless Nature's wilderness. . . .

The United States sent also to Arizona an Indian agent to fill the place of Mr. Poston resigned. [George W.] Dent was his name and he too resigned and was succeeded by G. W. Leihy of New York.[2] Mr. Leihy was installed as agent but a short time when he took occasion to send a direction from La Paz (his headquarters) to Prescott to the effect that the citizens about mining camps and elsewhere should not unnecessarily kill the Indians but to capture them to go on a reservation, which he proposed to prepare for them. But little heed was given to his order, because the citizens of that day could furnish but scanty rations for themselves and they were very sure not to attempt to furnish them for Indians gratuitously and guards also to watch them, while holding them prisoners. But, however, some fellow, who the old citizens called green, became guilty of the humane act of sparing the life of an Indian whom he captured and delivered to the officers at Ft. Whipple. These officers gave the generous fellow slight thanks for his generosity, but received the prisoner and sent word of the fact to the agent at La Paz. Although it was over two hundred miles and over a desert country, the humane agent, his clerk, and two soldiers traveled the weary way and safely landed at Prescott after the prisoner.

They took their captive and started on their return trip to La Paz. About three days afterward, their mutilated bodies were found in the vicinity of Date Creek, west of Prescott, where I, with others, had had a little breeze with the Apaches upon our first visit to the place. The clerk's head had been taken from his

[2] Conner's order of events is not accurate at this point. When Charles D. Poston was elected Territorial delegate to Congress, he was succeeded by George W. Leihy, previously of the Territorial Council, as superintendent of Indian affairs. Leihy and party, consisting of his clerk and two Indians, one of whom was an Apache-Mohave, were attacked by Indians about forty-five miles from Prescott while returning to La Paz. The attack occurred on November 18, 1866, when Leihy and the clerk, H. C. Everts, were killed, and the clerk's head was severed from the body and taken by the Indians as a trophy. George W. Dent then succeeded Leihy as superintendent of Indian affairs of Arizona Territory. *Report of Indian Affairs by the Acting Commissioner, 1867,* 154–55.

body and hidden, or at least it never was found. The prisoner was the only one to escape destruction, while it was in his behalf that so much trouble and danger was incurred by the agent and his unfortunate associates. The agent's head was flattened between two rocks, indicating the mode of the Pimas in the destruction of those who fall in their power, or it might have been done in retaliation for the smashing of Apache heads on the raid previously described.

In this same locality perished Chas. Cunningham and Geo. Bell, and about in the same way.[3] They were rash enough to travel in this locality in the daytime and therefore forfeited their lives and gave a permanent name to the unholy place. I presume that there are but few citizens of central Arizona who do not know where Bell's Cañon is. My recollection of it is that it is pre-eminently befitting the character of the savages in whose range it is located and the necessities of the other inhabitants associated with them, by an all wise Providence. Its vegetation consists of cactus and its other inhabitants are coyotes, wolves, centipedes, tarantulas, and rattlesnakes and whippoorwills and destined to remain unchanged, for I cannot conceive what civilized man would want to stay there for. I confess some weaknesses upon this particular subject, for one of those men once did me a neat favor, which was very essential to my everyday wants. I had previously met one of them in the wilds of central Arizona before dry-goods stores came in fashion and he divided his limited supply of clothing with me of which I stood sadly in need. This incident was forcibly brought to mind long after its occurrence in the winter of 1867, on the San Gabriel River in California, when that stream overflowed its banks, changed its bed, and swept houses from El Monte into the sea.

A woman and two children clung to a rocking house and were barely recovered before the building started for the ocean, and after the excitement was all over I was surprised to learn

[3] The report of George W. Dent cites the place where Leihy was killed as Bell's Corner. Barnes, *Arizona Place Names*, 43, maintains that the site was named after Bell, but the companion of Bell was another prospector by the name of Sage, both of whom were killed by Indians in 1864.

that it was the widowed wife and orphan children of my friend Chas. Cunningham, who gave me clothes and who perished at Bell's Cañon by the hand of the Apache. But I shall quit the record of unfortunate events at least for the time and retreat again to my cabin in Prescott, and give a short account of the phenomenal elements of Arizona by only a recitation of particular circumstances noted by my own observation. It has already been stated that snow had fallen at Prescott to a depth of from eight to fifteen inches, and I knew the snow to lay in patches all over the twenty- or thirty-mile plain north of the town, until late in the spring in April and after lying thus for weeks, without perceptible decrease, still in patches, it would go off suddenly. But while lying on the ground for weeks, the weather was a little cool, but pleasant. And the periods of the rain-fall, as before stated, are confined to probably a little over two months in the fall of the year. And there was a little probability of more rain before and after these seasons as there was a snow in August during the several years that I was there. I never noted the time of the falling of the first frost in the vicinity of Prescott in the fall of 1863, because our little party of explorers had lost all days and dates, but its first greeting in the fall of 1864 came on the night of the ninth of September, and also in the fall of 1865, it likewise first fell on the night of the ninth of September. In 1866 the first frost to fall was on the ninth or the tenth of September, and again on the ninth of September in the fall of 1867, at about the date that this witness left the country. This was exceedingly regular, but in view of the constantly slow, listless, steady, and passive nature of this peculiar climate and its passionless elements, these facts do not appear strange to me, but rather to the contrary, very natural.

That dry and worthless plain north of Prescott may become a splendid agricultural land after spots of it are plowed and shaded sufficiently to keep or at least to increase moisture there to an extent sufficient to invite stray and flying clouds, which have either left their current or else have not yet a fixed nucleus. A fixed desert is simply inanimation fixed, and hence, of course, it is regular and more regular than it is possible for living, breathing, and moving elements to become and more especially so in view of the ever active and constantly changing, artificial necessities of humanity. . . .

On a warm night in 1865, whilst in company of three or four others, in the town of Prescott at or about midnight, my attention was called by someone present, to an unusual appearance northwest toward Granite Mountain, which had already been described. It was an exceedingly large transient, luminous body and it was slowly and steadily moving toward the west. It was light and brilliant and seemed to have been suspended in the atmosphere at an equal height of Granite Mountain, the summit of which the meteoric phenomenon appeared to be slowly approaching. Like a full moon suspended in the heavens amongst the passing clouds, it gave us ample time to observe its steady course. As it appeared to approach the summit of this mountain eight miles distant, it began to color into an increasing shade of pink, thence to a deep burning passionate red and then burst into a thousand fragments like a bomb-shell against the summit of the mountain and went out. Presently there came upon the night air the deep tone of an explosion, like the low tone of a distant cannon once exploded and then silent. . . . I should have thought that we might have been mistaken as to its distance in the night, as it was, had not other parties four miles below Prescott and four miles nearer, described it just as we saw and heard it. Its reality thus became the strangest part of it. It may have arisen from the bed of the lake, which has been described previously as lying at the eastern foot of Granite Mountain and subsequently drained. And the same into which I had previously waded waist deep to rob the floating bird's nest from whence I waded out after the robbery, followed by a covey of old birds swimming after me threateningly, thus forcing a humiliating reality of the ludicrous but just comparison with the achievement of Gulliver when he waded the sea pulling after him the whole fleet of the enemy to deliver up to the Lilliputians. This single instance of any meteoric discovery in Arizona was the only one I ever saw or heard of in that country and the largest I ever heard of existing in any country. . . .

There was an Assay office established by Alexander Mehan in Prescott and located in a little log cabin about fourteen feet square on Granite Street. It contained a bunk, a pair of scales, some cooking utensils, and an operator.

This shop was soon macadamized inside and out with quartz specimens from the various mines, requiring the aid of grams, decagrams, cupels, blow-pipes, etc. It appears that this preparation was intended for the study of Mineralogy instead of Geology, but there were more geological than mineralogical specimens tested. The proprietor kept open doors and his establishment soon became the center of central Arizona.

The excitement of daily new discoveries of blossom rock (as it was called) constantly created and increased the demand for scientific tests, consequently the Assayist was kept busy for nearly a year. Prospective fortunes made the gold hunters industrious and they never lacked for encouragement as long as they accompanied the specimen to be tested by the usual fee of ten dollars.

The Assayist always arrived at satisfactory conclusions by his scientific investigations, because he always told the applicant just what he wanted to believe about the value of his mine. This infant establishment soon grew to an importance before which the United States Patent Office would pale in its palmiest days. I think that some of the most prominent officers in the Territory had stock in it and patronized it liberally to make it prosperous. Each lucky fortune hunter would depart from this patent office buoyant and hopeful and energetically beat his way back to the mountain wilds, where his fortune lay concealed, bearing the important secret in his bosom and the proof of a working test on a piece of paper, a certificate from the Assay office. Yes, he had a working test all added up in black and white and figures wouldn't lie and as to whether the Assayor would or not, he never stopped to inquire. In fact he cared nothing about the Assayor anyhow. But he very naturally felt that the additional advice he received to the effect that it was prudent to keep his business to himself until he got his mine open and additional claims located for his friends, was important. Secrets in such matters in the mines are very important things. The advice was slyly given and it was worth that much more on that account.

Every man who took a specimen to the Assay office to test, left with the consciousness of having a very valuable personal confidant in the person of the Assayist. He always came to the conclusion that he was one of the select few at headquarters and he therefore would keep his own counsel and only make known the important fact which he possessed to a very few prudent personal friends. The reason was obvious, for if everybody knew how rich the mine was, everybody would want to buy out the adjoining claims and perhaps in a little while he might be able to exchange other mining stock for the said claims adjoining his and he therefore kept his Assay certificate of calculations in his pocket. Pretty soon, however, some other fellow less prudent than himself and who also has been to the Assay office and is in good standing there, cautiously draws out his bill of rights, wondrously added up. To offset this, miner No. 1 now draws out his schedule of prices and triumphantly reads—"Gold per cent .21½, Silver .32, Antimony, .16¾, Lead 7¼, Copper 13½, Sulpher, .6 &c. This was a very rich specimen only leaving three per cent of it for quartz. These two miners thus became allied to each other for mutual protection and agreed to keep the secret from all the world except a few personal friends whom they desired to post. They are greatly elated to think that each had had the good fortune to stumble on an extraordinary rich mine and to be kept posted from headquarters. Presently each intimates the circumstance darkly to a personal friend and joyfully receives the intelligence that the friend has also a flattering prospect evidenced by an official chart fresh from the Assay office, which he refuses to display until they step aside out of sight so as to count up the per cent of gold, silver, zinc, antimony, &c, without interruption.

They look at the important paper altogether, and being very cautious, they won't risk counting it out loud and conclude the investigation therefore by nods, winks, and glances. These fellows finally took a long breath and returned to the mining camp while in their hearts they thanked Heaven for their good luck and pitied the rest of the population for their want of it. What selfishness. If they had all—the whole camp—become warm personal friends, they might all have had the pleasure of openly congratulating each other over their respective fortunes evidenced by the same or a similar official patent from headquarters and praised the Lord for having been the luckiest camp of miners in the mountains. Each man thus thought that he was the best posted individual in the mines, but when they began to be neighborly, brotherly, and trusting with each other, behold, and it was discovered that there was not a badly posted man to be found in all the land of Israel. This was a well-organized arrangement at headquarters and embodied some of the best principles for the control of man known to cunning rulers. It is the beauty of this mode of government that so enchants the wily speculator all over the land. But suffice it to say that this usually successful and crafty mining region art, like all others, served out its usefulness and slowly and gradually went out of style and finally died dead of old age, without drawing a tear, except from headquarters.

But new situations produced new necessities and the result of this death was to organize companies, and individuals of which would throw all of their mining stock into hotch-pot and send it on to New York by some defunct Assayor as agent for all the owners, to swindle capitalists out of their money, after which the agent always made his escape to parts unknown. . . .

It was claimed during these early settlements by those who professed to be Geologists and Mineralogists (some of whom were amongst the military) that the accepted theory would show that the broad belts of Arizona and New Mexico were essentially Laurentian, if there is any way to learn what that means. The Laurentian rocks were supposed to comprise the great portion of the areas colored Eozoic. The name seems to have been applied to a system in 1855. And it was supposed that if a subdivision of the Laurentian should be found practicable, it was claimed that a portion would prove to be older than the Atlantic seaboard, and it was ascertained that this formation lay also at the bed of the Colorado River in Arizona. But whatever may have been their conclusions, it is certain that Arizona is plentifully filled with metalliferous veins, and until those regions are better studied and scientifically tested by competent Geologists, no practical interests can be taken in any theory by those who are actually operating in the new mines of that country.[4] A bill was once said to have been introduced into the Oregon Legislature, providing for a Territorial Geologist. A member from some of the mining districts who strenuously opposed the bill declared that "When you come to dig in these 'ere mountains, you'll find a heap of rocks that the books don't know anything about." The bill was lost.

The formation in Arizona is a conglomeration and compared to the Atlantic coast—a modern chaos. There did not in any of her infant mines appear to be any primitive stratification of any particular materials. Gold, silver, iron, copper, lead, antimony, &c, with each one's train of numerous attendants, all seemed to have but little choice as to locality or surroundings. It is true that *lodes* can be traced on the surface, but their interminable dips, spurs, and angles are confused and deceptive on the surface and, for ought I know, to the bottom. They indiscriminately commingle without any reference to the kind or class of minerals adjacent or in juxtaposition. But perhaps and very probably—it is my own fault that it appears to be a "mighty maze without a plan," and whether it is or not, I confess that from my personal observation, it is a monstrous confusion without any apparent hope of explanation, either through the imagination or orderly calculations. However, it is my modest opinion, whether or not it be extracted from that "mighty maze with a

---

[4] It would seem that Conner had access to a geological map from the terms used here. Note the use of the phrase, "areas colored Eozoic."

plan," that we could more effectually discern the multiplicity of plans which those geological materials must have laid out before digging, than by any other process yet submitted. Scientists may indeed find a theory that will reach the question, but it will not be equally correct with one which the same ability might frame to discover the hidden participants in a game of hide-and-go-seek.

Yet while delving amongst the interstices of the rifts existing under the surface in Arizona, without reference to the character of the minerals sought, there is found a wonderful uniformity in its materials, closing the cracks and seams. And this material only differs as does the quality of mortar used in the construction of brick houses at the same period, while the character of the quartz taken from one lode differs so palpably from that taken from another in the same vicinity, that any novice with slight attention can easily detect that difference. This is true and it matters not whether the lodes are each silver or gold bearing or one of the one and one of the other. The black or chocolate colored shale may mark the base of either, or both. The same may be found overlaying the mortar-like substance above referred to, which is evidently a kind of a clay-shale, colored according to the circumstances of its position and location. And these conditions are also dependent upon and owing in some degree to the different conditions in which the main body of the lode is left by a greater or less subjection to the action of fire at the time of upheaval. The feldspar also usual in the casing of quartz veins of whatsoever kind of mineral differs in color and stability and yet may be the same in hornblend or pyrite lodes. So also, with the yellow or cream colored marl, which it is said after its subjection to different conditions even in different lodes, when found alternating with clay or soapstone, produce the most singular conglomerate of all—the puddingstone. This is not correct in fact. It is never found in quartz ledges. My conclusions are: theory or no theory, that is all the mines near together in Arizona, whether of gold, silver, lead, tin, iron, &c, have their crevices and clefts filled with the same putty-like substance, and whether called marl, shale, feldspar, clay, or soapstone or talc, it had nothing to do with the character of minerals contained in the ledge. With these few pretensionless remarks, I shall leave the subject except so much as require to give an explanation of the formation of the puddingstone (so called), according to my personal observation alone.[5]

William's Fork heads not far north of Prescott City, and is a tributary to the Colorado. For miles in extent it is but a cañon—a meandering gorge with perpendicular, craggy wall of rocks and probably in places many hundred feet in height. At the head of this cañon where it debouches out up stream, or rather where all the rivulets, gulches, and arroyos of the country converge to open into this gorge, I found some splendid specimens of puddingstone, so pronounced by our geologists at Prescott, where I conveyed samples of it. The clumps of barren and broken hills all about the head of this cañon were of almost all shades of color, from black volcanic to white. Each rivulet and hollow had its own peculiar shade of little boulders and pebbles, worn spherical and oval by attrition. When the rains came, they washed these pebbles out of all the hollows in the neighboring vari-colored hills and brought them in such quantities to the entrance of the gorge that they choked it up, thereby elevating the original bed of the stream some ten or twelve feet higher.

Subsequently the water found its way through this embankment of stones and pebbles over against the right bank of the stream and washed out the debris again to the old bottom of the river. After getting a start, the water from time to time caved off the embankment of cemented pebbles and steadily widened the stream again toward the left bank where there was only a remnant of the embankment left, which when I saw it in 1864 constituted the left-hand wall of the beginning of the

---

[5] A puddingstone is defined as "a popular term of a conglomerate consisting of well rounded pebbles in an abundant matrix." C. M. Rice, *Dictionary of Geological Terms*, 327.

Prescott, one stage beyond the town of Conner's day.
(From James H. McClintock, *Arizona: The Youngest State,* II.)

cañon and was probably twelve feet in height. This wall was caved over toward the stream a little and really parts of it overhung the shallow water at its foot. It was nothing more than a mass of small stones and pebbles firmly cemented together. I noticed some solid white quartz pebbles in it, which seemed to have formed there, but I knew they had not. When the wall last slabbed off, some of the pebbles and stones broke into two parts, one part adhering in the wall, and the other to the falling fragment. A few of the pebbles drew out of the wall, leaving a half-spherical cavity while the convexed half adhered to the slab and *vice-versa*. In breaking some of the fragments the mass would break directly through the pebbles, like any other solid stone, leaving like colors on each piece to match its corresponding color on the other. Some of these fragments that fell off of the wall had laid in the running water until they had worn smooth, forming a beautiful variegated surface of all distinct shades of color. Some of the pebbles were evidently harder than others, but the whole mass of a fragment was hard and solid. I took some small fragments with me to Prescott, where they were pronounced by professionals to be exceedingly pretty specimens of puddingstone. My recollection is that the wall showed unmistakable evidences of having been deposited there by different layers at different times. Now all that remains to be said is, if this was not the geological puddingstone of the scientists, it was a conglomerate which answered the purpose and as fine a counterfeit as could be formed and the mode of its formation so palpable—I think, to be mistaken, and an unnatural substance to form in the casing of a quartz lode. . . .

The redoubtable Smith . . . was with a little camp of miners, was located high up on the Colorado and not far from that stream engaged in prospecting for new diggings. Their supply of provisions was scanty, having to transport them a long distance on these docile little animals—Mexican donkeys. The Indians here, like they were everywhere else in hostile regions, were continuously hanging around in the neighboring rocky defiles, watching for all opportunities to kill a "pale face," or capture a donkey for a roast.

These annoyances continued until some ten of the "boys" concluded to go in search of them and teach them a lesson. After the necessary preparations were made they began their march and penetrated the rocky wilderness for nearly twenty miles. They lay concealed in a cañon all one night and sent out a spy in the morning to discover camp-smokes. The messenger having taken his position on an adjacent hill, soon discovered the smoke from a ranchería arising out of the woods, perhaps two miles away and came back and reported accordingly. The party immediately proceeded toward the ranchería and finally came to a well-used trail coursing directly toward the ranchería through the timber.

They followed the trail for a few hundred paces, then turned out of it into the woods and proceeded back a little distance and took their position in some rocks, commanding the trail at a short range, and concealed themselves in line. A signal to be made by the approach of the savages to a certain point in the trail was agreed upon. The most of this party were armed with double-barreled shotguns and thus became quiet to await the coming of their game. It was but a little while here in the morning of a sunny day and in the shady woods, before thirteen "braves" all painted up came silently along the trail in single file from the direction of their camp. The concealed enemy had it so arranged that each one was to shoot the savage whose position in his own line corresponded with his own number, so as to divide their compliments as largely as possible amongst the savages upon the first volley.

When they arrived at the proper place in the trail and opposite the "pale face's" ambush, the latter let loose their deadly and well-directed fire, taking the savages completely by surprise and killing and disabling all of them except one. This fellow ran but the left-hand barrels of those "big" guns stopped his flight within less than a hundred paces. They considered this a very neat "job" and proceeded thence to the ranchería which they found deserted. The remaining residents had heard the reports of those terrible guns and escaped perhaps to neighboring camps to stir up volunteers for resistance and perhaps aggressive measures. These men, well knowing the Indian character, and being fully conscious of the weakness of their little force, began to retreat toward their own headquarters. It is natural, when once away from a guilty scene, for the assailants to become more quiet and less trepidatious. So with those men they became careless and began to scatter in order to hunt game on the return trip. Some Indians came on the trail and luckily the first shot only wounded one of the "boys" who escaped to some others, followed by the savages, and the result was a little conflict which brought all the white men together except Smith, who was missing. The men gave away and fell back as they defended themselves for five miles, the savages wounding several of them slightly. But the savages were unable to detain them long enough for their reinforcements to come up and therefore the men kept falling back, until they became near enough home to get the supposed protection of a permanent camp and the result was, that the savages deserted the contest and the adventurers arrived safely into their headquarters at dark, pretty well worn out. These fellows were in the habit of taking with them while hunting game an empty sack in which to carry venison. But on this occasion they only got one small deer near home and that was after pursuit was abandoned.

There was now a general expression of regret at the loss of poor Smith, who was still missing. Thinking that it might be possible for him to have become lost in the wilderness, they fired signal shots for him at intervals, after each of which, someone would remark the uselessness of it, as Smith had gone to his happy hunting ground. The tired men began to get their suppers and otherwise to repair the wear and tear of the day. Large campfires were built and frugal repasts provided in order for final disposal, around which all parties were arranged in sitting postures on the ground. The night became dark and bright fires were therefore kept up, as the only light had on those occasions.

Presently all ears were open to hear the sound of a footman's approach. Suspense was short, however, for Smith came walking into camp puffing and blowing with his sack of venison on his back, looking much fatigued. Shout after shout of triumphant gratification arose upon the night air as Smith sat down his sack before the fire. No, he had not seen any Indians on his return trip and didn't understand the situation, and knew nothing of the fighting on the home route nor of his own supposed destruction. He therefore turned to the boisterous "boys" and demanded to know what they were all going crazy about. Another shout without explanation only served to give Smith the sulks and he quietly turned to his sack of game and caught the bottom corners, and emptied the contents out on the ground before the fire, which consisted of four or five Indian heads. They came tumbling out of the sack like so many pumpkins and bounced and rolled about upon the ground. This stayed all mirth and levity. The men all forgot what they were doing and stared at the ghastly spectacle in mute surprise. The open eyes of the death head gazed blankly by the firelight at whatever direction the accidental position of the head gave them.

Smith stood carelessly looking at his property without saying a word. The "boys" thinking that he too had to fight his way back and that these heads were captured on the way, all asked in one voice, "Why, Smith, where did you get those heads?" "These is the heads we killed this morning," he replied without taking his eyes off of them. "Well, what in the d—l did you bring them here for?" was again asked. "To git the brains to tan my deer hides, what you 'pose?" he answered quietly. This brought out a furious laugh, which some one brought to a close by saying, "Smith, I always thought that you was the biggest fool in the mountains, and now I know it." This angered Smith a little and he sharply replied, "Fool; oh yes, I am a fool. You carry a little venison for twenty miles, when you kin get a deer close by any day, while it 'taint every day you kin git Ingun heads. Now who's the biggest fool, me or you. The best buckskin I ever seed," he continued, "was tanned with Ingun brains."

MINING THE QUARTZ LODES

After quite an amount of sharp shooting the subject was dropped and Smith was left in peaceful possession of his ghastly property to use in any way that suited his fancy, and he tanned his deer hides with the brains. While he was storing away his ghastly plunder, preparatory to getting his supper, he gave a little chuckle and consoled himself by saying that before that rancheria could bother any more, a new "crop of Inguns" would have to be planted there. Some of the men pretended to believe that Smith was going to have a feast upon those heads and watched him on several occasions in a manner to attract his attention. Smith finally became annoyed and turned upon his supposed spy and shouted loud and angrily, "Clear out from here you fool, do you take me for a d—n wolf? I'll shoot you like I would an Ingun directly." . . .

The Pima Indians and also the Maricopas have for many years been raising corn and wheat on the Gila away across the deserts, and for that matter so have the Apaches raised patches of both in Arizona. But the first field of corn we have any account ever raised in central Arizona was planted and cultivated by Brown and Postle, a little over twenty miles north of Prescott, at the first location of Fort Whipple near the head of the Verde River.[6] This crop was harvested in 1865. The following year found an increased number of acres planted upon the same premises, of both wheat and corn, by the same men. The humble instrument of these notes, in conjunction with a friend, also conceived the idea of farming, pursuant to which design we located adjoining and west of Brown and Postle's premises three hundred and twenty acres of land. It was quite a pretty piece of land, being an inclined plain and therefore easy to irrigate.

---

[6] The site to which Conner is referring was Postle's ranch, which was some twenty-two miles northeast of Prescott. Robert Postle was an officer in the 1st New Mexico Cavalry, who, when mustered out of service, squatted on the previous site of Fort Whipple in the Chino Valley. Barnes, *Arizona Place Names*, 343–44. Conner served in the third legislative assembly as a member of the lower house from Yavapai County, under the name of Daniel Ellis. His residence was recorded as Postle's ranch and his occupation as a farmer. *Journals of the Third Legislative Assembly of the Territory of Arizona.*

There was no such thing as raising corn on uplands in that country, without irrigation, and but poorly upon the bottom lands. Indeed corn cannot be grown there at all upon other than swampy lands, without irrigation.

We purchased one third of the water right of Brown and Postle which of course adhered to the premises as a farm right, afterward. This land was thickly set in heavy sage-brush and during the spring of 1866 we cleaned off about eighty acres and planted it in corn and raised about ten bushels to the acre. We also planted about three acres of barley, which only grew about eight inches high. It was never gathered, but the corn was and cribbed. We gave twenty-two and a half cents per pound for seed corn and barley, with which to plant this ground. Before we began to plant, we had numerous *acequias* or water ditches for irrigating purposes to construct and also a house, out-houses &c, and a corral for stock. We were compelled to convey all the timber used about this ranch from the woods in the vicinity of Prescott, over twenty miles distant, except the posts of which the corral was constructed, which we hauled from some cedar glades situated about five miles west of this ranch. This corral of cedar posts was constructed by digging a deep ditch around a rectangular piece of ground in which the posts were inserted against each other perpendicularly, forming a stout wall of upright posts, hard to displace.

The capacity of the corral was sufficient for the enclosure and safe keeping of a hundred and fifty head of horses. This was the second crop ever raised and harvested in that country. The alkaline in this new land blighted the crop very materially. We cribbed this corn in the fall of 1866, or at least that which was left of it after the Apaches took their rents out of it, which they were constantly doing after dark. They would come into the field after night as thick as blackbirds and sit leisurely around the shocks and husk corn and fill three bushel buckskin sacks and leave, loaded down to the guards, and then send their neighbors for more on the following night. They at last came in such numbers that they began to think that the few hands about the place feared to attack them. I sent a double-barrel shotgun down there by a young man who proposed to sojourn at the place awhile for their express benefit.

When night came on the lords of the soil came for their rental as usual, and arranged themselves around the number of shocks necessary to give them all room, and proceeded to business. Two of the hands went around the field to the lower and farther end from the house and concealed themselves behind the shocks. The young man with the double-barreled gun proceeded directly toward them cautiously, and came in close range, raised his gun, and clicked it at them. The savages heard the sound and stopped their noise just in time to hear another click. But the young man found that his gun refused to go off and he therefore drew his pistol and fired as the savages arose and fled. In their flight they came in the vicinity of the two men concealed at the lower end of the field, whose guns did fire and killed a savage each. They drew pistols and crippled others of them before they were out of reach, and came back to the house. Upon investigation, the young man's gun was found to be already empty, having been fired by some one else during the evening, who failed to recharge it. On the following morning they found quite a number of buckskin sacks half filled with corn, sitting around the shocks, and also the bodies of the two "braves" who fell in the legitimate exercise of providing food for their papooses. One of them had his whole crown lifted off above the eyes by an ounce rifle ball. The men hung these bodies at the lower end of the field, upon a tripod built of three poles for a scarecrow, similar to the action taken by old ladies sometimes, to keep the hawks away from the chickens. Months subsequently I was on the ground and saw parts of the disjointed skeletons of these savages scattered about where the wolves had left them. But this little warning broke up their claims to a part of the crops and the remainder was as before stated, cribbed, and for aught I know is still there, for there was no market for it, and there was still some of it on hand when I left the country. My associates in this new ranch and corn crop were Geo. Banghart and E. G. Peck.

The military held the treasury of central Arizona those days, and the Government was the only market for corn within a thousand miles and the officers would have let their stock starve before they would have purchased grain from a man raised in a slave state. We could not have sold this corn to the quartermaster at any price, even when he was paying from six to ten cents per pound for it.[7]

Then besides, the army in the Territories always had its pets and flunkies and perhaps always will have. Suffice it to say I quit farming, but as a rule the officers of the military and civil service were gentlemen and well understood the inconveniences of this isolated situation. This insignificant malice generally arose amongst the lower characters of the civil and military service. This was the first corn ever raised on that soil since the flood and I left it that fall and was not on the place at all during the following year. But when I saw the situation and understood it, I took my last view of my unrequited labor by a peep through the cracks of that crib at my corn and departed without making any disposition of it, and have never seen the premises since only through my imagination, when reflecting upon the various trials and painful struggles successfully overcome around and about my first, last, and distant farm.

My experience in this matter brought vividly to mind a bit of advice which I heard by an old camp follower to his friend of less experience. It was in the earlier part of my career, when I was not sufficiently informed to give it proper attention, but subsequent observations hurled back the light words of "Old Jimmie" . . . upon my recollection with all of its truth, naked and plain. He said that the best way to get along out on the frontier and on the plains and to have a good easy time, was to go with the troops and get in with the quartermaster. He said

---

[7] Provisions were purchased from the farmers around Prescott because the quartermaster bought barley at $17 per hundredweight and hay for $35 a ton in 1866. Swor, *Development of Prescott*, 75–76.

that he had tried it for years and he had learned to do everything that the quartermaster told him to do, no matter what it was, and that it was always right, provided he held his tongue about it himself. If an officer asked him where he was going and what he was going to do, he said that he would tell him in his own way, but he would never risk saying that the quartermaster had sent him to do it. Jimmie said that even if he knew that he was doing right, he had to do it by himself, without bringing in the quartermaster's name. He said that the understanding of this rule without any questions about it, was the main point, and especially about new settlements or mining camps.

Jimmie said that he had no trouble to make money at all, when he thus got on the "blind side" of the quartermaster (as he expressed it) because the quartermaster was always on the "blind side" of the commanding officer. He said that no quartermaster ever told him to brand a government mule with the letter "C" (which stood for condemned) but that he somehow or other always knew when to do it without any words about it. An officer, he said, would never stoop so low as to inquire of a citizen or miner as to where he got his mule, after seeing the letter "C" branded upon it, and that he never in his life heard the quartermaster say anything about it, more than that the Indians were getting the mules every few days and that the Government would have to soon furnish more. Jimmie said that the commissary stores always spoiled fast in the neighborhood of ranches and mining camps and would have to be burned after being condemned. He said that he saw a sergeant sell twenty blouses at Santa Fe and reported them burned. Saddles, bridles, boots, shoes, and overcoats, all says Jimmie, can be condemned for burning, but he never saw any of them burned. Contracts for furnishing hay, also, he said, was a "big thing" and in short when a fellow got in all right that there was no little thing about it. He stated that the biggest speculation he was ever in was not far from Santa Fe, New Mexico, when the Government employees' back wages were all paid off with quartermaster vouchers. He said that the quartermaster furnished him the money with which to buy up the vouchers from hands, some of which he got for ten cents on the dollar.

Jimmie thus continued at great length to give a wonderful story of his convenient mode of money making, as he expressed it, which was made just by picking it up. The enthusiasm of the old camp follower's discourse came to me as before stated, unbidden, several years subsequently. I was at Fort Whipple, near Prescott City and saw nearly a wagon load of plunder lying off some distance from the post in a pile preparatory for burning. It lay under after dark and an acquaintance of mine bought a set of new whippletrees out of the pile, for which he paid seven dollars and fifty cents. The rest of the pile was sold out in the same manner. But subsequently another pile of new goods was thus laid out to burn and a lieutenant happened to discover it and took his position near by and refused to depart until it was really burned and then proposed to the quartermaster if that work was to be continued, to burn the fort and have done with it. But old Jimmie said that he was always sharp enough to 'spose that the officers knew nothing of such business. I shall never forget my surprise at the acknowledgment of a sergeant of having disposed of a quantity of soldiers' clothing by private sale and then of making the required affidavit to the proper distribution of the same amongst the soldiers. He was soon after his desperate and volunteer confession, killed by the Indians not far from Prescott. . . .

Visits to Sonora and La Paz

HAVING COMPLETED some sample sporadic subjects just previously, I shall proceed the regular course of incidents as they transpired. It was toward the fall of this year [1865] that a Theatre building was completed and a second part under way of construction. Bowers & Bro. imported a set of sax horns and a brass band was organized and put into successful operation. This and many other enterprises looking to a constant improvement was pushed forward with success.

About this time while a body of men were making preparations to go east again to chastise the marauding savages, a herd of cattle was attacked within a half-mile of Prescott. The affrighted animals dashed into town with arrows sticking into them and bellowing frantically. One of them was a frightened bull, which had his pluck warmed up in the mêlée and he dashed at some school children, who escaped in different directions. The enraged brute then deserted the children and gave chase to a merchant, Mr. Wetheimer, in a red wrapper, who happened to be out of his store, and ran him to the door, and stopped and pawed and examined around there for some time, as though he wanted to go in.[1] The savages killed quite a number on the attack and escaped as usual. But the party of men who were organizing to go in search of them completed their preparations, to the number of fifty, and took up the route by the Big Bug District and proceeded thence southeast and crossed the Agua Frio by the table lands lying along that stream. This party's destination was already settled and it took up a pretty direct line of march toward the fertile valleys of the Salt River and other tributaries of the Rio Gila. The supplies of the party were limited and before reaching the objective point, it was arranged to send twenty men to the Pima Indian Village for flour. This gave some time to loiter and six of us therefore halted to examine some quartz lodes. Night came on before we were through with the ledges, and therefore we determined to stay in the vicinity for the night and encamped upon a high rolling country amongst the scattering rocks and low, stunted chaparral. Before night, however, we had discovered on one of the quartz ledges the remains of black and red paint, where some of the savages had very recently completed their war toilet. This paint had not entirely dried on the stone and we therefore had two of our little party of six stand sentinel at the same time. After camp duty was all over and our blankets were spread for a night's rest, the guardsmen took their places and the night was quite dark. A Georgian, whom we called John, and Jake, a Dutchman, were sentinels for the forepart of the night, and were to be relieved at midnight by two others.[2] The remainder of the party retired for the night into their blankets and were soon asleep, leaving the camp as silent as were the sentinels. Peace pervaded all the elements while everything on earth appeared still and lifeless.

[1] Aaron Westheimer, or Wertheimer, a native of Germany, aged thirty-three, was listed as a trader possessing a personal estate of $3,000 in the *1864 Census of Arizona*, 183–84.

[2] Jake could have been again Jacob Schneider of the original Walker Party who was born in Germany. Conner to Hall, May 10, 1910, CONNER MANUSCRIPTS. From contemporary newspaper account, however, Conner seems to have erred in the dates because the Prescott *Arizona Miner*, May 25, 1864, presents a signed article by Henry Clifton, a member of the party, in which the incidents are given essentially as written by Conner. Clifton spells the name of Donohoe as "Donohugh," and clearly shows that the expedition took place in March and April, 1864.

Our four happy men thus slept soundly all night without the least disturbance. The gray dawn of morning began to approach gently as the sable curtain of night drew away. One of the sleeping men, whose duty had been assigned as relief at midnight, being apprised of approaching daylight, becoming frightened for not having been called up, to take his place on guard, suddenly sprang to his feet with his rifle in hand, and exclaimed, "Why, what is the matter, Jake? Where are you?" This brought all the rest of the sleepers to their feet, surprised and ready for war on the shortest possible notice, all of whom expected to receive a volley from the savages, who had stealthily killed John and Jake on their posts. But when Jake was discovered crouched behind a little stump of chaparral with his gun at make-ready, and covering John's locality about thirty yards distant and John in about the same position, watching Jake, the problem was solved.

The situation was at once so ludicrous and unexpected that the two thoroughly disgusted sentinels were greeted with a spontaneous, jolly laugh that immediately changed the whole face of the landscape.

Jake was the first to get his self-control and arose from his concealment full of explanations and assaults upon John's ignorance. He vigorously exclaimed, "Shon vas shust like a fool, shumping into does pushes all night, and conglude to keep him dare; fir I vas not much shleep anyhow." "But Jake," interrupted John, "didn't you see three Apaches rush down the hill just before midnight?" "No, no, I didn't see no Inchens all night." John became disgusted and Jake had gotten the start of him and triumphantly maintained his ground. John persisted and Jake received the hearty laughs of the party with complacency. Humiliation had not taken root amongst the tender fibers of his heart all for nothing, and he successfully displayed his home-spun indignation at John's presumption to trying to make it appear that he too had been frightened during the night. Jake's Dutch beat John's English and the latter gave up the contest, but had seen the Indians in spite of all that Jake could say.

The contest, however, was lost amongst an additional and accruing duties, and the business of the morning was proceeded with as usual. As soon as breakfast was over we discovered an accumulation of skulking savages in an adjacent ravine and this served to convince John that he was correct, and the rest of us that we were not going to be given sufficient time to prospect the quartz lodes and we therefore beat a hasty retreat in search of the main body of men who we found encamped on some tributary of Salt River in the afternoon of the same day.

Twenty of our men departed for the Pima Village for supplies. I don't think that any of the party were certain whether we were on a tributary of the Salt River or the Gila. At all events we encamped here a few days to give our men time to return with supplies. In the foothills of a large sharp spur overlooking this pretty little valley there was a fine looking sharp quartz ledge in the fragments of which gold could be detected with the naked eye. Also some good prospects from the dirt in the neighboring ravines were found without extra pains. . . .

Animation sparkled in the clear atmosphere and to strike out of the encampment seemed to be the inclination of the whole party, and a general move therefore was determined upon. . . . We harnessed up our pack animals, took a direct line to one of the prettiest valleys, and again encamped, unpacked, and turned the mules into an Apache wheat field and placed a guard around them to keep them there. The patch of wheat contained probably three acres. This was late in the year, but their crop was late and whether it was a second crop or not I cannot say, but it was a fine one. The stock were thus permitted to destroy this fine patch of wheat while we engaged ourselves in throwing up a stout brush corral which contained about an acre of surface. On the following day the savages to the number of nearly a hundred visited our encampment and came within the enclosure. They seemed to take no exceptions to our apparent breach of neighborly conduct of pasturing their wheat patch out of existence, but on the contrary looked exceedingly cheerful and mixed pleasantly with the "pale faces." But that encampment of white men were too well experienced to be thus caught off their guard. Still we were not ready for the fracas because of the absence of twenty of our party after provisions. To trust them was fatal and to attack them would have probably been fatal to the safety of the absentees. Therefore to prevent the savages from giving the signal of attack became the great consideration.

Their principal chief was sought out and a man was stationed near him with a double-barreled shotgun to kill him in case he gave any signal. The old fellow noticed the neighborly conduct of the man with the blunder-buss and to dispel all suspicions, he quietly seated himself upon the ground and thence reclined upon his elbow. Some of the rest of their leaders were similarly provided for, but when this old leader saw a heavy, stout, and red-complected Canadian come and lay down carelessly upon the ground in front of him, he became uneasy. The Canadian then quietly drew a heavy revolver from his scabbard and began to toy and play with the cylinder in a leisurely, careless manner by whirling it around on its axis. This act took all the coolness out of the old "brave." Indian-like, he knew that actions spoke louder than words, and he began to feel that his guilty intentions were discovered by the very silence about him. He glanced around the corral and uttered a very slight guttural.

Every eye about him was riveted upon him in an instant. He trembled and became nervously anxious that his quiet goose-like order should go into effect. Three or four of his warriors walked off and passed out of the corral through a gap left for passing the mules in and out. These were quietly followed after a moment or two by another little batch in an orderly way and continued until there were not a half-dozen left.

The old "brave" was evidently relieved after his warriors were gone and asked in broken Spanish why all the whites kept their arms in their hands while in camp. He was informed that it was for the same reason that the great Chief's braves did the same thing and the great Chief ought to know that brave warriors always kept their arms in their hands except when asleep.

He finally took his leave in a friendly mood and promised to come back on the next day but failed to do it.

This old Indian found that his trick was too well understood to avail him and he therefore had no further investigation to make in that quarter, and when our men arrived from the Pimas it was in vain that we tried to tempt them into the corral again. "The splendid little parlor," was that of the spider, but the fly refused to the last and this golden opportunity of having a "big killing," as it was expressed, was lost forever. After working with them two or three more days without success we deserted the place and penetrated a rolling rocky chaparral country toward the north and encamped in a sterile, bare land to rest only at noon. But when we moved out of the brush corral camp, six or eight of the party remained behind and got possession of three Indians who entrusted themselves to their mercy and hanged them on a cottonwood with some pack ropes which were thought could be spared. This was regretted, for it was not worth the while of so many men going to destroy three savages. The open breach of good faith could not be justified, for even policy's sake for such small results. It was evident that these savages had coolly plotted our destruction by the cheapest mode practical, but we were equally guilty. The party was not organized to whip them into surrender merely, but to destroy them as the only means of having peace in the country.

We halted at the second camp referred to and within about three hundred paces of a low dividing ridge of quite a scope of naked barren country. As soon as the animals were unpacked, a young man in the party with whom I was but little acquainted, who called himself Purdy, walked to the top of the ridge and halted amongst some granite rocks, from which to look at the country beyond the ridge from the camp. He had hardly halted, however, when the savages arose from the rocks about him and fired a fatal volley upon him and lanced him after he fell. Four of us immediately ran to his assistance and so quick was the work done that when we reached him, he was stripped of all his clothes except his shoes, and he had risen to one elbow, trying to get up.

The savages retreated down the opposite side of the hill and fired at us from behind the rocks. But when two of our men passed our wounded friend and began a regular fire on the savages it had the effect of keeping them behind rocks until the remaining two of us caught up the unfortunate man and took him down to the place of encampment. But he never lived over three minutes after laying him down upon a blanket previously prepared for him. He exerted himself greatly to speak as we took him between us and he blew and bespattered our faces with blood in the effort, but failed to get out an intelligible word. No one knew where he was from or where his friends could be found and it was supposed that his efforts to speak were intended to give some such information. But it was futile, he was buried a little distance from the spot without a coffin of course and left to the lonely companionship of wolves and the most sterile and lonely country in Arizona. . . .

In less than three hours from the time we tarried here we were moving off again and the sadness of this peculiar situation was really oppressive. On looking back at our comrade's broad and unkept cemetery the place seemed more than ever forbidding. A clump of sorry looking chaparral half hidden by a pile of naked rocks here, a lonely cactus loaded with balls of straw-colored thistles there, and naked ground streaked with little knobs of ridges and knots everywhere. I do not suppose that any one of our party has ever seen that place again.

We were soon out of sight, however, and looked to other matters more important to the living at least, and traveled until night through a still desolate country and as the sun sank slowly behind the western mountains we again halted for the night without water, and where there was no grass for the mules. Fatigued bodies were soon in the blankets and silence supreme took its beginning with the darkness of night. The guard allowed the herd of mules to wander off two hundred yards or more in search for grass that they never found, and left the sleeping men scattered about here and there promiscuously and comparatively unprotected.

Late in the night a shower of arrows came in amongst the men all about the encampment unaccompanied by any noise whatever except the slapping of bow strings and the thuds of the missiles as they struck the ground. Although this silent and dark attack was intended to kill as quietly as if the arrow had fallen from the sky, it created enough noise in the still night to awaken nearly every man in the camp. But there was no bustle or confusion. There could be indistinctly heard low voices arousing their nearest comrade like city people do in awakening a bedfellow upon the suspicion that there is a burglar in the adjoining room. An arrow stuck into the ground so near me that I reached out of my blankets and found it by feeling for it and poked my bedfellow in the ribs with it to be sure that he was awake. The wily savage always gives back under such circumstances however, for fear of meeting stray balls in the dark.

Our men spread out a little and silently awaited the development of poor "Lo's" ultimate intentions. But it was not long however before Donohoe, a red-headed Irishman, came with a steady and business-like step from the herd of mules where he had been on guard and walked into camp. He stirred up a little fire made from trash and chaparral in silence. When the fire blazed up an arrow could be distinctly seen sticking through his neck. Two or three of us went to his assistance immediately. He stood quietly and as unconcerned as if there was nothing the matter, although the arrow passed between his windpipe and the neck bone and lodged giving it the appearance of being located through the center of his neck. The feathered end stood horizontally more than two feet while the business end projected through the neck on the opposite side about four inches, still holding its flint point. Dr. A[lsop?] cut the long end off close to the skin and succeeded in pulling the piece with the barb on it through and out. While this process was going on two or three of us were keeping up the fire for light sufficient to perform the operation, but in the meantime we were watching the performance right earnestly. Donohoe noticed this and became annoyed at it. Whilst standing with his chin held up stoutly, thus to give a good chance to the operator, he strained his eyes down upon us and in a petulant way queried—"What in the h—ll are you all gazing at—didn't you ever see an Indian's arrow before?" Someone answered that he had seen many but not in such a curious place as this one.

The arrow was finally extracted, however, after which Donohoe spit just a little blood and retired into his blankets in silence. Someone had gone to take his place on guard and the animals were brought up nearer to the camp, and silence again reigned over the little isolated and beleaguered company. . . .

Donohoe on this the following morning arose with the rest of us, stout and hearty, except that he could not talk a bit, but he refused to ride a mule and preferred to walk like the rest of us, and did it successfully and did guard duty as ever and made just as good if not a better warrior than before. He recovered his speech in about ten days or two weeks and finally recovered entirely from his wound without ever losing any time. From this locality we bore toward the Gila again and encamped in the vicinity of where the Agua Frio nearly loses itself in the sands of the desert. . . .[3] We were detained at this forsaken place for several days. The savages came in sight and showed themselves under a white rag which they desired us to consider a flag of truce. They came to the number of ten or more within easy speaking distance and to make the matter more interesting to us, they presented to view two little red-headed white boys, evidently captives and probably fruits of some of their horrible and hidden crimes. These children were evidently too much alike not to be akin to each other, and were probably brothers. They were quite naked and appeared to be about eight or nine years of age. We determined to capture them and therefore took kindly to their overtures for a pow-wow. The Apache is wary and understands right well what it takes to interest a pale face. After showing both boys they divided their squad and one division came quite near us, with one of the boys only. They thus

[3] The Agua Fria sinks into the desert near Beardsley station on the Santa Fe Railroad.

secured their safety because they felt sure that we would not fire upon them for fear of losing the boy that they kept out of our reach and they also kept the nearest one so close to them that it would be doubtful shooting at least, that would kill a savage without hitting the boy. Thus they tampered with us the rest of the day. We now began to believe that the savages had showed the little pale faces for the purpose of detaining us until they could accumulate in such numbers as they desired.

We therefore decided to remain and accommodate them in order to get an opportunity to capture those unfortunate children. Everything was quiet during the night and the question as to how to get at the merits of the subject on the following day was fully discussed and left in an unsatisfactory shape to sleep on. It was a rugged and bleak sterile land and too much like chaos to find anything or anybody after being once lost sight of. Morning dawned beautifully, . . . but no living soul was in sight. . . . We were about to prepare to start when a signal smoke in the distance arose majestically and curled slowly away toward the west. A little later and our savage friends again presented themselves with one boy only. We worried with them all another day without getting any satisfaction upon which we could rely. A part of them did indeed come close enough to us to have enabled us to have captured the boy dead or alive, but that was not in the least satisfactory, for the probability was that they would have slaughtered the child themselves before it could have been taken by us. And then if we had succeeded, the fact would have been the sure destruction of the other. It was decided that if one had to remain a captive that it would better that both remain, because the two together might prevent each other from forgetting their language and be able thereby to plot an escape themselves, whereas one would despair alone. We remained over another night and another morning came but poor "Lo" never put in an appearance more.

In calling to the boy in English and in Spanish he never flinched or spoke a word or appeared to understand. He may have been a captive from infancy for there are many who have been thus taken and kept by the Apaches for years. We moved on in the afternoon without accomplishing our object and directed our course toward the Agua Frio, determined to proceed to the settlements which were yet more than a hundred miles away. We never saw nor heard of the little captive waifs again. Upon passing the Agua Frio on our return trip I noticed a little preparation for burning human beings alive, exactly like one I had previously seen in and near the mouth of the Hassayampa. Irotaba, our old chieftain guide, showed it to me when we first entered that stream under his guidance. It was the spot he said where the Apaches had burned three of his "braves" to death. Two or three little willows had been plaited together like they make wicker work to extend the victim while he is secured between them over a little hole in the ground filled with fire. . . .

We returned to the settlements and learned upon our arrival that the troops at Ft. Whipple had kept their horses saddled nearly constantly for the week previously, to repel feints against the town and fort. I went into Prescott on the following day and saw an excitement in which men were leaving their business houses hurriedly with their guns in their hands to protect the village. I now concluded to desert the Indian war altogether and to move my headquarters over on the Hassayampa in the vicinity of the first old mining camp ever made in those woods, by the original exploring party. . . .

Pursuant to this determination I borrowed a donkey upon which to carry some provisions to that creek where I had arranged to join a little camp of prospectors at the old cabin and corral. Being trepidatious about traveling in daylight while there were so many Indian ambushings going on in those woods, I waited until after dark to start. My friends were already at my destination and I therefore had to go alone five or six miles of the way. The rainy season had set in and it was a dark and gloomy night to begin with. Accordingly after dark I set out to pass through these woods over the well-known trail made by the Walker Party on first arriving in the country and the same on which Goodhue fell on the occasion of Sugar-foot-Jack's exploits, and by the way, the same whose course was marked for years afterward by the fragments of Charley's red shirt, as he tore it off of himself. My gentle little burro walked ahead of me and kept the meandering trail unerringly in the gloomy darkness of the night, which was quite dark and damp. After passing over the highest point in the woods along the trail, the narrow way, turned down a creek which the trail alternately followed and departed from for a short distance.

I was familiar with the trail by daylight and knew that at a certain point ahead of me it ran between the end of an old fallen pine tree and the tall stump from which it had broken. The tree lay at right angles to the trail. On passing between the end of the log and the stump my little animal suddenly sidled off out of the trail affrightedly and halted, and I ran against it. These little animals are reported to be good and cool judges of approaching danger and I gave full credence to this one's judgment immediately, and cast a glance along the log near the ground and saw the object of affright in the shape of two glaring eyes which looked fearful. They were just low enough to the ground to assure them to be the eyes of a ferocious and crouching wild beast. My heavy pistol was cocked and pointed at the eyes in an instant. For it was customary in those narrow passways to rely upon a pistol more confidently because of being short and handy for quick work with one hand. I was then carrying one of those in my hand, when I made the discovery of this monster crouched in the dark. But on the next instant I detected that one eye was a trifle smaller than the other and therefore held steady to examine it a moment longer and gained in confidence because it didn't spring. Upon a final examination it proved to be two specks of the phosphorescent substance sometimes known by old hunters as fox-fire.[4] My ludicrous position which I left that I was occupying came into my mind, and the sense of relief and amusement coming at the same time prompted a hearty laugh, but I discovered before I got away from there that it was but a

[4] Fox fire is defined as "the luminescence of decaying wood due to a certain fungus."

grim effort, and really the darkness of the night suggested putting my hand to my mouth to see whether I was really laughing or not. I turned finally to my little docile animal to start again, and found that the lazy little donkey had settled its opinion and was standing half asleep. . . .

I passed down the trail until I came to where the woods became more level and open, but it was growing darker all the while, and a storm was inevitable. As the thunder began to roll and rain drops began to fall, the donkey even failed to keep the trail.

Pretty soon the storm began in earnest and pitchy darkness settled over these old woods, so that nothing could be seen between the flashes of lightning. The elements warred with a fury, which forbid further progress altogether. While I would be looking for the trail or rather feeling for it, I would lose the locality of the timid and frightened little donkey and therefore have to wait for a flash of lightning to find him again. . . . Except that just before daylight the sorry cry of a lonesome wolf broke the stillness of that dark, portentously silent space occasionally; but day did come after an exceedingly long night and brought with it its beauty and its danger, although I proceeded on my dubious way and arrived in safety at the old cabin and corral where I found my friends in a terribly perplexed mood. They had driven a stake down into the dirt floor of our old pioneer cabin, led their two mules up to the door and tied the picket ropes to the stake and slept by it. The Indians during the storm had stealthily approached and cut the ropes and departed with the mules, which the owners had not missed until the break of day. The rain had hidden the foot-prints of the departing animals and hence there was nothing to show which direction they had gone. This fact however was of but little importance, since if it had not rained, the animals would have been just as effectively lost after being once out of reach. . . .

After my two friends lost their mules we all moved down stream and took lodgings near the Tanks. And prospecting was prosecuted for a week or ten days, and until my friends were captured and killed up in the chaparral hills toward the head of Copper Creek. The manner of their death was of course never known. It happened to be my day to keep house, but when the savages came by and laid seige to my cabin and passed on without tarrying long enough to burn me out, I knew that they had done some mischief somewhere in the vicinity. But they took the little donkey with them. I was engaged in washing a pan of dirt to see if there was any gold in it near the cabin in the shallow water of the creek, when they fired at me. They failed to touch me, however, and on retreating into the cabin, I dropped my pan. While one of them was attempting to get it, the rest kept up a fire on the house until he failed and gave up the pan and left. It was nearly night and on finding that my friends failed to put in an appearance, I became satisfied that they had perished. Late in the night I left the cabin, made my way to Walnut Grove, to the little grove of trees where I had laid unconscious with fever alone with the Walker Party, where I found assistance and on the following morning returned in search of my friends and found their bodies greatly mangled on Copper Creek. One was named Sharp, from Los Angeles, California, and the other was Williamson, an Eastern man. I was but little acquainted with them. Sharp's head was cut off and sitting upright upon a boulder, in the point of a little spur formed by the junction of a little gulch, with Copper Creek. The party separated after burying the bodies and left, some for Walnut Grove and the rest for Prescott. Thus ended this little prospecting expedition.

Winter began to become settled and inclement, and my inclination to leave the constant turmoil of the country increased and finally settled into a determination to do so. Pursuant to this design, I accepted an invitation to go with a small party to Sonora in Mexico and departed during the coldest weather of that winter. . . . Suffice it to say that our party of about a dozen arrived in Sonora after traversing a desert country for nearly three hundred miles, and found the country in a worse uproar than Arizona. There were still some French troops in the state, and the factions for and against the late effort to establish an empire were as hostile as ever. The consequence was that our small number were compelled to beat a hasty retreat out and across the line into Arizona again, for safety. Each faction was hostile to all the human race, and as we were a neutral party, we were the enemies of both. I learned that in 1864 the United States had sent one thousand stand of arms from a fort in California to Arizona, with which to fight the Indians. These arms were shipped to Ft. Yuma on the Colorado and from thence to an agent at Tucson, Arizona. This agent sold the arms to the Governor of Sonora with which to fight the French.[5] But as to the details of this affair being proper for such a sketch of the wilderness, as is presented in these notes, I doubt, and therefore I will leave it for the historian of a latter date to settle if any settlement should be found necessary.

A company of Mexican soldiers also crossed the line into Arizona and accepted service under the United States to fight the Indians and did good service. But upon our return trip to the Rio Gila we had a conflict with the Apaches, in which H[yram] M[ealman] of the old Walker Party was killed. I am under the impression and was at the time that he was killed by some of the Mexicans and not by the Apaches. But, however, as it did seem that it was the order of the day to kill, and to do nothing else but kill, there was but little attention paid to the manner of doing it. Still having the intention of deserting the country, I crossed the deserts east of La Paz toward the Colorado. In this desert land, some parties had discovered some silver-bearing quartz ledges, upon which quite an amount of work had been done. I halted at the encampment and found the agent of a San Francisco company was employed in working two mines not far apart with Mexican labor. I remained some months at these

[5] It is evident that some arms assigned to Governor John Goodwin of Arizona Territory found their way into Mexico. On October 15, 1864, Governor Goodwin reported that rifles and ammunition had arrived at Fort Yuma and were shipped to Tucson, Arizona. William S. Oury, acting mayor of Tucson, then loaned the rifles and ammunition to Governor Pesquiera of the Mexican state of Sonora. The numbers of rifles in this transaction, however, is given as only 140. *Journals of the First Legislature of the Territory of Arizona*, 132–33.

mines with the determination to avail myself of the first opportunity to depart for California.

Within a few months the agent departed for the states, leaving me in charge of the mines—the company's property, and twenty or thirty greaser laborers of every shade of color from white to black. The agent left another agent in La Paz about thirty miles distant, as he passed through. The company shipped its money to the La Paz agent with which to pay for labor and supplies, and it was in vain that I attempted for some months to get relief out in this vast desert. I could get supplies sufficient by sending the Mexicans across the desert to La Paz for them, which was regularly done. The company refused to leave the mines and property in the care or under the control of a Mexican under any circumstances, and I could not leave the place without abandoning the property to open robbery, which would have speedily followed. It was but seldom that I could hear from any part of the world at all and when I did, it was by the arrival of straggling greasers from Sonora, a country not necessary to be heard from. The only water within twenty or thirty miles was in a weak spring about two miles distant under a naked cliff surrounded for many miles by totally naked, barren wastes. It was carried to the mine in ten-gallon kegs, for the use of the hands. The coal used for sharpening the tools was burned in small kilns, made most of sage-brush.

The straggling greasers always came hungry and thirsty, and this mining camp became the headquarters for all the Mexican tramps who by any means learned of its existence in the country. They are great thieves and all who were not employed in the mines would hang around in the distance, like hungry wolves, until they were nearly starved and the moment my back was turned, they were being issued rations by some of the hands. They began to become so exacting that they threatened to assault the commissary and help themselves, and actually prepared for it after warning me that I was the only American amongst them. I learned the facts through some of the better disposed and found that ten or a dozen of the employed hands were engaged in the conspiracy. Forewarned is forearmed, it is said, and I remedied the matter by quietly employing about fifteen more of the stragglers under exacting conditions, before they were to be paid and set to work. After this was all accomplished, I discharged an equal number of those who desired to join the stragglers in the robbery. I knew that this was the dangerous point and therefore acted vigorously by going to each one and starting him off immediately. One fellow stubbornly informed me that I could not take off my belt of "big" pistols, and drive him from the camp. But I didn't give him time to rally for a conflict and in less than two hours I had the camp again clear of stragglers and in running order. This is only a fair sample of the Mexican way of doing business, and the cause of their failure in all things except robbery. Give them a dominating majority and they will rob the richest country in the world into poverty by making and increasing adherents by a division of the spoils. It takes as prompt and vigorous action to deal with them in peace, as it does in war, and equally as much vigilance. I had by this time lost sight of my main object—that of leaving the country, and employed my time in planning a mode of leaving this camp of greasers to the conduct of those who loved to manage a band of thieves and robbers. In two months more I succeeded in having the company of another white man once more. M. L [?], who came to take charge. But before leaving I desire to describe a peculiarity of one of those mines. The shaft was one hundred feet in depth or thereabouts when I left it and had to be blasted all the way down.

Yet the material was not rock or regular quartz or stone of any description, but a tough, light-colored substance of the color of putty. This was the regular formation of the earth itself, and not particularly of the lode. By blasting it would be broken into large heavy fragments like stone in a quarry. This dead substance was totally without any stratification or granulation whatever, and I presumed that the earth in that particular region was all of the same material. The strangest discovery of all was of the fact that no fragment which I ever examined from any depth, was without plain and distinct pictures of diminutive plants on it, or in it. I could rarely break a piece without exposing the same delicate little photograph traced in black lines, leaves and all. I have broken fragments, probably of the weight of twenty pounds, into ounce pieces, and found a new photograph on a part of it at every fracture. Sometimes, a part of the plant would be on one fragment and the other part which matched it, on another. And thus it was with the material from the bottom of this shaft and also from a tunnel at the bottom, which ran horizontally twenty or thirty feet. The little bundle of flowers, like a diminutive bouquet, thus pictured all through this singular stone would measure but little over a half-inch in height. The tiny leaves of the shape of those of mistletoe, and less than the twelfth of an inch in diameter, studded the delicate stems thickly —being set quite against each other. I pretend no explanation, but wondered whether these were seaweeds and whether this country was ever the bottom of the ocean; and lastly whether the material thus blasted out of the ground was really formed from the soft sediment at the bottom of the deep. But however, these are the facts and I shall here leave the matter to be settled by some geological botanist or somebody else, and assure the undertaker that for aught I know, this clay-stone, shale, or whatsoever it may be properly named, may reach a thousand feet deep and mixed all the way with the remains of perished flowers. In conclusion, I will merely state that I subsequently noticed little plants exactly like those described above both as to size and appearance, growing on those deserts, with their tiny leaves lying close to the ground, and looking more like a painting than living vegetation.[6]

Sea shells are also found scattered extensively over this sterile barren country two hundred or more miles from the Gulf of California.

---

[6] Although one cannot be absolutely certain what Conner is describing here, it is possible that he saw manganese dendrites, a secondary crystalline growth of manganese occurring from solutions, which have the branching appearance and size noted. There are also areas on geological maps near La Paz showing volcanic tuft, which could have been the material without stratification which Conner found.

Taste All Gone—the Adventure Ends

IT WAS NEARLY or quite midsummer before I took my departure from the desert camp. Having learned that quite a party of immigrants were passing up the Colorado and destined for Prescott, I took my sudden leave of this Tierra del Fuego of the North Temperate Zone and succeeded in cutting the travelers off and joined the procession.

In spite of all my calculations I again found myself at Prescott within four weeks after my departure from the greaser camp. Indecision as to another departure baffled all preparations in that direction for the time and I joined two friends for the purpose of hunting game for a few days. This trio obtained a light spring wagon and team and proceeded to Granite Mountain northwest of the town, already described as being about eight miles distant. We arrived in the evening and encamped at the upper edge of the bed of the lake, also previously described. Preparations for the morrow's hunting was being made when we discovered approaching by the road from the direction of California quite a cavalcade of well-dressed white men to the probable number of twenty.

They had one ambulance for the elder men and the rest were

well mounted on horseback. This was quite a sight, to see so many neatly appareled tidy looking men in one party. Indeed it really appeared to me that they were monstrously extravagant to be wearing white linen shirts for everyday wear and tear. But they did it and looked so innocent too, as though they didn't feel that they were doing anything wrong or guilty or useless waste. They drove up within thirty yards of us and halted as it was nearly night and began to make preparation for camping. Our trio set up at our camp on the wagon tongue under a long juniper tree, quiet and ragged.

The strangers took no notice of us, for some time, but just about dark an elderly gentleman walked leisurely over to our camp and politely asked if we were hunters. He was informed that we were not professionals, but would be in that line for a few days only.

He then asked if we could sell him some venison and on being informed that we had just arrived and had not yet time to obtain any, he bowed and quietly withdrew to his camp. He was very neatly attired and wore spectacles which fact did not look half so extravagant as wearing clean and sound clothes. After dark another of their party came over and we were surprised to see an acquaintance in the person of Dr. W[?]. The Doctor informed us that the gentleman who first stepped over to see us was Major Stympson of Baltimore and that he was a representative of some capitalists there. He also informed us that New York and Philadelphia capitalists also had each a representative in the party, whose name have escaped me. The Doctor had been on to those cities to raise mining companies for the working of gold and silver mines in Arizona.

Pretty soon their party was in readiness to start and the elderly gentlemen got into the ambulance and the young men mounted their horses.

One by one the young men rode up to the ambulance and handed their guns in, to be hauled. One of my friends, who was an experienced Indian fighter and who had also taken quite a fancy to the Major, for his polite bearing, remarked promptly to us that that would not do. He looked on a moment longer as the young men were putting their guns into the ambulance, and suddenly jumped up with the remark that he would tell them that that would not near do. He walked rapidly to the ambulance and told the gentlemen that the men should not invite attack by storing their guns away and that the road from thence to Prescott was as dangerous as any in the whole country, and that they had to go through the "Point of Rocks," and that if they were not attacked in that condition it would be because there happened to be no Indians on the route that day. He described the danger of passing through the "Point of Rocks" and insisted that if they should be attacked that they would never be given time to get their guns out of the ambulance and to go on that way was equal to going without arms entirely.

    I shall never forget the polite and gentlemanly demeanor of Major Stympson, as he smiled and politely thanked my friend for his friendly caution and added that he had no fears in the least for his safety. Because, he said that the ignorant savages could never be a match for these young men who were all just out of the army of the Potomac. In vain did G[eorge] B[anghart] plead and explain that that fact made no difference whatever if they should be attacked in that condition. The Major smiled and bowed good naturedly, as the ambulance moved on, carrying the guns intended for defense, while the young men followed on horseback without arms. How dangerous it looked and how strange it appeared that those men after their attention was drawn to the fact, were still so grievously mistaken as to their situation. Any experienced man would have sooner gone alone, by all means, than to have entrusted his safety with that party of mistaken men. They, however, got through safely to Prescott, but it was the same reason that an unarmed man could have followed over the same road at the same time with impunity, because there happened to be no savages on the route on that occasion. When they departed from Prescott for the mines, I understood that the Governor urged the same thing on them and also to get experienced men to make the circuit of the mines with them. They got guides, of course, for the trip and owing to the fact that the ambulance could not go through the gorges and hills in the various mining districts, they were compelled to carry their arms in their hands, thus insuring their safety. They made the trip through the various districts, and examined the mines with which they were much pleased, came back to Prescott, and remained a little while. Our hunting excursion had ended and our little party of three had returned to the town and were there when this investigating party returned. After becoming satisfied with their observations the Major and his party took their leave by the same route which they had come.

They had learned while at Prescott that there was another mine, Sacramento, not far from the road on the route to California and concluded to examine it as they returned. A shaft had been sunk upon this lode called "Sacramento Lode," which lay upon a rocky chaparral spur. The owners had suspended operations upon it, and the mine for the time had been deserted. This party when arriving at a point on the road opposite the mine, they left the ambulance with a few of their men at the road, to wait until the rest of them went up to examine the mine, which was in sight of them. As the party ascended the hill and was crossing the head of a little rocky arroyo near the shaft, the savages arose from behind the rocks all around them and poured into the surprised party a deadly volley, which killed all of them but one, who escaped to the ambulance. The party at the ambulance escaped by fast driving. Major Stympson fell with the rest. Assistance was sent and the mutilated bodies interred, except perhaps Major Stympson, whose remains I was informed had been taken to Ft. Mohave to be embalmed for the purpose of moving to Baltimore.[1]

[1] The party to which Conner refers was led by a Dr. Willing, who had previously been interested in several mines near Prescott during 1864 and 1865. He was accompanied by James H. Stimpson of Baltimore, a Mr. Hyde of New York, and others. After a brief survey of the region around Prescott, the party departed for California via Hardyville. Before reaching that town on the Colorado River,

TASTE ALL GONE—THE ADVENTURE ENDS

Those who had met the gentlemen were much pleased with them, and valued their acquaintance highly and also looked upon their visit as an important step toward turning the attention of the capitalists thither. But the sad termination of those unfortunate men blasted the hopes of speedy assistance from capitalists and served to add to the desperate character of the Indian war and postpone indefinitely the development of the material resources of the country. The savages were thus capturing and killing Anglo-Saxons all over the country, the incidents of all of which could not be put into a large volume.

During the winter of 1866 previous to my departure for Mexico, Capt. Thomas Hodges was commissioned by the Governor to command a body of Rangers, which was organized to search for the savages.[2] He was successful from the beginning to the end of his efforts. The first move he made was to go in the direction of Ft. Mohave and near the road where Major Stympson and party were subsequently massacred. Here he learned the locality of a rancheria by the smoke arising from it early in the morning. He moved always under the cover of night. After discovering the position of the rancheria he kept his men concealed during the day and surrounded it during the night. Upon the dawn of day they attacked the camp and killed every member of it . . . except three squaws, who were permitted to escape through one of the gaps between the mountains within a short distance of some of the men. On this occasion he lost only one man killed and several wounded. He continued these night marches and became so successful that poor "Lo" had something else to do besides looking for victims. On one of these occasions the Captain sent three men out on an investigating

---

they were ambushed by Walapai Indians in the Sacramento Mining District, where Stimpson, Edward Yonker, Frank Mesner, and H. H. Altman were killed. Prescott, *Arizona Miner*, August 10, 17, 31, 1867.

[2] Thomas Hodges served as sergeant-of-arms of the third legislature of Arizona Territory. In this session a bill authorizing the establishment of a group of rangers was approved in the lower house but failed in the council. *Journals of the Third Legislature of the Territory of Arizona Territory*, 116, 120, 128. McClintock, *Arizona*, I, 193, identifies Tom Hodges as a well-known gunman who also served as a guide to the United States troops in Arizona.

excursion with orders to fix the localities of all probable rancherias, evidenced by the smoke of fire, and to return before night and make their report. They stealthily felt their way for several miles and finally made a discovery of an abundance of smoke and thought that it was only the mountains on fire. After being satisfied that so much smoke was the work of Indian scouts, because of being too incautious for the conduct of the wily savage in building a rancheria, and they concluded to approach it and surprise the lone spy and make short work of him. Accordingly, they crept through the chaparral, meandering gorges and arroyos until they came close to the little clump of pine trees from whence the smoke ascended. There was not more than an acre or two of this stunted woodland situated in the lap of the mountain side. A little sharp ridge came down the mountain and descended into the chaparral country and bordered the lowland woods which stood behind it. Our adventurers came finally to a long-sought position on the opposite side of the ridge from the smokes. They all got ready and crept upon the side of the little ridge with their arms ready for action and cautiously peeped over and beheld with amazement about one hundred "braves," all busily building wigwams for their papooses, all within easy gunshot. According to the testimony of one of those adventurers, the trio unconsciously ducked their heads all at once and cast a surprised glance at each other and without a word turned and crept away, without consultation or consideration other than cautious expedition. They succeeded in getting out of hearing in safety and beat a hasty retreat for the balance of the way to their friends and reported the facts. They promised to render obedience to order henceforth and forever and begged leave to be excused thereafter from the duties of reconnaissance.

Night came on [and] the whole command moved out in quest of the little clump of timber and after tedious stumbling through the broken country for some hours, came in sight and began to move in the slow and stealthy order necessary to such business. There were about fifty of them and it took them nearly all the night to surround the woods and to get each in his assigned place. But they finally did and the whole party laid impatiently awaiting the tardy approach of daylight.... But it came at last quietly and silently opening the dark passages between the trees.... The triumphant soul is quickened as men arise from their unholy concealment with ready rifles for bloody work, and behold the ground dotted thickly with half-finished wigwams, a stake here, a hoop planted there, while bundles of material strew the ground all around and about, but no living creature in sight.

Our spies or their tracks had been discovered and the result was quite natural. But if they had been discovered while peering over that little ridge the day previously the christening of that new camp with such dainty sacrifices as would have been offered up, would have embalmed the spot with a tenderness imperishable as the legends of a cause lost forever. There would have been neither cause nor occasion for tears. One of this trio was the Territorial translator of the laws into the Spanish language and was appointed by the Legislature.[3] The party left this unfinished rancheria in quest of others and found them and, in the language of the day, made some pretty good "killings." While on this subject I will stop and bring up the various threads of scattering incidents which have been left behind. It is now the incidents of the summer of 1867 near the close of my experience in Arizona. And in order to keep pace with a general run of facts I shall have to go back to the fall of 1866 for a little space. The Third Legislative Assembly convened on the third day of October of that year.[4] Ball rooms had long been in frequent use by this date. And the ladies were in attendance quite often upon the sittings of the Legislature.

At this term there were many bills offered for the purpose of

---

[3] Alexander McKey was translator and interpreter in 1865, and Octavius B. Gass filled the position in 1866.

[4] Conner, as Daniel Ellis, from Postle's ranch, Yavapai County, served on six standing committees but did not serve on the Ways and Means and Mines committees as he did in the previous session. *Journal of Third Legislature of the Territory of Arizona.*

establishing some uniform plan of fighting the Indians into subjection. A grand scheme (in one instance) for the purpose was drawn into the shape of a bill and introduced by and through the influence of some speculators in the lobby. The lobby members of this Legislature, like they are everywhere, I presume, were the smartest members of the body, for some of those fellows knew how to draw up a bill the way they wanted it without assistance. The bill in question provided for the proper equipment of one hundred rangers to be divided into four squads, all of which were to co-operate with each other. The captains were to receive five dollars per diem for this regular service and the privates three.

The raw material necessary to feed one soldier at that time cost a dollar per day, amounting to four dollars per day for one hundred privates each, and twenty-four dollars per day for four captains. The provisions of the bill only divided the troopers into two classes, captains and privates. Altogether their food and salary was to cost four hundred and twenty-four dollars per day, to be kept up constantly.

More than twelve thousand dollars per month, and over one hundred and fifty thousand dollars per year, was proposed to be paid by this bill. Now what were the resources from whence the Territory had to raise the money? At the end of that fiscal year the country about Prescott paid in the shape of taxes a little more the rise of seven hundred dollars, which was more than half of the taxes collected in the whole Territory. The full account of taxes collected in Arizona that year was between thirteen and fourteen hundred dollars. Yet a hard battle was fought by lobby members, in conjunction with other members, to pass a bill providing for an expenditure of over twelve thousand dollars per month and the bill came very near passing. Had that bill succeeded, there was a certain gentleman living not far from Ft. Mohave, who would have furnished these rangers about ten or twelve thousand dollars worth of supplies, for which he would have ultimately received one hundred and fifty thousand dollars in Territorial bonds drawing interest at five or ten per cent. This debt would have hung over that Territory like a dark cloud for generations at least, the property of their heirs of the deceased. It would have been paid off in installments, each equal to the original costs of the goods. . . . The bill failed by one or possibly two votes.[5]

The next expedient to rid the country of the Apaches was embodied into a bill which provided for paying one hundred dollars apiece for scalps, similar to the provisions made in some states for catching foxes. This one was also lost by a small majority. The reason that it failed was owing to a defect in the bill, wherein it failed to provide any means by which the speculators could become the necessary link in securing a division of the bounty without subjecting their own scalps to uncertainties.[6] It became a vexed question and there seemed but little hope of securing the means of subduing the Indians, without putting the Territory hopelessly in debt by paying ten dollars to some scheming politician for every fifty cents worth of supplies furnished. It became a passion with some of the most voracious speculators to get the Territory to issue them a grand fortune in bonds for a trifle. This determination became impudent and bold and success under any pretext would have issued the interest-bearing bonds which would have been immediately transferred to innocent parties, and thus become a standing incubus upon the country for many years. The citizens of Arizona today owe more to the patriotic members of her Third Legislature than they are aware of. All of those schemes fell through, by the merest preponderance and left the volunteer troops the task of fighting the Indians in their own way, resulting in some of the incidents I have already mentioned, while under the command of Capt. Hodges. He was an effective operator against the Apaches, as previously stated, and his men fought without money or price. There was a circumstance which

---

[5] The bill in question here passed the lower house, with Conner voting in the negative, but it was defeated in the council. *Journals of the Third Legislature of the Territory of Arizona,* 116, 120, 123, and 212.

[6] This bill does not show in the *Journals* by an identifiable title.

transpired at Prescott during that year which I thought I would pass over, but as it was in some degree connected with the above state of affairs there, I will give an outline of it. . . .

The war in the states had ceased and a regiment of United States soldiers under the command of Gen. Gregg came to Arizona via California, and five hundred of them, with their general, to Prescott, the capital of the Territory at that time.[7] Three soldiers came ahead of the command, when they learned or believed that they were near their destination, and without halting at Ft. Whipple, one and a half miles below the town on Granite Creek, but they came on up to the town. They went to the first saloon they reached and took drinks, and proceeded thence to a store on the upper side of the Plaza, and bought some goods which they took away without paying for them. As they left the store they told the clerk to charge them to the "Fourteenth," their regiment. They proceeded around the public square to several stores and repeated the same or similar acts, over at each house.

They came around to Granite Street to the store of H[?] and not being aware that a runner had gone ahead of them, informed the clerk of their conduct, they entered the store and asked for goods. The clerk quietly walked around the counter as though he was going to wait upon them, reached up to a shelf and took down a heavy six-shooter and told the soldiers that they had just one minute to get out of the house. They were at first incredulous and seemed very indignant at the clerk's conduct, and told him that they were members of the "bloody Fourteenth," just from the Potomac, and that the regiment was nearly to the fort just below town. Silently the clerk drew out his watch, by which to time them, in such a winning way, that they did back out of the store and finally left in great indignation, leaving some right interesting promises behind. In depart-

---

[7] J. Irwin Gregg was a colonel and brevet brigadier of the 8th United States Cavalry, and commanding officer of the District of Prescott with headquarters at Fort Whipple. The 14th Infantry, however, was scattered throughout the various military establishments in Arizona. Heitman, *Historical Register*, 477; *Report of the Secretary of War, 1866*, 448–49.

ing for the fort they called by the saloon to get more drinks and revealed the circumstances to the barkeeper, who was a jolly, wide-mouthed fellow, and he advised them that they were acting a dangerous part and to take his word for it, and not attempt under any consideration to repeat such conduct. They persisted that they were just from the Potomac and that that clerk knew what he was doing. C. J[?], for that was the bartender's name, good humoredly insisted that they should remember that everybody in the country was armed on account of the Indians and that they were the most reckless soldiers in any country, totally without encumbrances in the way of women and children. The barkeeper here treated them to drinks to allay their passions, but they went off to the fort dissatisfied. The whole command had arrived and heard the story of the experience of the three soldiers in town. After dark, thirty or forty of them came up into town and visited the said bartender, whom they treated kindly. They informed him that they had learned that they had arrived into a country where the clerks drew pistols upon soldiers for asking to look at goods in the stores. The barkeeper tried to explain to them their situation, all of which they hooted.

They took their leave and proceeded to another saloon in a body. This room may have been fifty feet or more in length, with the bar in one end. The room was constructed lengthy in proportion to the width, so as to make room to arrange beer and gaming tables throughout its length. There had been long since a large beer brewery in Prescott. The house was bounded by the street and its entrance was near the end so that on passing into the door, a customer would find himself in front of the bar counter, which ran across the end of the room. While the proprietor stood behind the counter he could see out upon the street through a large window, which came nearly to the floor at the end of the counter around which he had to walk to get to his post of duty.

This room was well lighted up when the soldiers all walked in and took seats. The proprietor was standing leisurely behind the bar, upon which he was leaning unengaged. Six ragged looking miners sat at some distance toward the other end of the room leisurely engaged in sipping their beer around the little tables.

Any man acquainted with the country could have seen at a glance that each of those dirty looking fellows with a brace of heavy pistols to their belts, were just down from the mountains after supplies. Tired and hungry, too, perhaps, they sat at the tables sipping their beer in silence. One of the soldiers arose and made a motion that they proceed to business as though there was no one present except themselves. The motion had its orderly second and they were pretty soon organized into a business shape, with a chairman, &c. One of their number was nominated for a bartender and his good qualities set forth to recommend him for the position. "He would not sell drinks quite so high as was the custom and would not draw pistols on customers like some clerks do in the dry-goods stores not far away."

When the barkeeper saw that they were in earnest, he quietly asked them if they were not strangers in that country. No, they said that the "bloody Fourteenth" were not strangers anywhere, but that they had just arrived. Their chairman now appointed five committeemen to oust the incumbent and to install the newly elect, while the proprietor protested that they were ignorant of what they were doing, and that if they would stay at the fort a week or two and until they became a little acquainted with the people, that his warning would become unnecessary. They hooted him in levity and reverted in contempt to the custom of drawing pistols on soldiers for making inquiries after goods. As the five committeemen walked around the end of the counter after the proprietor to put him out, he remarked that if they were determined to put him out that he would come from behind the bar on his own accord, and did so, leaving the five soldiers behind the counter.

Just at this point the six old miners, whom the soldiers had not as yet deigned to notice, quietly arose in one body, drew their heavy six-shooters, and without a word or command, began to fire on the soldiers as rapidly as they could shoot. The soldiers crowding toward the door in their surprise, blocked it up as the miners advanced upon them, keeping up the fire. The five committeemen, who were behind the bar, made no effort to get to the door, but made a dash at the large window and carried it with them into the street, sash and all.

The whole catastrophe passed and was over in an incredibly short space of time, and as strange as it may appear, there was only one soldier killed dead on the spot, and he was caught by one of the miners in one arm and stabbed to death with a sheath-knife. The rest, variously wounded, escaped to the fort. This occurrence raised the animosity at the fort to its highest pitch. The officer who delivered the proclamation declared the people of Central Arizona had for a long time been praying the aid of the United States against the Apaches, and that on the very day of his arrival they killed and crippled nineteen of his men.

The excitement arose and increased with great indignation on the following day when a sergeant was reported to have had one hundred volunteers from amongst the soldiers to come up and "clean out the town," at it was expressed. All the miners who happened to be in town after supplies quickly deserted the place and left that night to the respective mining camps of the country. The consequence was that before night on the following day, the woods all around Prescott was full of their encampments, and they were still arriving. About dark they collected into the town and held a miners' meeting at which they made fiery speeches. Some of them boldly moved to appoint a committee to wait on the soldiers, to learn if they came to assist the Apaches, and that the proper way was to go after them right away before they became settled. Someone in his speech said that they had become so accustomed to abusing women and children in the States that they would never quit and that he was in favor of giving them a little foretaste of what they might expect, to begin with. All of this was going on within hearing of the Governor's Mansion, and there never was collected together a more dangerous enemy, according to their members, than was this crowd of ragged miners. Evidently a war footing had been reached, and these inflammatory speeches were not to be hooted at, for those men could have defeated several times their own number in their own woods and in their own way. Finally, the Governor appeared on the stand, and his conservative remarks had a quieting influence and, besides, he was well liked by the people. Disturbances were more than once checked by the respect felt for our chief magistrate by the populace.

On the following day there were still many miners loitering about the town, shooting their pistols at the trees in the public square. The soldiers seemed to be confounded by the situation. One of them afterward told me that he was actually afraid to go into a saloon after refreshment, where there were a party of miners drinking. But however that may have been, I know that that little looseness was the last of the kind that ever occurred about Prescott as long as I knew the place, and if that shooting party of miners were ever tried for that night's work, I never heard of it. . . .[8] Still it may have been that the . . . bold conduct of those six old miners might have been beneficial in the end by forcibly defining the respective rights of citizens and soldiers.

At any rate it did do it, and the consequence was that peace reigned supreme so far as the whites were concerned and mutual respect sprang up which dispelled all animosity to such an extent that wounded citizens would go to the post hospital for treatment. I remember that a Georgian, who had always been a warm sympathizer with the South, during the war, was in the hospital under treatment for wounds when I left the country. This conservative state of affairs was owing to the wisdom of the Governor's administration, which in a candid mind acquainted with the facts, admitted of no questions. A better selection for a Chief Magistrate for the Territory at the time could not have been easily made.[9] Those Indian-fighting miners were as a class as bold and reckless a set of men as could be found in any country, but yet life was as secure amongst them as anywhere. I was

[8] This incident might be the foundation of the story that citizens of Prescott robbed and beat a squad of soldiers about 1867. *Arizona: A State Guide*, 236.
[9] Here Conner refers to Richard C. McCormick, third governor of Arizona Territory.

amongst them for years and in countless Indian skirmishes with them, and if I ever felt a pang of trepidation for my safety amongst them from the beginning to the end, I have no recollection of it. Incidents of accidental discharges of fire arms amongst the miners were exceedingly scarce. It is among green recruits where it is proper to have a care about having one's brains blown out, when it is least expected. I cannot recall but one instance at this time where a miner in Arizona killed his friend by the accidental discharge of fire arms.

During the year of 1866 the General commanding the department, and by the way, an ex-commander-in-chief of the army of the Potomac, visited Prescott.[10] He was received at the State House by the Territorial officers in wholesome Arizona style, with big boots on the outside the pants. Speeches of welcome and other appropriate attentions toward a distinguished soldier was enthusiastically indulged. The brass band came out and played Hail to the Chief &c. He finally took his leave well pleased with his visit.

With these few running remarks of the town, country, and condition of things generally, I will betake myself again into 1867 to my cabin in Prescott, where I had kept an intermittent residence for several years. To bring up a few threads, also about that town, I will mention the fact that the first brick kiln ever burned in central Arizona was erected during the latter part of 1866 and the forepart of 1867.

About one hundred and fifty thousand bricks were put in this kiln by Martin and French, aided by the humble compiler of these notes. This was the only enterprise of the kind which had been undertaken up to my final leave of the country.

There was no sale for the bricks after they were burned, sufficient to encourage another attempt, for more than half of them were still in the kiln when I last saw it. The first brick

[10] Major General Irvin McDowell was commanding officer of the Department of California at this time, while General H. W. Halleck commanded the Division of the Pacific.

house ever built in Prescott, or the part of one, was erected on the Plaza by one Campbell, and the writer hereof is not appraised of any second one having ever been erected since, but I presume doubtlessly there has been many, ere the present. While burning this brick kiln, provisions at Prescott gave out. There seemed to be nothing but liquors and hardware for sale at any of the stores. The last supplies of anything which could be eaten were the products of Indian labor on the Colorado River—diminutive, black-eyed peas. They were much smaller than buckshot and scarce in quantity, in proportion to their size. The whole supply had been speedily divided up amongst the needy and everybody was in need, and the portion coming to the brick-yard hands amounted to about one peck. There was no salt, nor any other seasoning to be had, and therefore their preparation was of the simplest process. To just boil them soft enough to eat, was all that was necessary.

The hands had at that time completed the kiln and were engaged in chopping wood in the neighboring forest with which to burn it. Upon being put to such straights for food all the men about the yard deserted the enterprise except three, for the purpose of hunting wild game. Three of us continued to chop wood for a day or two, when another left in quest of venison. This left two who continued to cut wood for nearly two weeks. There was a few inches of snow on the ground during the time, which kept our beans from spoiling. But toward the last my plucky comrade, who was a Texan, put all in the kettle and cooked them at once, and after cooling and standing thus from day to day they soured. He ate some of them anyway, remarking that they would still do for pickles, and that one had better eat pickles than nothing. But it proved a failure for the spoiled mess sickened his stomach and vomited him generously. When he was through this last exercise he kicked the camp kettle out of doors, picked up his gun, and walked off into the woods, and I saw him no more for nearly a month. I went to what was known as Miller's ranch, one mile northwest of Prescott and joined the

TASTE ALL GONE—THE ADVENTURE ENDS

inmates of the premises in a frugal meal upon boiled corn.[11]

On the following morning I returned to my cabin, happy. I had only about thirty-six hours more to do without food, for the wagon train arrived from California late on the following day, bringing peace and plenty. The results was that the kiln was soon burned and made a fine quality of bricks. The Texan came back in about a month and again took up quarters with me. He said that he loved to chop wood in the snow while he lived on black-eyed peas, but not over ten days at a time, especially when they were sour. This good-hearted fellow made my cabin his headquarters as long as I remained there. During that summer he found an exceedingly rich piece of quartz in the woods on the east side of Granite Creek and we engaged ourselves searching over Prescott's town site for nearly a month in quest of the lode from whence the fragment came. At last we stumbled on to a ledge which we took to be the long sought prize. It slightly cropped out of the ground beyond the woods up in the rolling chaparral hills about a half or three-quarters of a mile southeast of the town. We located it and began work immediately and continued to delve and blast until we had a shaft about forty feet deep. We found some quartz of the exact character of the rich specimen referred to about halfway down this shaft, but only a small seam of it. The barren quartz of the main lode appeared to have swallowed up the rich little streak.

During the sinking of this shaft, the Texan did the blasting and picking and his assistant drew out the debris with a windlass. While working at the windlass and after the shaft was nearly thirty feet in depth the Apaches began to skulk about the chaparral, which thickly clothed the rolling hills around the shaft and in the vicinity, so constantly, that I began to use the stone taken out to build a wall for protection around the works. The savages discovered this and fired on me from a chaparral ridge

[11] Samuel C. Miller, one of the original members of the Walker party, established a ranch some seven or eight miles northeast of Prescott which was burned in 1865 by Indians and was known subsequently as Burnt Ranch. Barnes, *Arizona Place Names*, 277.

about sixty paces away without effect other than to temporarily stop the work. The Texan was afraid to stay in the shaft longer for fear that the Indians would either kill or cripple me so that I could not help him out, and such failure would leave him at their mercy.

The only remedy was to build a solid wall around the open shaft four or five feet high, which was done and the work resumed. They fired upon us several times, but the locality was too near town for them to lay siege to our temporary fort with any hope of success. But one morning when we went up to begin the work of another day, we discovered that the savages had been there during the night and cut the windlass rope into short bits and threw them into the shaft and also pitched in the windlass and platform. Upon these they heaved the rocks of the wall, thus destroying all hope of progress without guarding the place during the night. We therefore finally abandoned the work altogether after reaching, as before stated, a depth of about forty feet.

We quietly retired to my little cabin in town and idled away the fleeting time, still poor and discouraged. I now set my time of departure so as to go with the next wagon train for California and impatiently waited for the time to roll around. I gave up all business and determined to leave, but the time was nearly a month off. To kill time I joined my Texan friend and two or three others in a leisurely loiter through the woods to Turkey Creek, a distance of about thirty miles. All of us were afoot, for there was no such thing as being enabled to keep a horse or mule, apparently, without holding it by the bridle reins all the while. We passed through the level and pretty woods known as the *Mesa*. This is an extensive tongue of high table land projecting out of our Big Woods eastward for a mile or more and suddenly breaks off abruptly and falls thousands of feet sheer down into the chaparral country lying between Big Bug Creek and Turkey Creek. This table woodland also lies between the two heads of these streams and its sides pitch abruptly down toward either stream and grow steep and deeper and the creeks descend until the apparent dead-level woods terminate abruptly as before stated. Upon this high point of table woodland, toward the east, the beholder can take one of the most romantic positions in the whole country. From this high and pretty place he can look down upon a chaos of ruined and wrecked country for miles in extent. The first ray from the east greets this point every morning promptly in advance of the surrounding country.

But it was a wilderness. As we passed down toward Turkey Creek I saw a deer climbing the hill with desperate efforts to reach the table land. It was a hard struggle, but he finally succeeded and passed over the brow onto the table, out of sight. We reached the Bully Bueano mill and found three men in the cabin, who were in charge of the company's property. Some of our party remained two or three days while others of them left for Big Bug District. The Indians perhaps saw some of the men leaving and thought that only one was left, and they therefore prepared to burn out the enemy. There were five of us still left and we sat up to a late hour and were all surprised to see an armful of firebrands thrown down at the door. But when one armful after another was thrown up the first one next before in quick succession, until a cart-load of brands were piled against the door three feet or more in height in less time than it would take to tell it, we gathered our guns for the evident fracas, which was intended. By the time we were in readiness, another line of savages followed the firebrand troop and by the same means succeeded in quickly piling armfuls of dry fuel upon the brands, thus extending the pile nearly to the eves of the cabin and above the top of the door.

This was quite a new mode of building a large fire quickly, but it was done and started within less than three minutes from the time the first fire was thrown down. The door opened inward and we therefore got to work to scatter the fire and wood before it burned brightly enough to light us up sufficiently for good targets. In the absence of sufficient light the savages fired upon us before the wood was out of the way. This gave another valuable suggestion, which was to dash a bucket of water on the fire and to keep it from shining brightly and to leave the wood until their opening volley was exhausted. After their excitement cooled down a little we dashed the wood and fire from the door. When their arrows began to come into the door we knew that their fire arms were exhausted, and then two or three of us kept up a steady fire out in the dark, while two of our party finished putting out fire. Augustus S[?], a Georgian, who was of our party, received an arrow near the stomach during the affray. When he pulled it out of himself the flint point pulled off and remained in his body, giving him a severe and dangerous wound. He recovered without ever extracting the ugly tenant. It is quite a science with the Apaches to be able to fasten a flint point to an arrow so that it will stand firm on entering and separate from the shaft upon pulling the latter out of the body.

One of the party felt his way through the darkness to Prescott and got the post surgeon to come and attempt the extraction of the arrowhead, but he failed because of it penetrating to the hollow. It was the beginning of the rainy season and I returned with the surgeon. We attempted to go back in the night and were caught in a rain storm, and the night became so dark that we were compelled to take refuge under a tree and await the coming of the morning.

I returned to my cabin and found my friend the Texan and took up my lodging quietly until the time came for taking my final leave of the country. Col. C[?], who was secretary of the Territory, asked me to remain a few months longer and go through Old Mexico with him.[12] I would have liked to have joined his party very much, but I had done so much overland traveling for seven consecutive years, I had a holy horror of deserts, and declined joining the Colonel's party. I subsequently learned that he did start and died en route in Mexico. I firmly held to my original calculations, which were to the effect that I should take the shortest route to civilization. The train of

---

[12] The secretaries of state for the Territory of Arizona during this period were Richard C. McCormick, 1863–66; James P. T. Slater, 1866–69; and Coles Bashford, 1869–76.

TASTE ALL GONE—THE ADVENTURE ENDS

wagons with which I was going set their time for departure, only a few days previously to the day set for the convention of the Fourth Legislature of Arizona, to be held at Prescott.[13]

This train was to start from Miller's ranch one mile northwest of the town. On the day of departure, I left my little cabin without an occupant and without an owner; I passed the Governor's Mansion, which stood alone, across the creek opposite the town and took my position on the little bench of high ground just back of the house on the road to Miller's ranch and stopped to survey for the probable last time the town and surroundings of Prescott. I had been accustomed to feel for a long while that my final departure would mark the most gratifying event of my life. But upon an actual departure, I found it very different, for when I looked back upon the town, with a long and steady survey, I felt an affection for its success and welfare which I had not before dreamed of. The associations about those old woods, now that I was about to leave them, had a curious charm for me never experienced before. One hundred and fifty paces to my right hand and a little back of the Governor's Mansion, under some little oaks, I could distinctly see the light picket enclosure, which marked the resting place of the first white woman of whom we have any knowledge of dying in central Arizona— the wife of the Governor.[14] Those kindly hands and that gentle demeanor had won many a rough miner's resolution back to the flowery path of rectitude. The little leaning trees hung weeping over that lonely grave, as my attention was directed toward them and remembered the generous impulses, which were always so easily awakened in behalf of the proud and humble alike. There were no partial angels hovering there. I cast a glance at the houses of the town and was really amazed to realize the great change. The town spread out, up and down the creek, and presented so many considerations at once that I almost felt that I was dreaming. I turned around and walked on—busy with my reflections, and was pretty soon out of sight.

[13] The fourth legislature of Arizona Territory convened September 4, 1867.
[14] Mrs. Richard C. McCormick died in the Governor's Mansion in 1866.

I arrived in time to start with the train, which in a short time was on the road and out of sight of the settlements, none of which I have ever seen again.

The wagon train halted at Granite Mountain for the night and proceeded on its journey to Skull Valley the next day. As we passed through this valley I saw the dried bones of forty or fifty Indians already referred to, bleaching in the sun. The Adjutant General Garvin of the Territory [15] took passage with us and in all there were about forty persons leaving the country, including two ladies and their husbands. We passed onto the Colorado, where we arrived in about two weeks after a dry, desert trip worthy of no notice here, save that it was as usual very trying upon the patience.... Our party passed the river in safety and landed upon the shore of California, out of range of the Apache at last. Now for the first time in seven years, I felt that self-defense against the savage was one of the considerations of the past, although there were some friendly tribes yet to meet. I had often thought how pleasant it would be to unbuckle my belt and throw it with its scabbards and pistols altogether into the sea, and as I pulled them off, when I had arrived nearly to the frontier settlements of California, I really concluded to preserve them for that purpose. But it was a long while before I could be accustomed to being without them, and I was constantly feeling that something was wrong, without thinking what it was, but on turning my attention to it I invariably found the annoyance caused by the absence of the heavy belt, which I had become accustomed to wearing.

Especially was this observable on arising from sleep in the morning, when for months I always missed something and would have to wait and think what it was. I have never carried a pistol or other arms since—*taste all gone.*

Now after crossing the river out of the range of the hostile Indians, I felt that there was nothing left to do on earth. In the

---

[15] William H. Garvin, resident of Prescott and listed as a native of Kansas, served as adjutant during 1866. *Journals of the Third Legislature of the Territory of Arizona.*

absence of excitable reflections I became listless and lazy, only when stirred up from habit, when not thinking of, or being conscious of, perfect safety. Here the force of habit played a capricious part for some benefit and stirred up the energies, whether there was anything to employ them or not. But everything appeared so tame and worthless that I felt that I was totally out of employment and out of reach of it. It was a long time before I was able to convince myself that I was not horribly demoralized. But as I take my leave of the hostile Indians, Apaches and all, I shall attempt to leave to them and to theirs my mite of that justice to which I consider them entitled.

A tribute to their natural firmness and constancy of purpose would be given to their leading and most marked characteristics. His unflagging, unyielding purpose to drive directly at the result of his conclusions and to enforce them or finally perish in the attempt is the leading trait of his character. He is incapable of knowing any law except that of his own will. When he fails to do whatsoever he pleases to do, his life is a failure and he is dead, whether respiration ceases or not. He cannot be bound to others by any contract, because he knows nothing of any valid contract but the one he makes with himself. If he surrenders anything in the considerations necessary for a mutual contract as we understand it, he considers his part thereto simply a free gift dependent along with his pleasure, which has only the effect of placing the opposite party under obligations to him for his condescension for making the agreement. He then loses sight of the real considerations of the contract and believes that when the opposite party asserts his freedom to any extent from that obligation, the contract is ended. He who makes a contract with an Indian and fails to consider poor "Lo's" consideration, knows but little of the Indian's character. His will, his pleasure is the real consideration above and beyond all else, with him, and the man who refuses submission to it constantly conceals all the minor consideration of a contract with him.

When the Indian is forced to accept the ordinary construction of the consideration of ordinary contracts without being looked up to (as the expression goes) by the opposite party, he is then subdued into another creature under which he sinks and loses himself as a natural consequence. His insignificance naturally follows in his own estimation and follows simply as a fact, in the estimation of all other races. The Indian cannot joke, nor does he ever attempt it. I have seen accounts taken from captives amongst the Apaches, of their wonderful endurance in running down and capturing deer in Arizona. I saw one not long since which appeared to have been published by an intelligent man in San Francisco, which was so exceedingly ridiculous that it seems but folly to mention it. I am acquainted with the deer as well as I am with the Apaches of Arizona and know that they could come about as near running a deer down in that country and capturing it, as the writer could of defeating some of our best coursers in a four-mile heat on the turf. But the Apaches do have one wonderful virtue of which we all might do well to consider, with a view to imitate it. They never fight amongst themselves and bruise one another's faces like enlightened people do. They never fly into a passion, and knock each other down, like we do in polished life. Nor do they become savage enough to kill a friend and say that it was done under a sudden heat and passion, like Christians do. All this is unknown amongst them. Even the children do not know how to become petulant and fight each other and to knock each other's teeth out. These customs seem to belong exclusively to the most polished races of mankind. And one other prominent charge I deem worth a single notice to wit: Their use of poisoned arrows. I do not suppose that there is one single instance of a responsible man ever charging an Apache Indian with ever having used a poisoned arrow or lance.

[Conner's narrative does not end here, but his adventures in Arizona are now concluded, for early in September, 1867, he made his way with the wagon train to San Bernardino, California. After spending a few months working in the orange groves and vineyards in the vicinity of Los Angeles, he moved northward to San Francisco. During the winter of 1867–68, Conner visited various places of interest in California, including the Yosemite Valley. Undoubtedly still looking for another opportunity to prospect and mine, he traveled inland again, this time to Virginia City, Nevada, but returned once more to San Francisco in the spring of 1868.

Failing to make his fortune in the western gold fields, Conner sailed for New York City in the spring of 1868 by way of the Isthmus of Panama and Havana, Cuba. After an unsuccessful effort to locate in Philadelphia the officers of a mining company who owned the Bully Bueno mine, Conner continued on to Bardstown, Kentucky, his birthplace and early home. For ten years Daniel Ellis Conner had traveled on the American frontier: in the gold fields of Colorado, in the mineral-bearing regions of New Mexico, and in the unexplored plateau wilderness of central Arizona. Now the high adventure had ended and at home he found himself a stranger.]

Bibliography

DOCUMENTS AND MANUSCRIPTS

Browne, J. Ross. *A Report upon the Mineral Resources of the States and Territories West of the Rocky Mountains*, 39 Cong., 2 sess., House Exec. Doc. No. 29. Washington, Government Printing Office, 1867.

The 1864 Census of the Territory of Arizona. Phoenix, The Historical Records Survey, 1938.

Conner, Daniel Ellis. Conner Manuscripts. Arizona State Library, Phoenix.

Conrad, David E. "Explorations and Railway Survey of the Whipple Expedition." Unpublished M.A. thesis, University of Oklahoma, 1955.

Department of War. *The War of the Rebellion: A Compilation of the Records of the Union and Confederate Armies.* 130 vols. Washington, Government Printing Office, 1880–1901.

Emory, William H. *Notes of a Military Reconnaissance from Fort Leavenworth, in Missouri, to San Diego, in California, including parts of the Arkansas, Del Norte, and Gila Rivers*, 30 Cong., 1 sess., Sen. Exec. Doc. No. 7. Washington, Wendell and Van Benthuysen, Printers, 1848.

Fish, Henry. Manuscript History of Arizona. Arizona Historical Society, Prescott.

Frémont, John C. *Report of the Exploring Expedition to the Rocky Mountains in the Year 1842, and to Oregon and North California in the Years 1843–'44.* Washington, Blair and Rives, Printers, 1845.

Journals of the Legislative Assemblies of the Territory of Arizona, 1864–1867. Prescott, 1864–67.

Journal of the Pioneer and Walker Mining Districts, 1863–1865. Yavapai County Recorder's Office, Prescott.

Report of the Commissioner of Indian Affairs for the Years 1864–1867. Washington, Government Printing Office, 1865–68.

Report of the Secretary of War, 39 Cong., 2 sess., House Exec. Doc. No. 1. Washington, Government Printing Office, 1866.

Swor, Robert L. "The Development of Prescott." Unpublished M.A. thesis, Arizona State College at Tempe, 1952.

MAPS

Arizona Territory

"Manuscript Map." Drawn by Lieutenant Richard C. Lord around the late 1860's showing the area northwest of Prescott, Arizona. National Archives. Record Group 77, U.S. 324 (78).

"Manuscript Map." Dated 1866, showing trails from Prescott to Wickenburg, to Fort McDowell, Arizona. National Archives. Record Group 77 (2).

"Manuscript Map of Arizona." Drawn in the 1860's. National Archives. Record Group 77, U.S. 324 (72).

"Map of the Territory and Department of Arizona." Compiled and drawn in 1885 under the direction of First Lieutenant T. A. Bingham, Corps of Engineers, United States Army.

"Official Map of the Territory of Arizona." Dated 1880. Compiled from surveys, reconnaissances, and other sources by E. A. Echhoff and P. Riecher.

New Mexico Territory

"Map of the Military Department of New Mexico." Dated 1864. Drawn under the direction of General James H. Carleton, by Captain Allen L. Anderson, U.S. 5th Infantry, Acting Engineering Office. National Archives. Record Group 77, W 83 (1).

"Map of New Mexico." Dated about 1869. Prepared in the Engineer's Office at Headquarters, 5th Military District, Brevet Captain William Hoelcke, United States Army in charge. National Archives. Record Group 77, W 603.

"Map of the Territory of New Mexico." Dated 1851. Compiled by Brevet Second Lieutenant John B. Parke, United States Topographical Engineers, assisted by Mr. Richard Kern.

"Old Territory and Military Department of New Mexico." Dated 1859, partially revised and corrected to 1867. Compiled in the Bureau of Topographical Engineers of the War Department. National Archives. Record Group 77, W 55 (4).

"Sketch of Public Surveys in New Mexico and Arizona." Dated 1866. Department of the Interior, General Land Office.

"Territory of New Mexico." Dated 1879. Compiled from the official records of the General Land Office and other sources, by C. Roeser, Principal Draughtsman, General Land Office. Record Group 49.

BIBLIOGRAPHY

"Territory of New Mexico." Dated 1883. Compiled from the official records of the General Land Office under the supervision of G. P. Strum, Principal Draughtsman, General Land Office.

NEWSPAPERS

The Arizona Miner, Fort Whipple, Arizona.
The Arizona Miner, Prescott, Arizona.
The Daily Arizona Miner, Prescott, Arizona.

BOOKS

Adams, Henry. *The Life of Albert Gallatin.* New York, Peter Smith, 1943.
Alter, J. Cecil. *James Bridger, Trapper, Frontiersman, Scout, and Guide: A Historical Narrative.* Salt Lake City, Utah, Shepard Book Company [1925].
Bancroft, Hubert Howe. *The Works of Hubert Howe Bancroft.* 39 vols. San Francisco, The History Company, 1886-89.
Barnes, Will C. *Arizona Place Names.* University of Arizona *Bulletin. General Bulletin No. 2* (1935).
Bartlett, John Russell. *Personal Narrative of Explorations and Incidents in Texas, New Mexico, California, Sonora, and Chihuahua.* 2 vols. New York, Appleton, 1854.
Benson, Lyman. *The Cacti of Arizona.* University of Arizona Biological Science *Bulletin No. 4* (1940).
Bolton, Herbert Eugene. *Coronado: Knight of the Pueblos and Plains.* New York, Whittlesey House [1949].
———. *Rim of Christendom: A Biography of Eusebio Francisco Kino, Pacific Coast Pioneer.* New York, Macmillan, 1936.
Brandt, Herbert. *Arizona and its Bird Life.* Cleveland, Ohio, The Bird Research Foundation, 1951.
Brooks, Juanita. *The Mountain Meadows Massacre.* Stanford, California, Stanford University Press [1950].
Browne, J. Ross. *A Tour Through Arizona, 1864, or Adventures in Apache Country.* Tucson, Arizona Silhouettes, 1951.
Caughey, John Walton. *California.* 2d ed. New York, Prentice-Hall, 1953.
———. *Gold is the Cornerstone.* Berkeley, University of California Press, 1948.
Chittenden, Hiram Martin. *The American Fur Trade of the Far West.* 2 vols. New York, The Press of the Pioneers, Inc., 1935.
Cleland, Robert Glass. *This Reckless Breed of Men.* New York, Knopf, 1950.
Conkling, Roscoe P. and Margaret B. *The Butterfield Overland Mail, 1857-1869.* 2 vols. Glendale, Arthur H. Clark, 1947.
Cosulich, Bernice. *Tucson.* Tucson, Arizona Silhouettes [1953].
Coues, Elliott. *Lists of Birds of Fort Whipple. Proceedings* of the Academy

of Natural Science, Vol. XVII. Philadelphia, Academy of Natural Science, 1866.

Cremony, John C. *Life Among the Apaches.* Tucson, Arizona Silhouettes, 1954.

Cummings, Byron. *First Inhabitants of Arizona and the Southwest.* Tucson, Cummings Publication Council, 1953.

Darton, N. H. *A Resumé of Arizona Geology.* Arizona Bureau of Mines *Bulletin No. 119* (1925).

DeVoto, Bernard. *Across the Wide Missouri.* Boston, Houghton-Mifflin [1947].

Elliott, Wallace W. *History of Arizona Territory.* San Francisco, Wallace W. Elliott & Co., 1884.

Farish, Thomas Edwin. *History of Arizona.* 4 vols. Phoenix, 1915–16.

Favour, Alpheus H. *Old Bill Williams, Mountain Man.* Chapel Hill, University of North Carolina Press, 1936.

Faxon, Charles W., and Gill, Mary W. *Manual of Trees of North America.* 2nd ed. Boston, Houghton-Mifflin, 1926.

Federal Writers Project. *Arizona: A State Guide.* New York, Hastings House, 1940.

Fewkes, Jesse Walter. *Antiquities of the Upper Verde River and Walnut Creek Valleys, Arizona.* Twenty-Eighth *Annual Report* of the Bureau of American Ethnology. Washington, Government Printing Office, 1908.

Hafen, LeRoy R. and Ann W. *Old Spanish Trail: Santa Fé to Los Angeles.* Glendale, Arthur H. Clark, 1954.

Hamilton, Patrick. *The Resources of Arizona.* 3rd ed. San Francisco, A. L. Bancroft & Company, Printers, 1884.

Heitman, Francis B. *Historical Register and Dictionary of the United States Army, from its Organization, September 29, 1789, to March 2, 1903.* Washington, Government Printing Office, 1903.

Hinton, Richard. *The Handbook to Arizona: Its Resources, History, Towns, Mines, Rivers, and Scenery.* Tucson, Arizona Silhouettes, 1954.

Hodge, Frederick W. *Handbook of American Indians North of Mexico.* 2 vols. Bureau of American Ethnology *Bulletin No. 30.* Washington, Government Printing Office, 1907, 1910.

Hunt, Aurora. *The Army of the Pacific.* Glendale, Arthur H. Clark, 1951.

Irving, Washington. *The Adventures of Captain Bonneville.* 2 vols. New York, G. P. Putnam's Sons [1895].

Jackson, Orick. *White Conquest of Arizona: A History of the Pioneers.* Los Angeles, California, West Coast Magazine, The Grafton Co. n.d.

Johnston, Abraham Robinson. *Journal of Abraham Robinson Johnston, 1846.* in Bieber, Ralph P. (ed). *Marching with the Army of the West.* Glendale, Arthur H. Clark, 1936.

Kearney, Thomas, and Peebles, Robert H., et al. *Arizona Flora.* Berkeley, University of California Press, 1951.

Keleher, William A. *Turmoil in New Mexico 1846–1868.* Santa Fé, The Rydal Press [1952].

BIBLIOGRAPHY

Kelly, George. *Legislative History—Arizona 1864–1912.* Phoenix, The Manufacturing Stationers, 1926.

Kortright, Francis H. *The Ducks, Geese, and Swans of North America.* Washington, The American Wildlife Institute, 1942.

Kroeber, A. L. *Handbook of Indians of California.* Bureau of American Ethnology, *Bulletin No. 78.* Washington, Government Printing Office, 1925.

Lavender, David. *Bent's Fort.* Garden City, New York, Doubleday, 1954.

Leonard, Zenas. *Narratives of the Adventures of Zenas Leonard.* Quaife, Milo M. (ed.). Chicago, Lakeside Press, 1934.

Lockwood, Frank C. *The Apache Indians.* New York, Macmillan, 1938.

———. *Pioneer Days in Arizona: From the Spanish Occupation to Statehood.* New York, Macmillan, 1932.

McClintock, James H. *Arizona—Prehistoric—Aboriginal—Pioneer—Modern.* 3 vols. Chicago, S. J. Clarke Publishing Company, 1916.

———. *Arizona: The Youngest State.* 2 vols. Chicago, S. J. Clarke, 1916.

Malone, Dumas (ed). *Dictionary of American Biography.* 20 vols. New York, Scribner's, 1935.

Monaghan, Jay. *Civil War on the Western Frontier, 1854–1865.* Boston, Little, Brown, 1955.

Morgan, Dale Lowell. *The Great Salt Lake.* Indianapolis, Bobbs-Merrill, 1947.

———. *Jedediah Smith and the Opening of the West.* Indianapolis, Bobbs-Merrill, 1953.

Murdock, George Peter. *Ethnographic Bibliography of North America.* 2d ed. New Haven, Connecticut, Human Relations Area File, 1953.

Nevins, Allan. *Frémont, Pathmarker of the West.* New York, Appleton-Century, 1939.

Nidever, George. *The Life and Adventures of George Nidever 1802–1883.* Ellison, William H. (ed.). Berkeley, University of California Press, 1937.

Pratt, Henry Sherring. *A Manual of the Common Invertebrate.* Rev. ed. Philadelphia, P. B. Blackinston's Son and Co., 1935.

Rice, Clara Mabel. *Dictionary of Geological Terms.* Ann Arbor, Michigan, Edwards Brothers, 1941.

Riegel, Robert Edgar. *The Story of the Western Railroads.* New York, Macmillan, 1926.

Sabin, Edwin L. *Kit Carson Days.* Chicago, A. C. McClurg and Co., 1919.

Shinn, Charles Howard. *Land Laws of Mining Districts.* Johns Hopkins University *Studies in Historical and Political Science,* Vol. XII. Baltimore, 1884.

———. *Mining Camps: A Study of American Frontier Government.* New York, Knopf, 1948.

Spicer, Edward H. *Pasqua: A Yaqui Village in Arizona.* Chicago, University of Chicago Press [1940].

Spier, Leslie. *Yuman Tribes of the Gila River.* Chicago, University of Chicago Press, 1933.

Swarth, Harry S. *A Distributional List of Birds of Arizona.* Hollywood, California, Cooper Ornithological Club, 1914.
Twitchell, Ralph Emerson. *The Leading Facts of New Mexican History.* 2 vols. Cedar Rapids, Iowa, The Torch Press, 1911–12.
Watson, Douglas S. *West Wind: The Life Story of Joseph Reddeford Walker.* Los Angeles, California, Johnck and Seeger, Printers, 1934.
Wellman, Paul I. *Death in the Desert, the Fifty Years' War for the Great Southwest.* New York, Macmillan, 1935.
Wilson, Eldred D. *Arizona Gold Placers and Placering.* 4th ed. rev. Arizona State Bureau of Mines, *Bulletin No. 135* (1933).
Wooton, Elmer O., and Standly, Paul C. "Flora of New Mexico," *Contributions from United States Herbarium,* 1915. Vol. 19. Washington, Government Printing Office, 1915.
Wyllys, Rufus Kay. *Arizona, The History of a Frontier State.* Phoenix, Arizona, Hobson and Herr [1950].

ARTICLES

Cheetham, F. T. "Kit Carson," *New Mexico Historical Review,* Vol. 1, No. 4 (October, 1926), 375–99.
Clendenen, Clarence C. "General James Henry Carleton," *New Mexico Historical Review,* Vol. XXX. No. 1 (January, 1955), 23–43.
Donnell, F. S. "The Confederate Territory of Arizona, as Compiled from Official Sources," *New Mexico Historical Review,* Vol. XVII. No. 2 (April, 1942), 148–63.
Farquhar, Francis P. "Exploration of the Sierra Nevada," *California Historical Society Quarterly,* Vol. IV. No. 1 (March, 1925), 3–58.
McKinnan, Bess. "The Toll Road over Raton Pass," *New Mexico Historical Review,* Vol. II, No. 1 (January, 1927), 83–89.
Ogle, Ralph H. "Federal Control of the Western Apaches, 1848–1866," *New Mexico Historical Review,* Vol. XIV. No. 4 (October, 1939), 309–65; Vol. XV., Nos. 1 and 3 (January and July, 1940), 12–71, 188–248.
Pettis, George H. "The California Column," *Papers of the Historical Society of New Mexico,* No. 11 (1908).
Reeves, Frank D. (ed.). "Albert Franklin Banta: Arizona Pioneer," *New Mexico Historical Review,* Vol. XXVII, Nos. 2, 3, and 4 (April, July, and October, 1952), 81–106, 200–52, 315–47; Vol. XXVIII, Nos. 1 and 2 (January and April, 1953), 52–67, 133–47.
Waldrip, William I. "New Mexico during the Civil War," *New Mexico Historical Review,* Vol. XXVIII, Nos. 3 and 4 (July and October, 1953), 163–82, 251–90.
Walker, Charles S. "Causes of the Confederate Invasion of New Mexico," *New Mexico Historical Review,* Vol. VIII, No. 1 (January, 1933), 76–97.

Index

Adams, George: 227
Agua Caliente, Arizona: 170 & n.
Agua Fria (Frio) River: 160 & n., 167, 207, 210, 225, 230, 231, 264, 310, 317 & n., 319
Albuquerque, New Mexico: 13
Allyn (Allen), Joseph P.: 156 & n.
Alsop, John T.: 141 & n.
American Fur Company: xv, xviii
Antelope Hill, Arizona: 131 & n., 216–17, 216 n.
Apache Indians: 18, 21, 22, 29, 31, 50, 52, 53, 54, 59, 71–72, 71 n., 191, 223, 245–46, 256, 263–64, 272; raids on settlements, 218 & n.; depredations, 257–58, 280–82; expedition against, 313–19; attributes of, 349–50
Apache-Mohave Indians: *see* Yavapai Indians
Arizona Territory: officials of, 156 & n.; territorial legislature, 158, 242, 247, 270 & n., 333 ff.
Arrastres (quartz mills): 285

Banghart, George: 306, 329
Bardstown, Kentucky: xxi
Bashford, Levi: 156
Battle Flat, Arizona: 250 ff.; participants in skirmish, 255 n.

Bear Creek: 57 & n.
Bell, George: 290
Bent's Fort, Colorado: xix
Beulah Valley, Colorado: xx
Big Bug Creek: 110, 113, 230
Big Bug mining district: 110 & n., 203, 229, 310
Big Burro Mountain: 33 & n., 43
Big Rump, Apache chief: 264–65, 265 n.
Big Rump Valley: 264–65, 265 n.
Bill Williams Mountain: 145 & n.
Binkley, Frank: 250 ff., 255 n., 283
Boggs, John M.: 143
Bonneville, Benjamin L. E.: xvii, xviii; meets Joe Walker, xiv; failure of enterprise, xv–xviii; originates Walker's California expedition, xvi
Bradshaw, John: xvii
Bradshaw Mountains: 160 & n.
Bradshaw, William D.: 159–60, 160 n.
Bully Bueno (Bueano) mine: 283–85, 345

Canby, E. R. S.: 19 & n.
Carleton, James Henry: 9 & n., 12, 13 & n., 130
Carson, Kit: xix, xx, 3, 10
Chiles, J. B.: xviii
Clark, John A.: 130 & n., 155

[359]

INDEX

Colorado River: 117, 122
Comstock Lode: xiii
Conner, Daniel Ellis: 3, 92–95, 193 ff., 199 ff.; sketch of, xx–xxi; observations on New Mexico, 13 ff.; prospecting, 237 ff.; trip to Colorado River, 271 ff.; criticism of assays, 293–95; observations on Arizona geology, 295–99; farming attempt, 303–306; trip to Sonora, Mexico, 322–23; superintends mines at La Paz, Arizona, 323–25; residence at Prescott, 341 ff.; leaves Arizona, 347 ff.; route to Bardstown, Kentucky, 350–51
Cooke's (Kook's) Spring: 23 & n.
Copper Creek: 96–97, 96 n., 322
Coronado, Francisco Vásquez: 68
Cosgrove (Crasthgrove), Joseph: 140–41, 141 n.
Crump, William: 184
Cunningham, Charles: 290

Date Creek: 216 & n., 289
Death Valley, California: xx
Delaware Indians: xv
Dent, George W.: 289 & n.
Dixon, John H.: 110, 135, 167, 183 & n., 282
Doubtful Pass: 61 & n.
Duffield, Milton B.: 156
Dunn, A. G.: 232

Ehle, Mary: 183 & n., 282
Elsinore, California: xxi
Emory, W. H.: 68

Finney, Frank: 135–36
Fontenelle, Lucien: xv
Fort Craig: 19 & n., 20
Fort Gibson: xv
Fort McLane (McLean): 32 & n.
Fort Osage: xiv, xv
Fort West: 47–48, 47 n., 57
Fort Whipple: 155 & n., 176, 225, 257, 287, 289
Fort Yuma: 77, 78 n., 137
Fraeb, Henry: xviii
Frémont, John C.: xix, 10

Gage, Almon: 156
Gallatin, Albert: 68
Garvin, William H.: 348 & n.

Gila River: xiii, 45, 68, 310
Gilliland (Gillilan), Francis G.: 8 & n., 92, 117, 182
Gilroy, John: xix
Georgia Gulch, Colorado: xx
Goodhue, George: 148–50, 151
Goodwin, John N.: 156, 261 & n.
Granite Creek: 111 & n., 155, 184, 191, 212
Granite Peak (Mountain), 185 & n., 186, 292
Gray, Jim: 3
Green River: xix
Gregg, J. Irwin: 336 & n.
Groom, Robert W.: 140 & n., 158, 283
Groomdale (Groom's Dale), Arizona: 223 & n., 261

Hanover College, Hanover, Indiana: xx
Hardyville, Arizona: 185 & n.
Hassayampa (Haviamp) Creek: 84 & n., 87, 92, 96, 98, 101, 102, 170, 223, 233
Hawk's Peak, California: xix
Henry, Frederic: 250 ff., 255 n.
Hodges, Thomas: 331 & n., 335
Howell, William T.: 159 & n.
Howell's Code: 159 & n.
Hudson's Bay Company: xviii
Humboldt River: xvi
Humboldt Sink: xvi

Independence, Missouri: xiv, xv
Iretaba (Irotaba), chief of Mohaves: 78 & n., 102, 195, 276–78; description of, 86–91
Irving, Washington: xvii–xviii

Jackson, Orick: xix
Jacquois Indians: see Yaqui Indians
Jay, Leroy: 207
Johnson, Thomas: 79, 101 & n.

Keyesville, California: xx

Lallier, William: 40
Lane, James Henry: 272 & n.
La Paz, Arizona: 193 & n., 271, 276, 289
Las Animas (Animus) River: 6 & n.
Leavenworth, Kansas: xx, xxi
Lee's Ranch: 190 & n.
Leihy, George W.: 289 & n.
Lennan (Lenon), Cyrus: 173 & n., 176

[360]

INDEX

Leonard, Zenas: xvi
Lewis, M.: 94, 182
Lount, George: 20–21, 99, 132
Lynx Creek: 102 & n., 109 & n., 113, 133, 201, 221, 222, 229, 233
Lyon, Jack: 79

McCleave (McClane), William M.: 48
McClintock, James H.: xx
McCormick, Richard C.: 156, 261–62, 261 n., 262 n., 288, 340 & n.
Mangas Coloradas: xxii, 34, 35 & n., 36, 41, 43, 54, 56, 72; description of, 36–37; death of, 38–39, 39 n.; rancheria of, 44, 55
Mangus: *see* Mangas Coloradas
Maricopa Indians: 66, 67 & n., 69, 72, 219 ff., 303
Maricopa Wells, Arizona: 66 & n., 103
Mealman, Hyram: 136, 323
Meek, Joe: xvi
Mehan, Alexander: 293
Merced River: xvii
Mescal: 107 & n., 115–17
Miller, Jacob: 186
Miller, Samuel C.: 94, 95, 109, 141, 202
Miller's Ranch: 342 & n., 347
Mimbres River: 54
Mining camp law: 100, 268–69; discrimination against Mexicans, 143 & n.
Mining claim notice: example of, 236
Mining frauds: 269–70
Mohave Indians: 195 ff.
Mono Lake: xix
Monterey, California: xvii
Moqui Village: xix
Moss, John: 87 & n., 195 & n., 277, 278
Mountain Meadows, Utah: xix
Mountain Meadows Massacre: 224, 224–25 n.

Navajo Indians: 70–71, 70 n., 129 & n., 219
New Mexico Territory: description of, 13 ff.
Nidever, George: xvii

Oatman Massacre: 75–77, 75 n., 77 n.
Osburn (Orsburn), John P.: 244 & n.
Osburn (Orsburn), Nettie: 281

Peck, Edmond G.: 241 & n., 306
Peeple (People), A. H.: 131 & n.
Peralta, New Mexico: 13 & n., 19
Pertenencia: defined, 268–69, 268 n.
Pikes Peak: 4 & n.
Pima Indians: 64–65, 67 & n., 69, 73, 74, 219 ff., 290, 303, 312
Pima Indian Village: 64 & n., 103
Pinole: 73
Pinole Treaty: xxii, 171 ff., 176–77 n.
Pinos Altos (Pene Alto), New Mexico: 33 & n., 36, 41, 42, 54, 55, 56
Point of Rocks, Yavapai County, Arizona: 212 & n.
Postle's Ranch: 303–304, 303 n.
Poston, Charles D.: 156, 159, 289 & n.
Prescott, Arizona: 111, 112, 132, 139, 155, 170, 176, 184, 191, 212, 223, 247, 258, 271, 280; townsite of, 135; naming of, 143; *Arizona Miner*, 228, 228–29 n., description of, 244; climate of, 291–92; incidents with United States troops, 336–40, 340 n.
Price, Sterling: 151 & n.
Pueblo, Colorado: xx

Ralston, Jack: xx
Raton Mountains: 4 & n., 5, 6, 7
Raton Pass: xxi
Ridgeley, Missouri: xx
Río Grande: 19, 37
Riverside, California: xxi
Rock Corral, New Mexico: 12 & n.

Sacaton Station, Arizona: 74 & n.
Sacramento mining district: 330, 330–31 n.
Salt River: 310, 312
San Francisco Mountains: 99 & n.
San Francisco River: *see* Verde River
San Juan Bautista, California: xvii
Santa Cruz Mountains: xvii
Santa Cruz River: 62 & n.
Santa Fé, New Mexico: 9, 12, 37
Santa Fé Trail: Mountain Branch, xx
Santa Rita copper mines: 54 & n.
San Xavier del Bac, Arizona: 63
Schneider, Jacob: 49, 50 n., 51, 52, 310–11, 310 n.
Shirland (Sherland), E. D.: 35 & n.
Sibley, Henry H.: 19 & n.

[361]

INDEX

Skull Valley, Arizona: 206–207, 206 n., 223, 257
Slack, J. B.: 241
Smith, Jedediah Strong: xvi
Smith, Van C.: 131–32, 132 n., 134–35, 135 n., 140, 217
Snake River: xvii
Sonora, Mexico: 34
Southern Route (to California): 27, 30–31, 32, 61
Stearn, Abel: xviii
Stein's Peak: 27 & n.
Stimpson (Stympson), James H.: 328–31, 330 n.
Sugarfoot Jack: exploits of, 148–50, 150 n., 265, 266–68
Sumner, E. B.: 137, 138 n.
Swain, G.: 227, 228
Swilling, John W.: 35 & n., 256

Taos, New Mexico: 12
Tucson, Arizona: 62, 63–64, 63 n.
Tuolumne mining district, California: xiii
Turkey Creek: 110 & n., 229, 250, 257, 261, 283, 286, 344
Turner, William F.: 156
Twaddle, Harvey: 214–15

Valverde, New Mexico: battle of, 19 & n.
Verde River: 48, 51, 155, 162, 219 & n., 225, 264
Vickory, G. H.: 283 n., 284
Virgin River: xix

Walker, Isaac: xiv
Walker, James T.: xix
Walker, Joel: xiv
Walker, John: xiv
Walker, Joseph Reddeford: xiii, xvii, xviii, xix, xx, xxii, 3, 5, 8, 9, 10, 12, 13, 19, 20, 21, 22–23, 24, 26, 27, 34, 42, 48, 51, 55, 56, 58, 62, 88, 89, 90, 96, 100–101, 111, 112, 129, 133, 145, 147, 193, 194, 198, 209–10; leader of Keyesville party, xiv; Indian trade, xiv; guide, xiv; Santa Fé trade, xiv; near Fort Osage, xiv; sheriff of Jackson County, Missouri, xiv; characterization of, xiv–xv, 201; visit to Cherokee Nation, xv; meets Captain Bonneville, xv; expedition to California, xvi; death of, xxii; physical decline of, 199; leaves Arizona, 200 & n., 279–80, 280 n.
Walker Party: 8, 134, 138, 169; members of, 103 & n.; description of, 245–46
Walker's Pass: xvii
Walker, Samuel: xiv
Walnut Grove, Arizona: 95 & n., 213, 322
Weaver, Pauline: xx, 104 & n., 131 & n., 136–37, 137 n.
West, Joseph R.: 37
Westheimer (Wertheimer, Wetheimer), Aaron: 309, 310 n.
Wheelhouse, H. V.: 101
Whipple, Amiel Weeks: 155 & n.
Wickenburg, Arizona: 85 & n.
Wickenburg, Henry: 85 & n.
Williams Fork: 272, 273 & n., 298
Wilmington, California: xxi
Wolf (Wolfe) Creek: 110 & n.
Woolsey, King S.: 170 & n., 171, 172, 173, 210
Wright, John T.: 40

Yaqui (Jacquois) Indians: 63 & n.
Yavapai (Apache-Mohave) Indians: 87 & n.
Young, J.: 189, 271 ff.

Zuñi Indians: 69 & n.
Zuñi Village: xix

BIBLIOGRAPHY

THE AMERICAN EXPLORATION AND TRAVEL SERIES

of which *Joseph Reddeford Walker and the Arizona Adventure* is Number 22, was started in 1939 by the University of Oklahoma Press. It follows rather logically the Press's program of regional exploration. Behind the story of the gradual and inevitable recession of the American frontier lie the accounts of explorers, traders, and travelers, which individually and in the aggregate present one of the most romantic and fascinating chapters in the development of the American domain. The following list is complete as of the date of publication of this volume:

1. Captain Randolph B. Marcy and Captain George B. McClellan. *Adventure on Red River:* Report on the Exploration of the Headwaters of the Red River. Edited by Grant Foreman.
2. Grant Foreman. *Marcy and the Gold Seekers:* The Journal of Captain R. B. Marcy, with an account of the Gold Rush over the Southern Route.
3. Pierre-Antoine Tabeau. *Tabeau's Narrative of Loisel's Expedition to the Upper Missouri.* Edited by Annie Heloise Abel. Translated from the French by Rose Abel Wright.
4. Victor Tixier. *Tixier's Travels on the Osage Prairies.* Edited by John Francis McDermott. Translated from the French by Albert J. Salvan.
5. Teodoro de Croix. *Teodoro de Croix and the Northern Frontier of New Spain, 1776–1783.* Translated from the Spanish and edited by Alfred Barnaby Thomas.
6. A. W. Whipple. *A Pathfinder in the Southwest:* The Itinerary of Lieutenant A. W. Whipple During His Explorations for a Railway Route from Fort Smith to Los Angeles in the Years 1853 & 1854. Edited and annotated by Grant Foreman.
7. Josiah Gregg. *Diary & Letters.* Two volumes. Edited by Maurice Garland Fulton. Introductions by Paul Horgan. Out of print.
8. Washington Irving. *The Western Journals of Washington Irving.* Edited and annotated by John Francis McDermott. Out of print.
9. Edward Dumbauld. *Thomas Jefferson, American Tourist:* Being an Account of His Journeys in the United States of America, England, France, Italy, the Low Countries, and Germany.
10. Victor Wolfgang von Hagen. *Maya Explorer:* John Lloyd Stephens and the Lost Cities of Central America and Yucatán.
11. E. Merton Coulter. *Travels in the Confederate States:* A Bibliography.
12. W. Eugene Hollon. *The Lost Pathfinder:* Zebulon Montgomery Pike.
13. George Frederick Ruxton. *Ruxton of the Rockies.* Collected by Clyde and Mae Reed Porter. Edited by LeRoy R. Hafen.
14. ———. *Life in the Far West.* Edited by LeRoy R. Hafen. Foreword by Mae Reed Porter.
15. Edward Harris. *Up the Missouri with Audubon:* The Journal of Edward Harris. Edited by John Francis McDermott.

16. Robert Stuart. *On the Oregon Trail:* Robert Stuart's Journey of Discovery (1812–1831). Edited by Kenneth A. Spaulding.
17. Josiah Gregg. *Commerce of the Prairies.* Edited by Max L. Moorhead.
18. John Treat Irving, Jr. *Indian Sketches,* Taken During an Expedition to the Pawnee Tribes (1833). Edited and annotated by John Francis McDermott.
19. Thomas D. Clark (ed). *Travels in the Old South, 1527–1825:* A Bibliography. Two volumes.
20. Alexander Ross. *The Fur Hunters of the Far West.* Edited by Kenneth A. Spaulding.
21. William Bollaert. *William Bollaert's Texas.* Edited by W. Eugene Hollon and Ruth Lapham Butler.
22. Daniel Ellis Conner. *Joseph Reddeford Walker and the Arizona Adventure.* Edited by Donald J. Berthrong and Odessa Davenport.